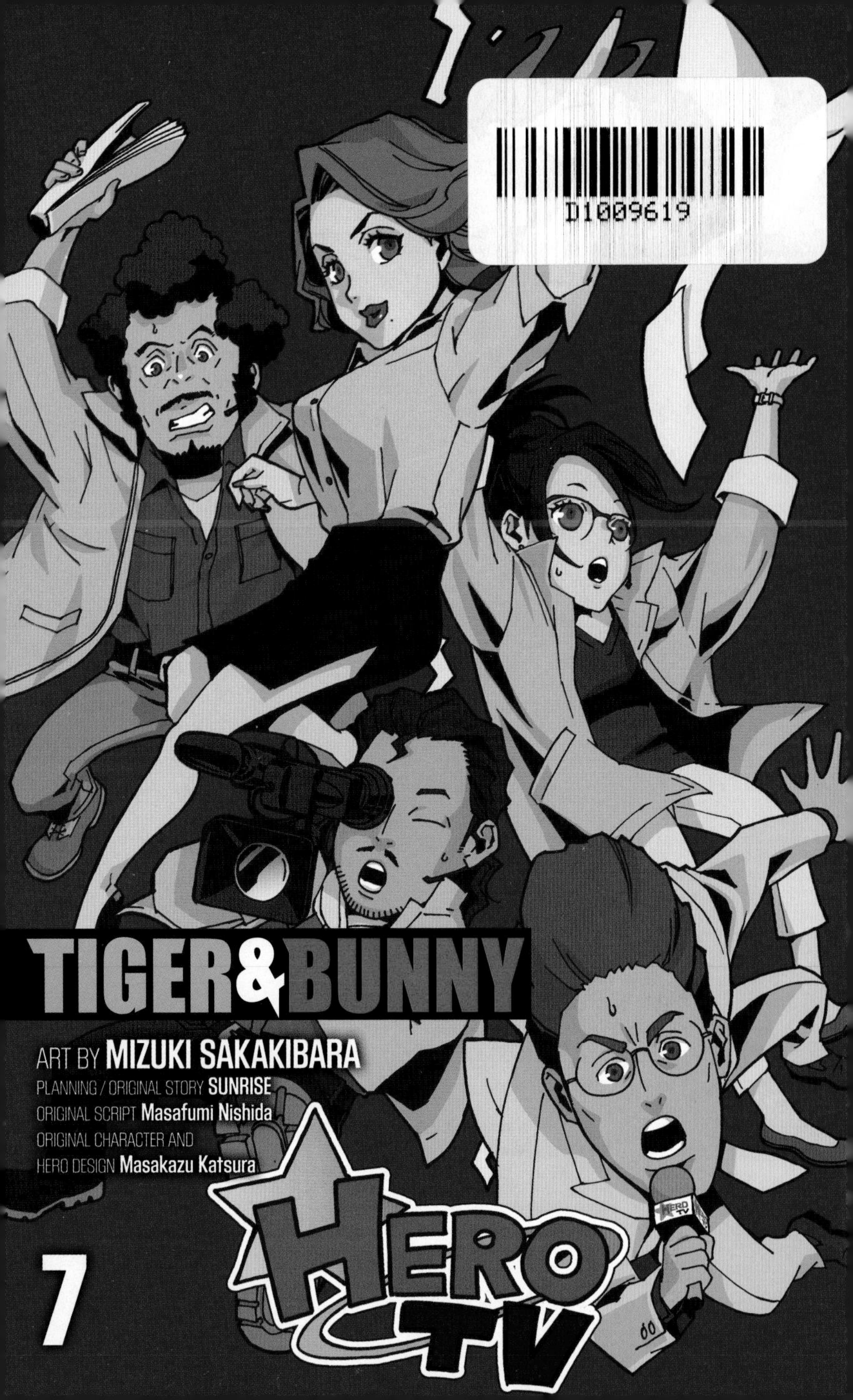
HERO TV

TIGER & BUNNY

ART BY MIZUKI SAKAKIBARA
PLANNING / ORIGINAL STORY SUNRISE
ORIGINAL SCRIPT Masafumi Nishida
ORIGINAL CHARACTER AND HERO DESIGN Masakazu Katsura

7

CONTENTS

#26   Confidence Is a Plant of Slow Growth, Part 3   003
#27   Confidence Is a Plant of Slow Growth, Part 4   035
#28   Confidence Is a Plant of Slow Growth, Part 5   067
#29   Confidence Is a Plant of Slow Growth, Part 6   101
#30   Confidence Is a Plant of Slow Growth, Part 7   135

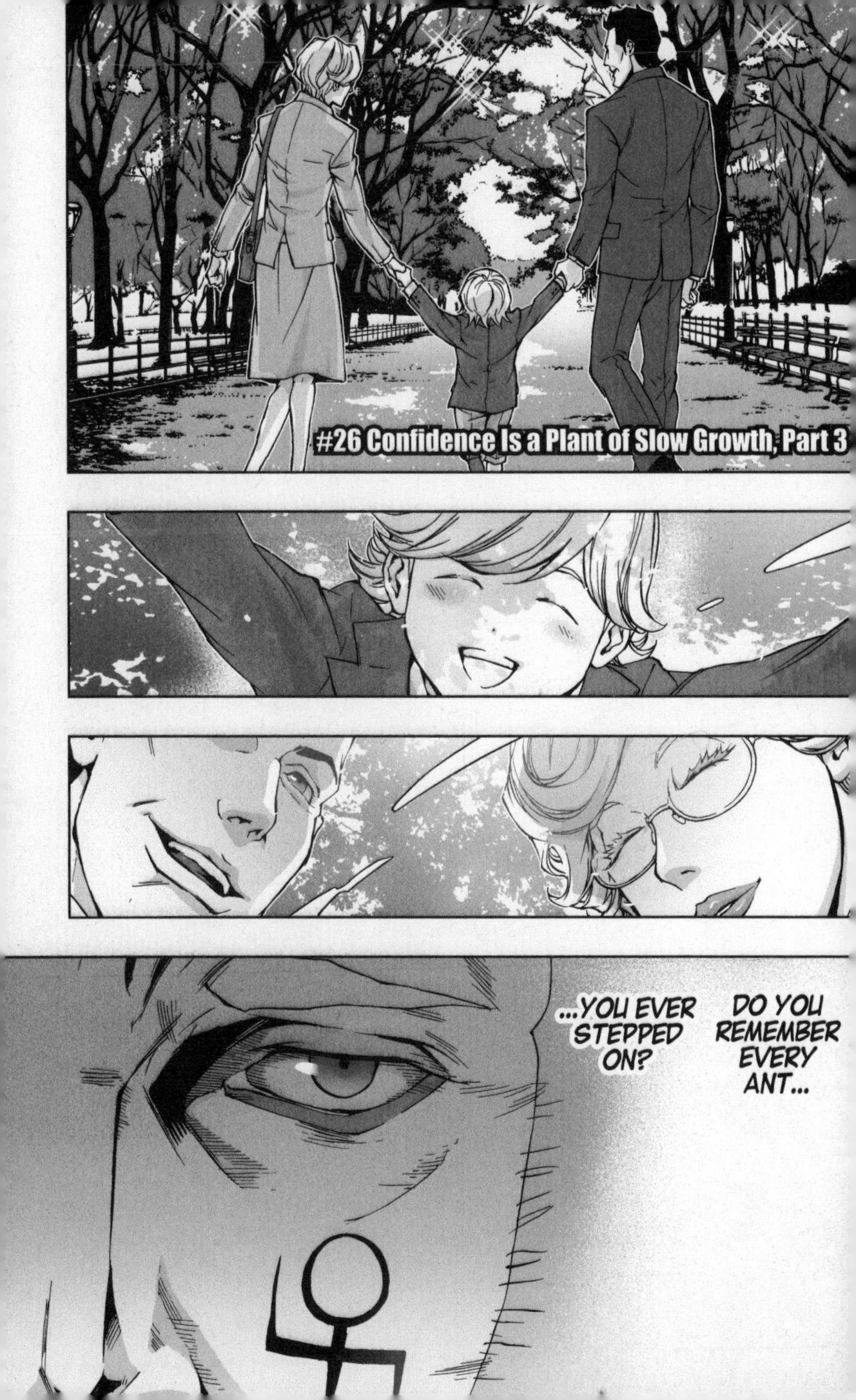
#26 Confidence Is a Plant of Slow Growth, Part 3
DO YOU REMEMBER EVERY ANT...
...YOU EVER STEPPED ON?

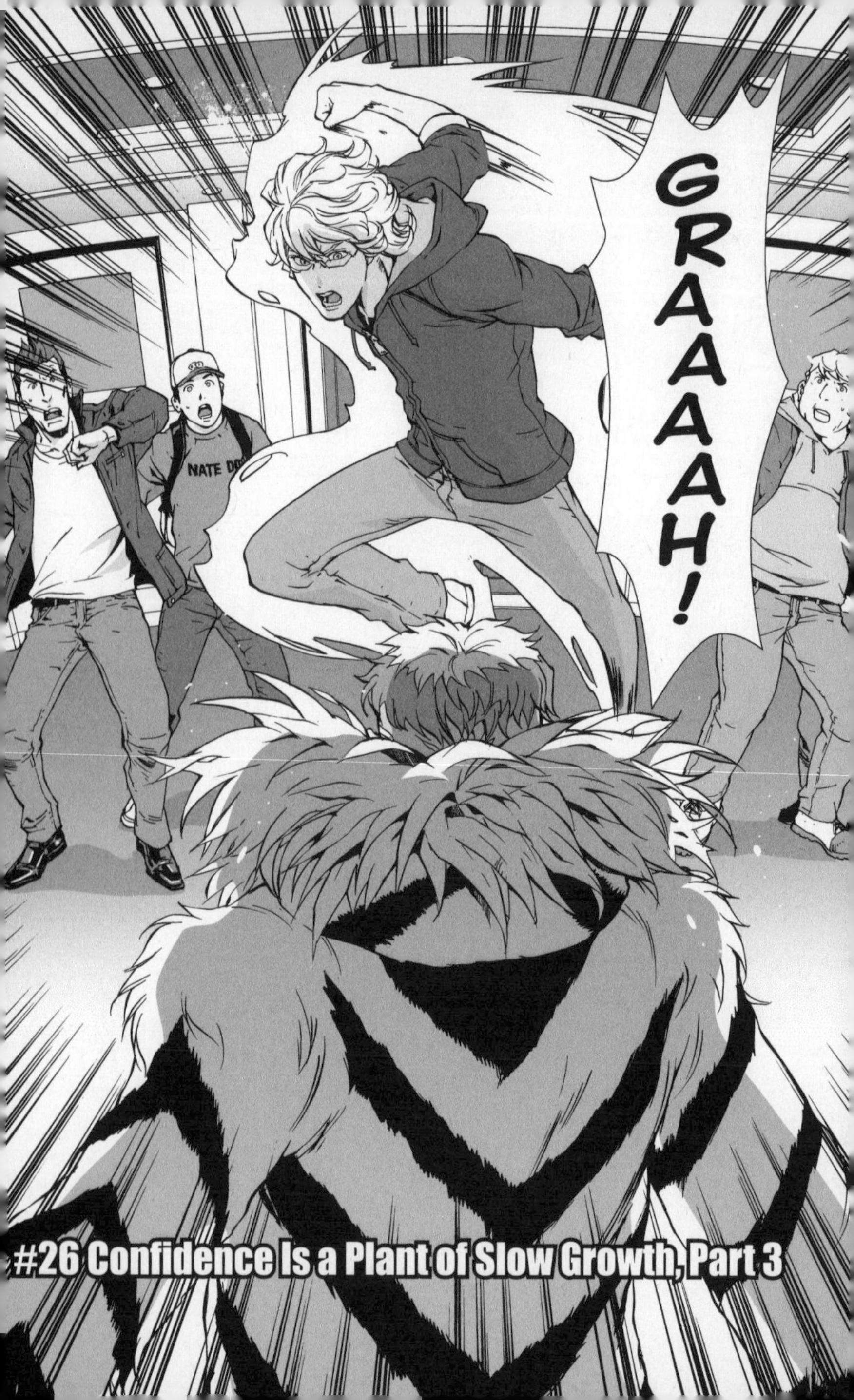
GRAAAAH!

#26 Confidence Is a Plant of Slow Growth, Part 3

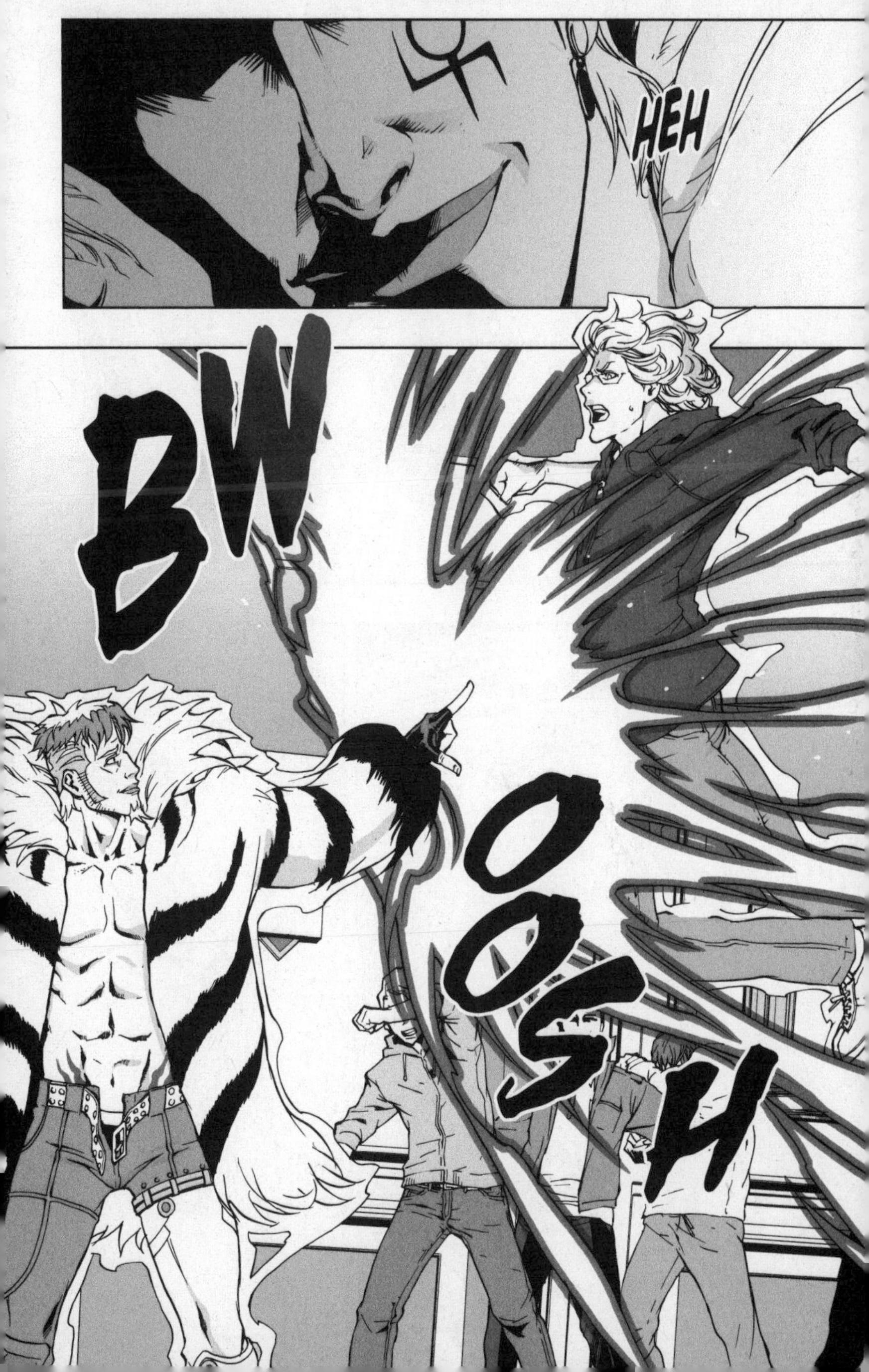
HEH
BWOOSH

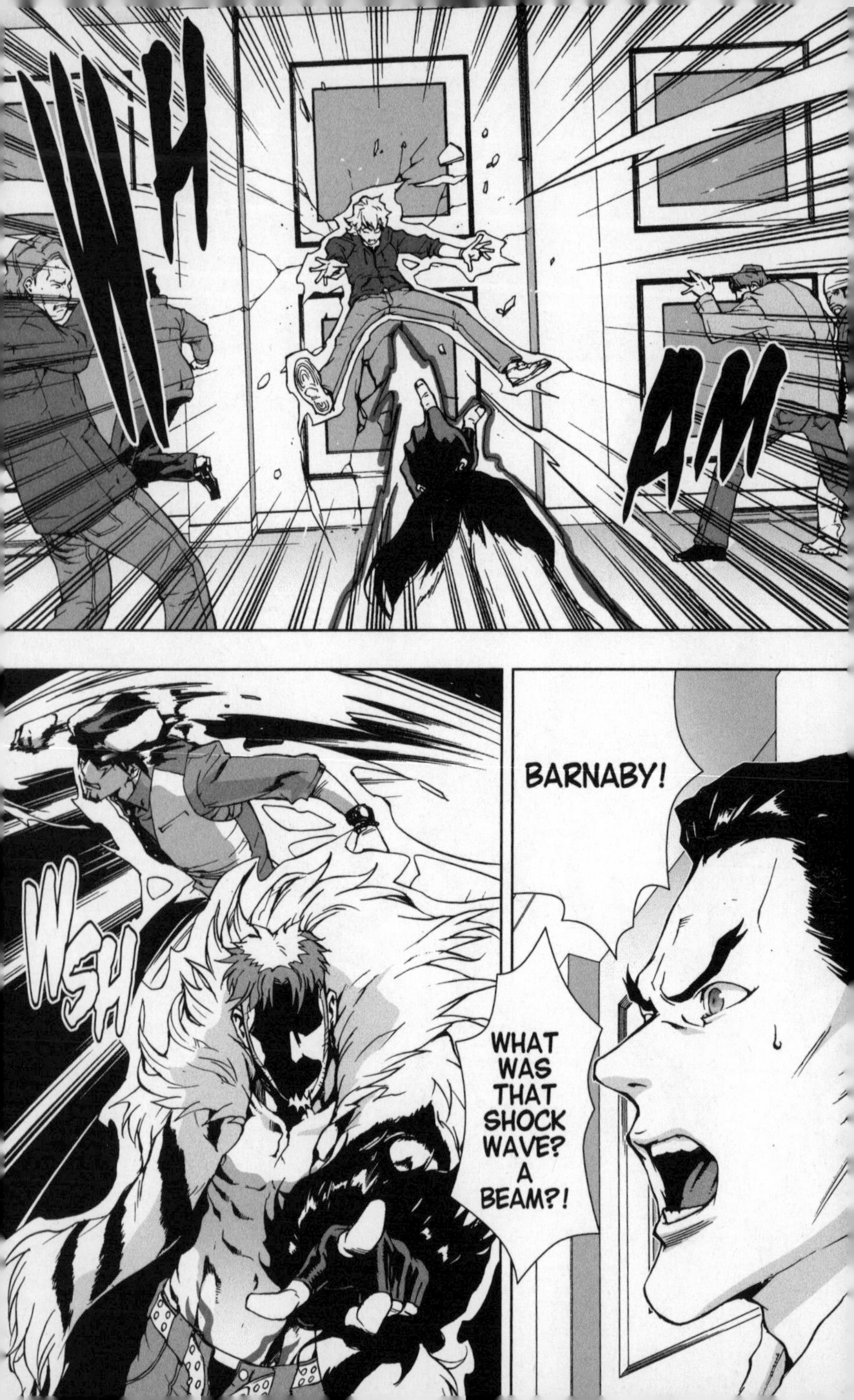
AM
BARNABY!
WHAT WAS THAT SHOCK WAVE? A BEAM?!
WSH

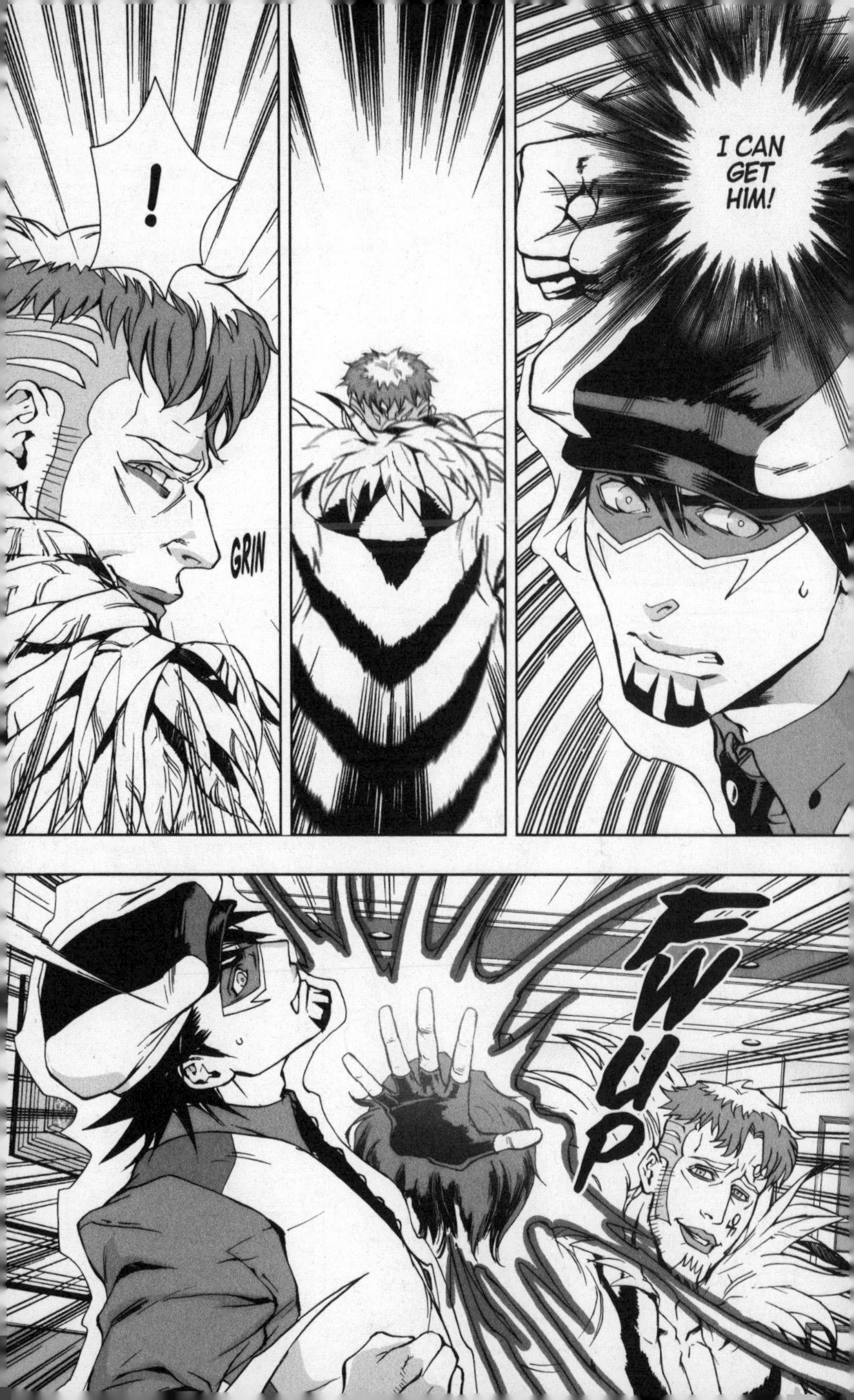
I CAN GET HIM!
!
GRIN
FWUP

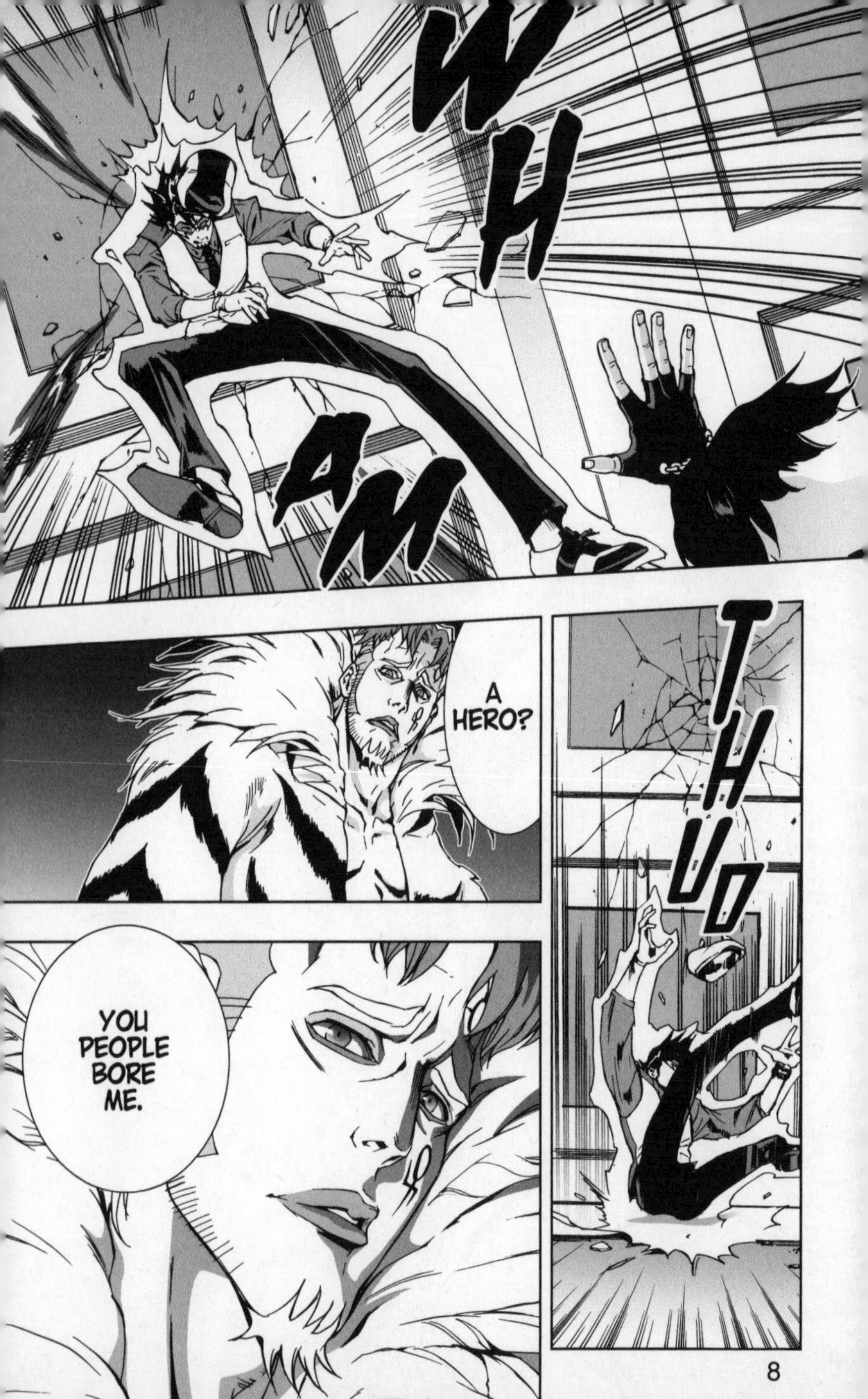
WHAM
THUD
A HERO?
YOU PEOPLE BORE ME.

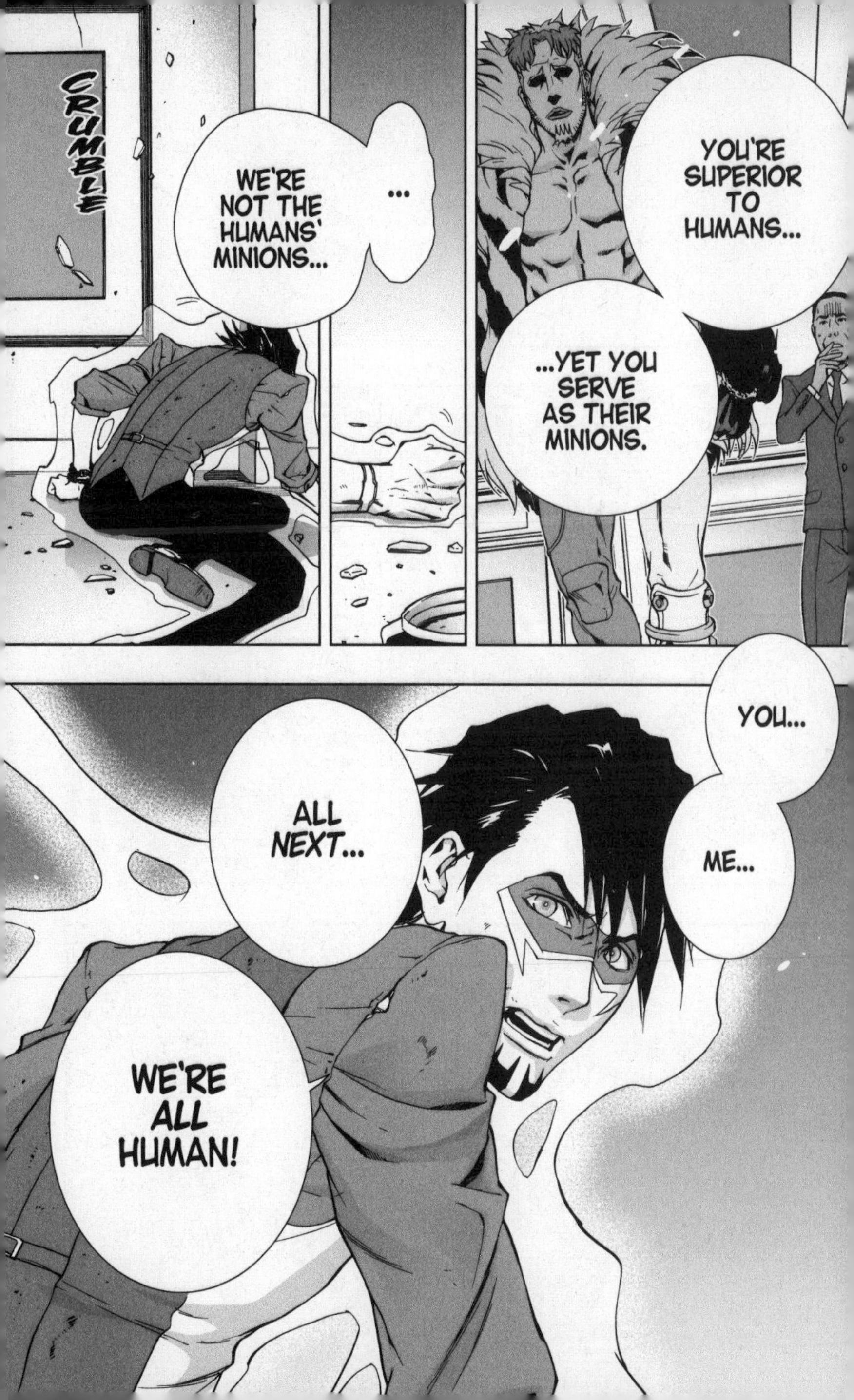
YOU'RE SUPERIOR TO HUMANS...
...YET YOU SERVE AS THEIR MINIONS.
...
WE'RE NOT THE HUMANS' MINIONS...
CRUMBLE
YOU...
ME...
ALL NEXT...
WE'RE ALL HUMAN!

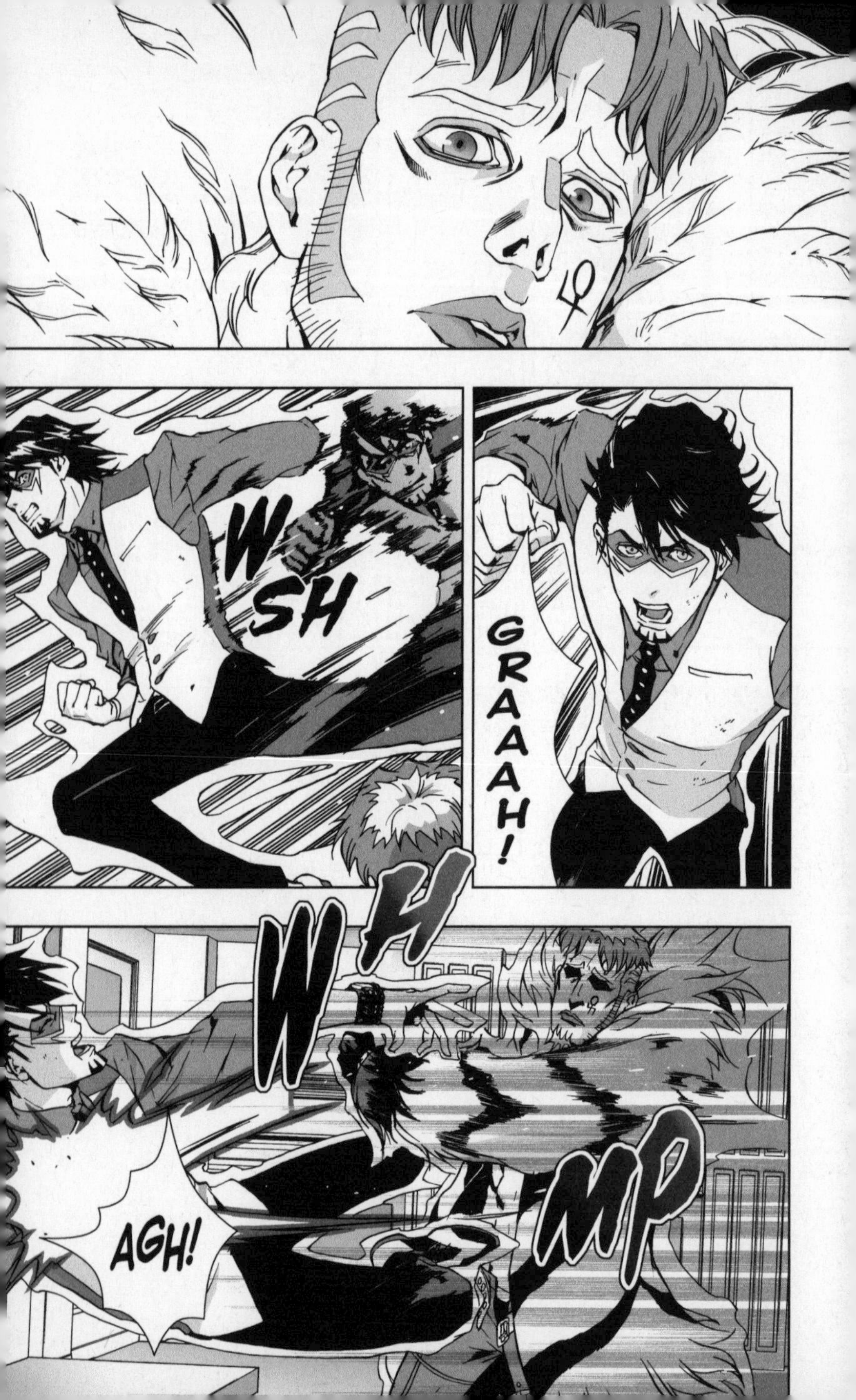
GRAAAH!
WSH
WH
MP
AGH!

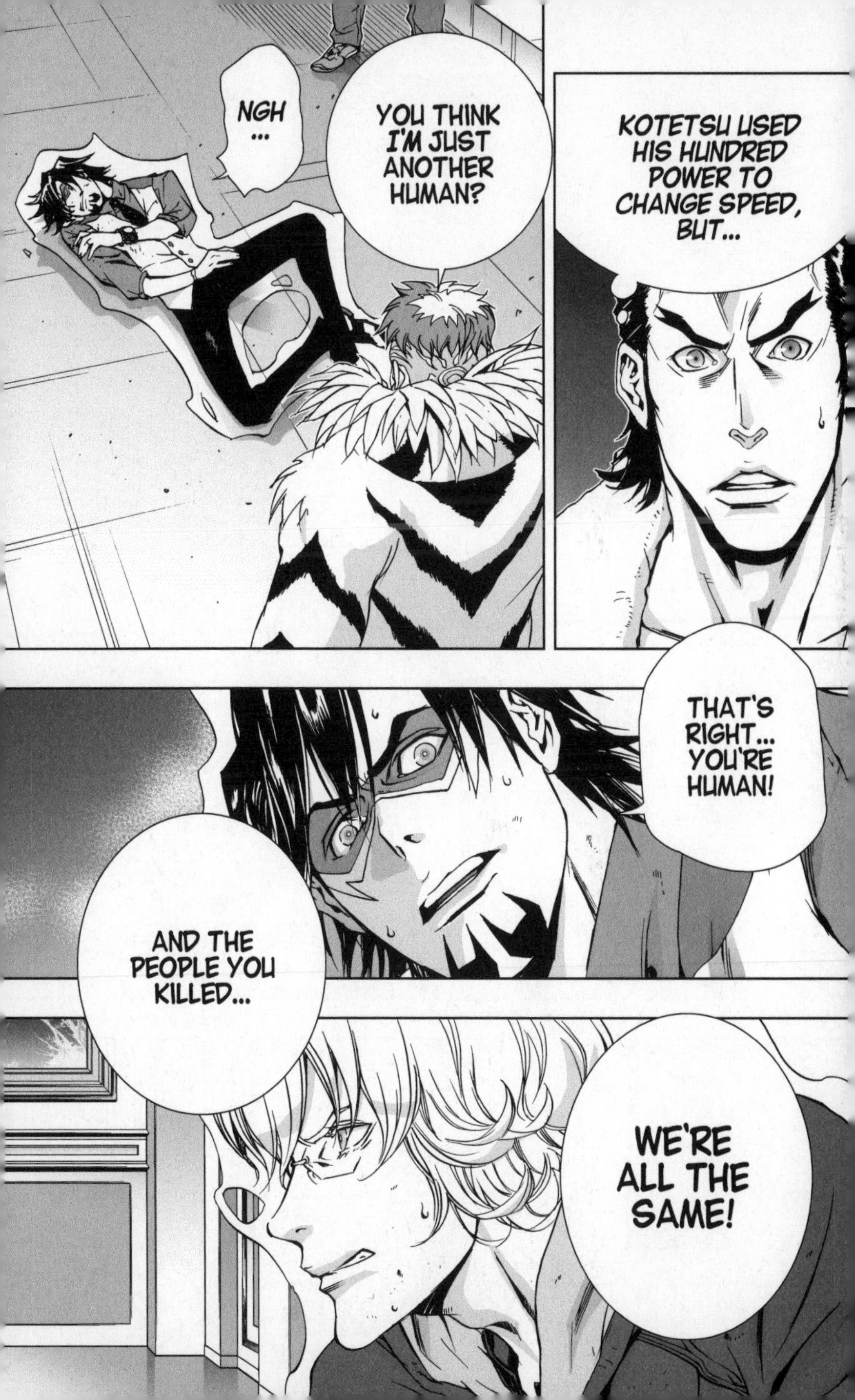
KOTETSU USED HIS HUNDRED POWER TO CHANGE SPEED, BUT...
YOU THINK I'M JUST ANOTHER HUMAN?
NGH ...
THAT'S RIGHT... YOU'RE HUMAN!
AND THE PEOPLE YOU KILLED...
WE'RE ALL THE SAME!

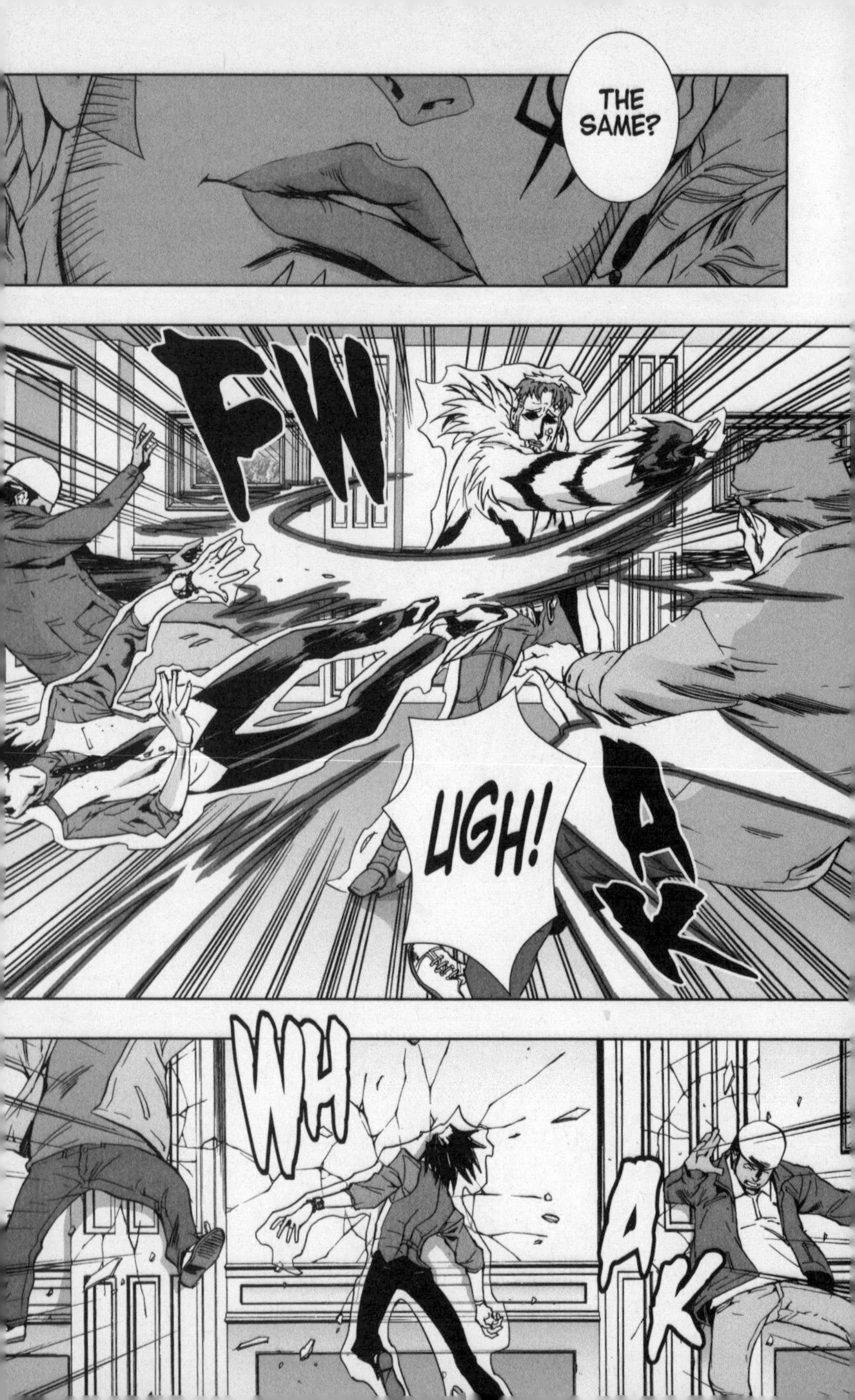
THE SAME?
FW
UGH!
AK
WH
AK

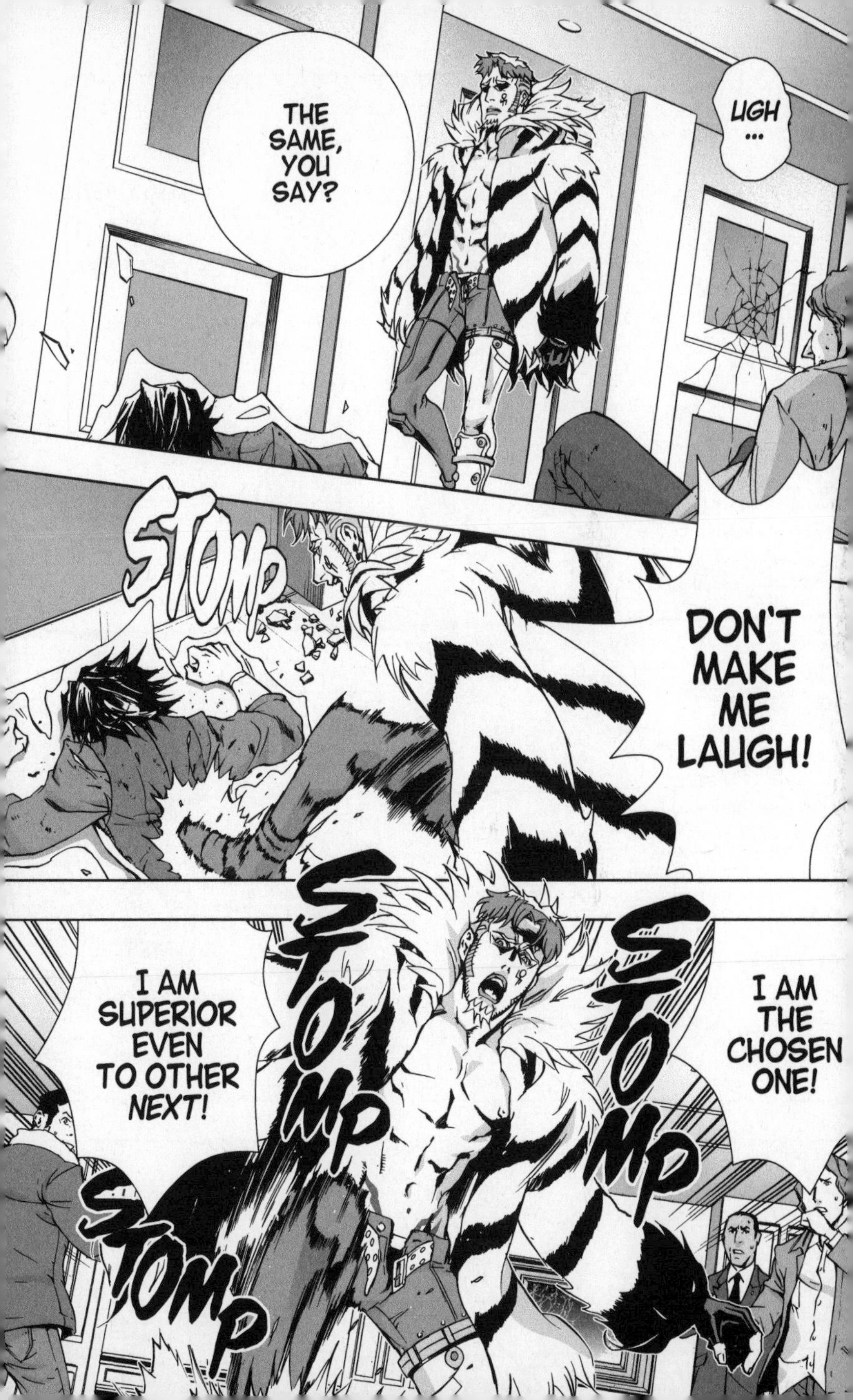
UGH...
THE SAME, YOU SAY?
DON'T MAKE ME LAUGH!
STOMP
I AM THE CHOSEN ONE!
STOMP
STOMP
I AM SUPERIOR EVEN TO OTHER NEXT!
STOMP

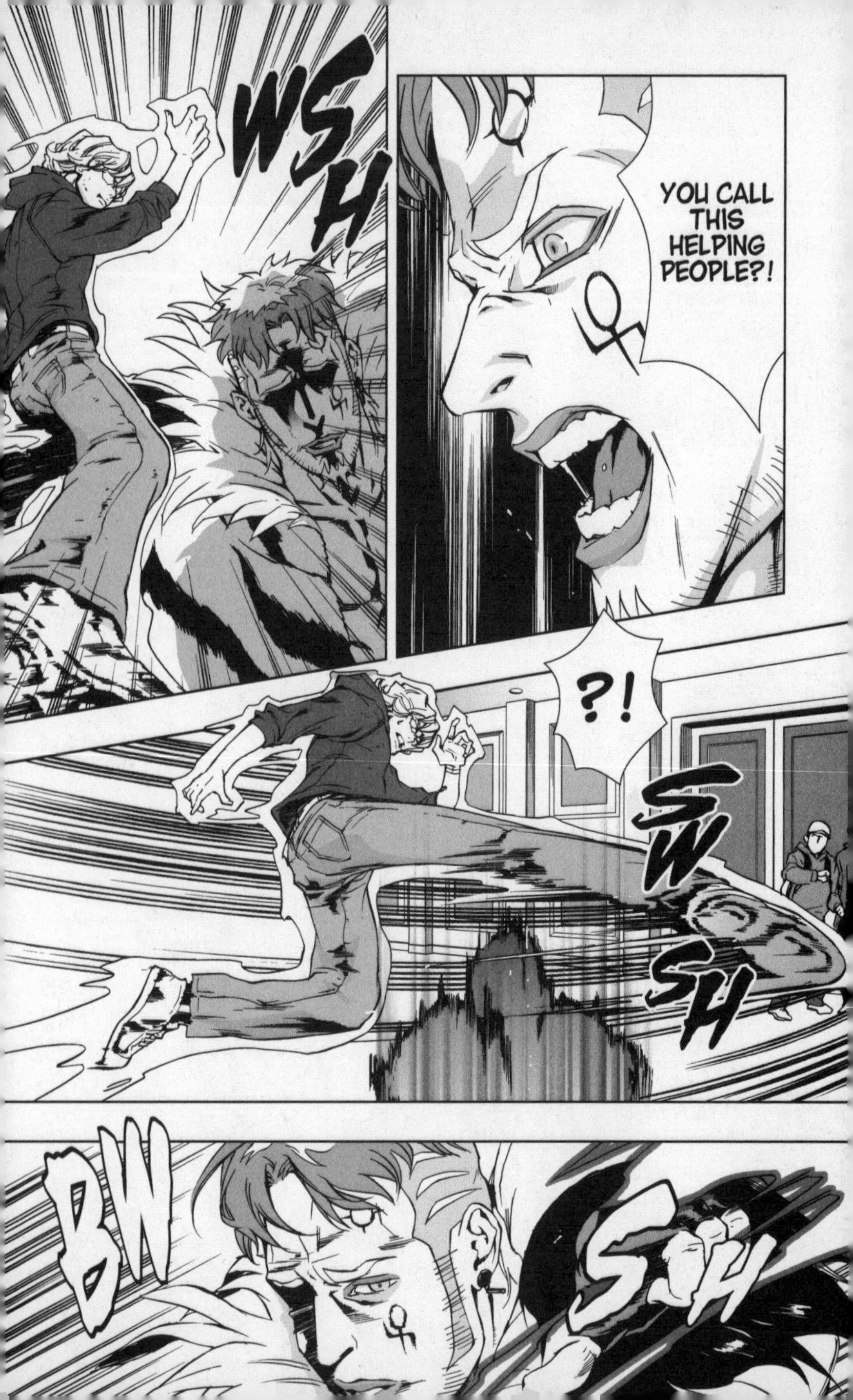
YOU CALL THIS HELPING PEOPLE?!
WSH
?!
SWSH
BWSH

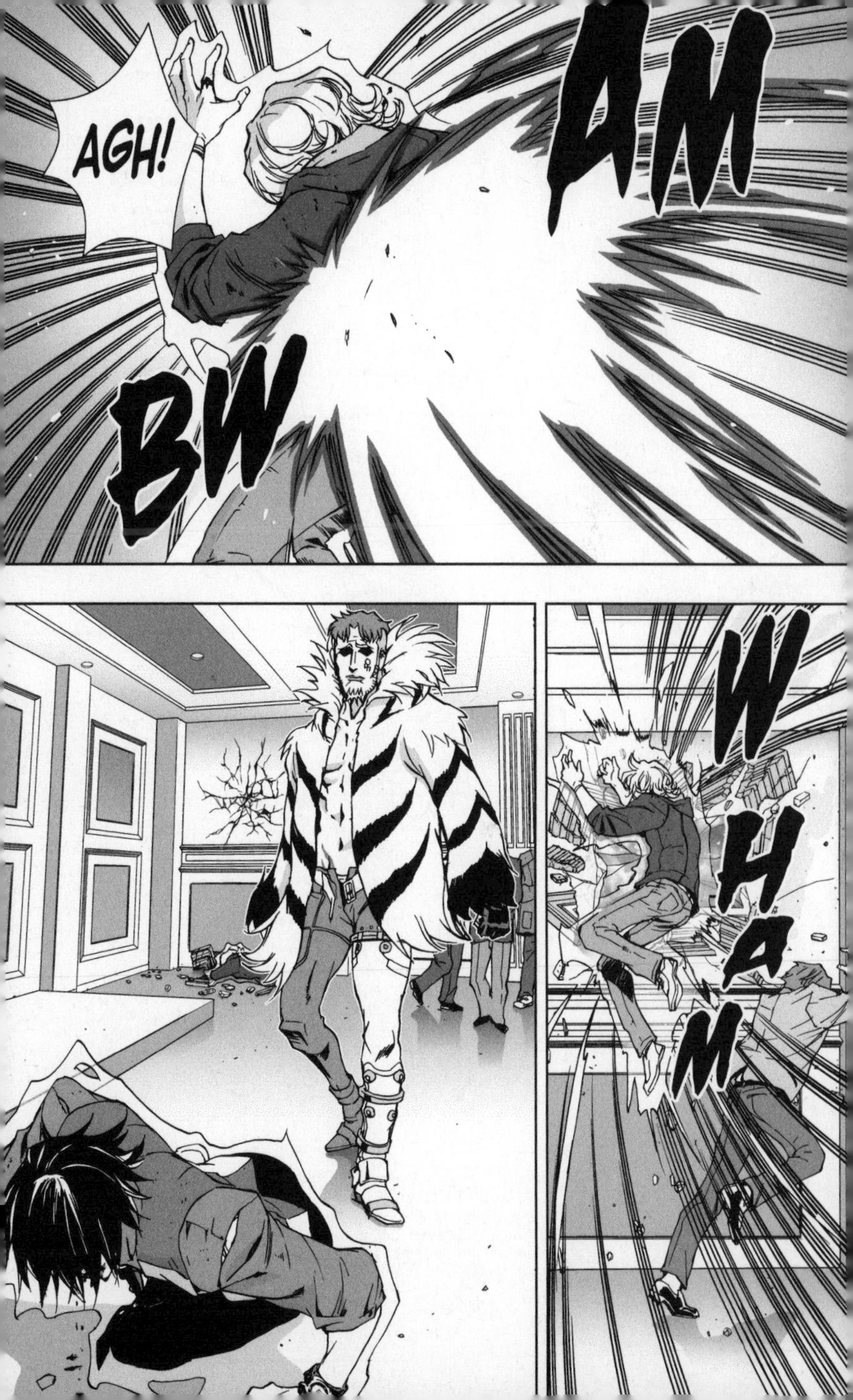
BWAM
AGH!
WHAM

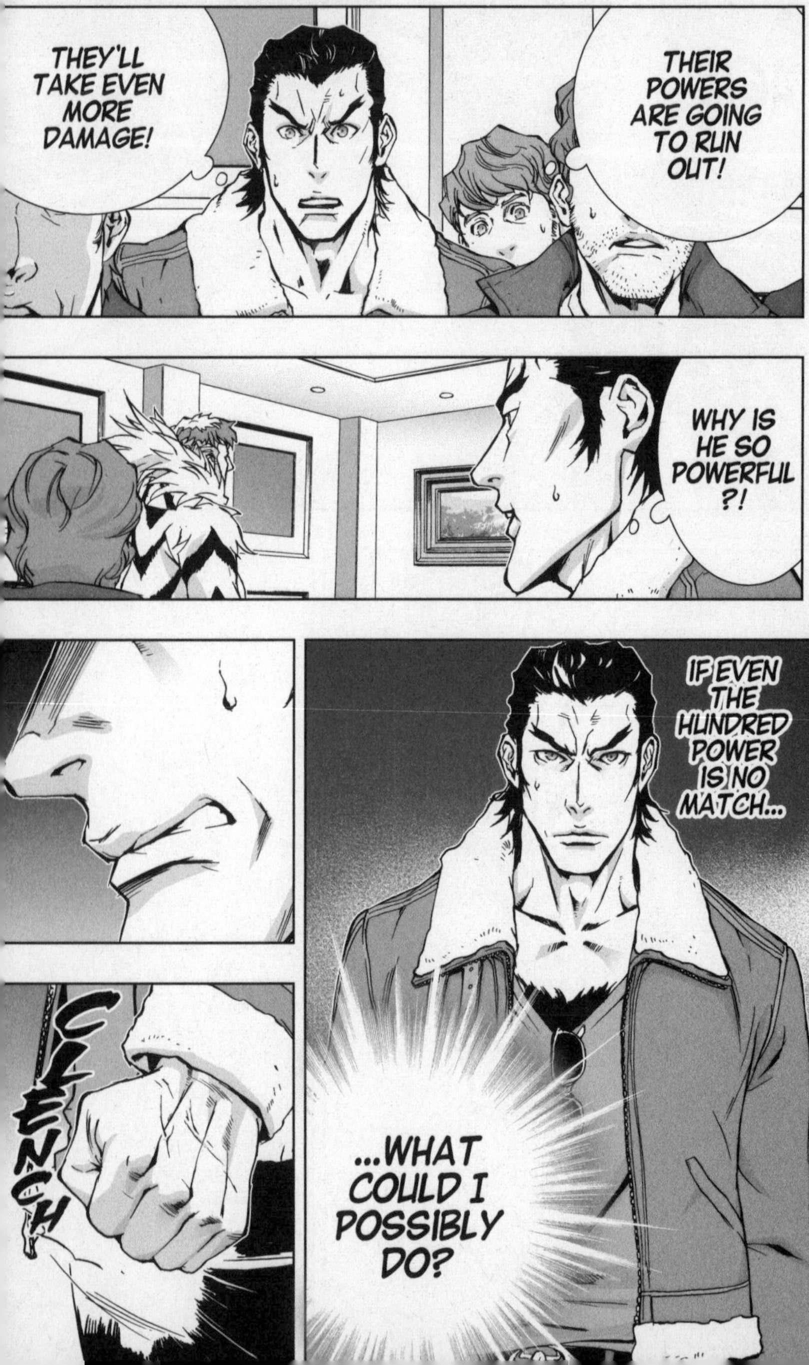
THEIR POWERS ARE GOING TO RUN OUT!
THEY'LL TAKE EVEN MORE DAMAGE!
WHY IS HE SO POWERFUL ?!
IF EVEN THE HUNDRED POWER IS NO MATCH...
...WHAT COULD I POSSIBLY DO?
CLENCH

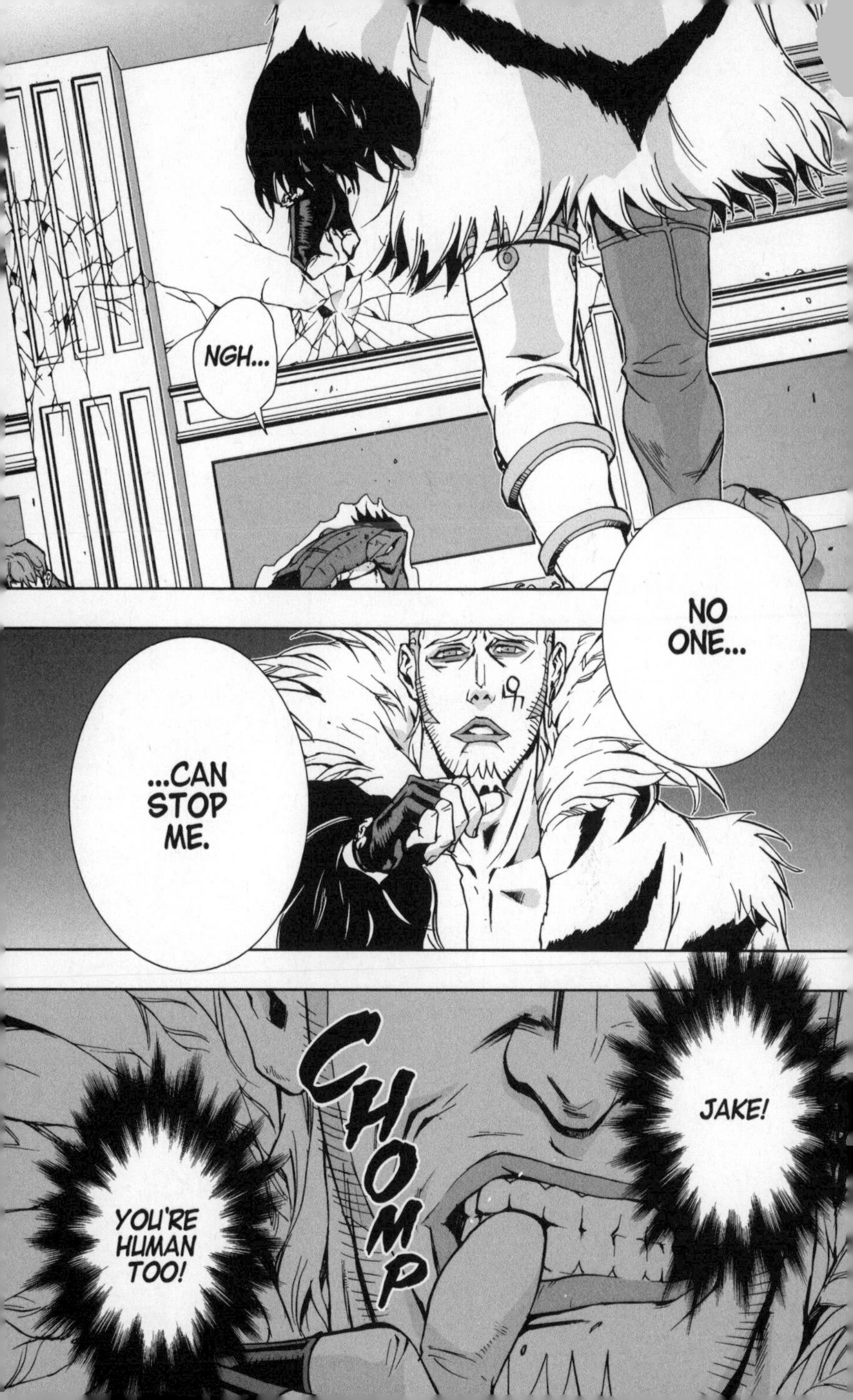
NGH...
NO ONE...
...CAN STOP ME.
JAKE!
CHOMP
YOU'RE HUMAN TOO!

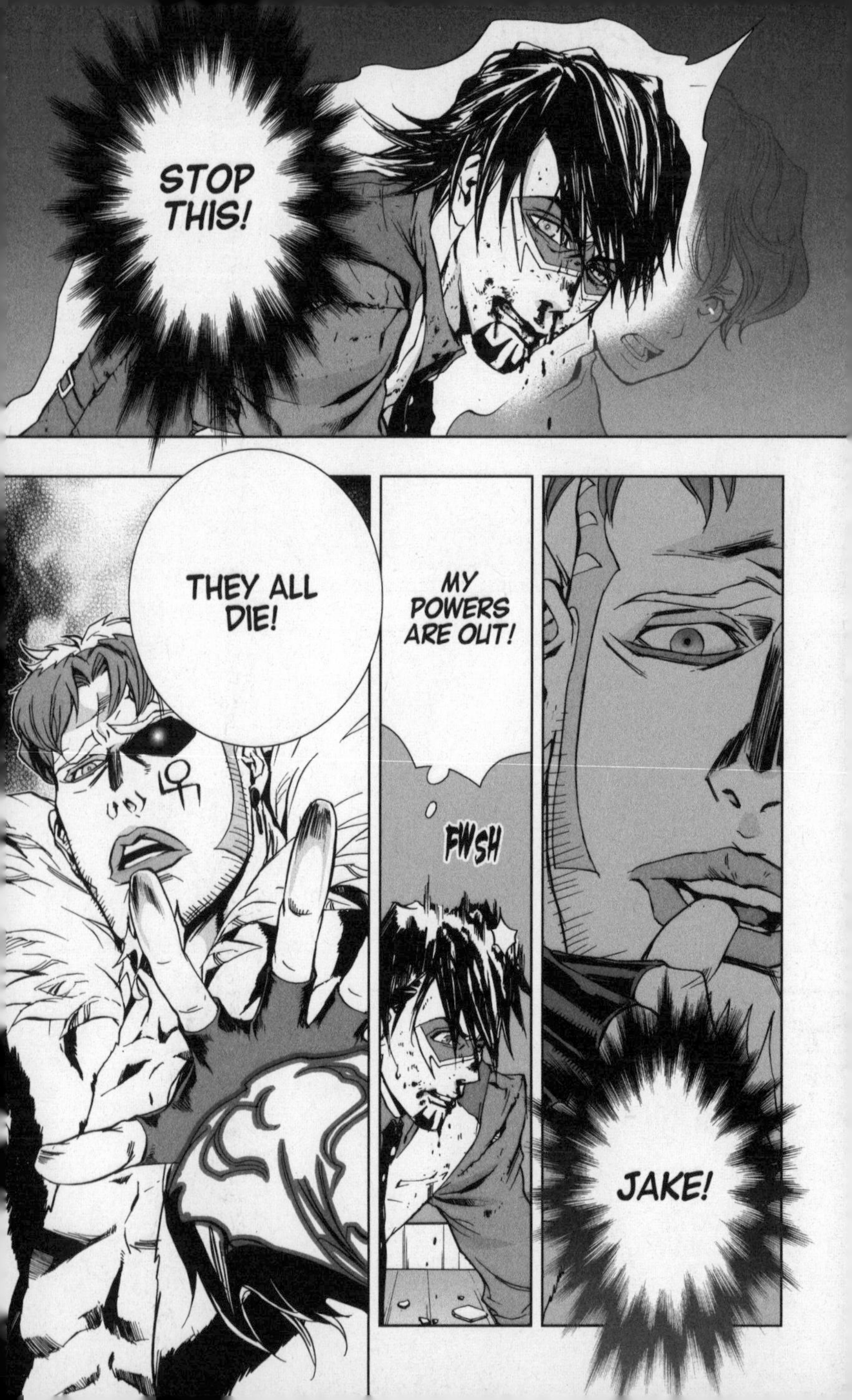

STOP THIS!
JAKE!
MY POWERS ARE OUT!
FWSH
THEY ALL DIE!

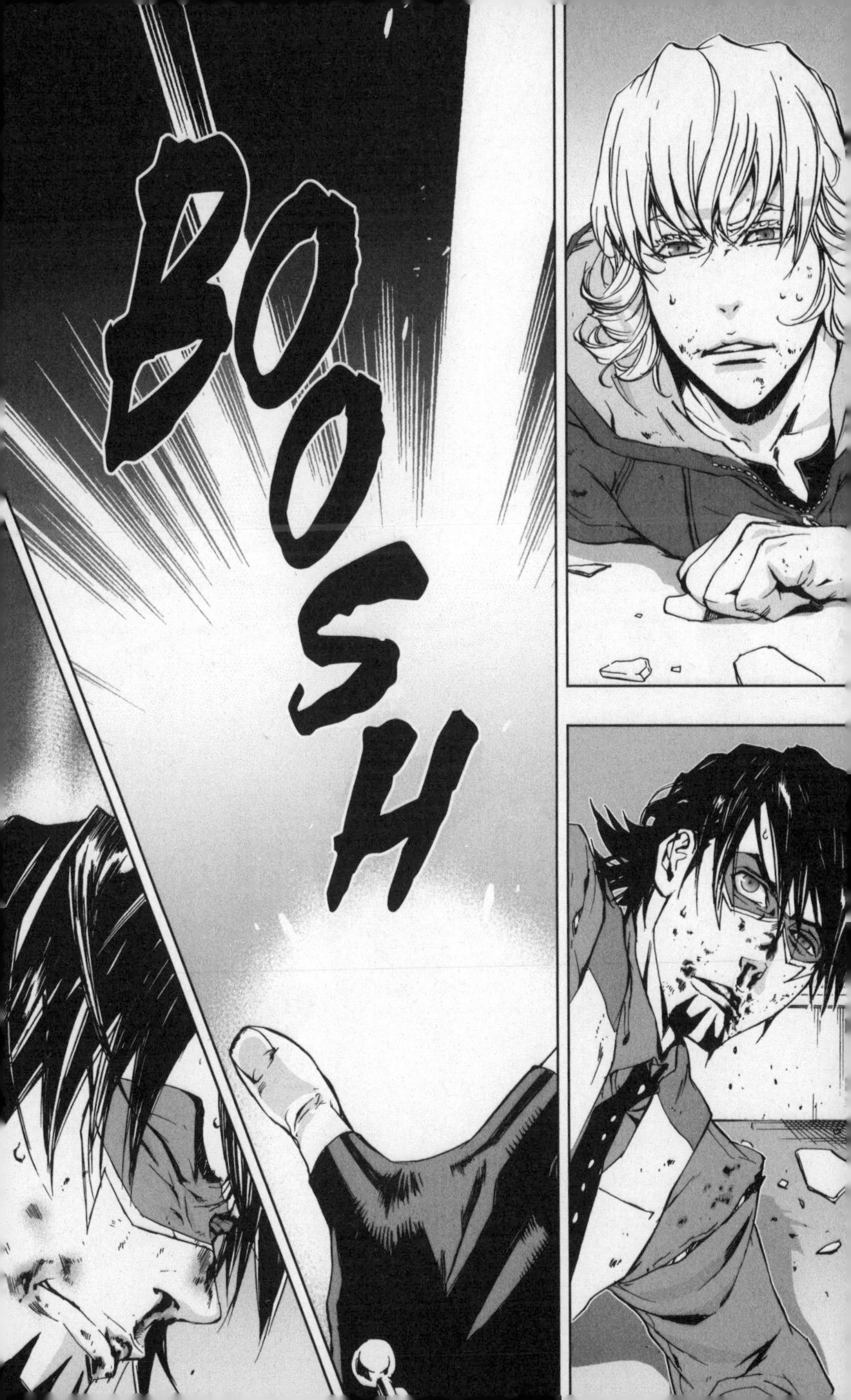
BOOOSH

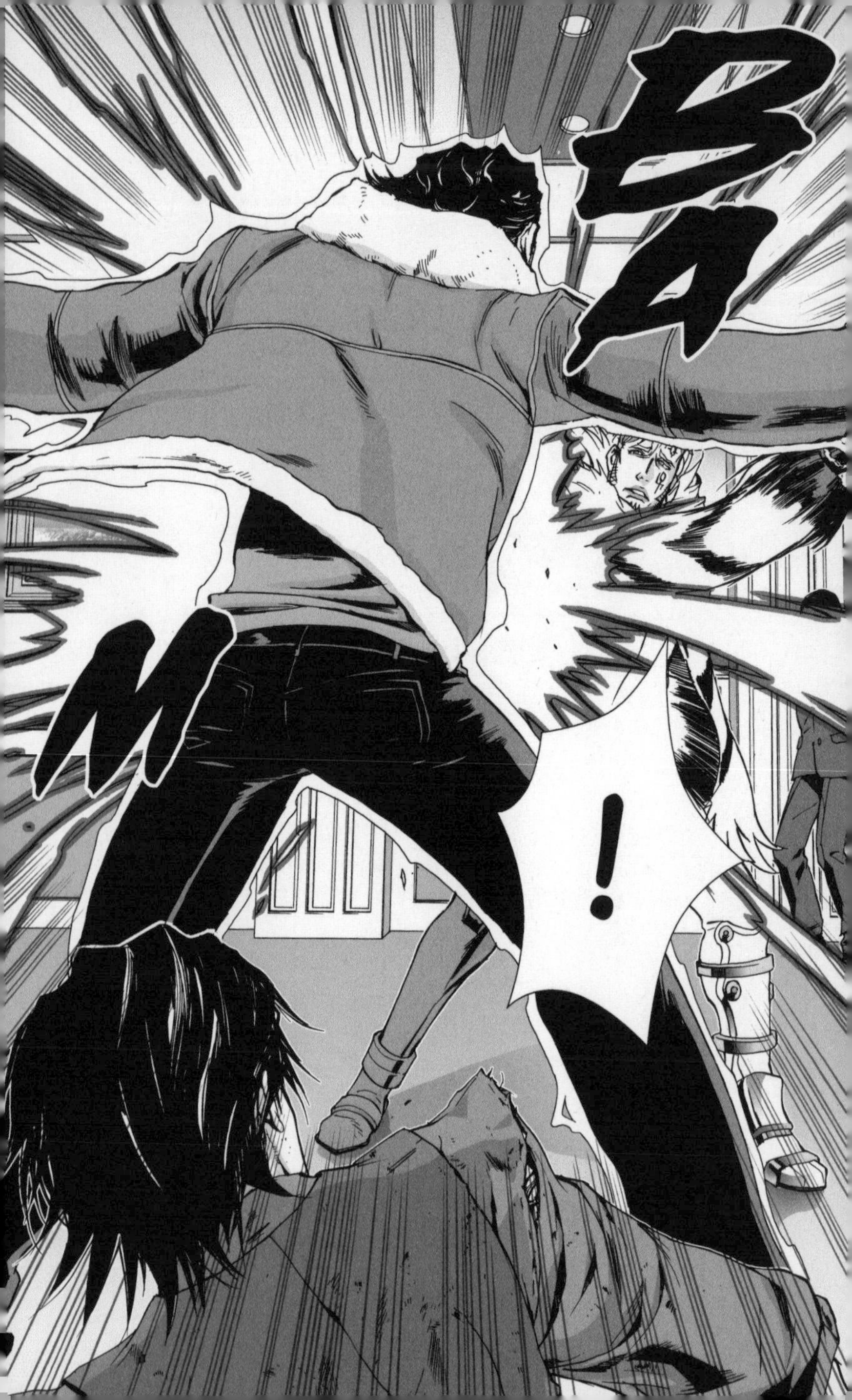
BAM
!

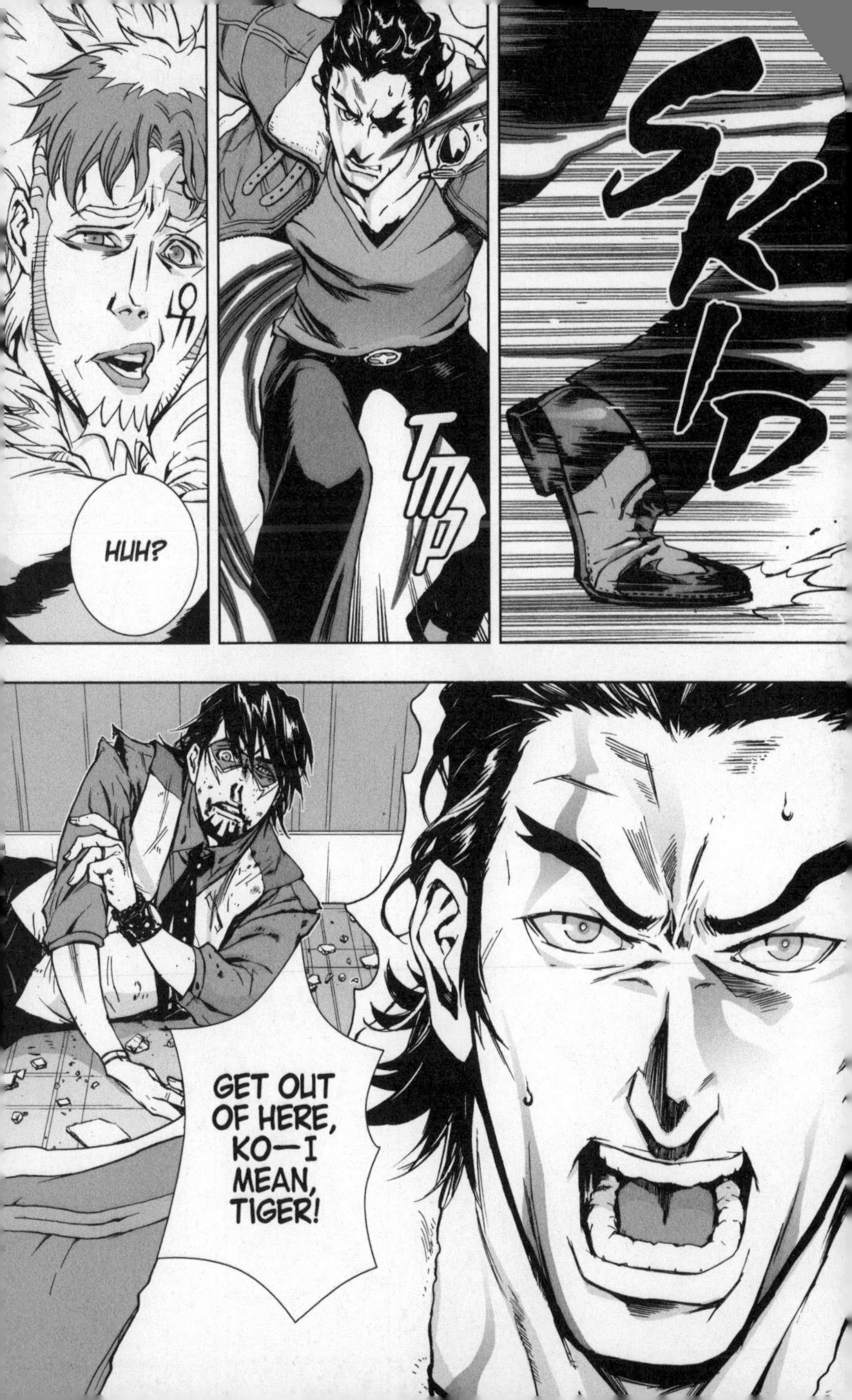
SKID
TMP
HUH?
GET OUT OF HERE, KO—I MEAN, TIGER!

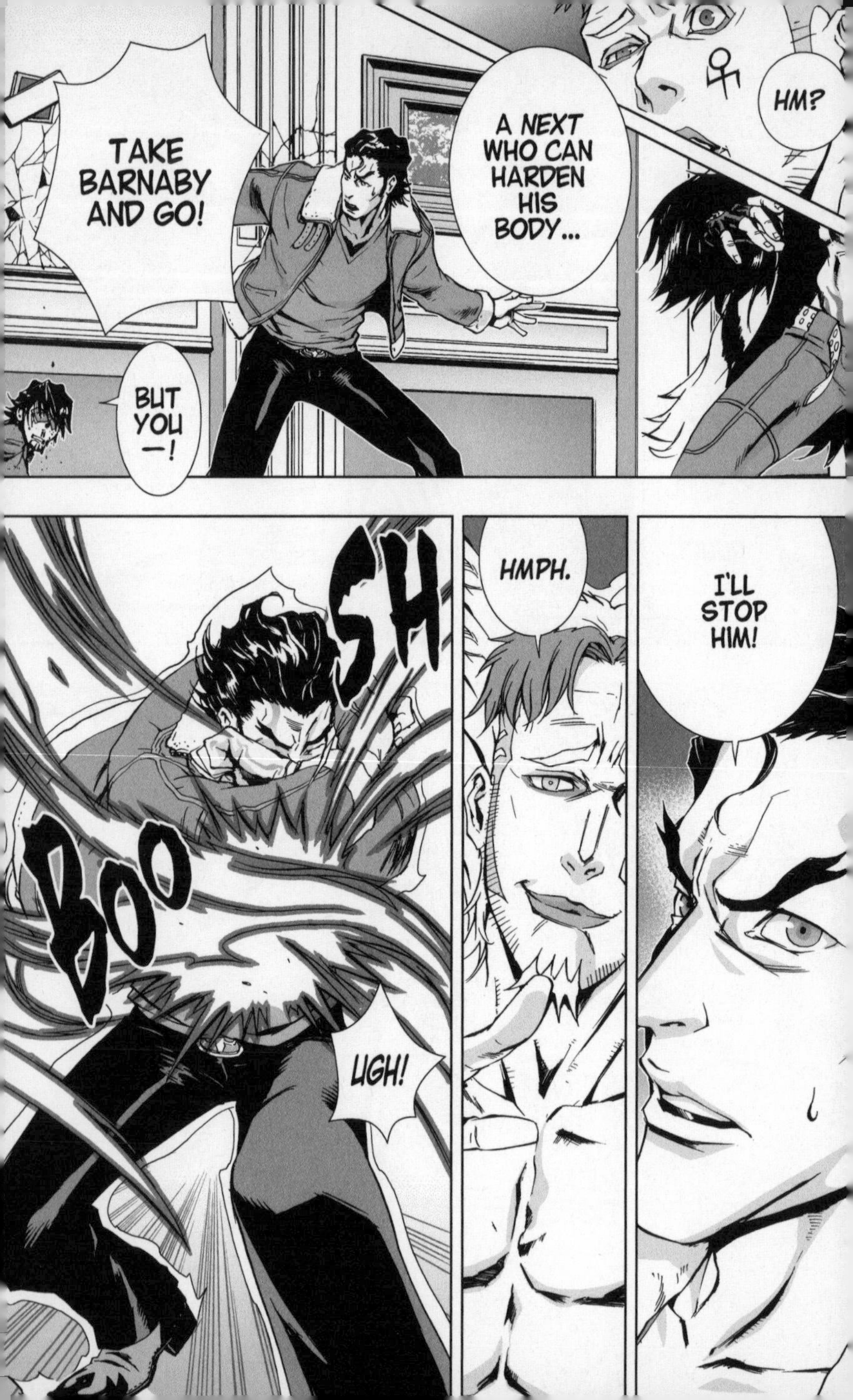
HM?
A NEXT WHO CAN HARDEN HIS BODY...
TAKE BARNABY AND GO!
BUT YOU—!
I'LL STOP HIM!
HMPH.
BOO
SH
UGH!

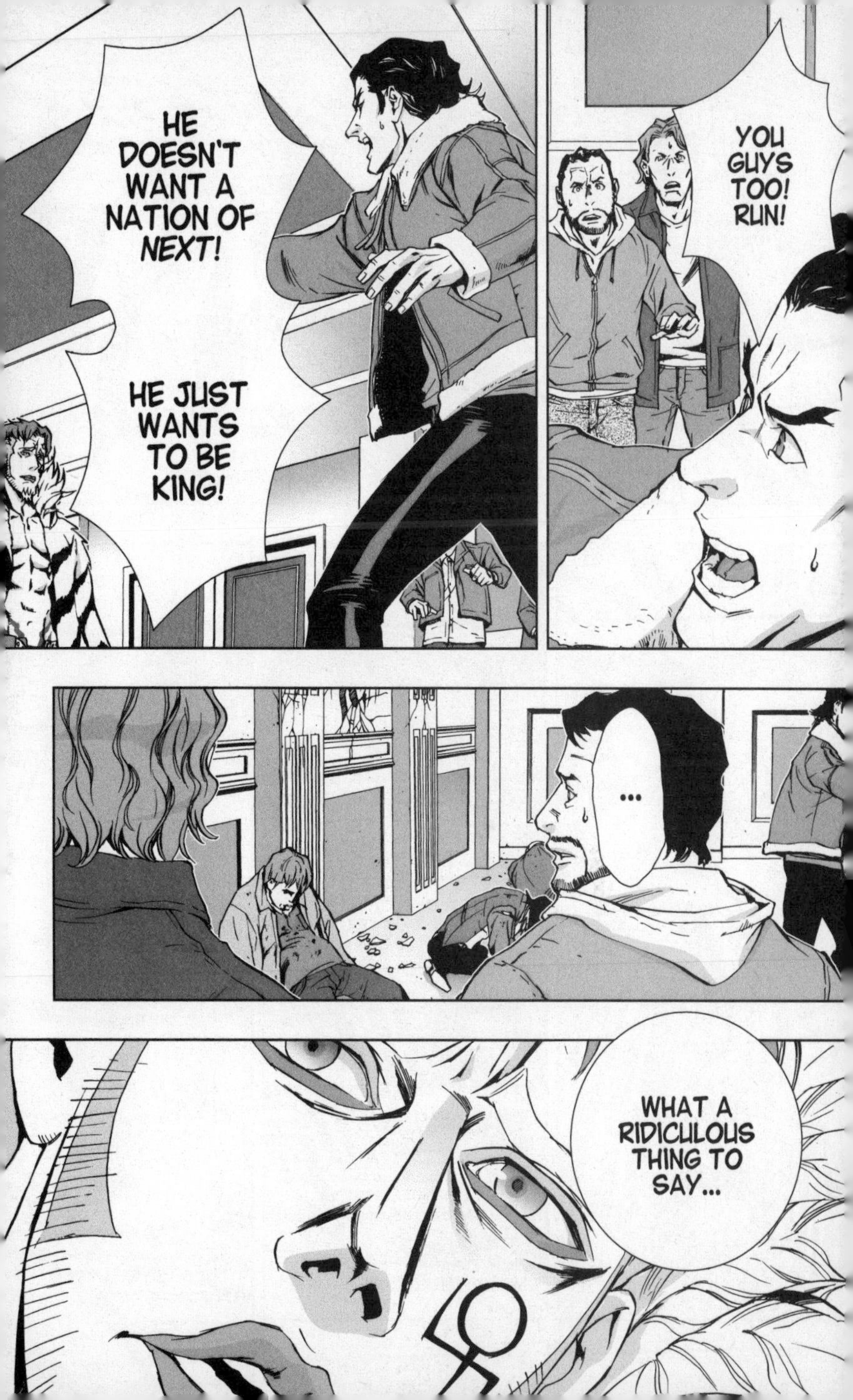
YOU GUYS TOO! RUN!
HE DOESN'T WANT A NATION OF NEXT!
HE JUST WANTS TO BE KING!
...
WHAT A RIDICULOUS THING TO SAY...

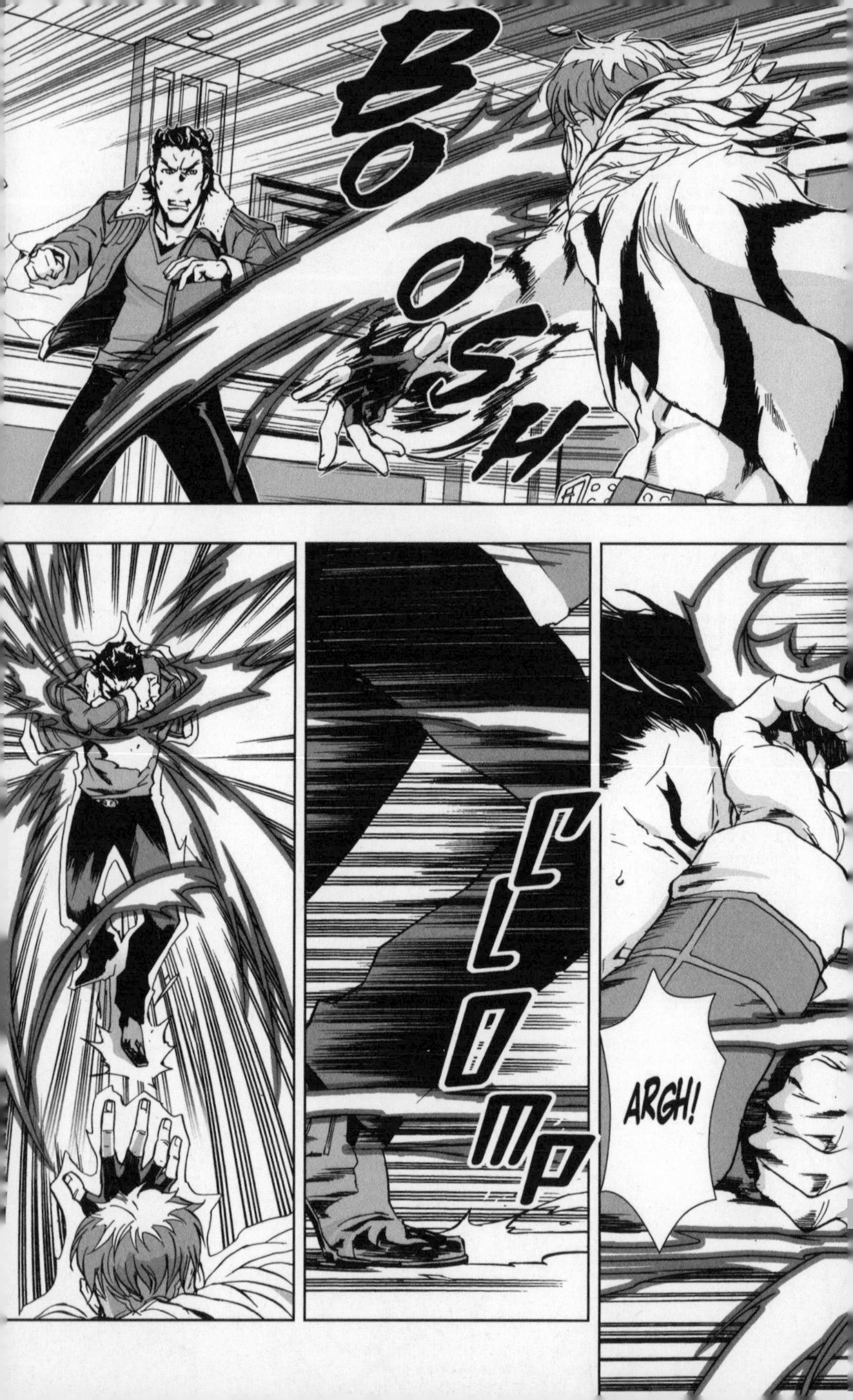
BOOSH
ARGH!
CLOMP

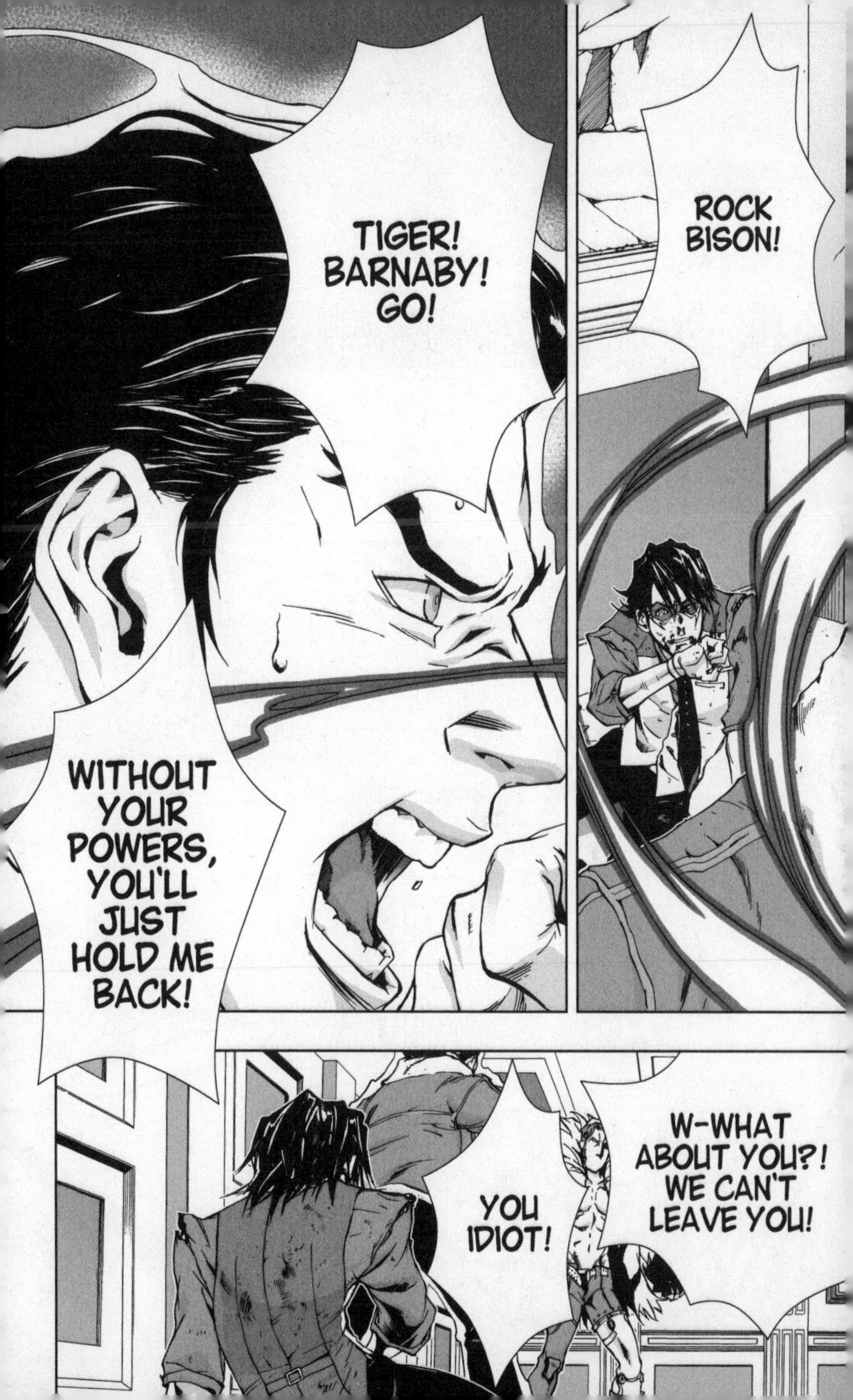
ROCK BISON!
TIGER! BARNABY! GO!
WITHOUT YOUR POWERS, YOU'LL JUST HOLD ME BACK!
W-WHAT ABOUT YOU?! WE CAN'T LEAVE YOU!
YOU IDIOT!

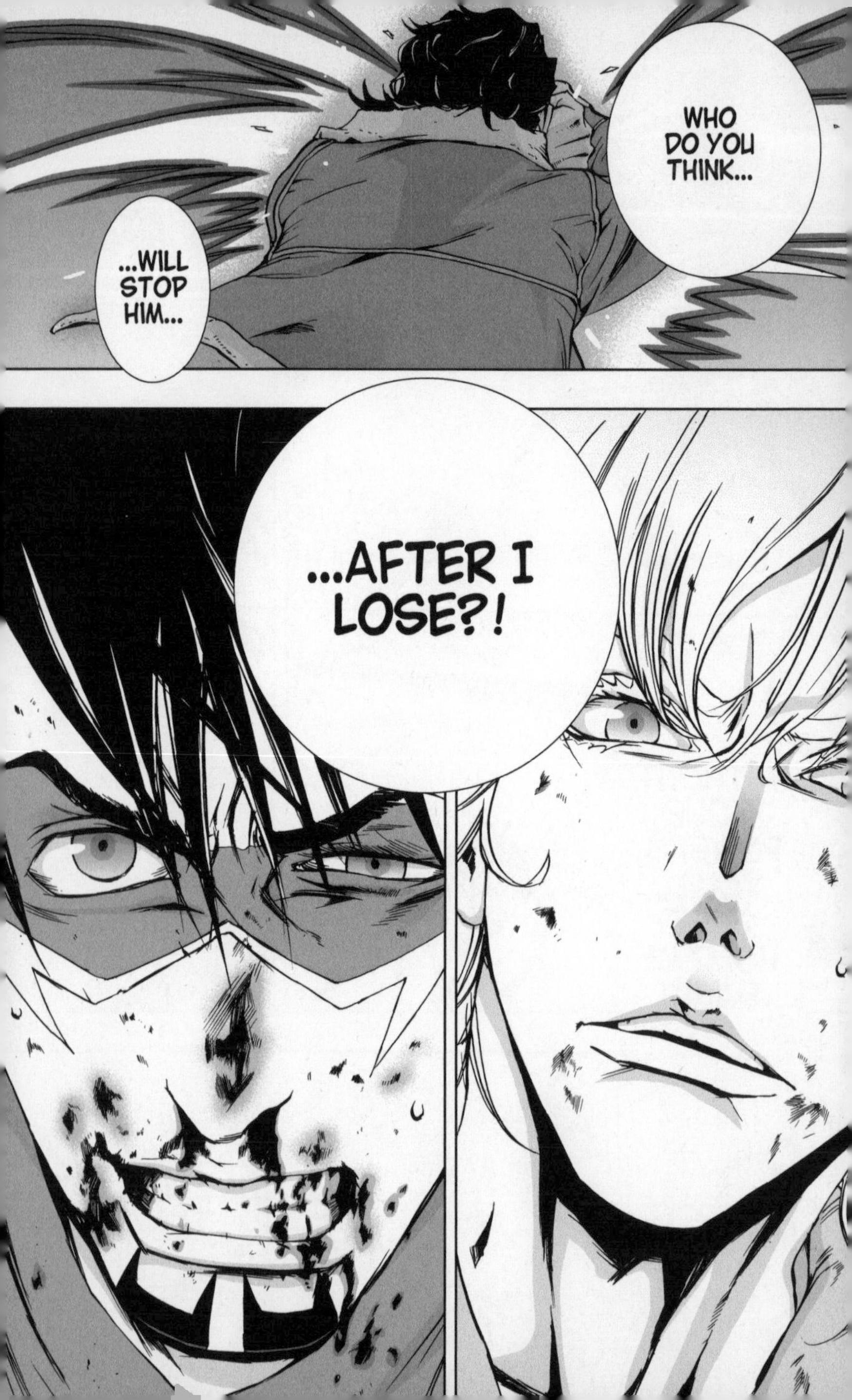
WHO DO YOU THINK...
...WILL STOP HIM...
...AFTER I LOSE?!

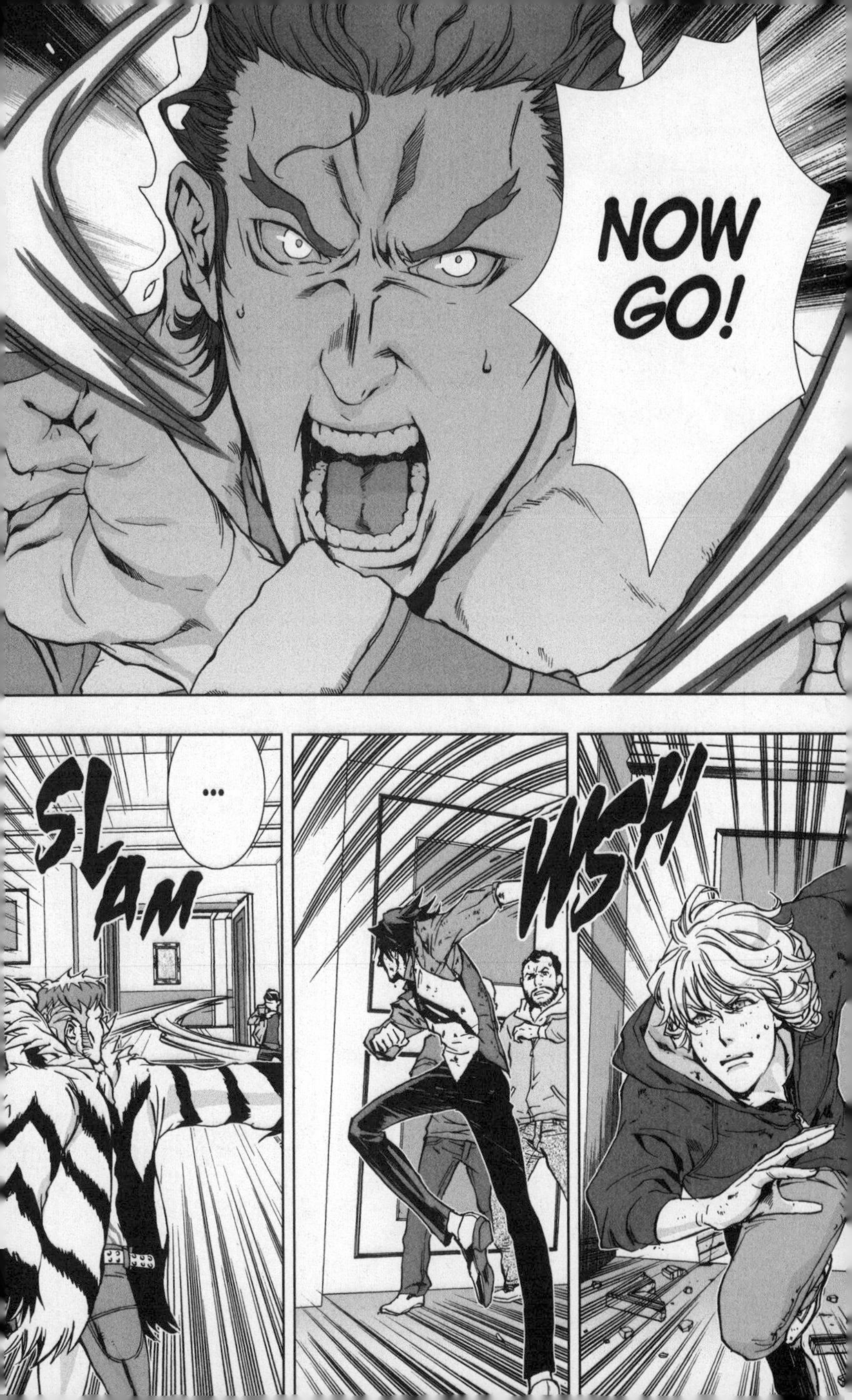
NOW GO!
WSH
...
SLAM

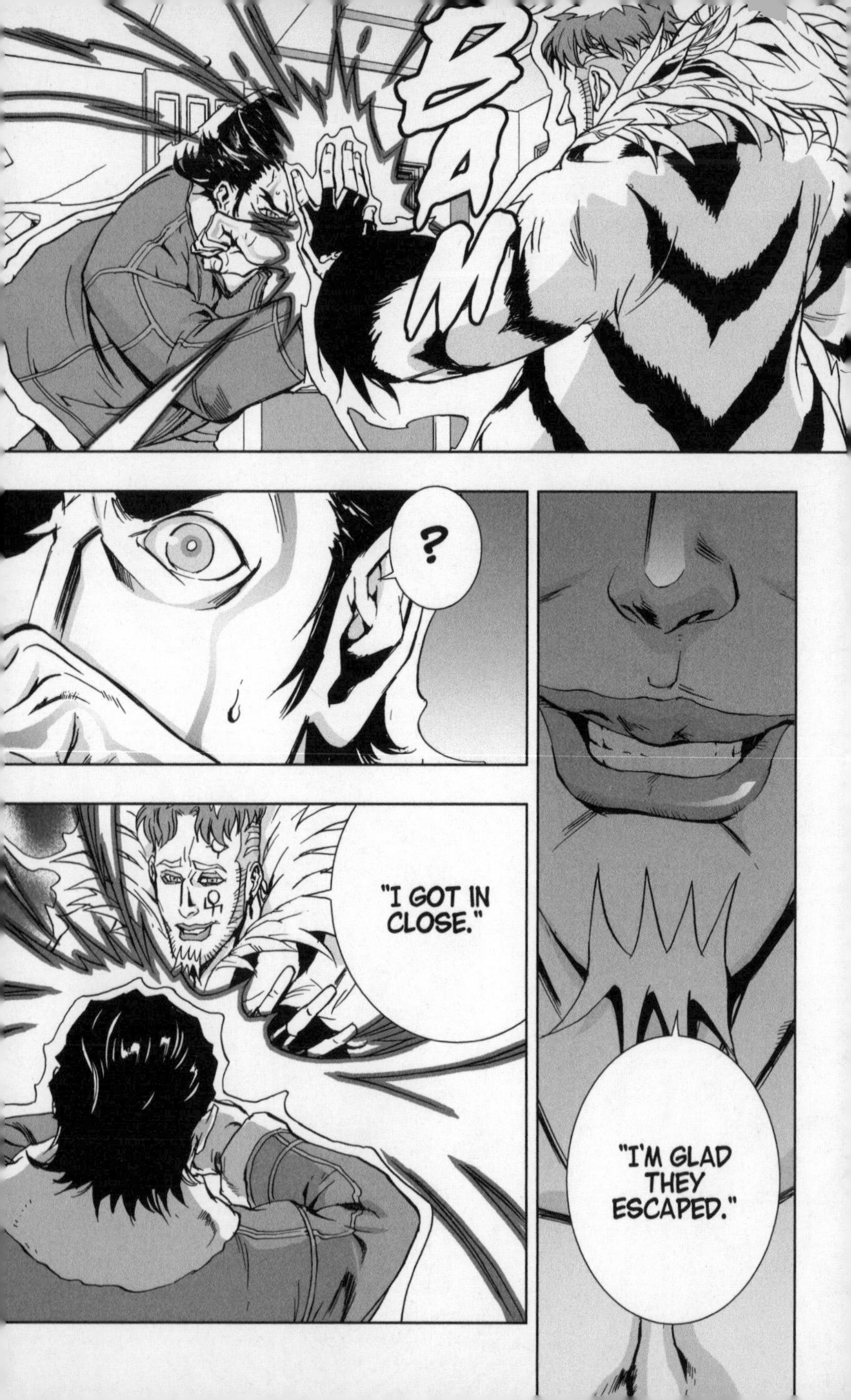
BAM
"I'M GLAD THEY ESCAPED."
?
"I GOT IN CLOSE."

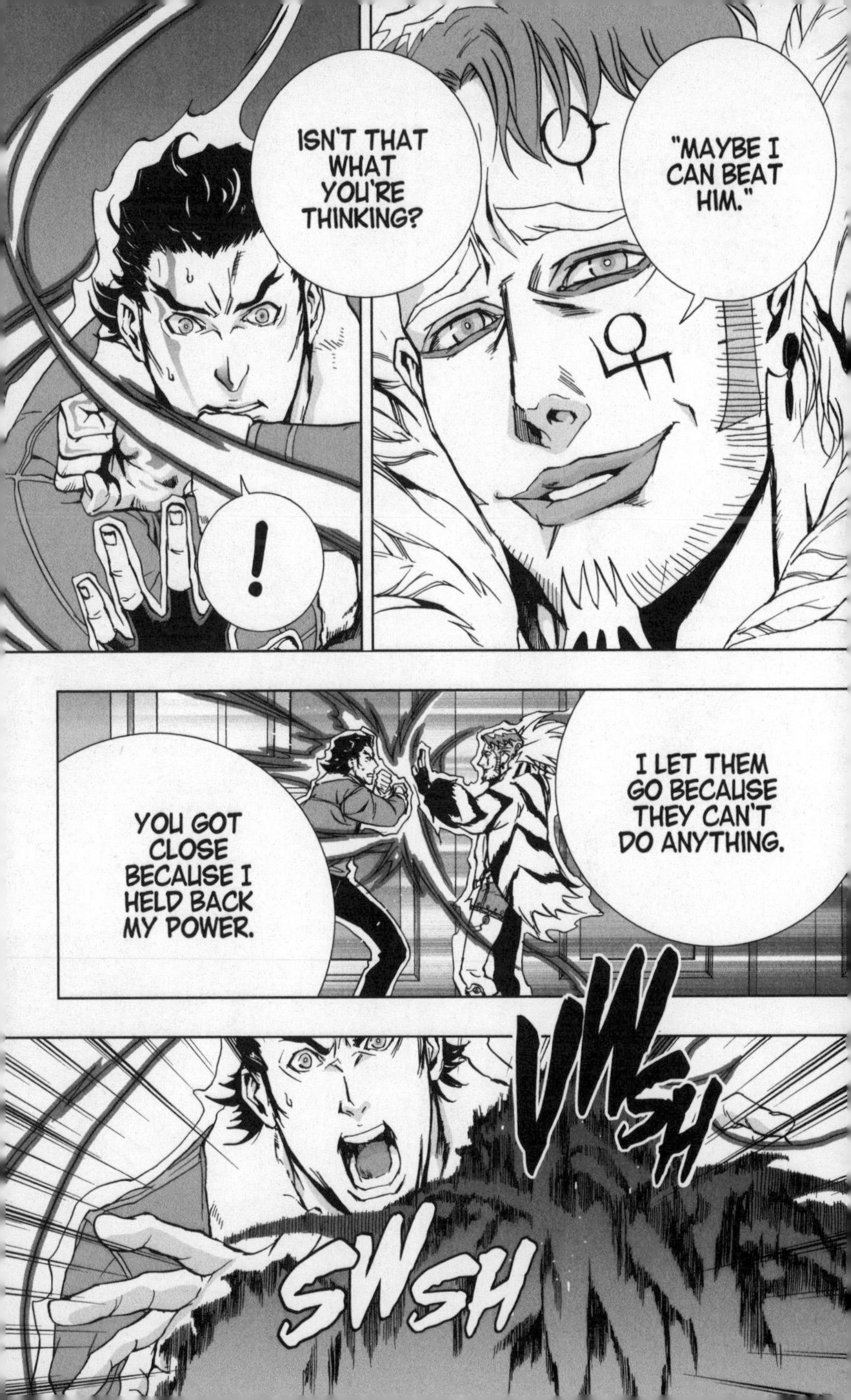
"MAYBE I CAN BEAT HIM."
ISN'T THAT WHAT YOU'RE THINKING?
!
I LET THEM GO BECAUSE THEY CAN'T DO ANYTHING.
YOU GOT CLOSE BECAUSE I HELD BACK MY POWER.
VWSH
SWSH

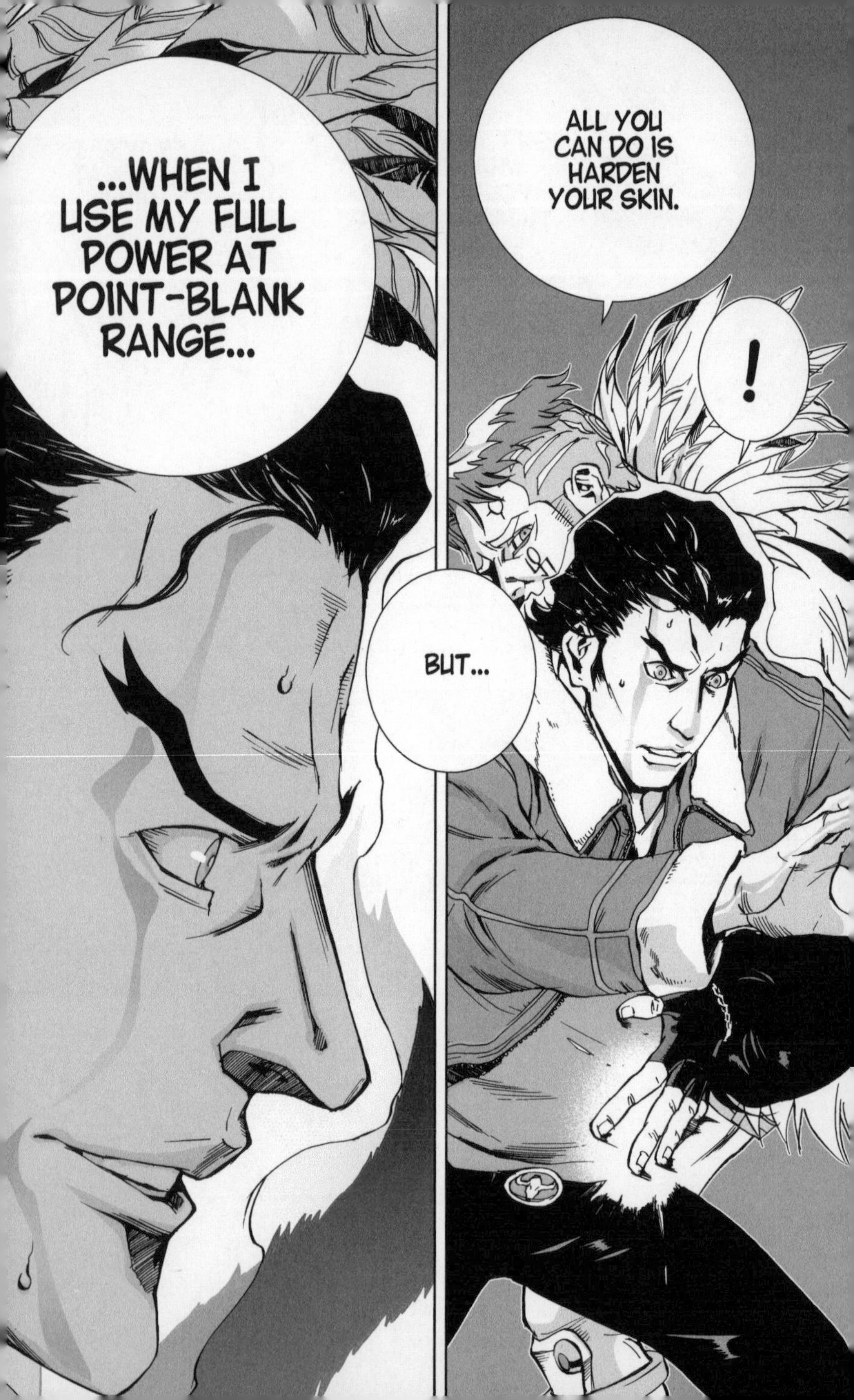
ALL YOU CAN DO IS HARDEN YOUR SKIN.
!
BUT...
...WHEN I USE MY FULL POWER AT POINT-BLANK RANGE...

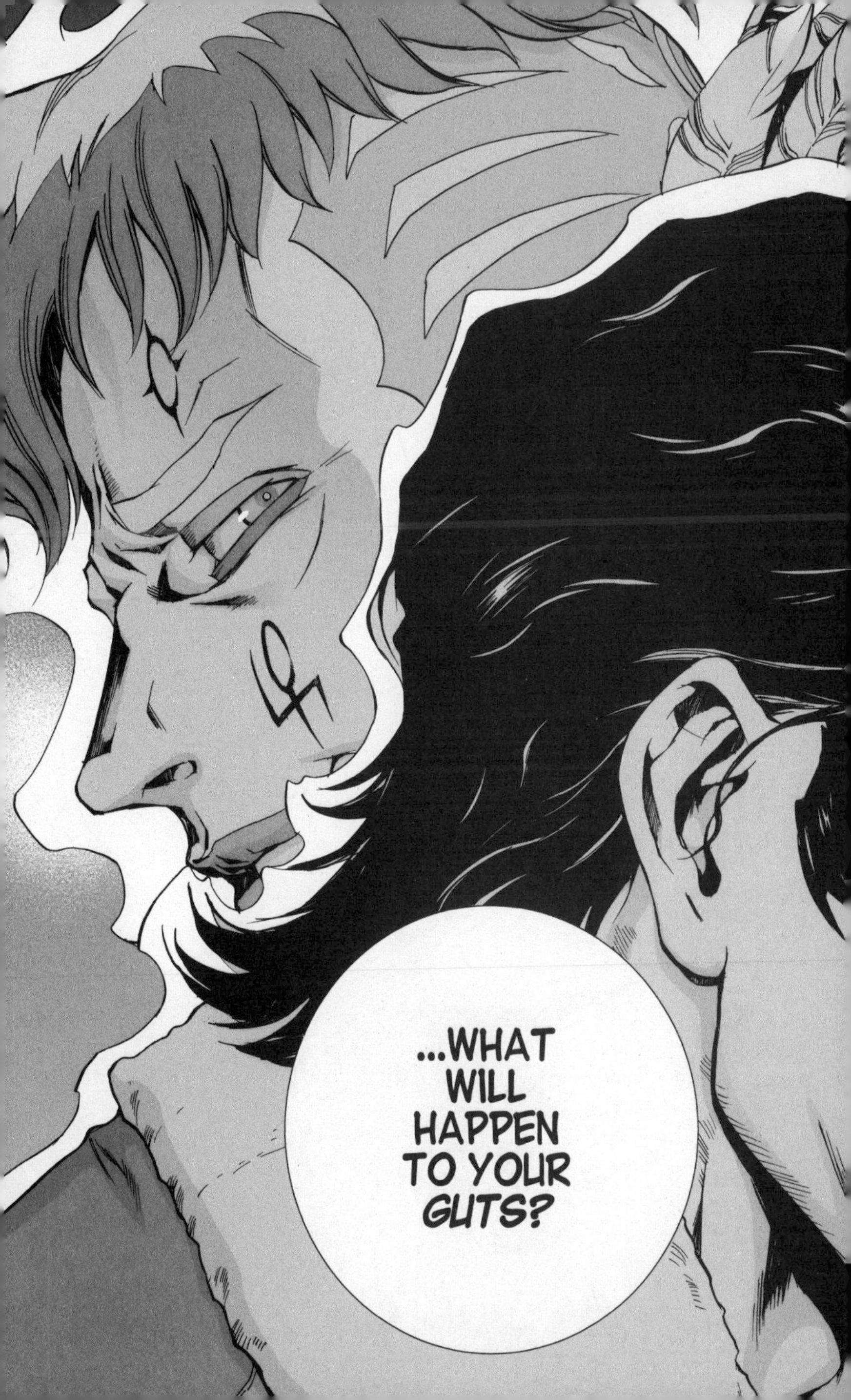
...WHAT WILL HAPPEN TO YOUR GUTS?

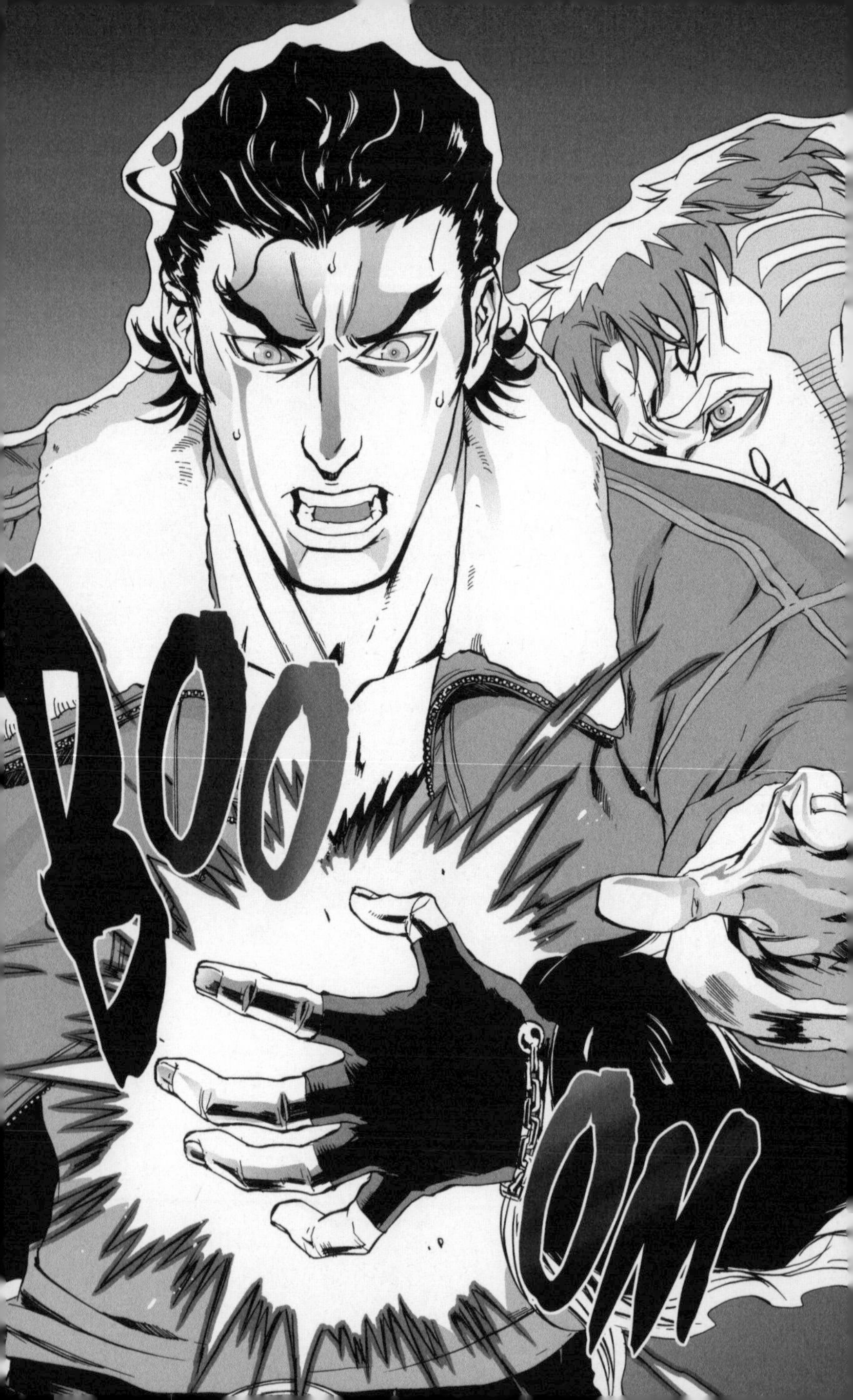
BOOOM

TIGER & BUNNY

TIGER&BUNNY

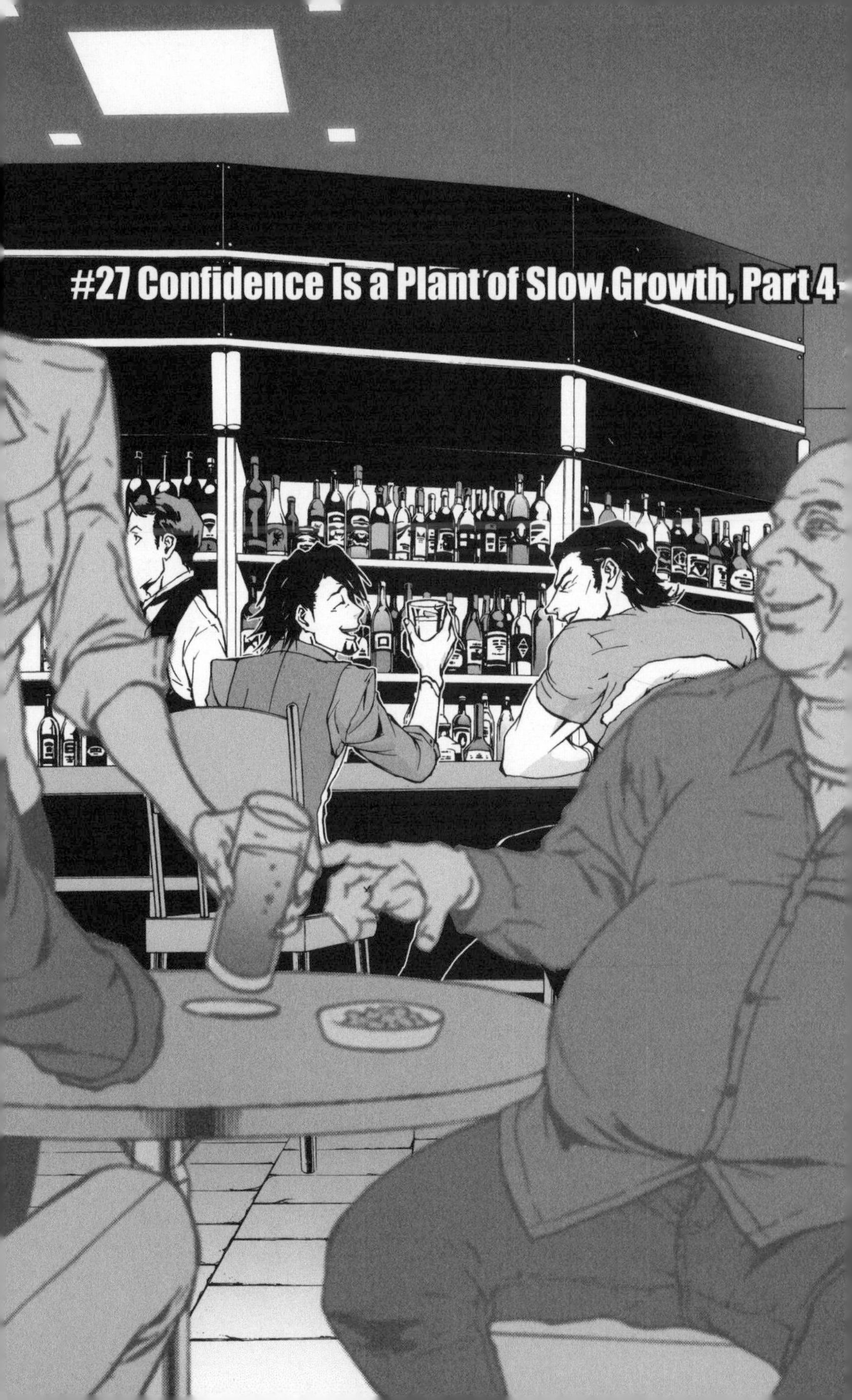
#27 Confidence Is a Plant of Slow Growth, Part 4

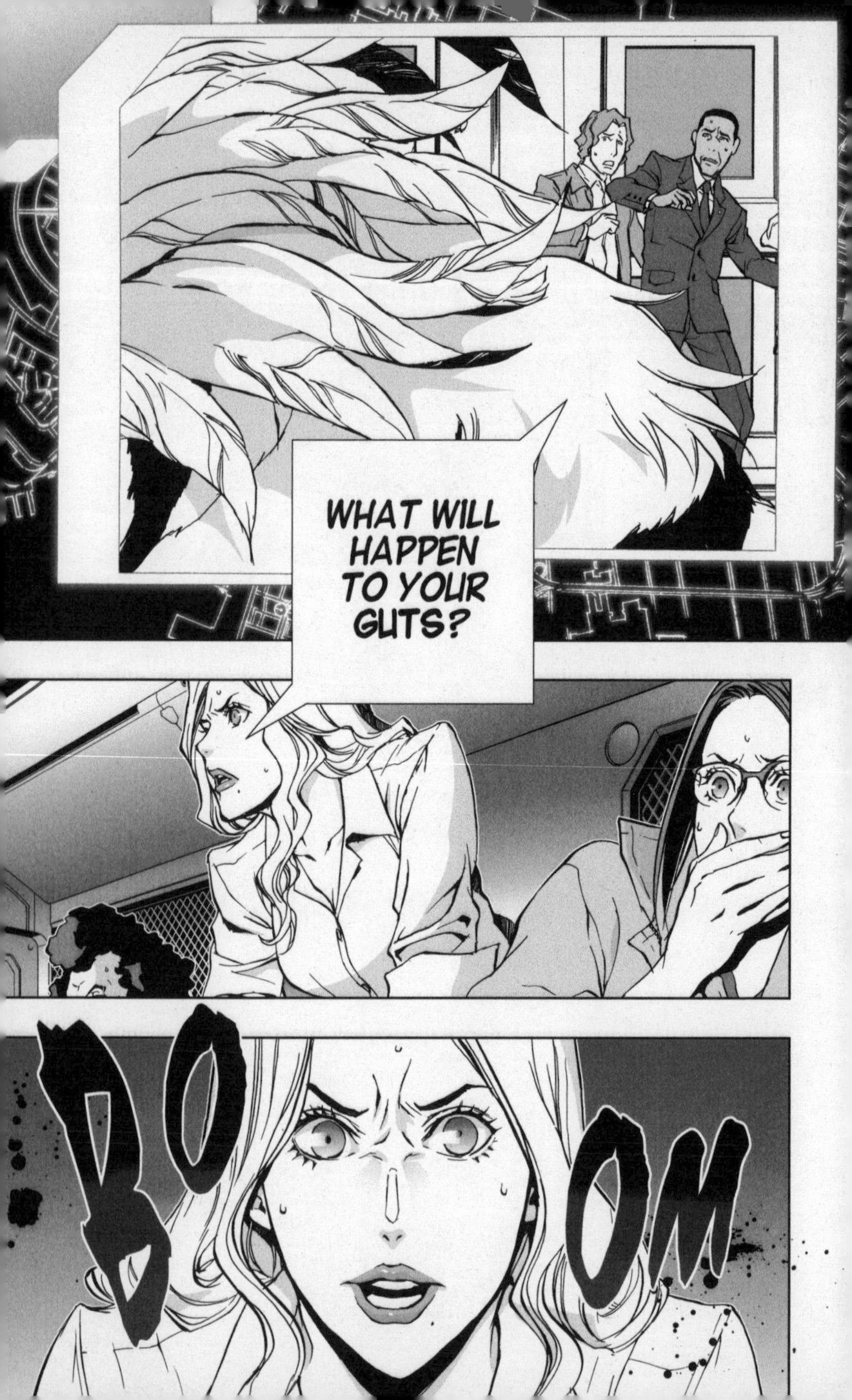
WHAT WILL HAPPEN TO YOUR GUTS?
BOOM

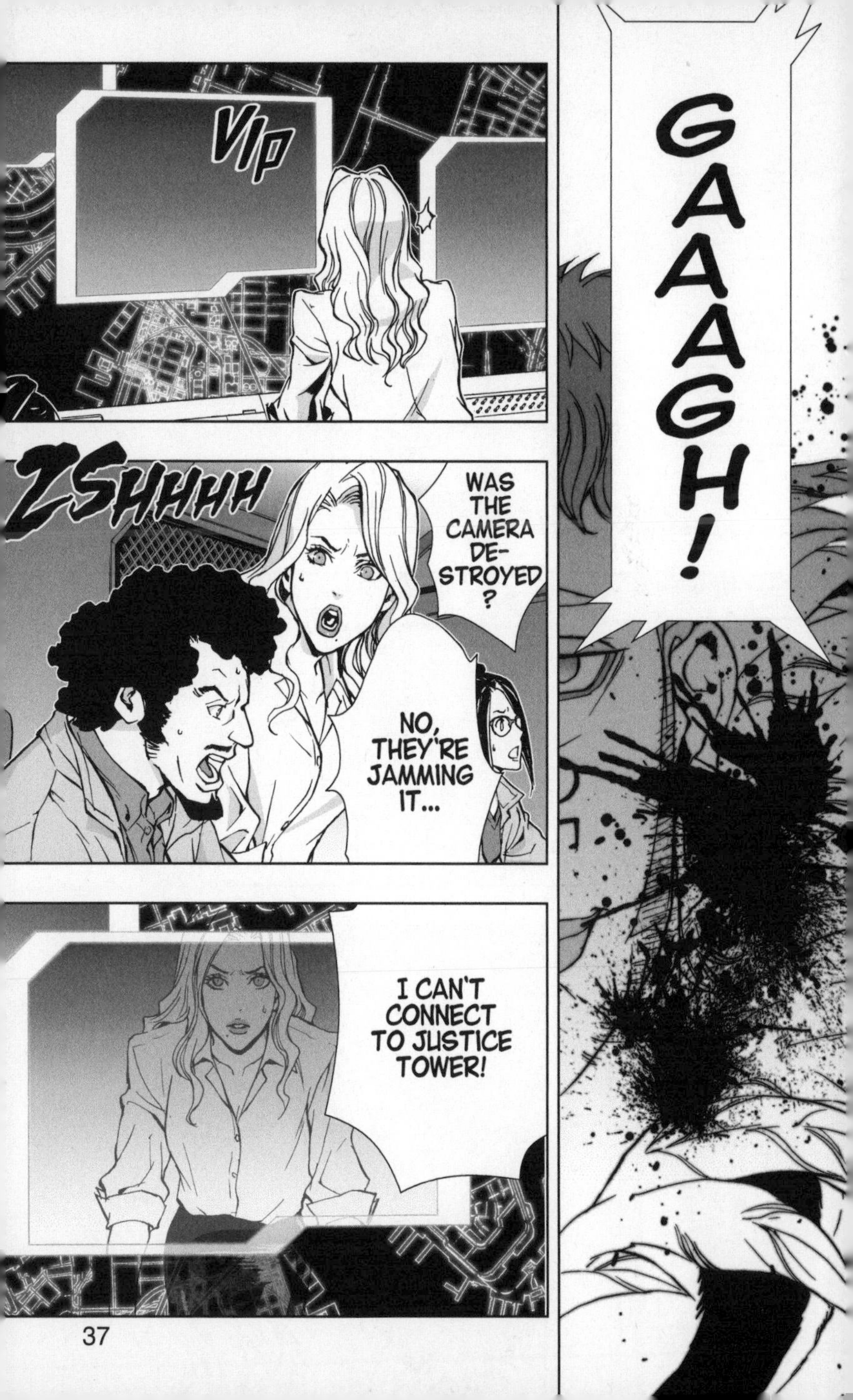
GAAAGH!
VIP
WAS THE CAMERA DE-STROYED?
ZSHHHH
NO, THEY'RE JAMMING IT...
I CAN'T CONNECT TO JUSTICE TOWER!

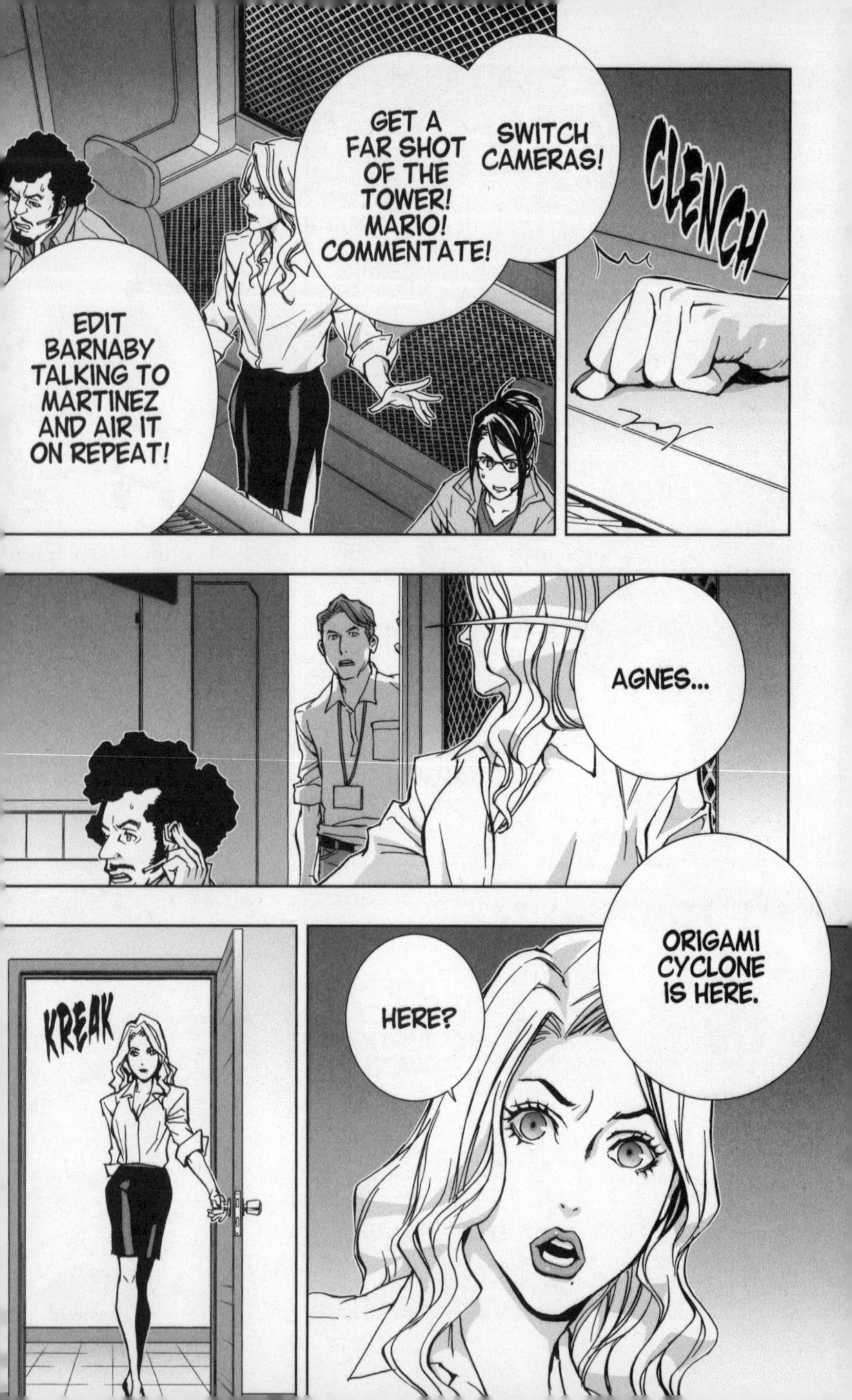
CLENCH
SWITCH CAMERAS!
GET A FAR SHOT OF THE TOWER! MARIO! COMMENTATE!
EDIT BARNABY TALKING TO MARTINEZ AND AIR IT ON REPEAT!
AGNES...
ORIGAMI CYCLONE IS HERE.
HERE?
KREAK

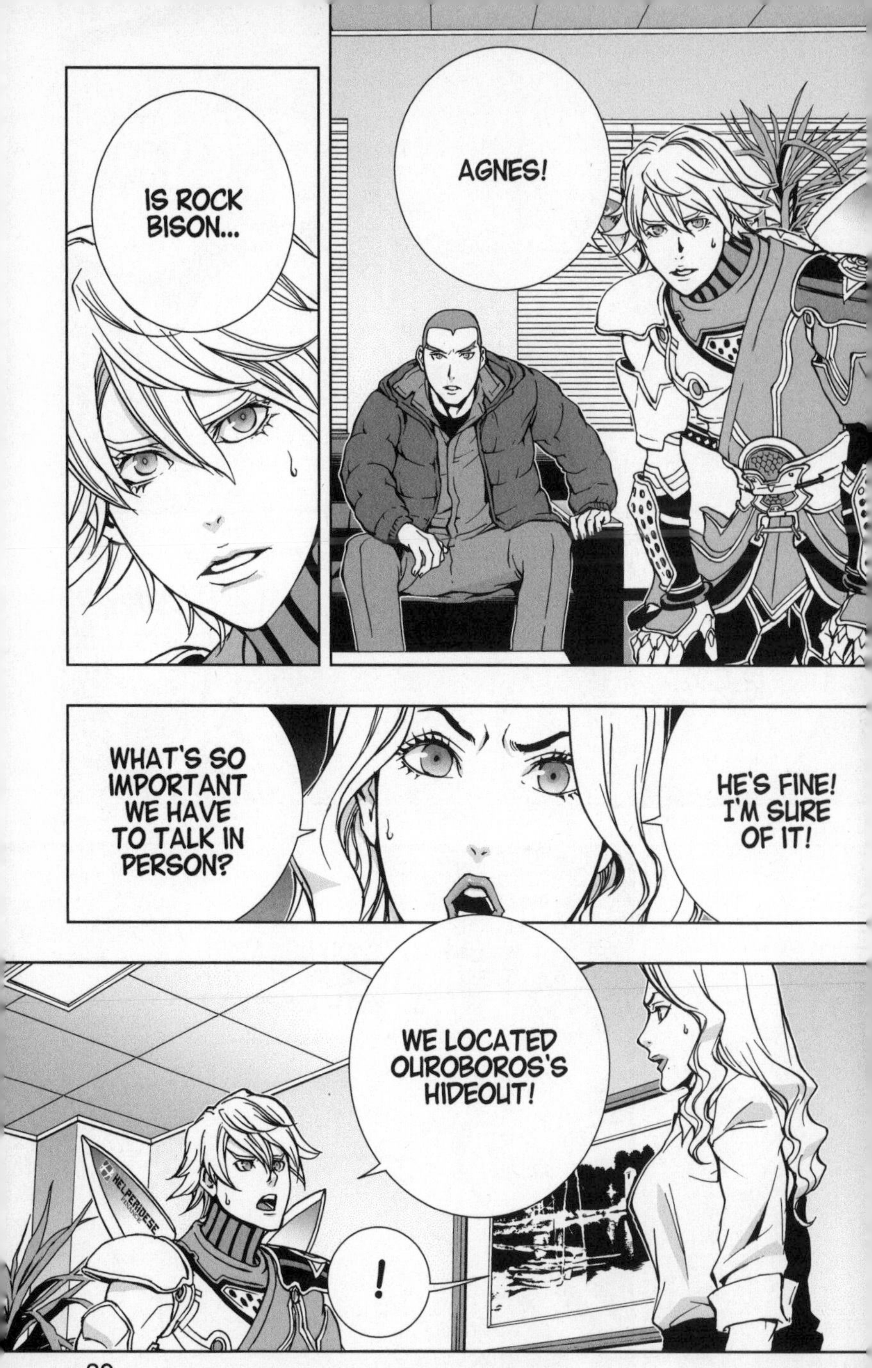
AGNES!
IS ROCK BISON...
HE'S FINE! I'M SURE OF IT!
WHAT'S SO IMPORTANT WE HAVE TO TALK IN PERSON?
WE LOCATED OUROBOROS'S HIDEOUT!
!

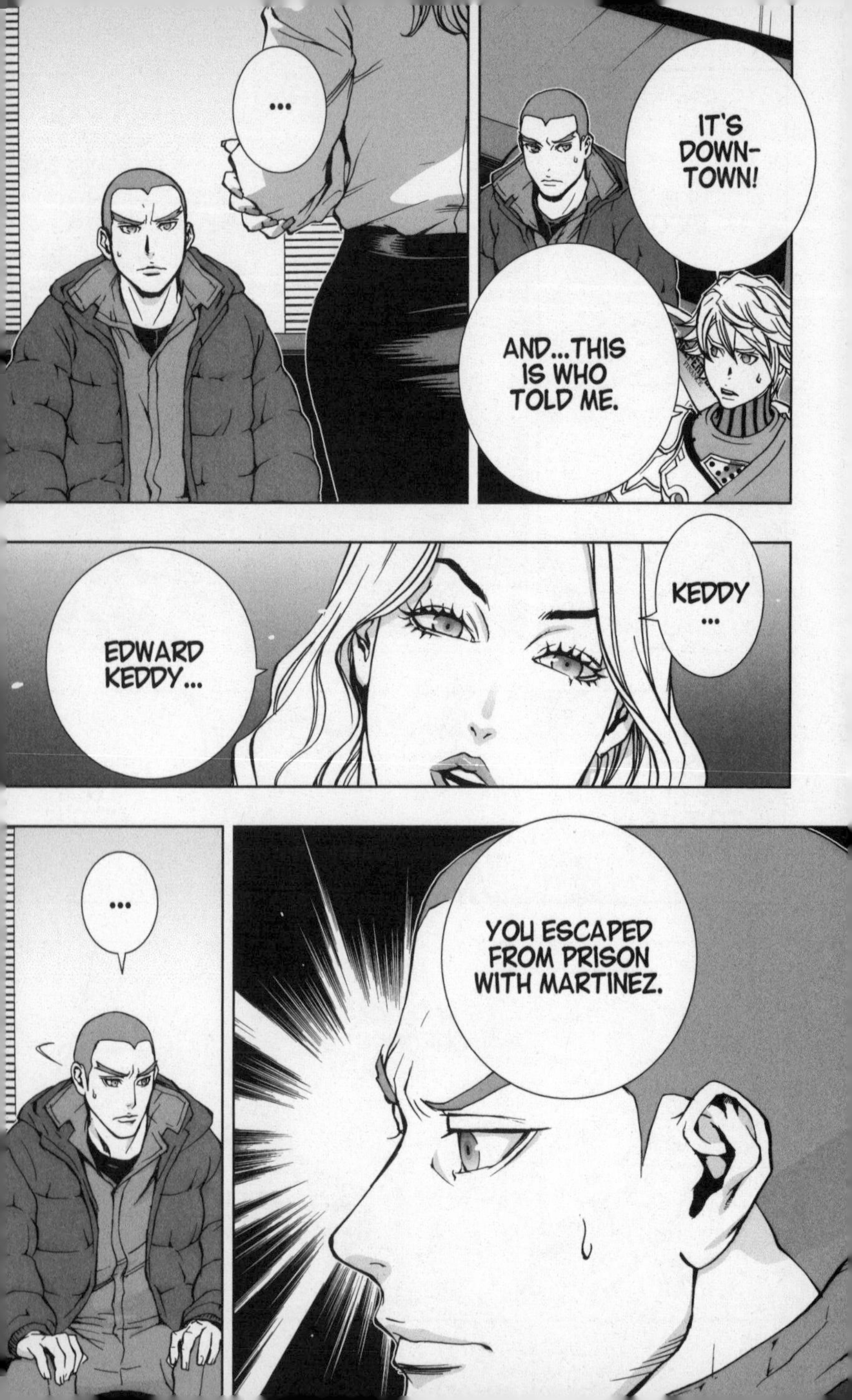
IT'S DOWN-TOWN!
AND...THIS IS WHO TOLD ME.
...
KEDDY ...
EDWARD KEDDY...
YOU ESCAPED FROM PRISON WITH MARTINEZ.
...

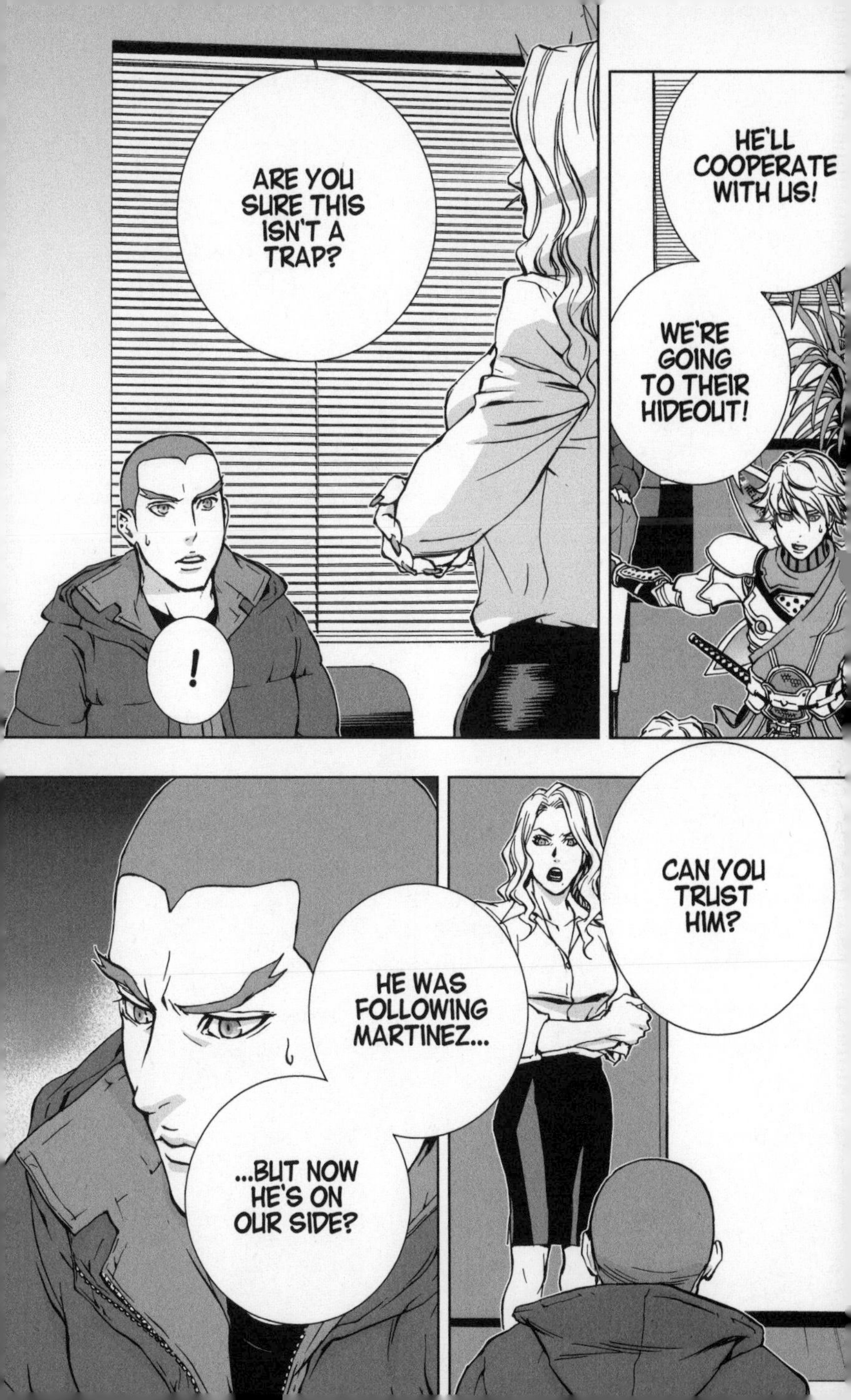
HE'LL COOPERATE WITH US!
WE'RE GOING TO THEIR HIDEOUT!
ARE YOU SURE THIS ISN'T A TRAP?
!
CAN YOU TRUST HIM?
HE WAS FOLLOWING MARTINEZ...
...BUT NOW HE'S ON OUR SIDE?

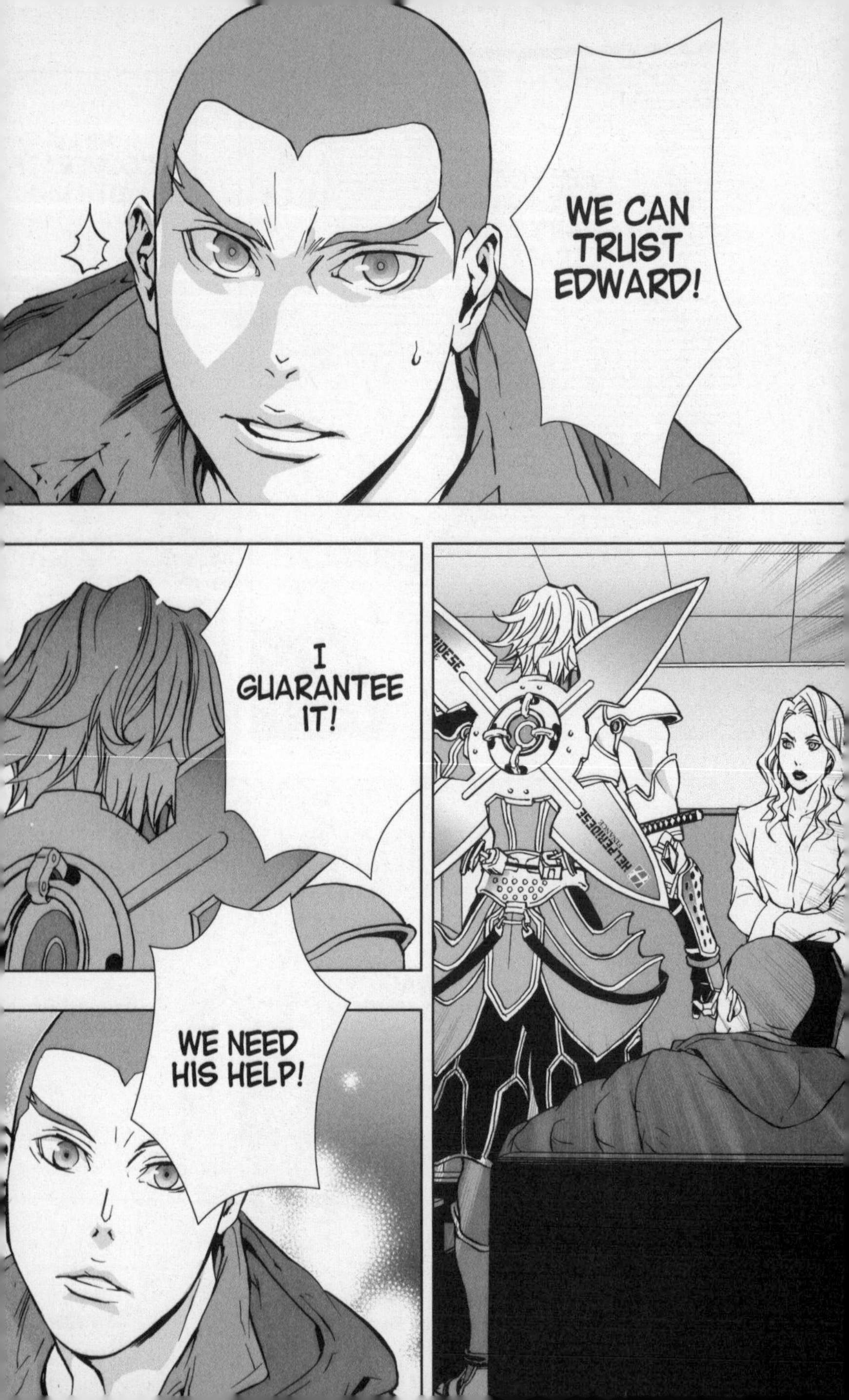
WE CAN TRUST EDWARD!
I GUARANTEE IT!
WE NEED HIS HELP!

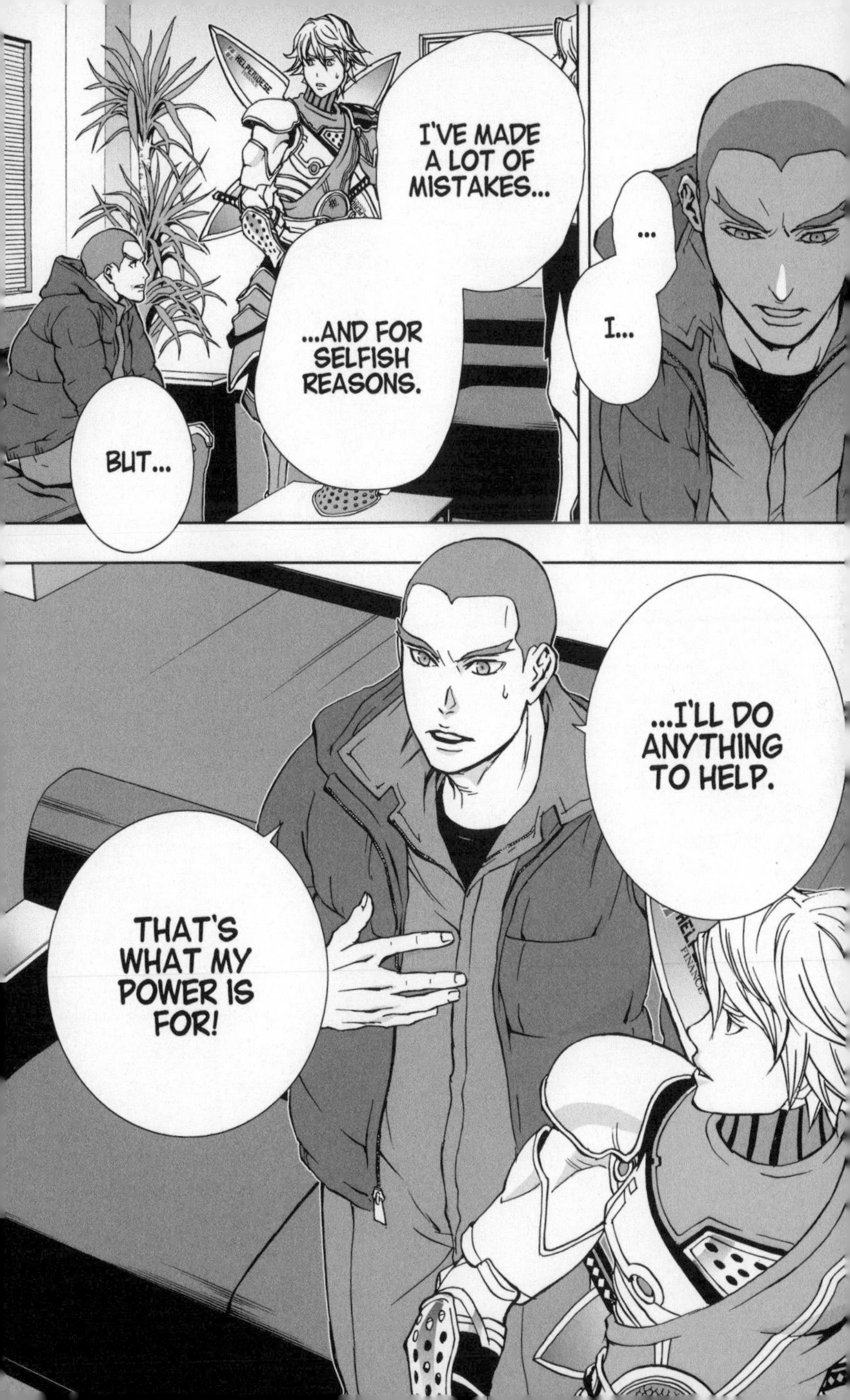
...
I...
I'VE MADE A LOT OF MISTAKES...
...AND FOR SELFISH REASONS.
BUT...
...I'LL DO ANYTHING TO HELP.
THAT'S WHAT MY POWER IS FOR!

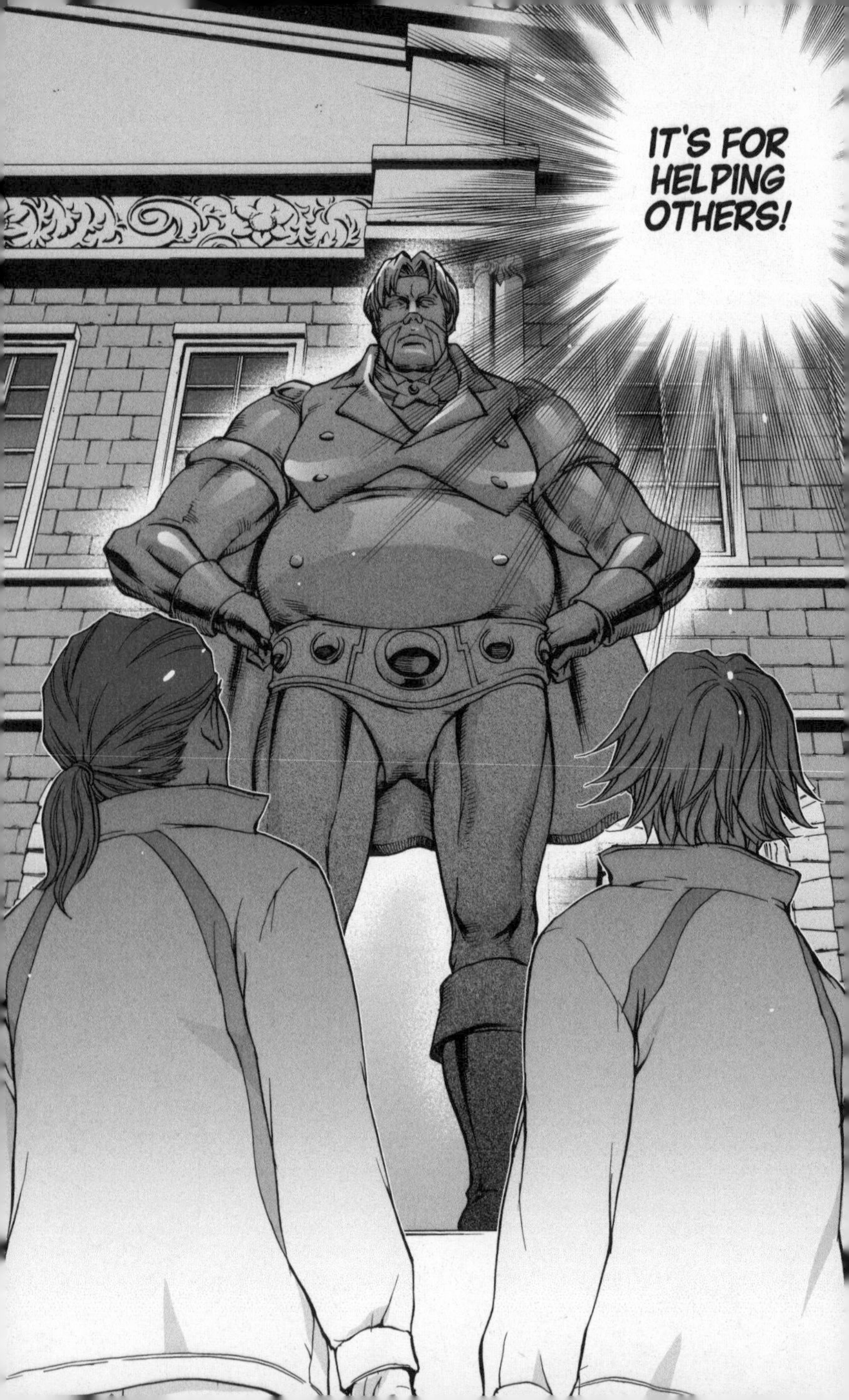
IT'S FOR HELPING OTHERS!

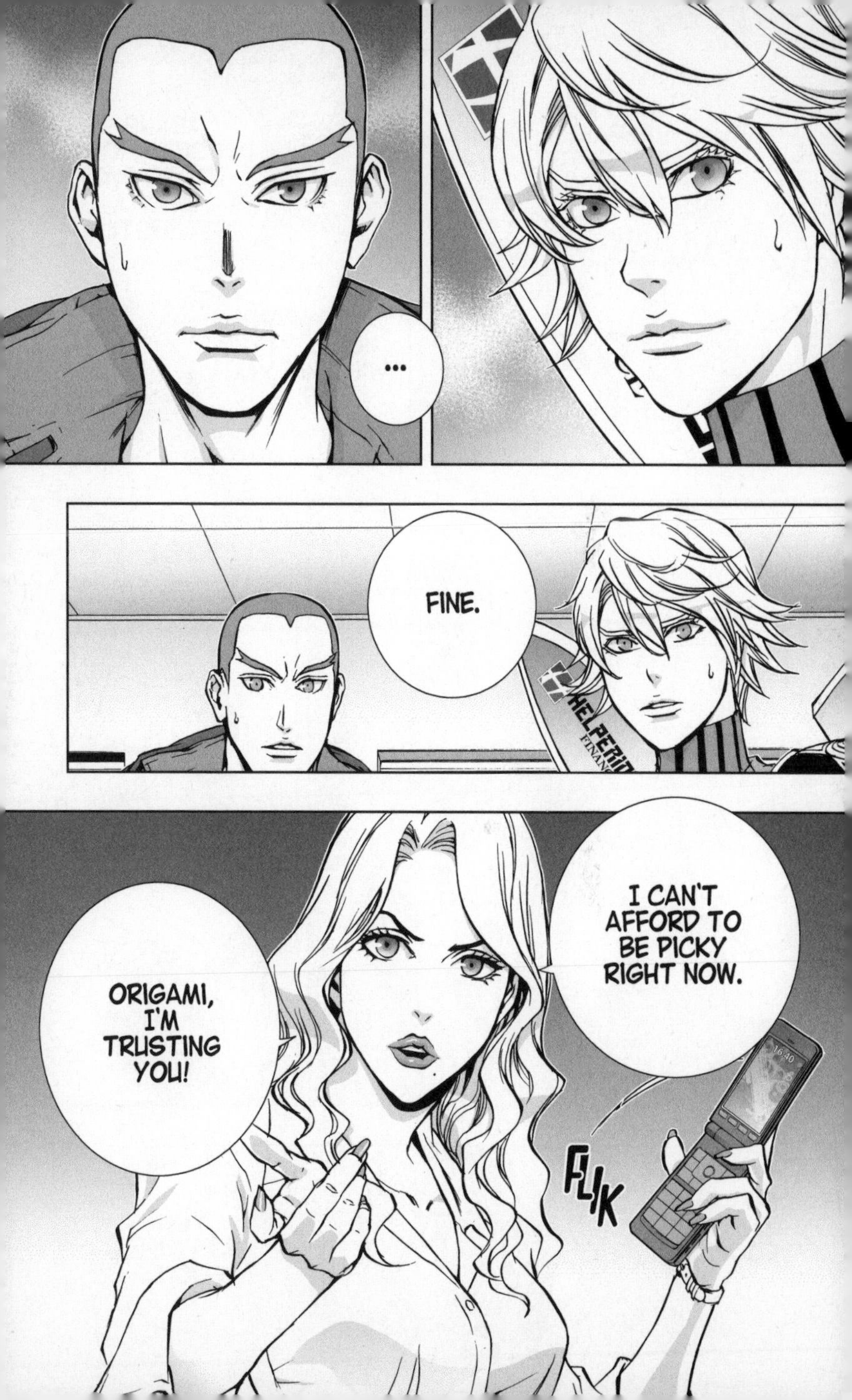
...
FINE.
I CAN'T AFFORD TO BE PICKY RIGHT NOW.
ORIGAMI, I'M TRUSTING YOU!
FLIK

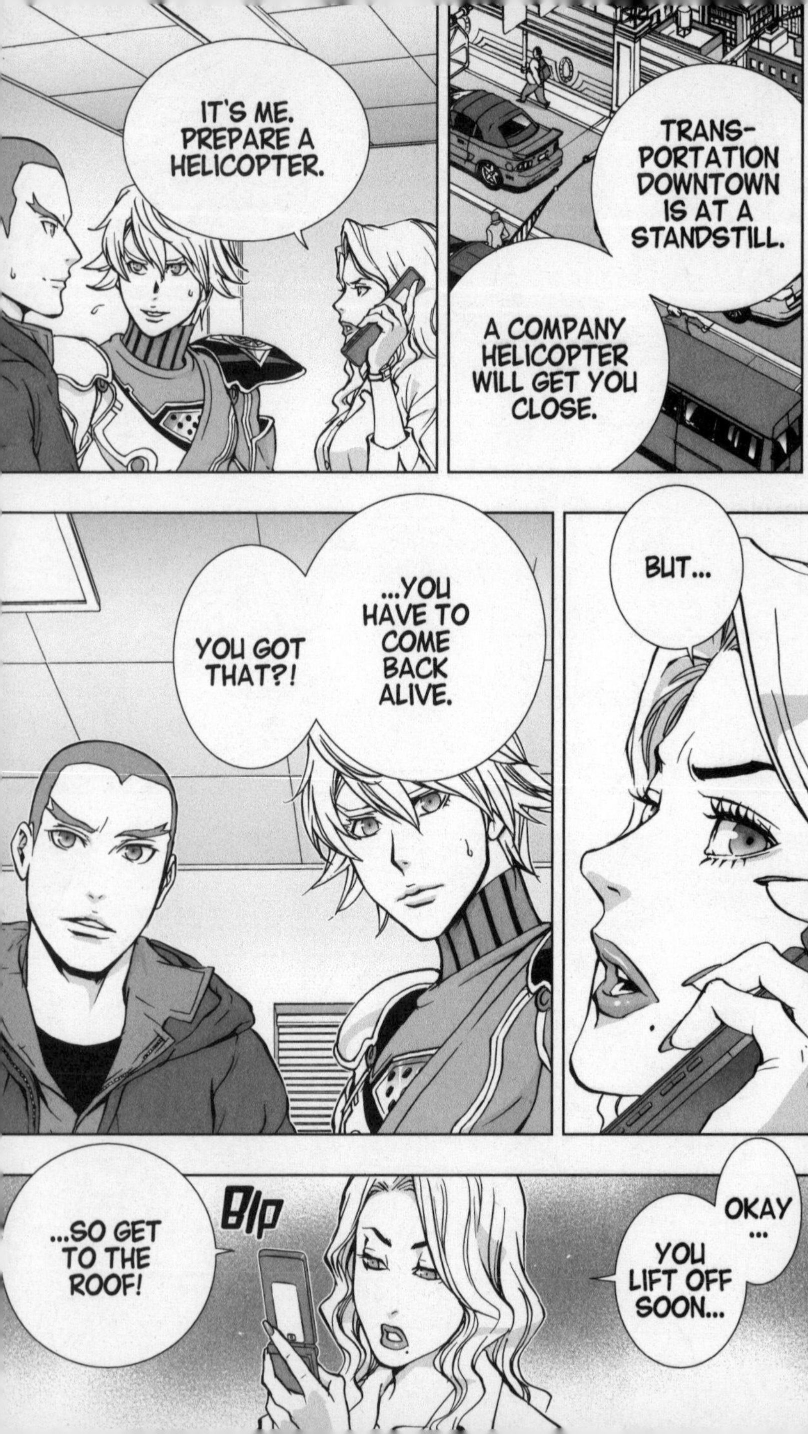
TRANS-PORTATION DOWNTOWN IS AT A STANDSTILL.
A COMPANY HELICOPTER WILL GET YOU CLOSE.
IT'S ME. PREPARE A HELICOPTER.
BUT...
...YOU HAVE TO COME BACK ALIVE.
YOU GOT THAT?!
OKAY ... YOU LIFT OFF SOON...
BLIP
...SO GET TO THE ROOF!

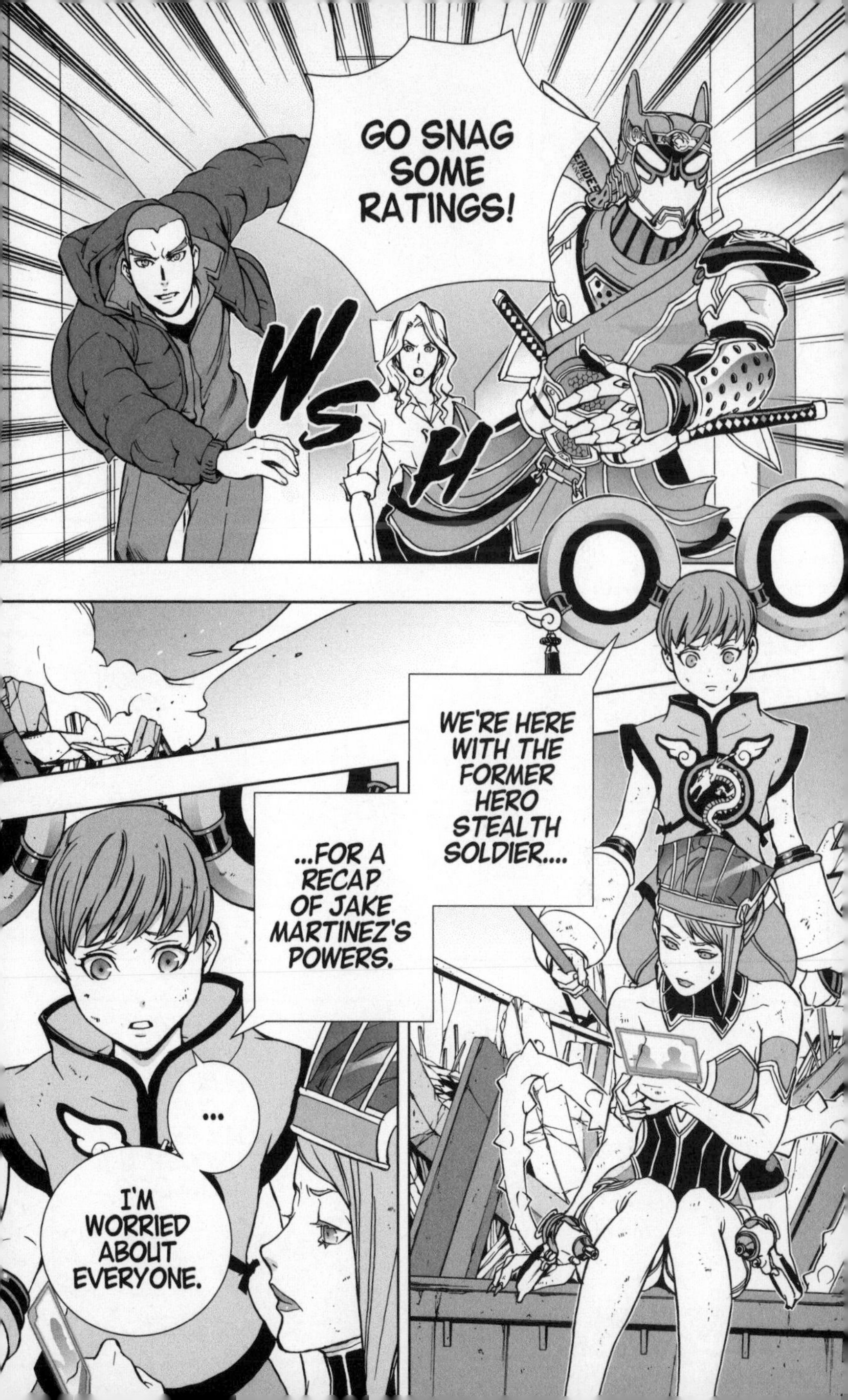
GO SNAG SOME RATINGS!
WSH
WE'RE HERE WITH THE FORMER HERO STEALTH SOLDIER....
...FOR A RECAP OF JAKE MARTINEZ'S POWERS.
...
I'M WORRIED ABOUT EVERYONE.

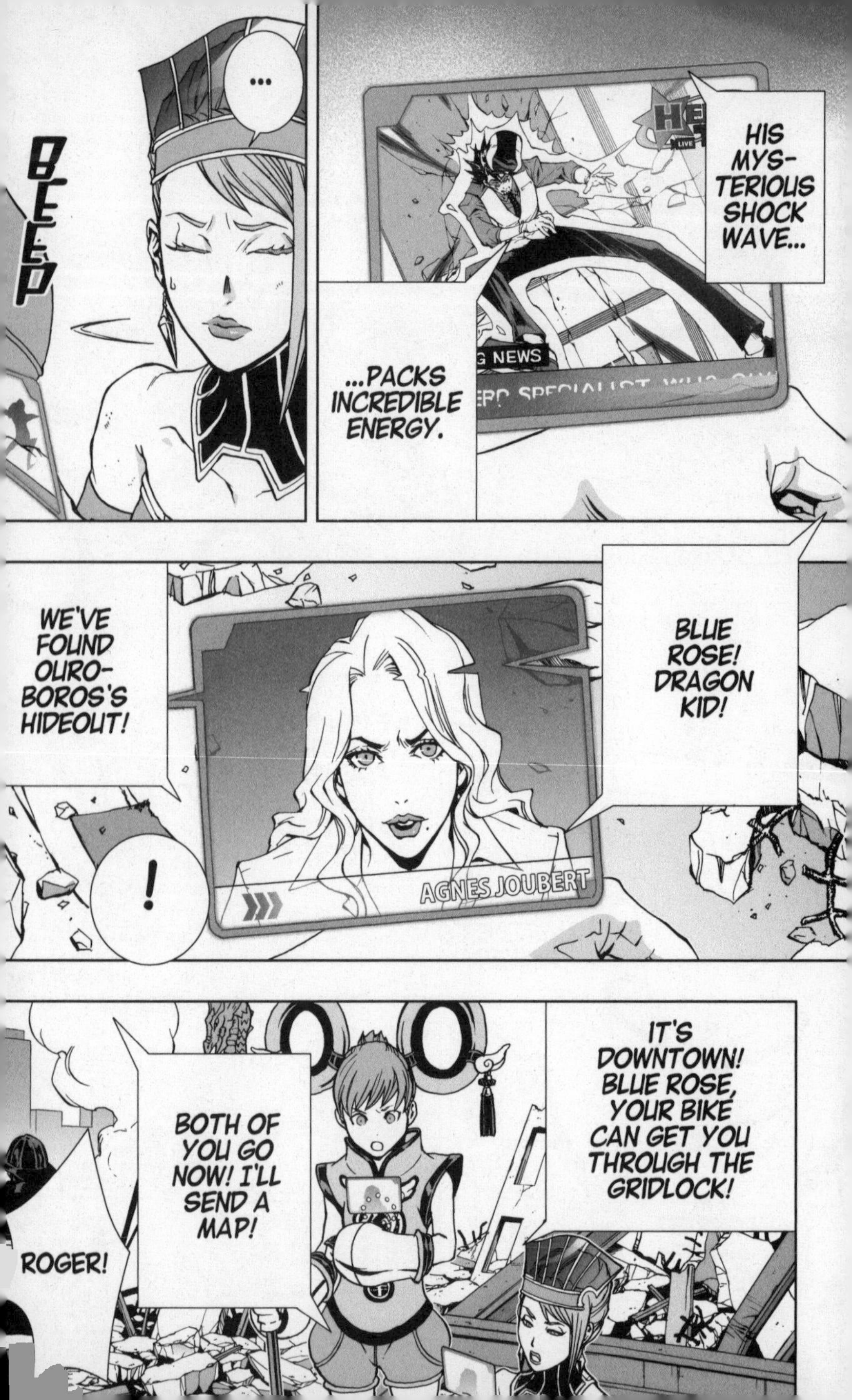
HIS MYSTERIOUS SHOCK WAVE...
...PACKS INCREDIBLE ENERGY.
...
BEEP
BLUE ROSE! DRAGON KID!
AGNES JOUBERT
WE'VE FOUND OUROBOROS'S HIDEOUT!
!
IT'S DOWNTOWN! BLUE ROSE, YOUR BIKE CAN GET YOU THROUGH THE GRIDLOCK!
BOTH OF YOU GO NOW! I'LL SEND A MAP!
ROGER!

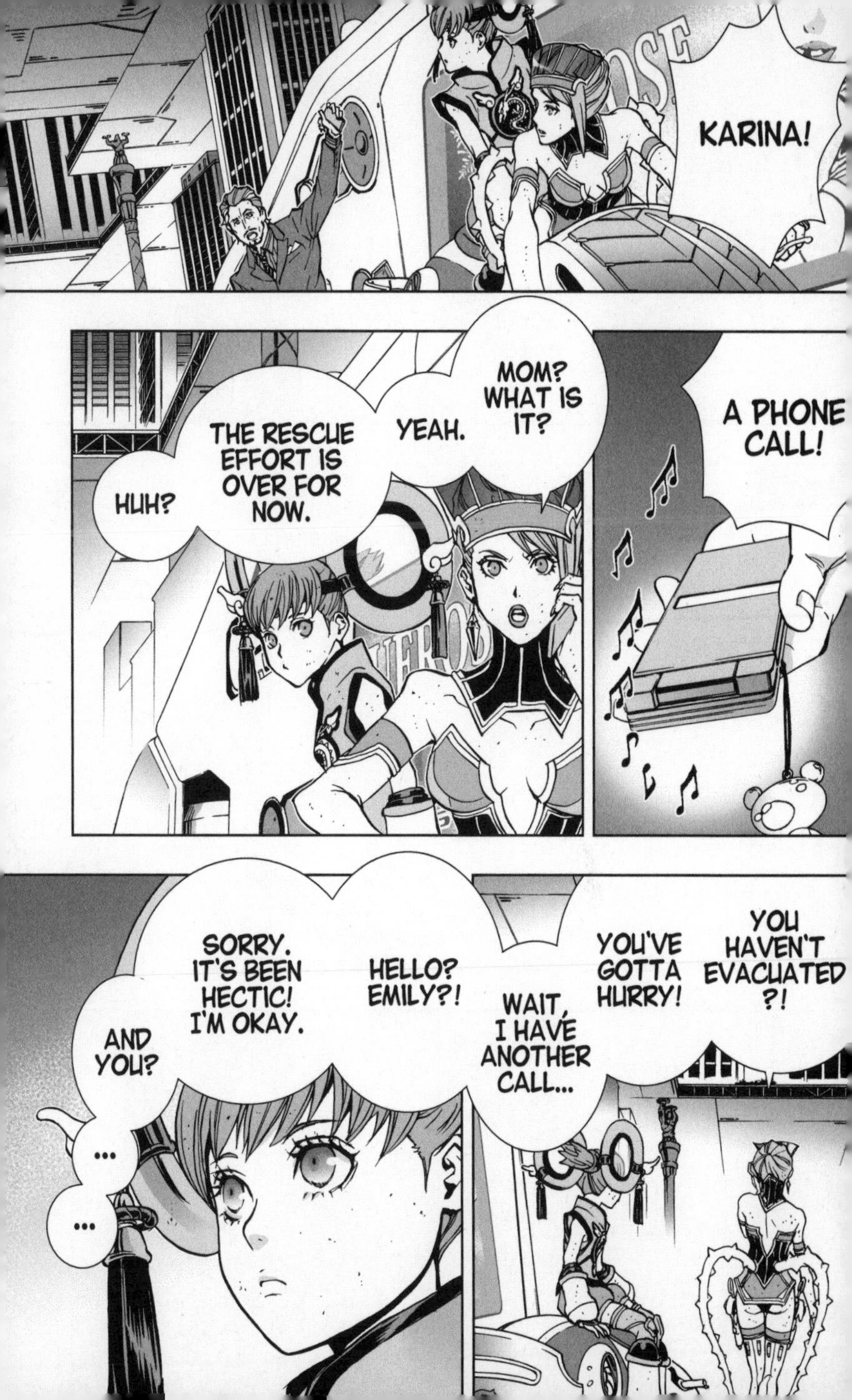
KARINA!
A PHONE CALL!
MOM? WHAT IS IT?
YEAH.
THE RESCUE EFFORT IS OVER FOR NOW.
HUH?
YOU HAVEN'T EVACUATED?!
YOU'VE GOTTA HURRY!
WAIT, I HAVE ANOTHER CALL...
HELLO? EMILY?!
SORRY. IT'S BEEN HECTIC! I'M OKAY.
AND YOU?
...
...

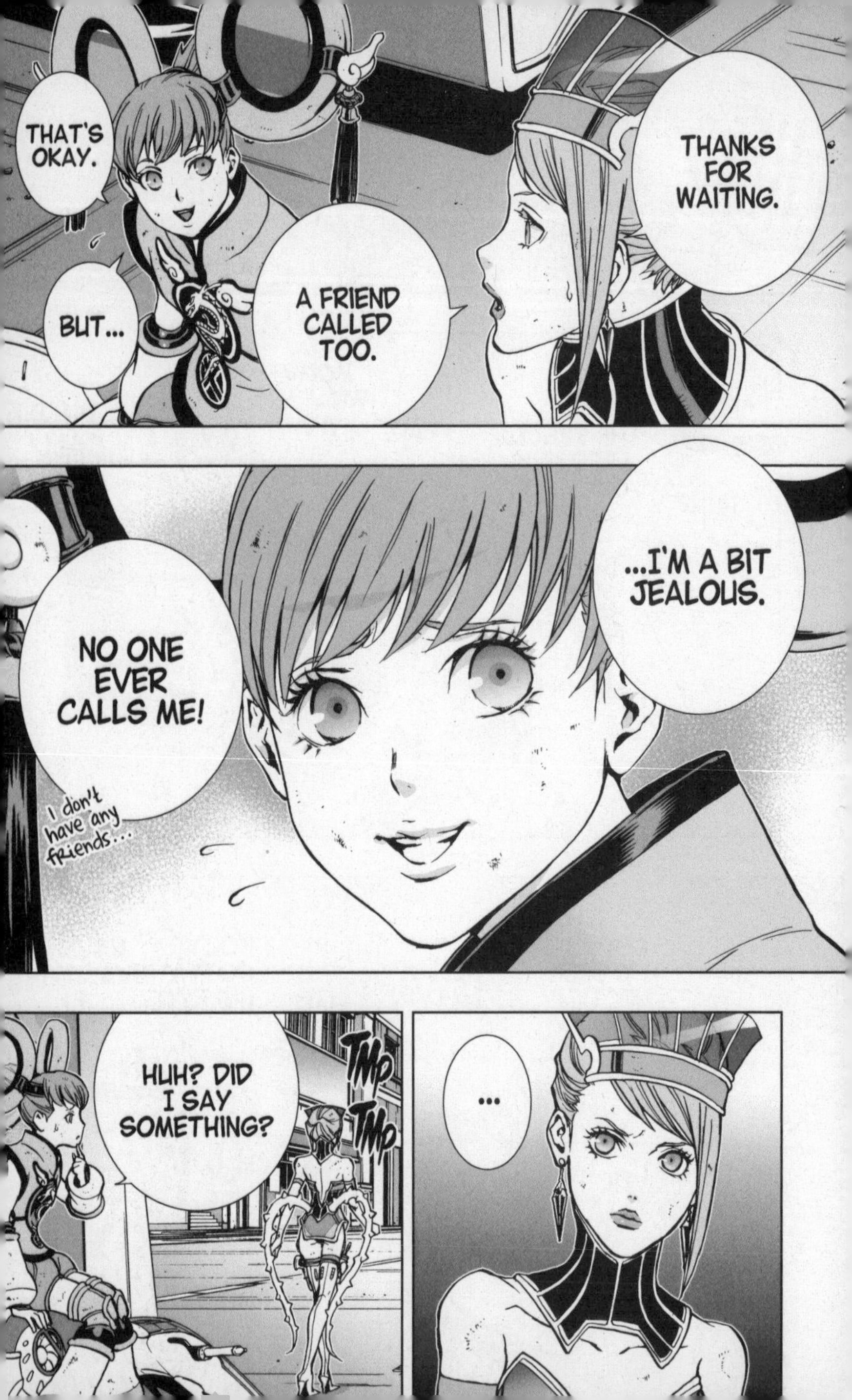
THANKS FOR WAITING.
THAT'S OKAY.
A FRIEND CALLED TOO.
BUT...
...I'M A BIT JEALOUS.
NO ONE EVER CALLS ME!
I don't have any friends...
...
HUH? DID I SAY SOMETHING?
TMP
TMP

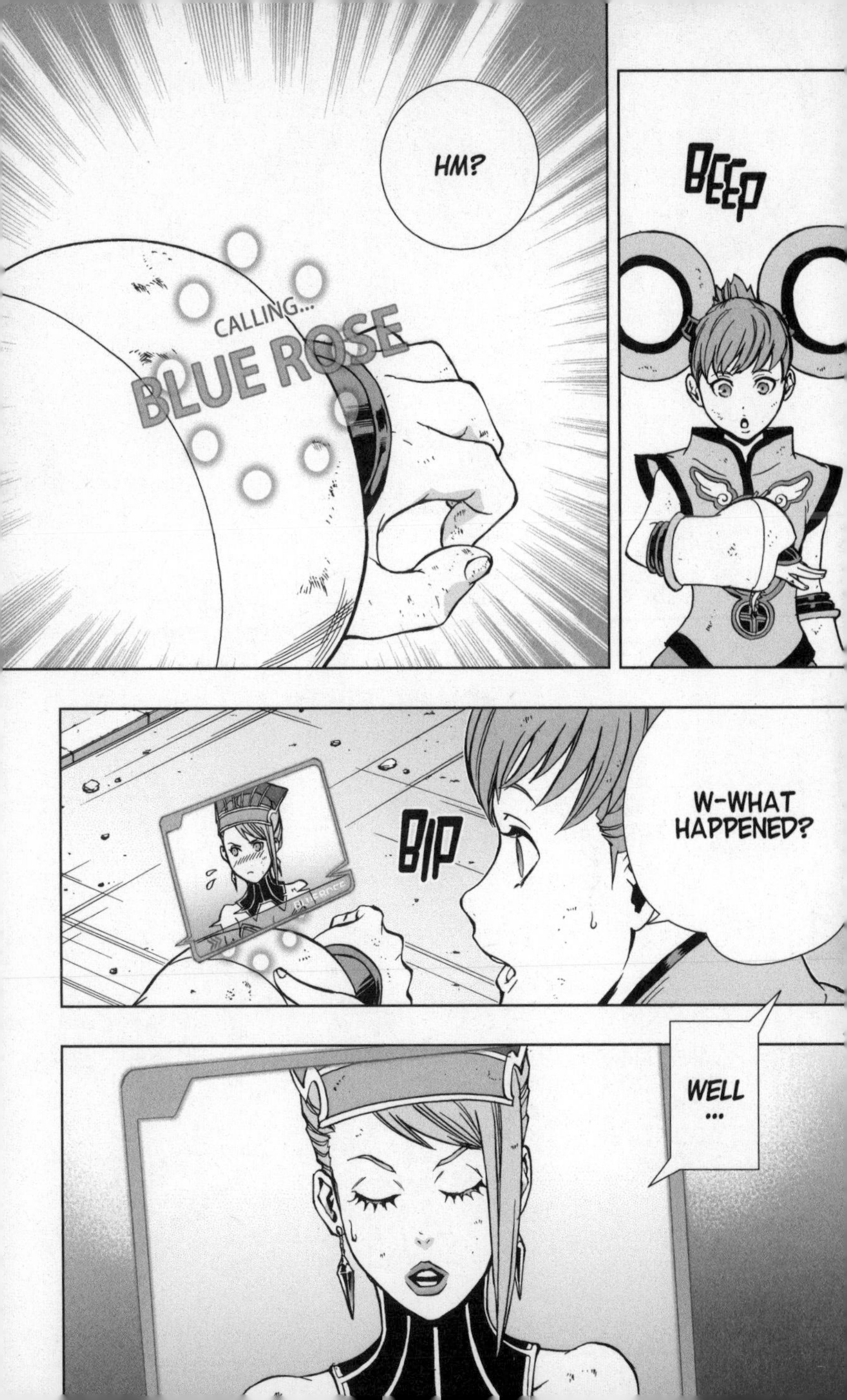
BEEP
HM?
CALLING...
BLUE ROSE
W-WHAT HAPPENED?
BIP
WELL
...

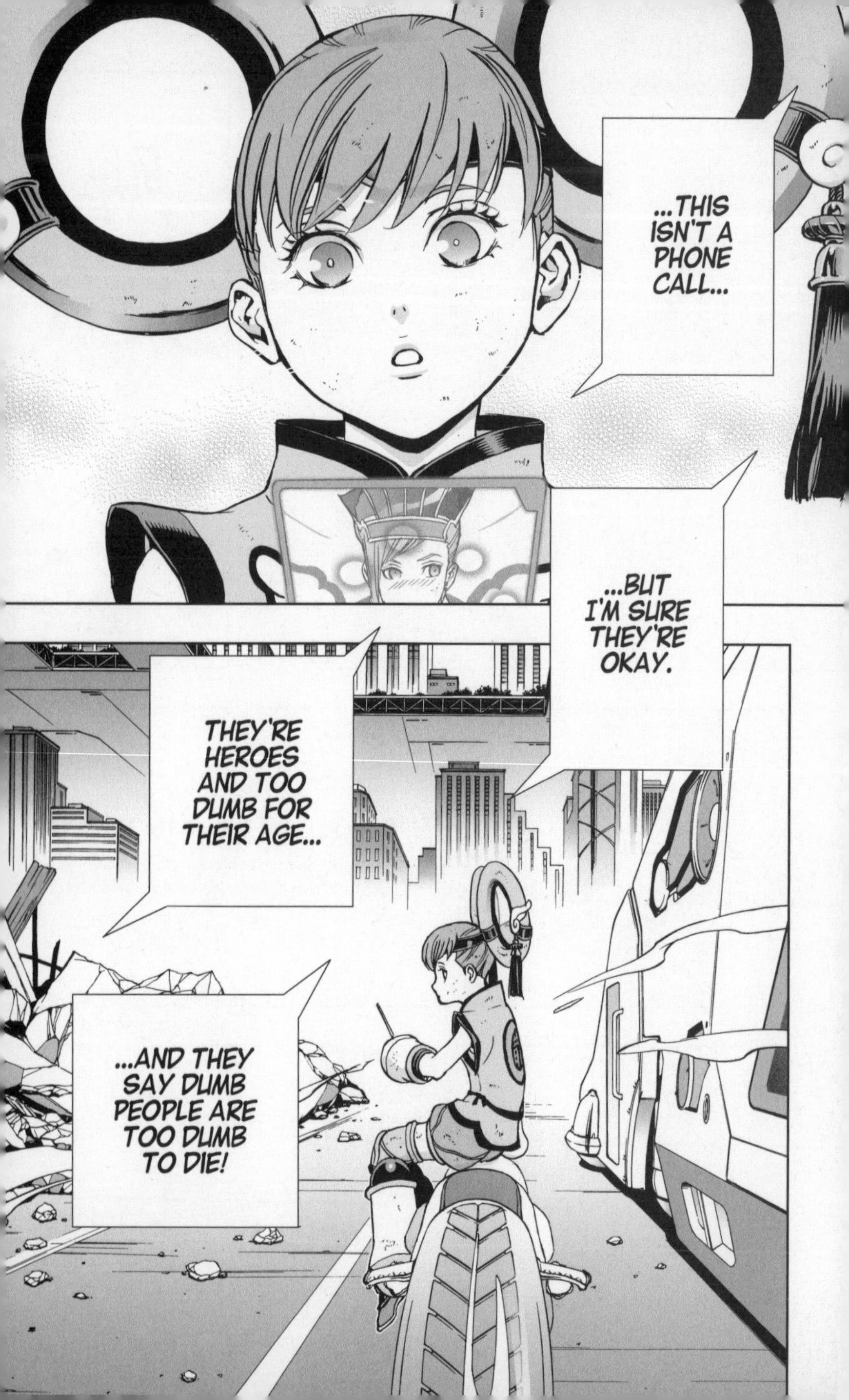
...THIS ISN'T A PHONE CALL...
...BUT I'M SURE THEY'RE OKAY.
THEY'RE HEROES AND TOO DUMB FOR THEIR AGE...
...AND THEY SAY DUMB PEOPLE ARE TOO DUMB TO DIE!

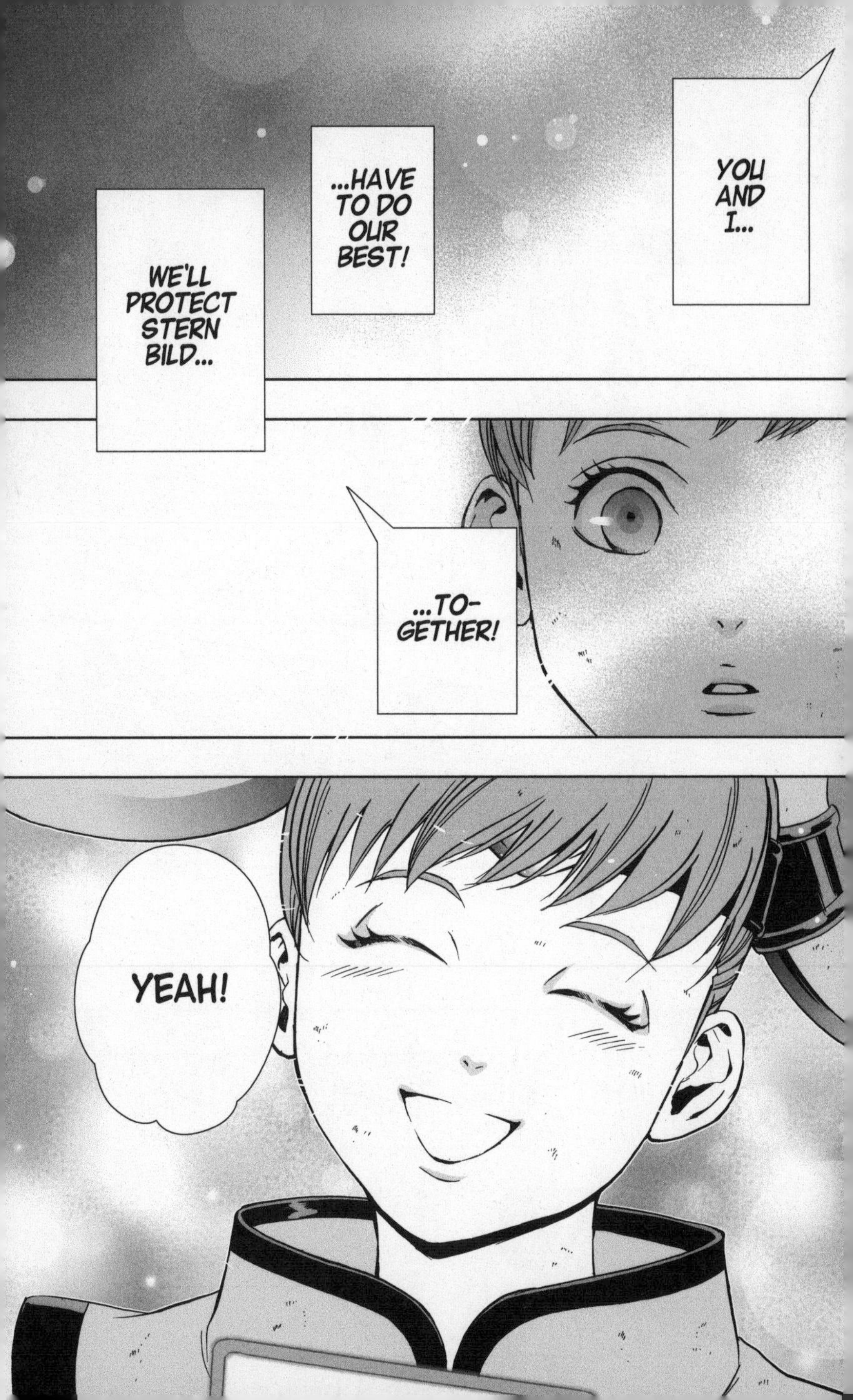
YOU AND I...
...HAVE TO DO OUR BEST!
WE'LL PROTECT STERN BILD...
...TO-GETHER!
YEAH!

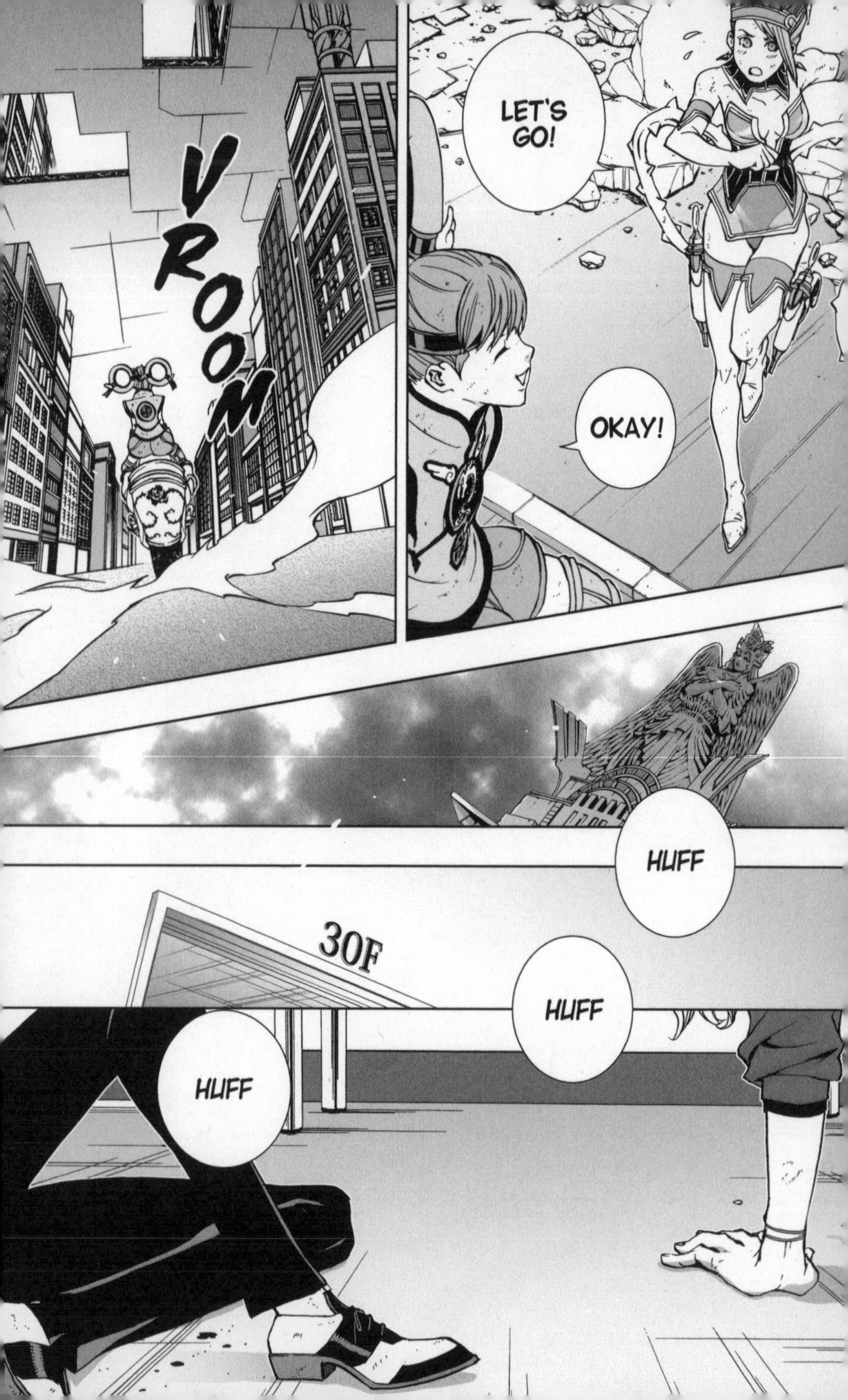
LET'S GO!
OKAY!
VROOM
HUFF
30F
HUFF
HUFF

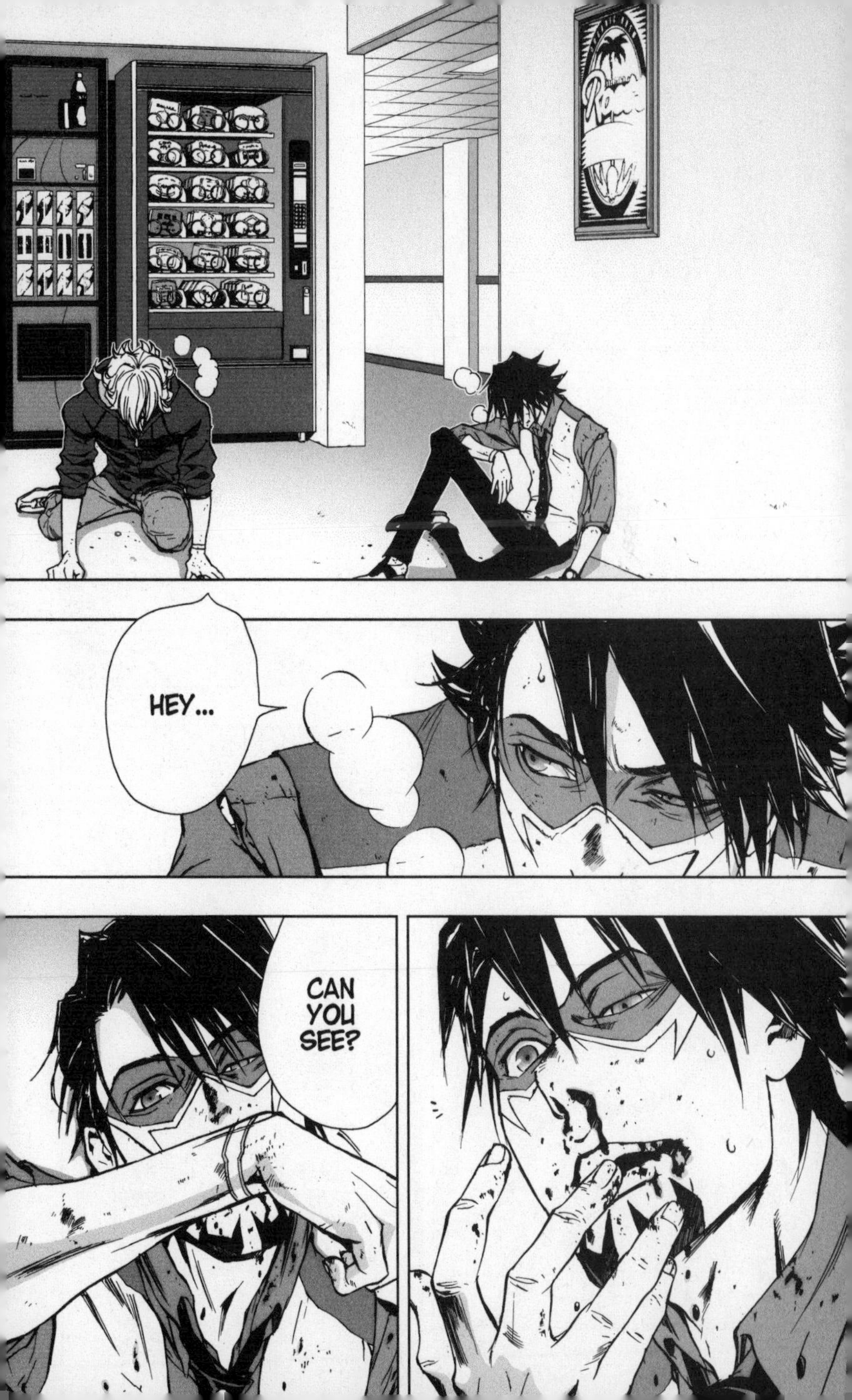
HEY...
CAN YOU SEE?

HUH?

YOUR GLASSES...

UGH

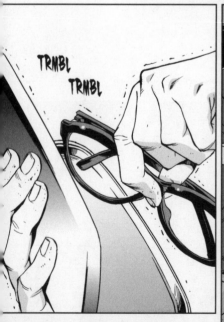

TRMBL
TRMBL

EVERY-THING IS BLURRY...

...BUT I HAVE MY DISGUISE GLASSES.

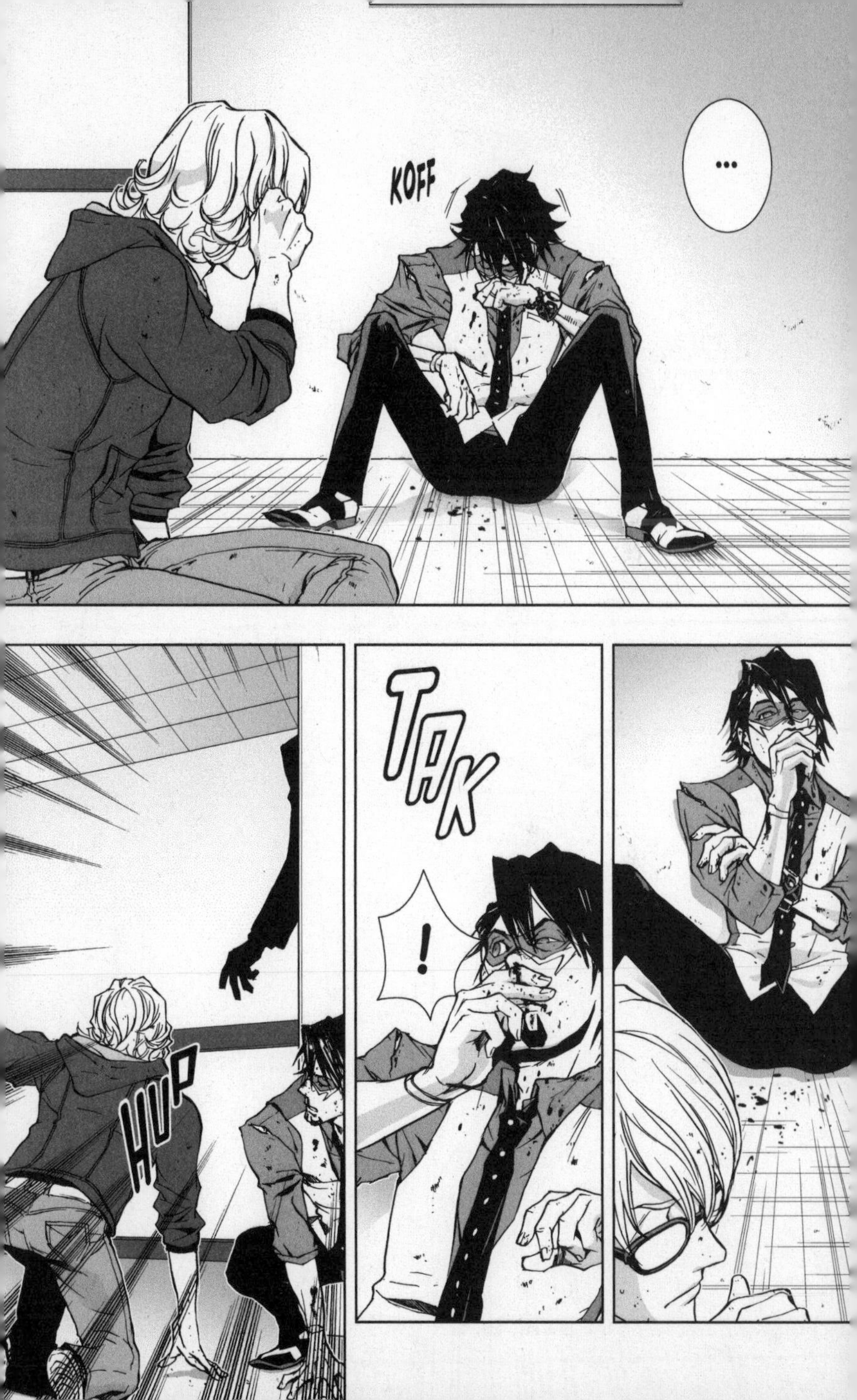
...
KOFF
TAK
!
HUP

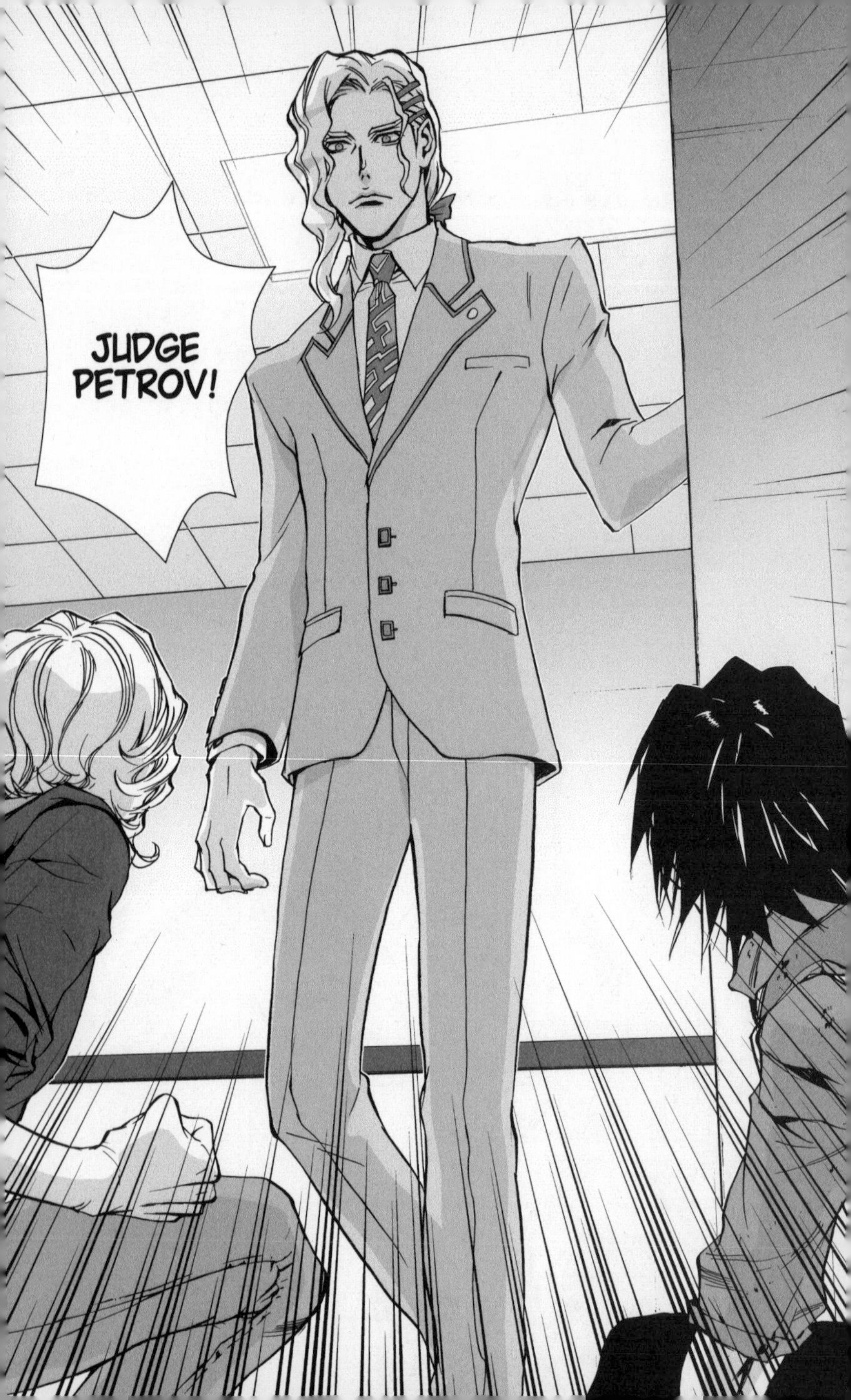
JUDGE PETROV!

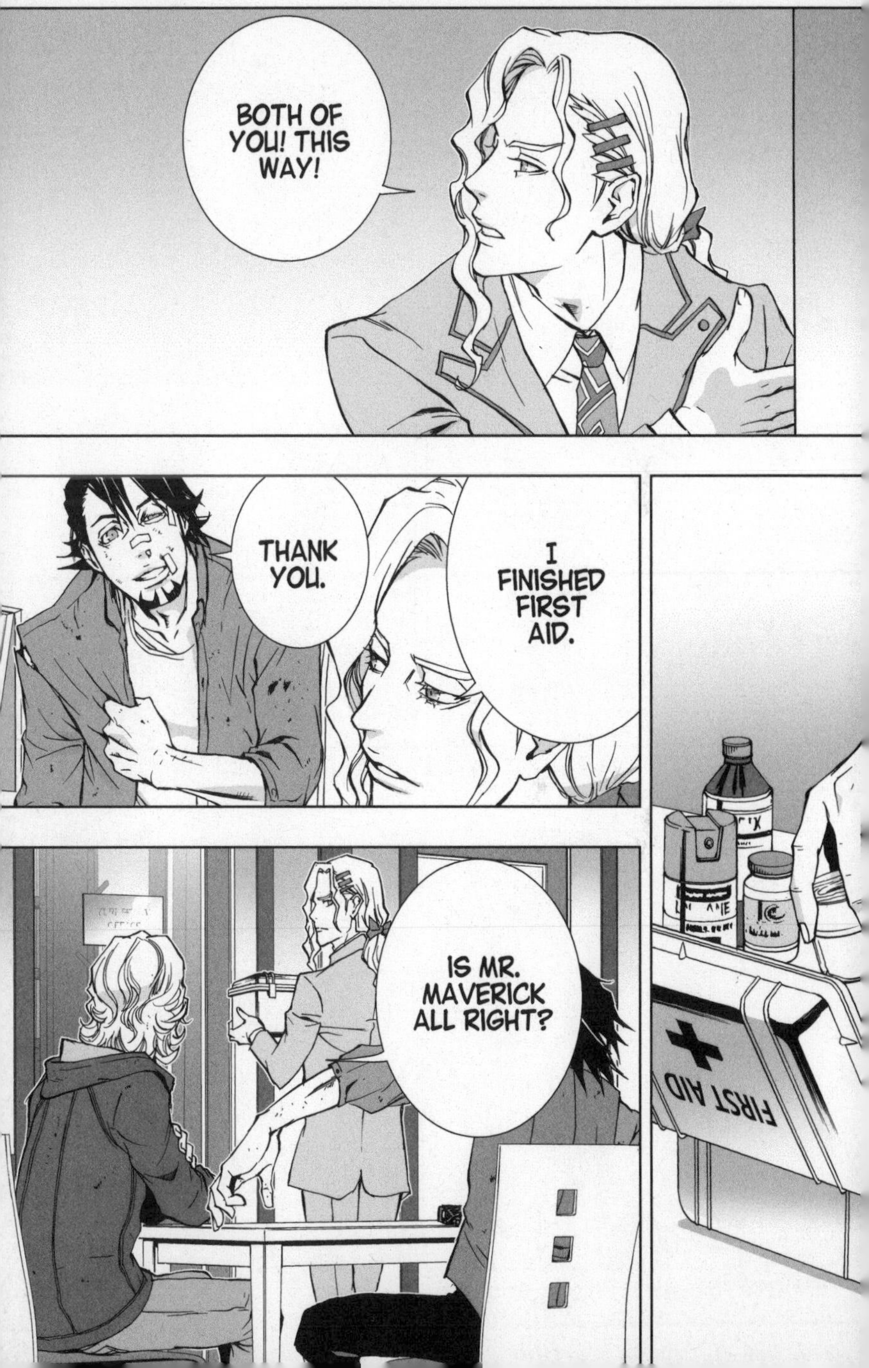
BOTH OF YOU! THIS WAY!
FIRST AID
I FINISHED FIRST AID.
THANK YOU.
IS MR. MAVERICK ALL RIGHT?

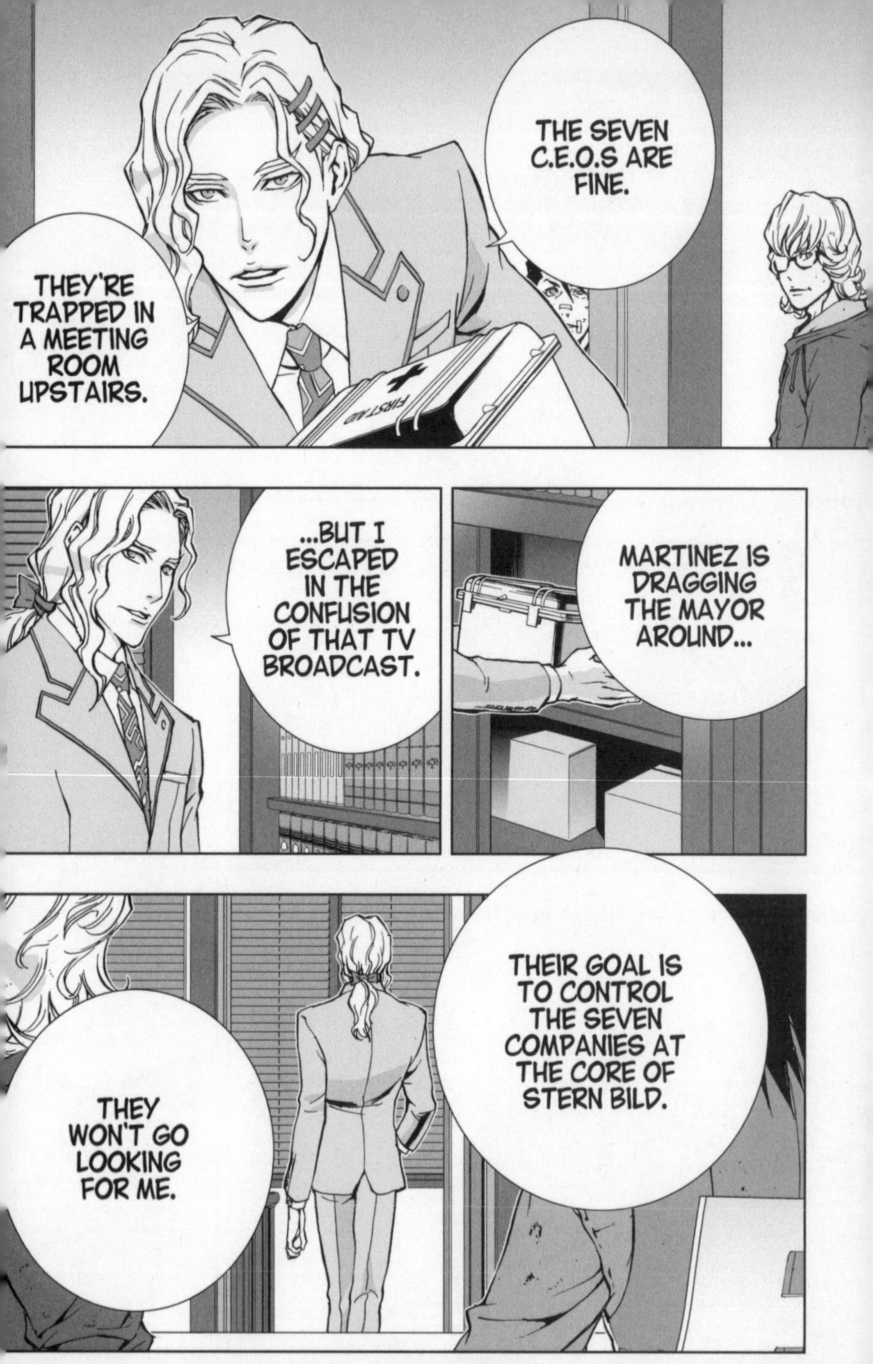
THE SEVEN C.E.O.S ARE FINE.
THEY'RE TRAPPED IN A MEETING ROOM UPSTAIRS.
MARTINEZ IS DRAGGING THE MAYOR AROUND...
...BUT I ESCAPED IN THE CONFUSION OF THAT TV BROADCAST.
THEIR GOAL IS TO CONTROL THE SEVEN COMPANIES AT THE CORE OF STERN BILD.
THEY WON'T GO LOOKING FOR ME.

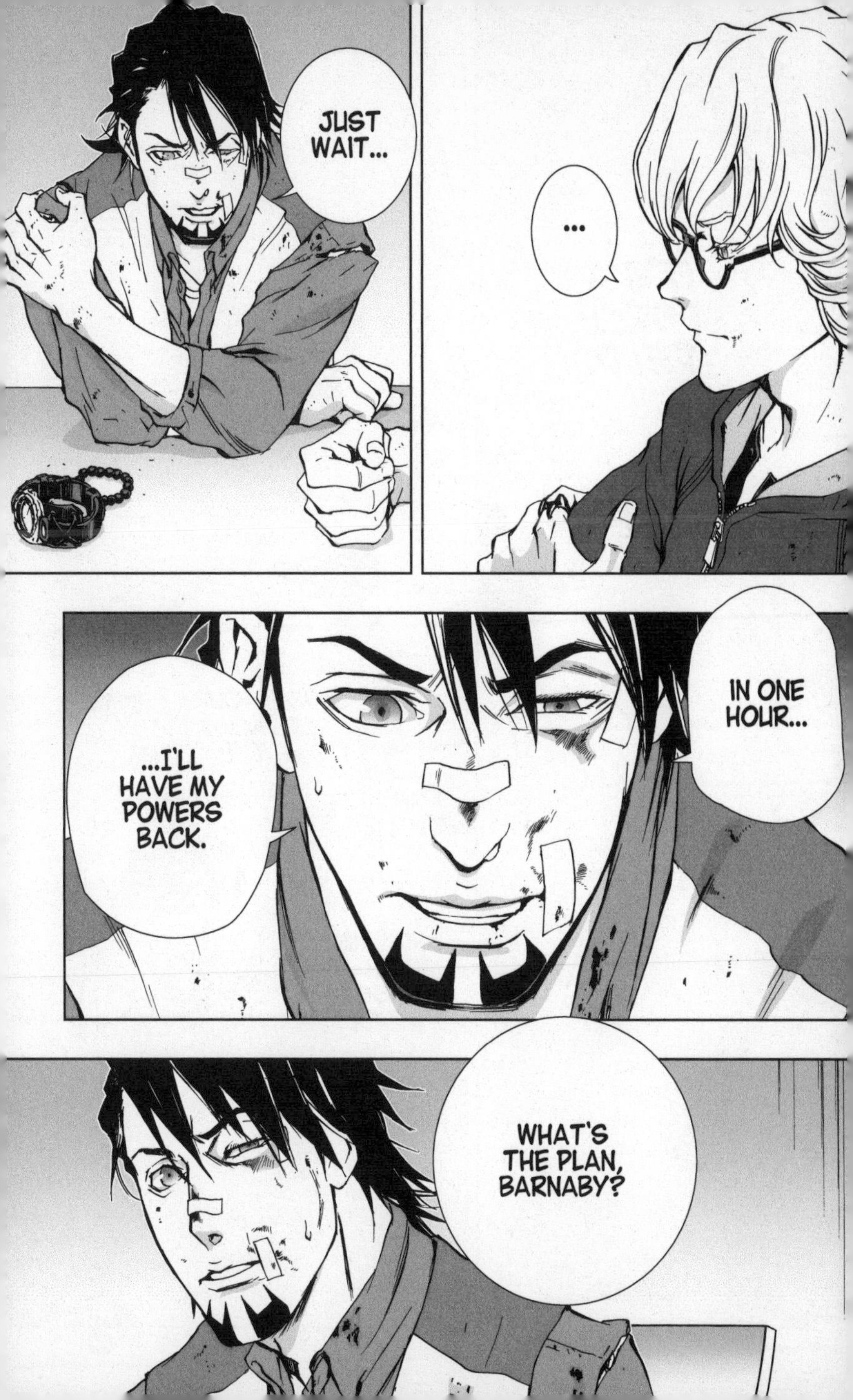
...
JUST WAIT...
IN ONE HOUR...
...I'LL HAVE MY POWERS BACK.
WHAT'S THE PLAN, BARNABY?

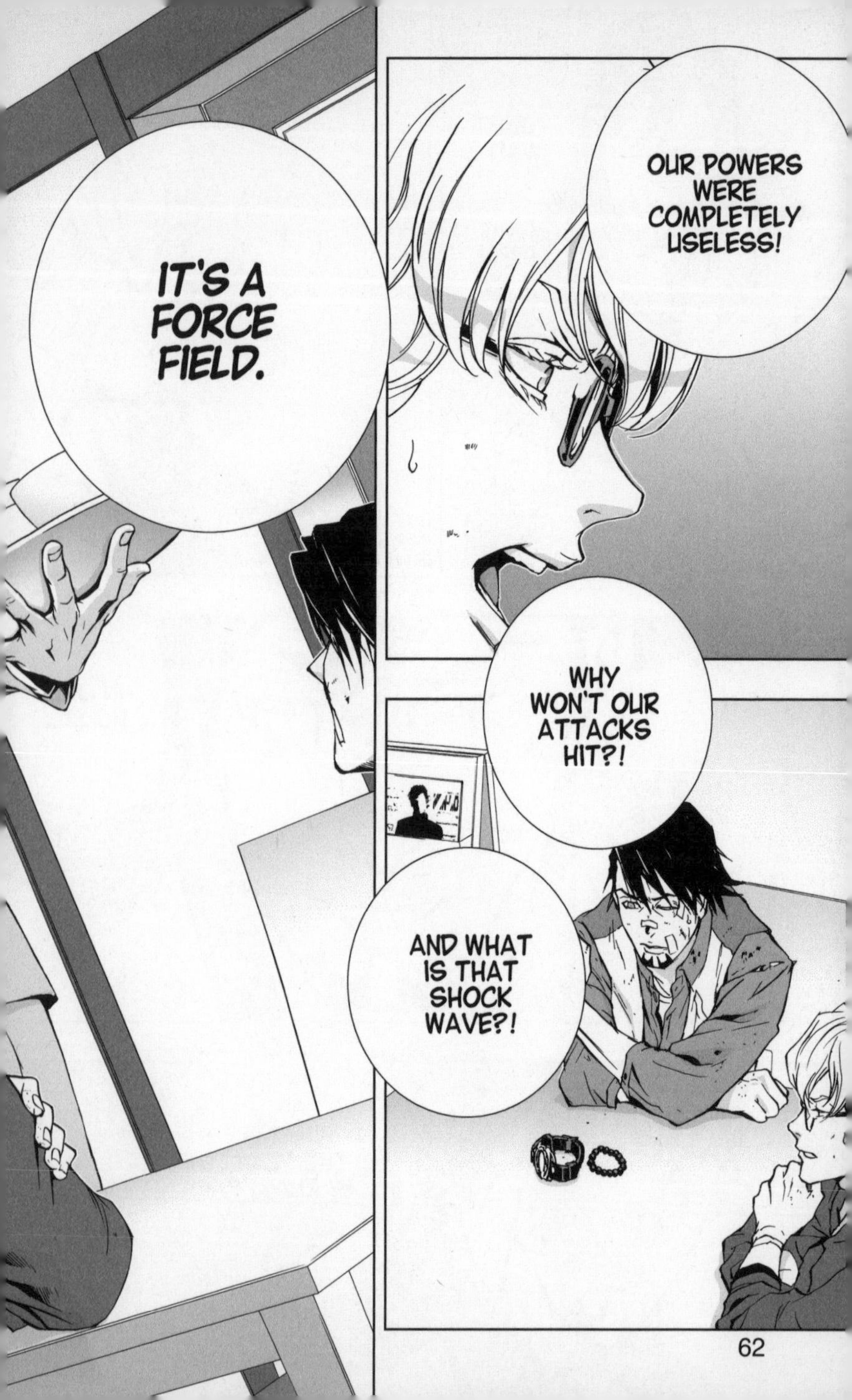
OUR POWERS WERE COMPLETELY USELESS!
WHY WON'T OUR ATTACKS HIT?!
AND WHAT IS THAT SHOCK WAVE?!
IT'S A FORCE FIELD.

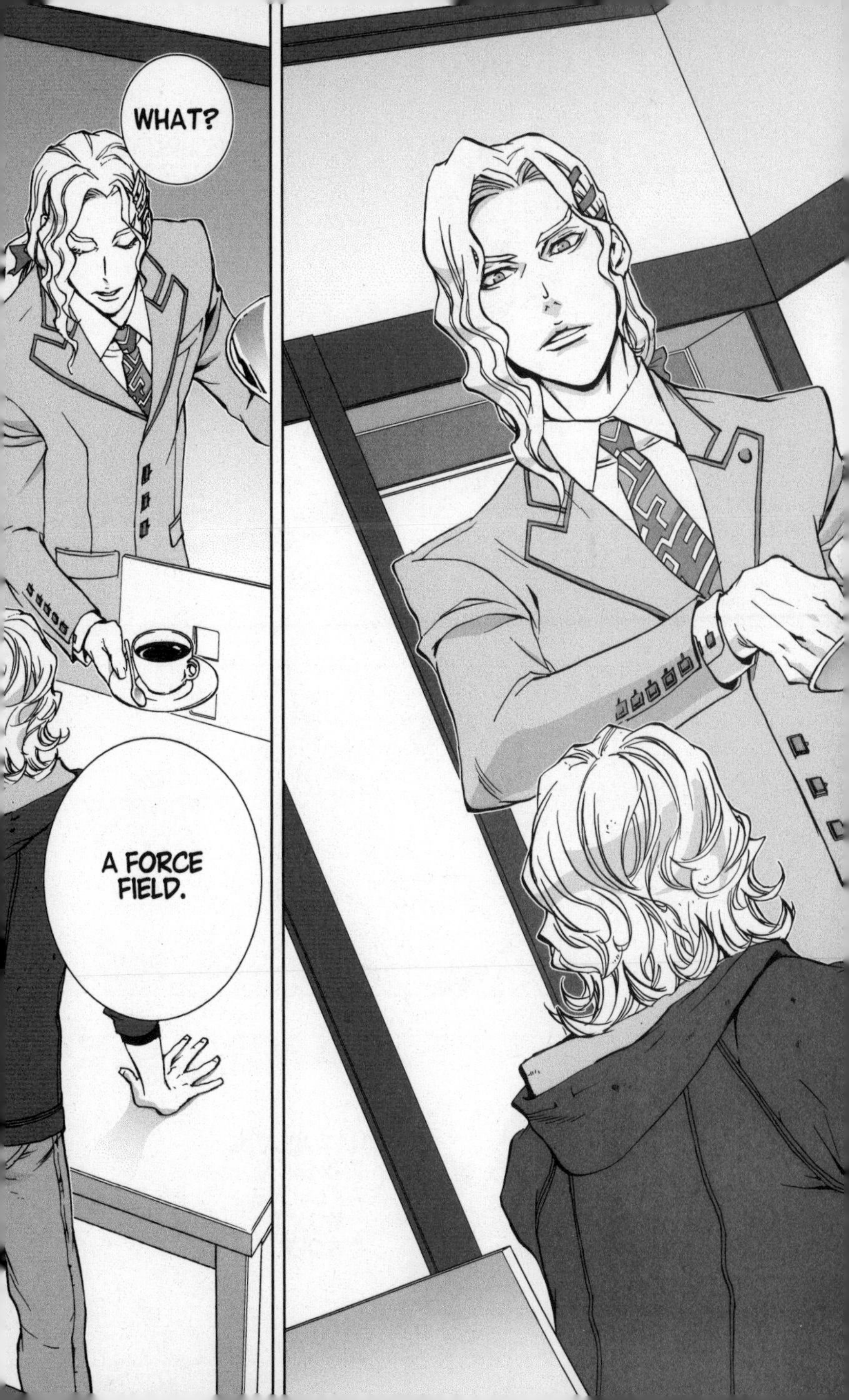
WHAT?
A FORCE FIELD.

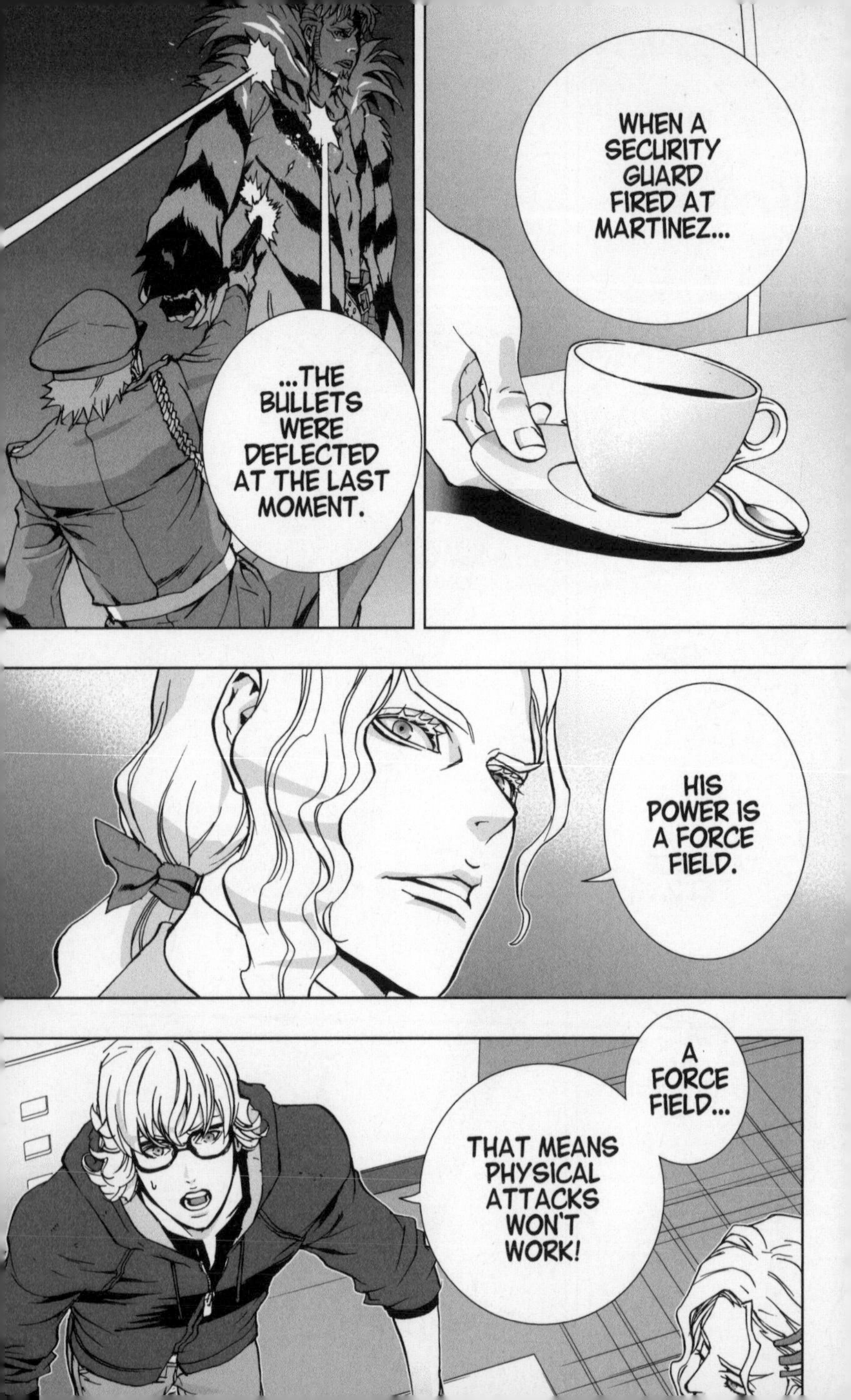
WHEN A SECURITY GUARD FIRED AT MARTINEZ...
...THE BULLETS WERE DEFLECTED AT THE LAST MOMENT.
HIS POWER IS A FORCE FIELD.
A FORCE FIELD...
THAT MEANS PHYSICAL ATTACKS WON'T WORK!

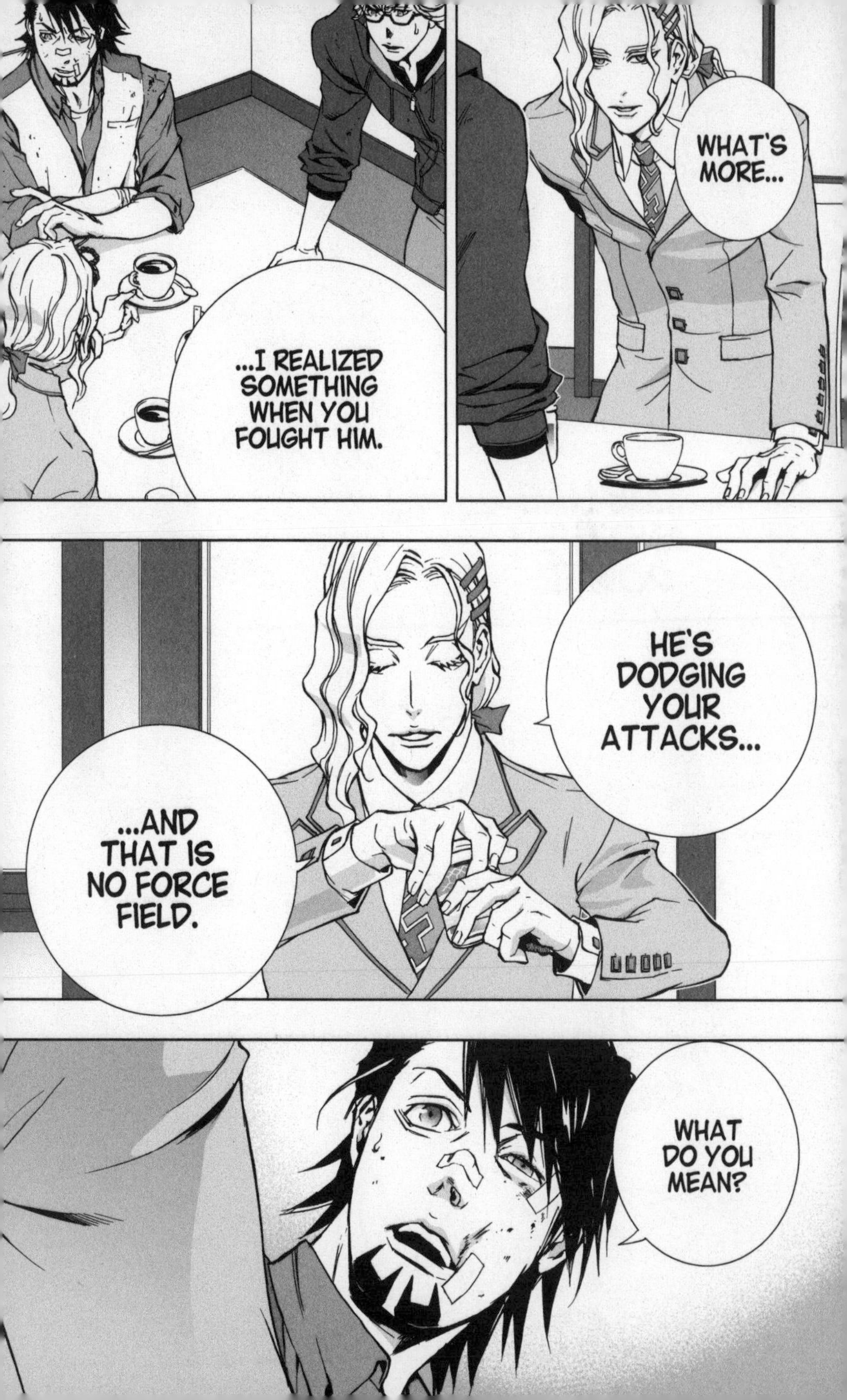
WHAT'S MORE...
...I REALIZED SOMETHING WHEN YOU FOUGHT HIM.
HE'S DODGING YOUR ATTACKS...
...AND THAT IS NO FORCE FIELD.
WHAT DO YOU MEAN?

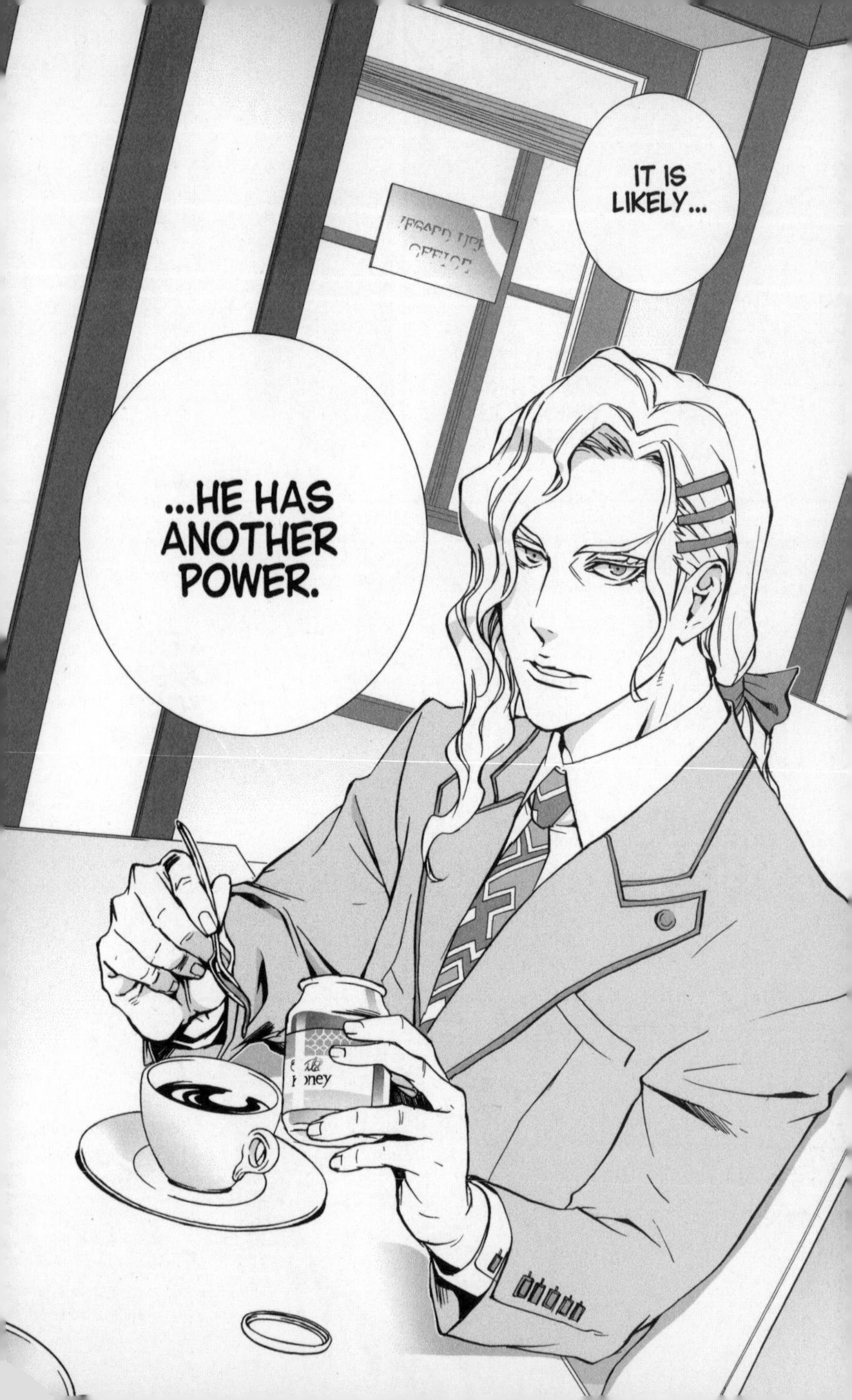
IT IS LIKELY...
...HE HAS ANOTHER POWER.

#28 Confidence Is a Plant of Slow Growth, Part 5

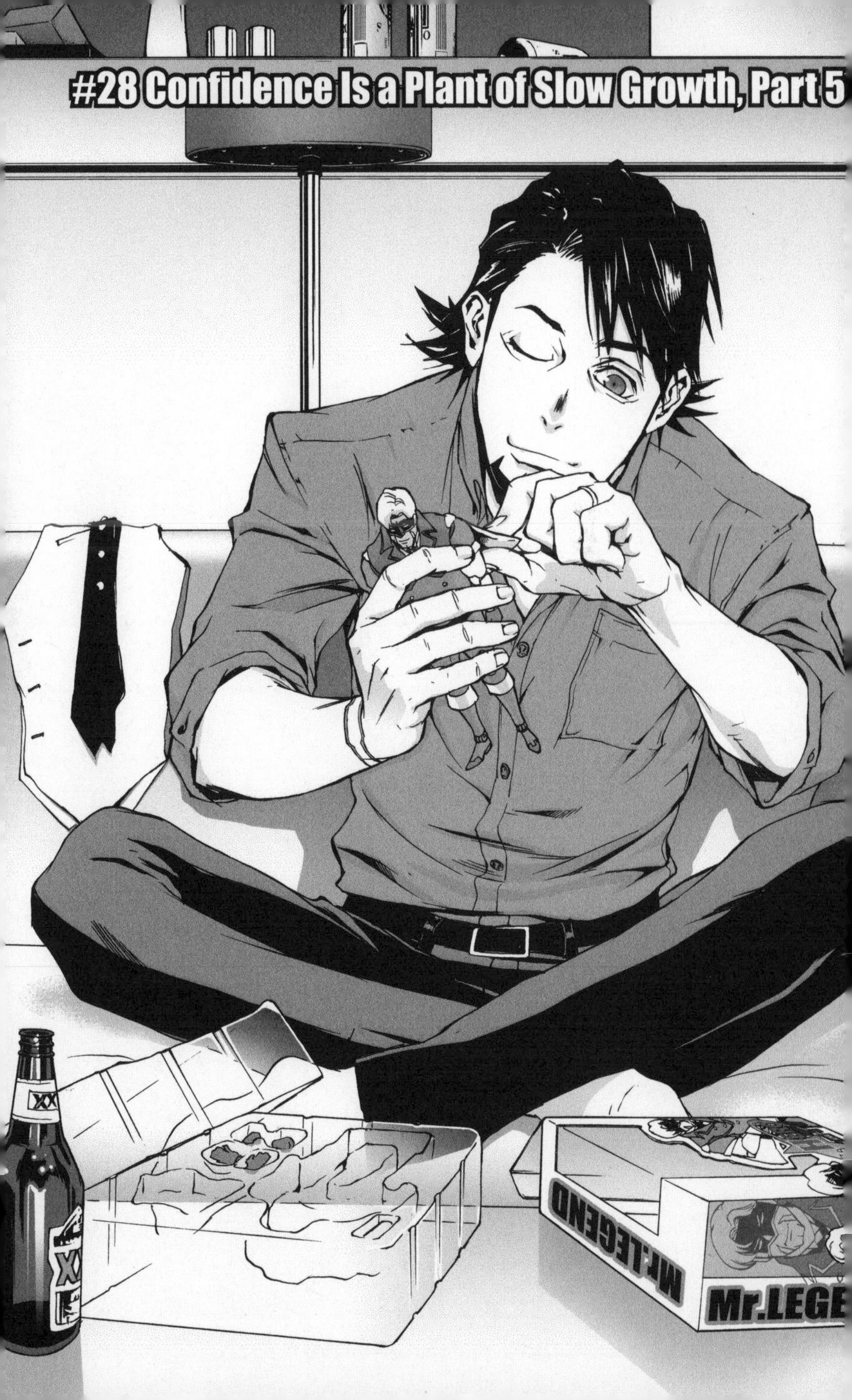
Mr.LEGEND
Mr.LEGE

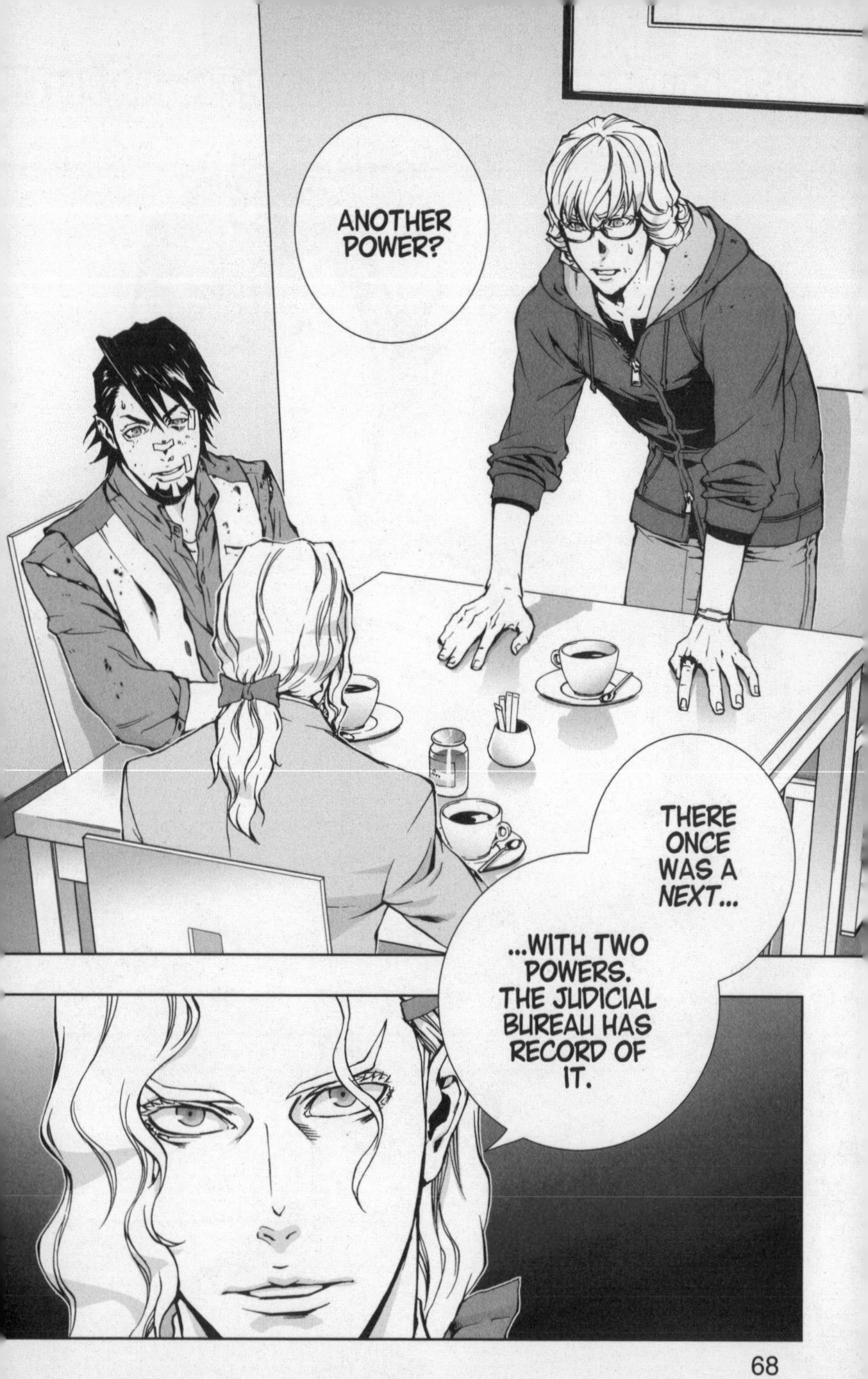
ANOTHER POWER?
THERE ONCE WAS A NEXT...
...WITH TWO POWERS. THE JUDICIAL BUREAU HAS RECORD OF IT.

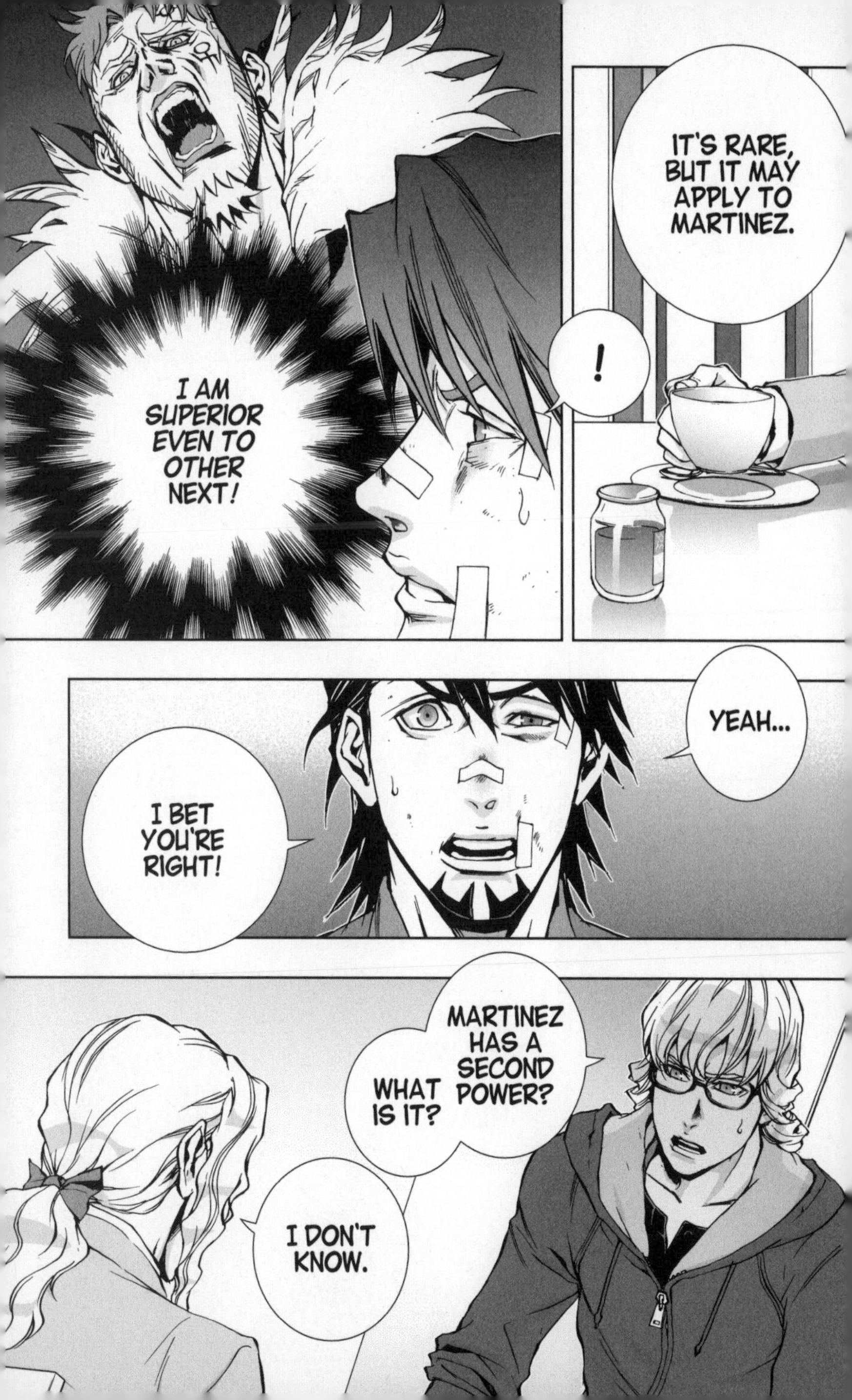
IT'S RARE, BUT IT MAY APPLY TO MARTINEZ.
!
I AM SUPERIOR EVEN TO OTHER NEXT!
YEAH...
I BET YOU'RE RIGHT!
MARTINEZ HAS A SECOND POWER?
WHAT IS IT?
I DON'T KNOW.

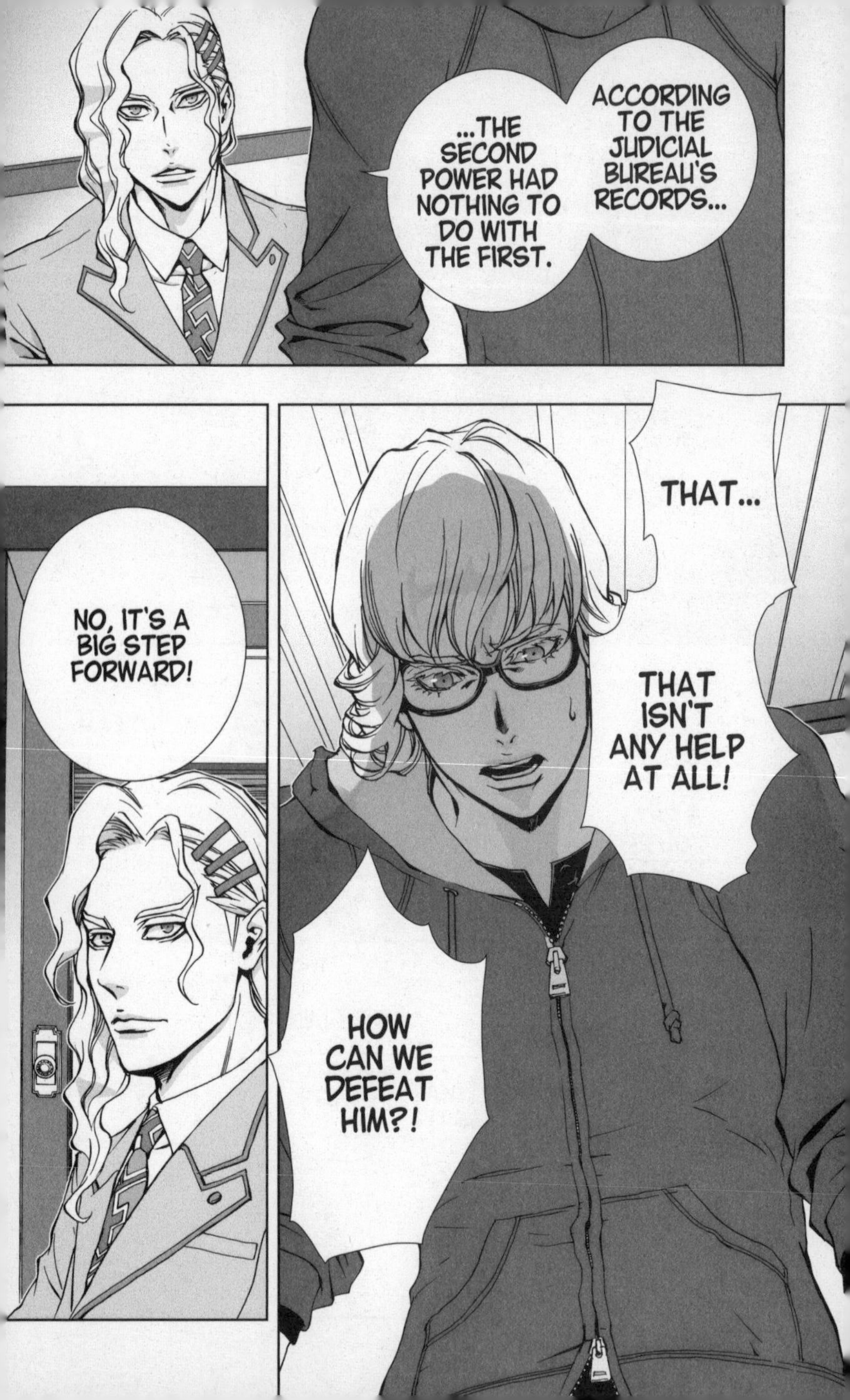
ACCORDING TO THE JUDICIAL BUREAU'S RECORDS...
...THE SECOND POWER HAD NOTHING TO DO WITH THE FIRST.
THAT...
THAT ISN'T ANY HELP AT ALL!
HOW CAN WE DEFEAT HIM?!
NO, IT'S A BIG STEP FORWARD!

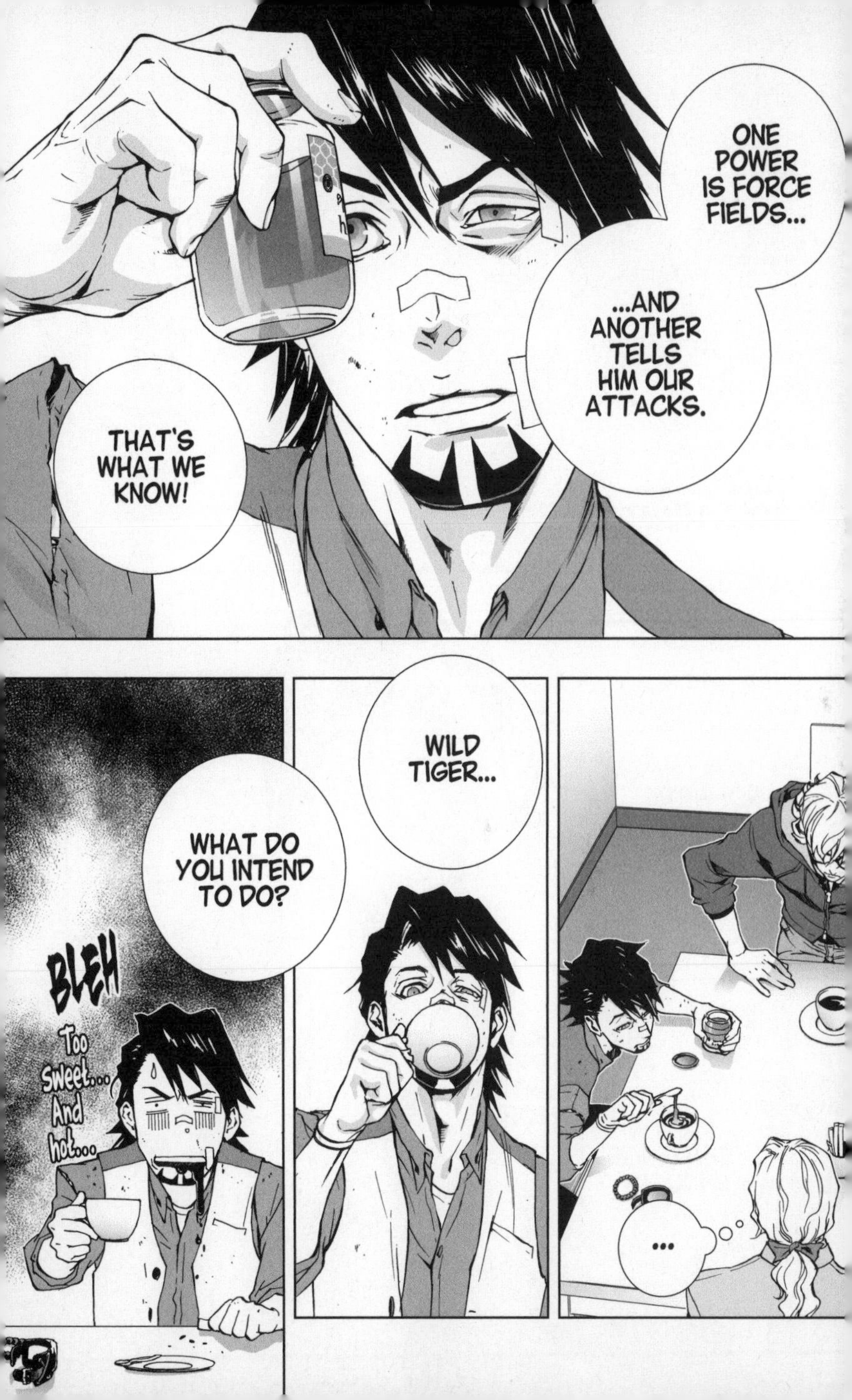
ONE POWER IS FORCE FIELDS...
...AND ANOTHER TELLS HIM OUR ATTACKS.
THAT'S WHAT WE KNOW!
...
WILD TIGER...
WHAT DO YOU INTEND TO DO?
BLEH
Too sweet... And hot...

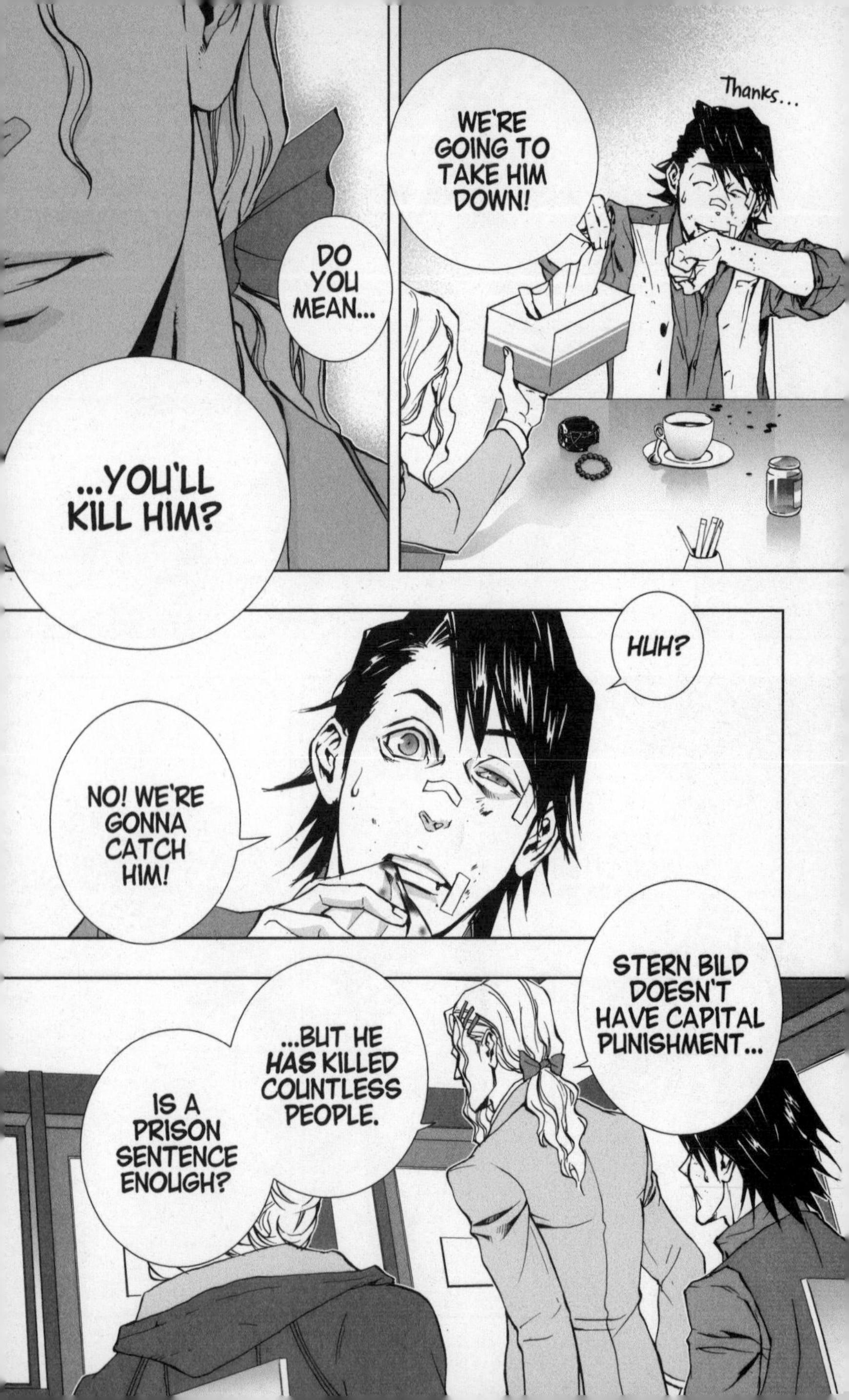
Thanks...
WE'RE GOING TO TAKE HIM DOWN!
DO YOU MEAN...
...YOU'LL KILL HIM?
HUH?
NO! WE'RE GONNA CATCH HIM!
STERN BILD DOESN'T HAVE CAPITAL PUNISHMENT...
...BUT HE HAS KILLED COUNTLESS PEOPLE.
IS A PRISON SENTENCE ENOUGH?

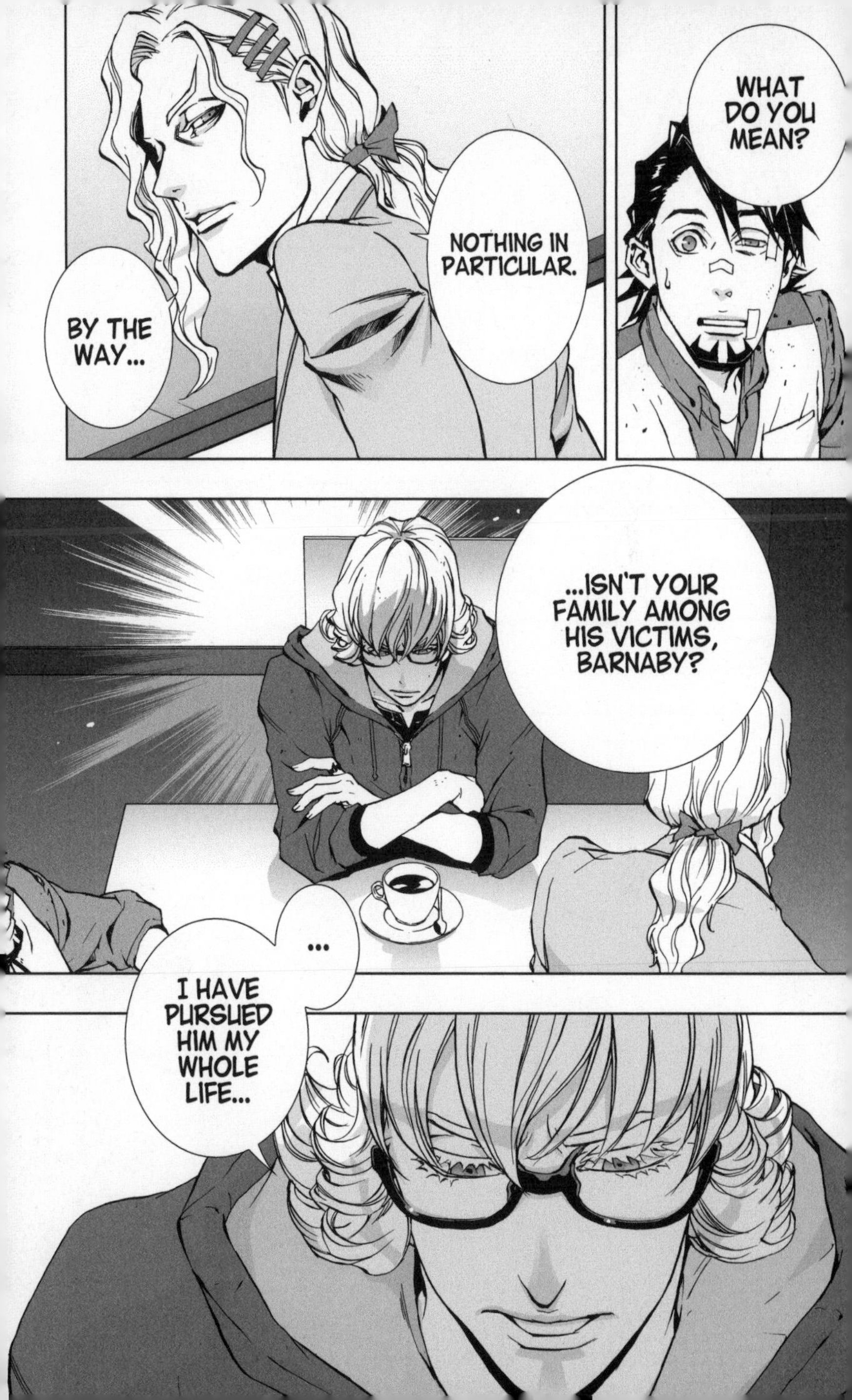
WHAT DO YOU MEAN?
NOTHING IN PARTICULAR.
BY THE WAY...
...ISN'T YOUR FAMILY AMONG HIS VICTIMS, BARNABY?
...
I HAVE PURSUED HIM MY WHOLE LIFE...

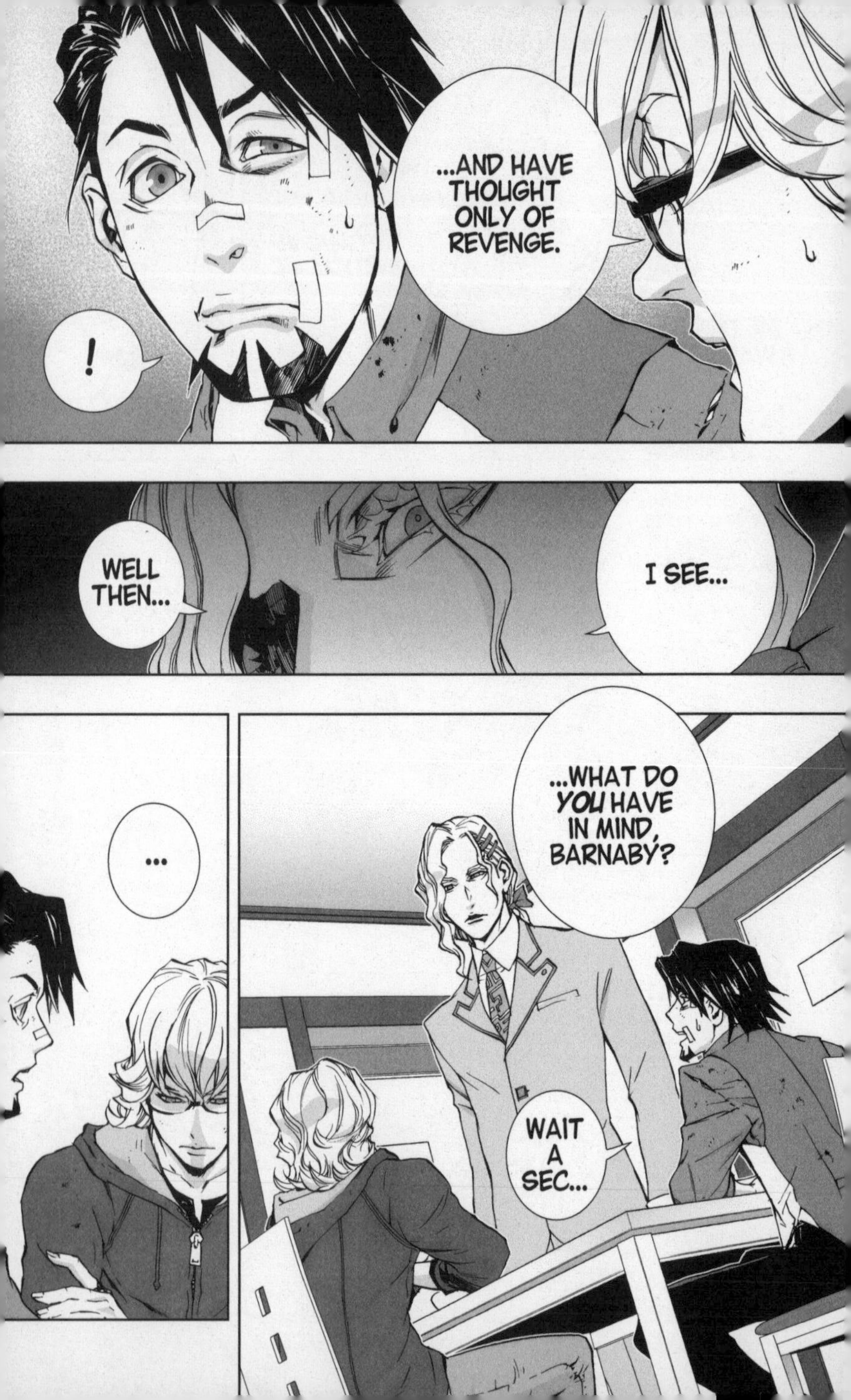
...AND HAVE THOUGHT ONLY OF REVENGE.
!
I SEE...
WELL THEN...
...WHAT DO *YOU* HAVE IN MIND, BARNABY?
WAIT A SEC...
...

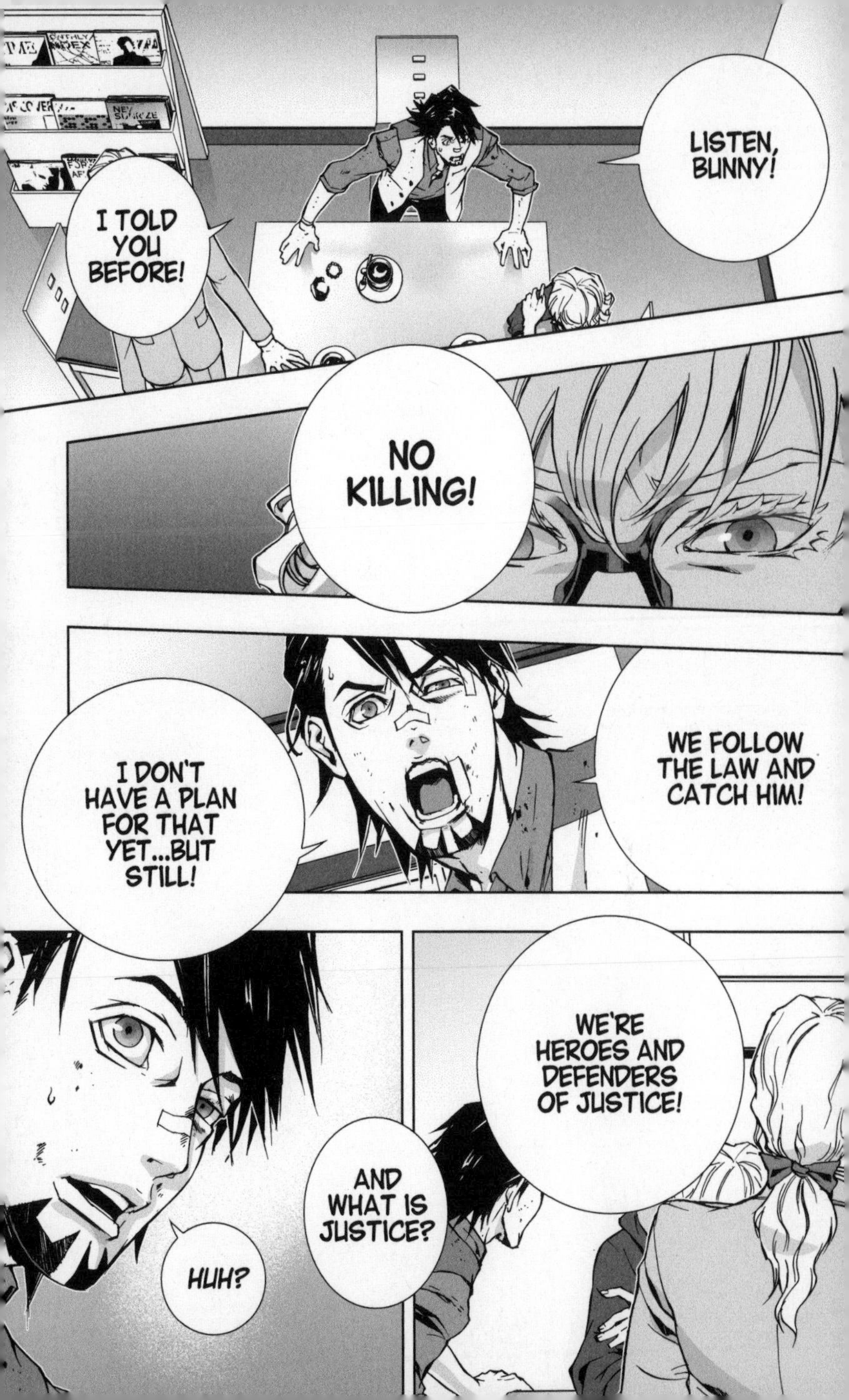
LISTEN, BUNNY!
I TOLD YOU BEFORE!
NO KILLING!
WE FOLLOW THE LAW AND CATCH HIM!
I DON'T HAVE A PLAN FOR THAT YET...BUT STILL!
WE'RE HEROES AND DEFENDERS OF JUSTICE!
AND WHAT IS JUSTICE?
HUH?

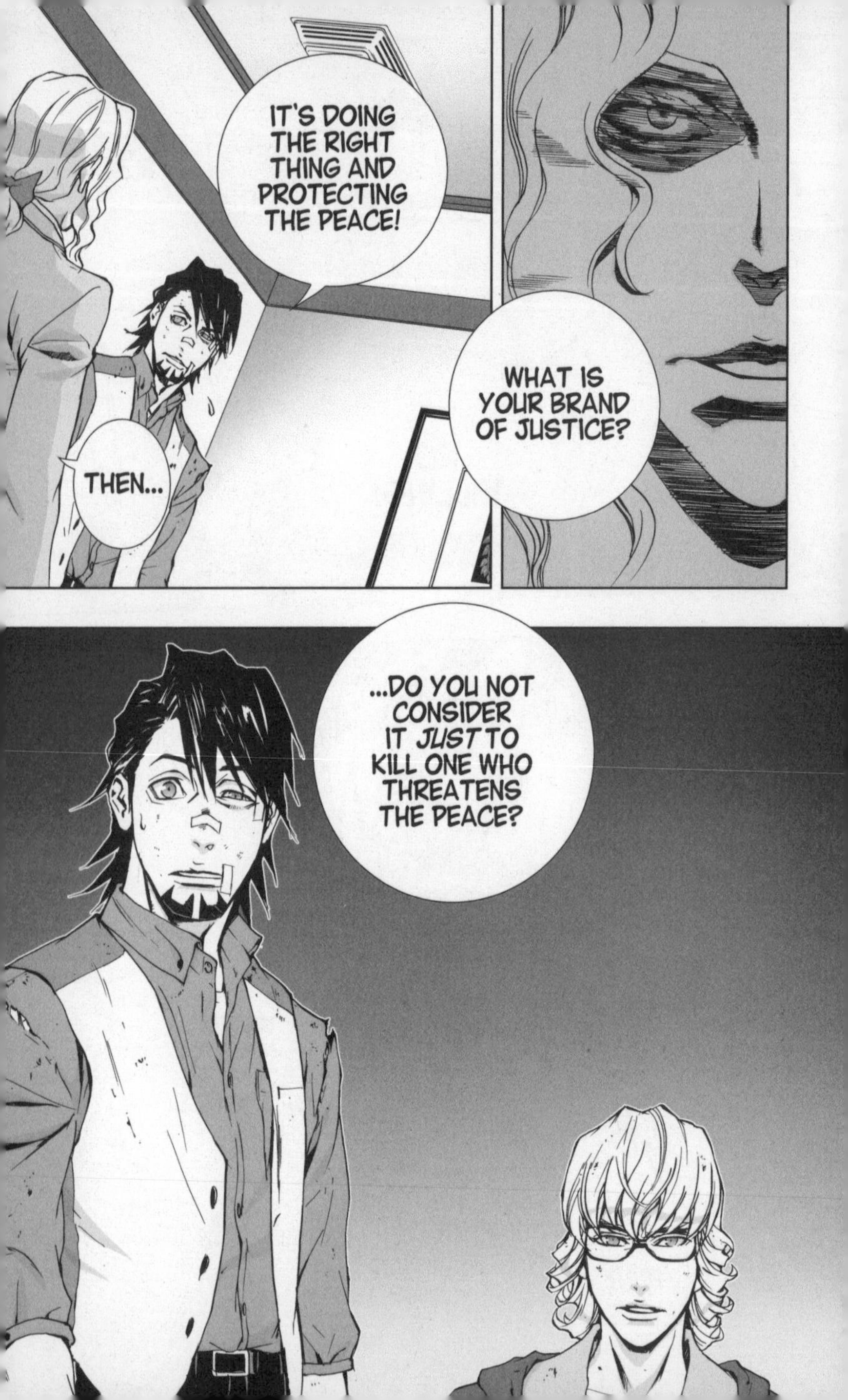
WHAT IS YOUR BRAND OF JUSTICE?
IT'S DOING THE RIGHT THING AND PROTECTING THE PEACE!
THEN...
...DO YOU NOT CONSIDER IT *JUST* TO KILL ONE WHO THREATENS THE PEACE?

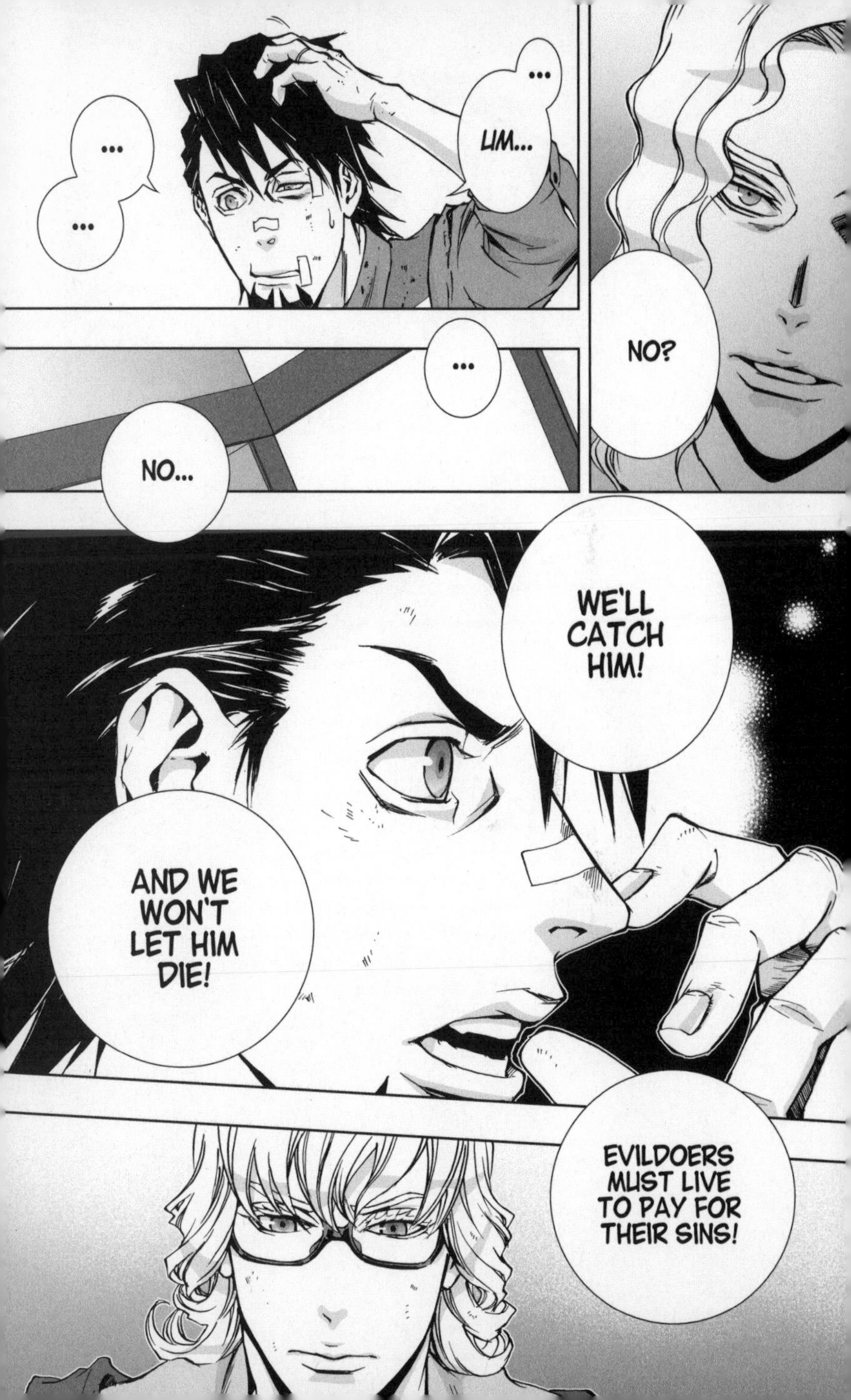
NO?
...
UM...
...
...
...
NO...
WE'LL CATCH HIM!
AND WE WON'T LET HIM DIE!
EVILDOERS MUST LIVE TO PAY FOR THEIR SINS!

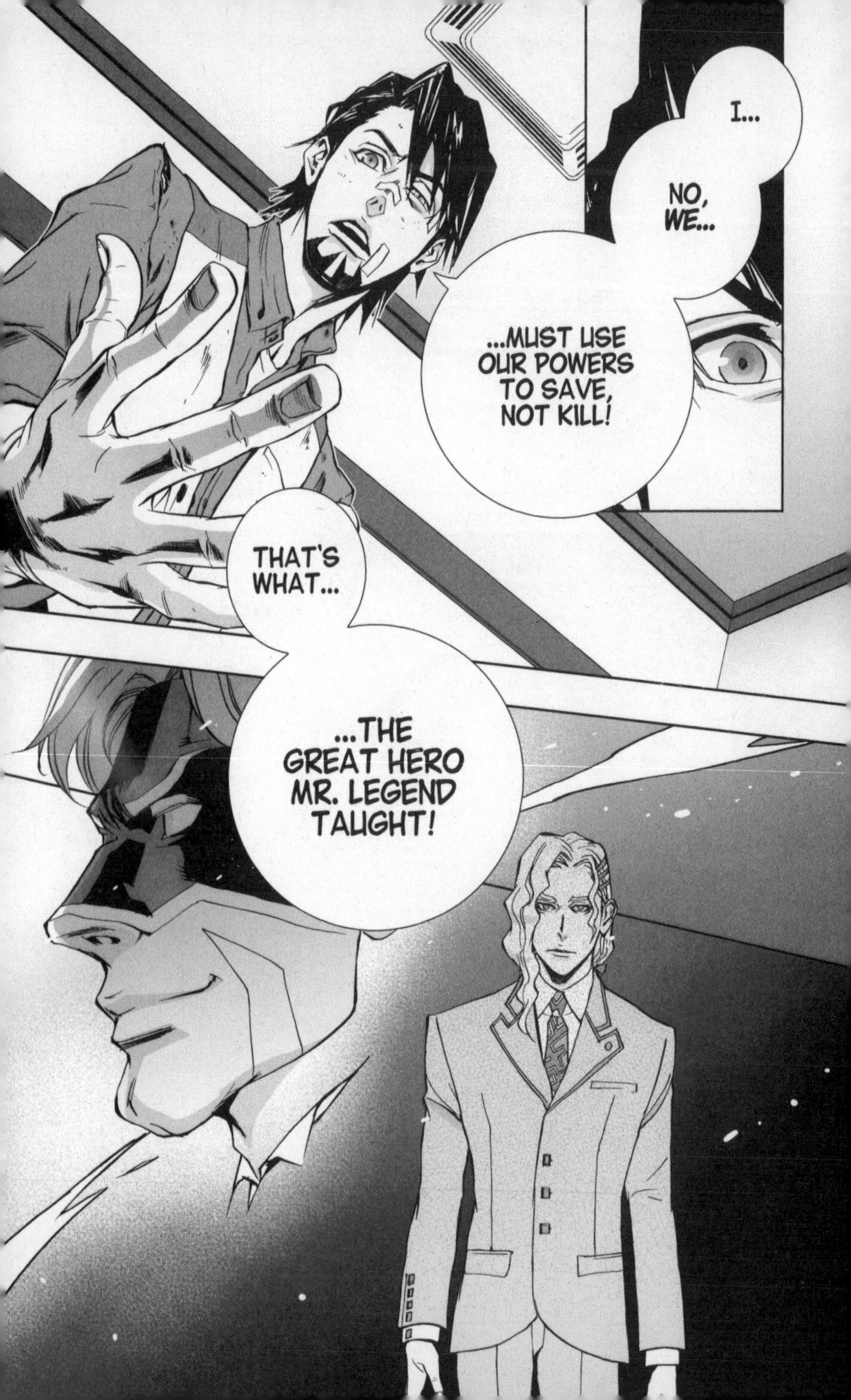
I...
NO, WE...
...MUST USE OUR POWERS TO SAVE, NOT KILL!
THAT'S WHAT...
...THE GREAT HERO MR. LEGEND TAUGHT!

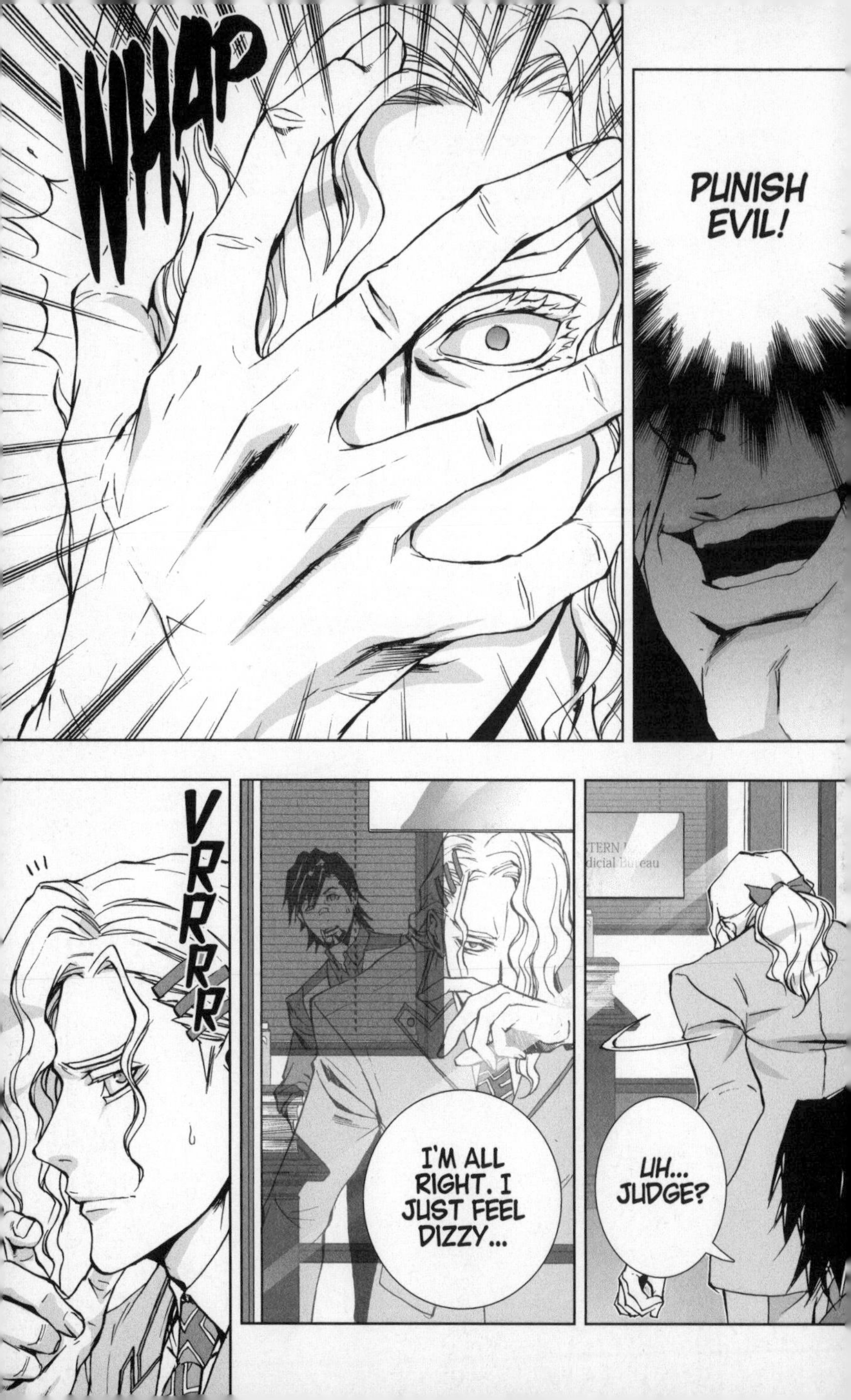
PUNISH EVIL!
WHAP
UH... JUDGE?
I'M ALL RIGHT. I JUST FEEL DIZZY...
VRRRRR

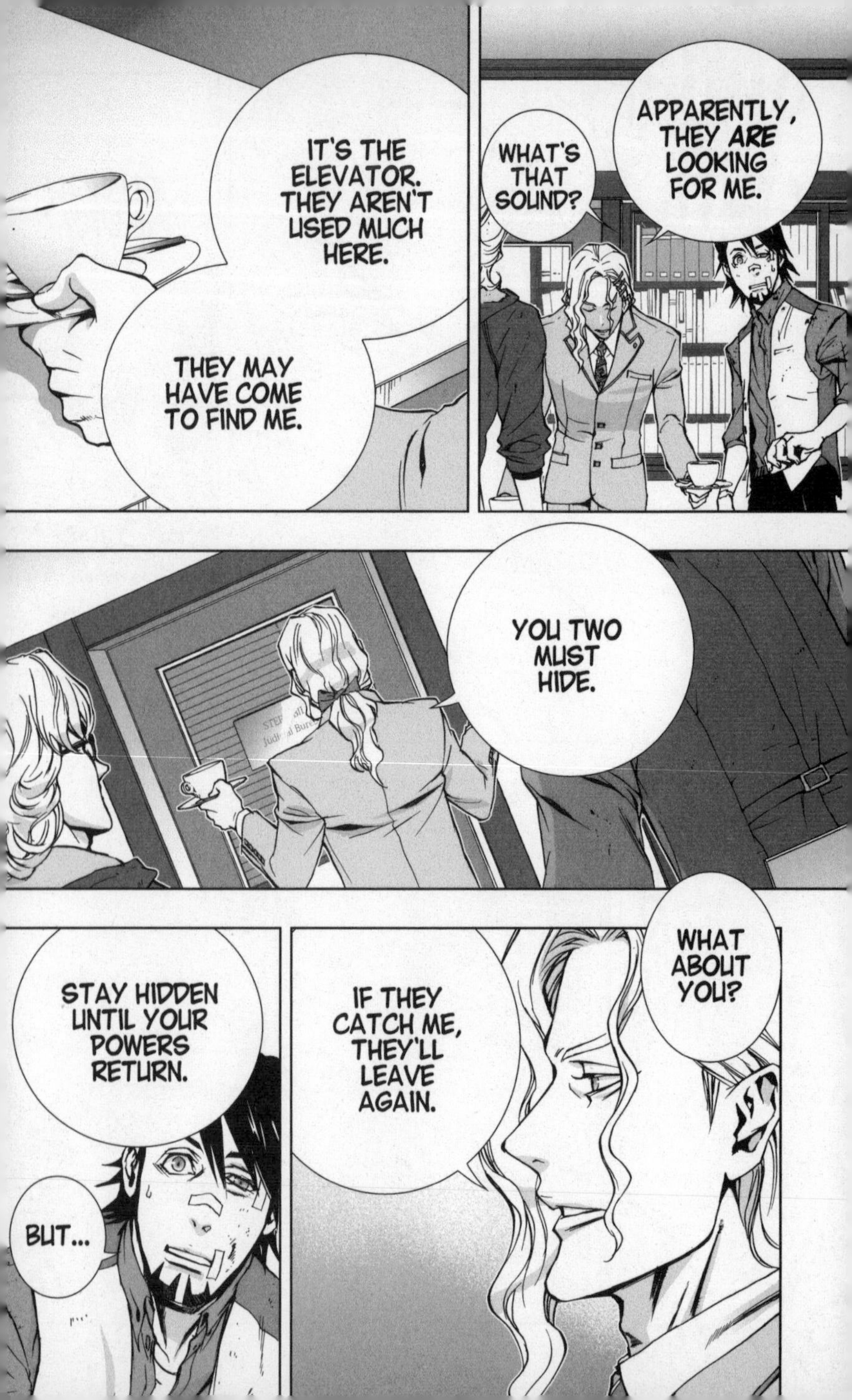
APPARENTLY, THEY ARE LOOKING FOR ME.
WHAT'S THAT SOUND?
IT'S THE ELEVATOR. THEY AREN'T USED MUCH HERE.
THEY MAY HAVE COME TO FIND ME.
YOU TWO MUST HIDE.
WHAT ABOUT YOU?
IF THEY CATCH ME, THEY'LL LEAVE AGAIN.
STAY HIDDEN UNTIL YOUR POWERS RETURN.
BUT...

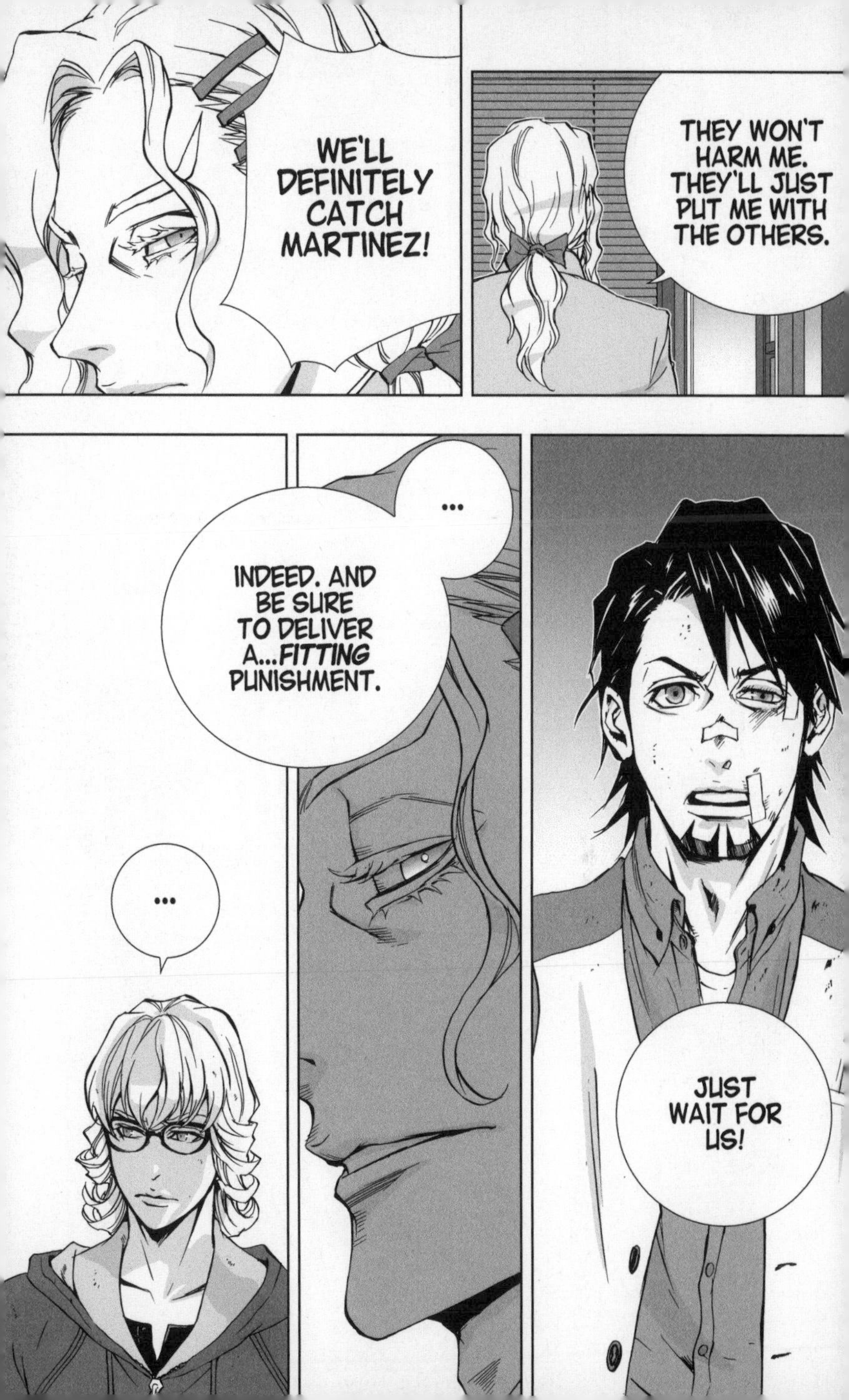
THEY WON'T HARM ME. THEY'LL JUST PUT ME WITH THE OTHERS.
WE'LL DEFINITELY CATCH MARTINEZ!
JUST WAIT FOR US!
...
INDEED. AND BE SURE TO DELIVER A...*FITTING* PUNISHMENT.
...

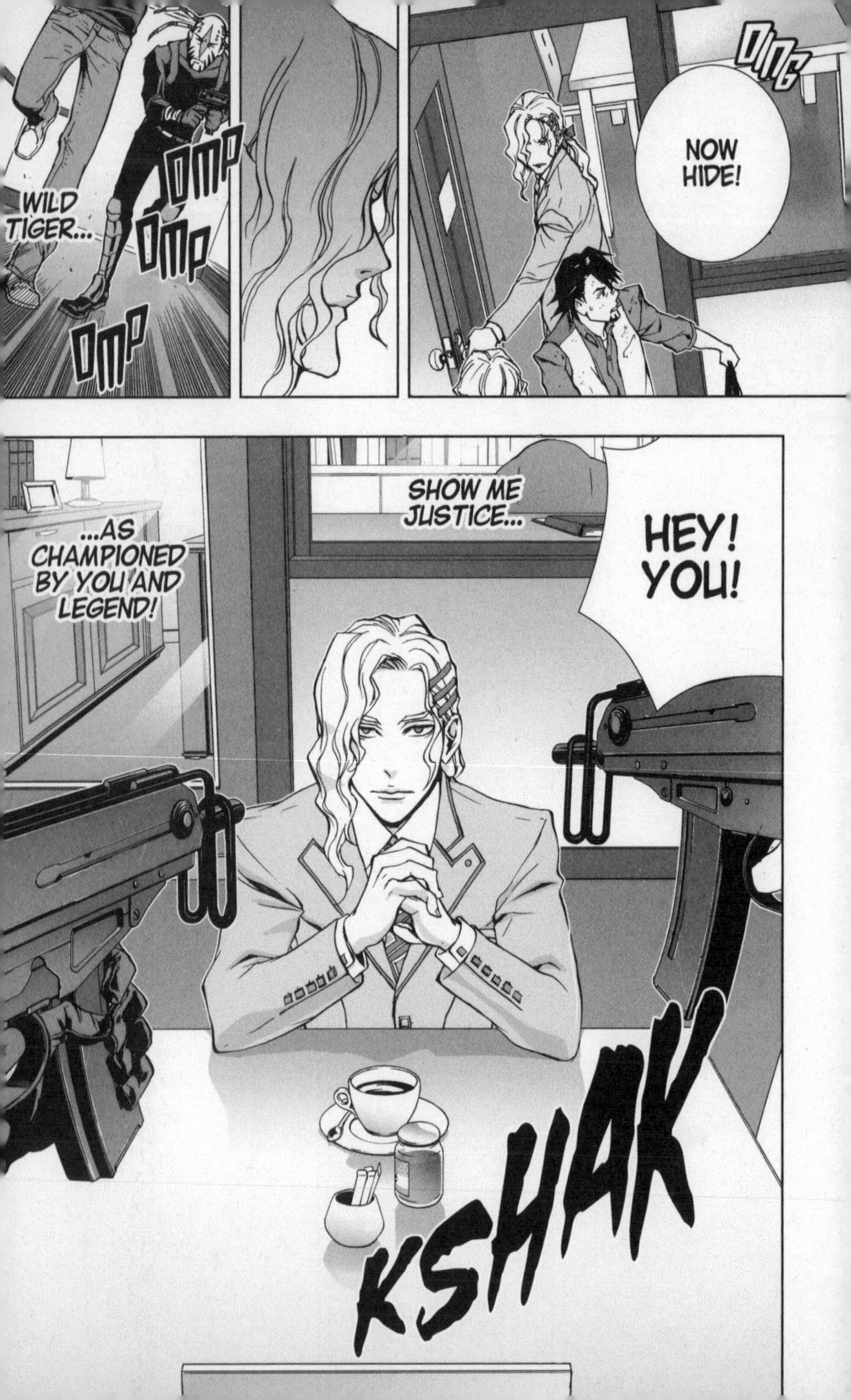
DING
NOW HIDE!
WILD TIGER...
OMP
OMP
OMP
HEY! YOU!
SHOW ME JUSTICE...
...AS CHAMPIONED BY YOU AND LEGEND!
KSHAK

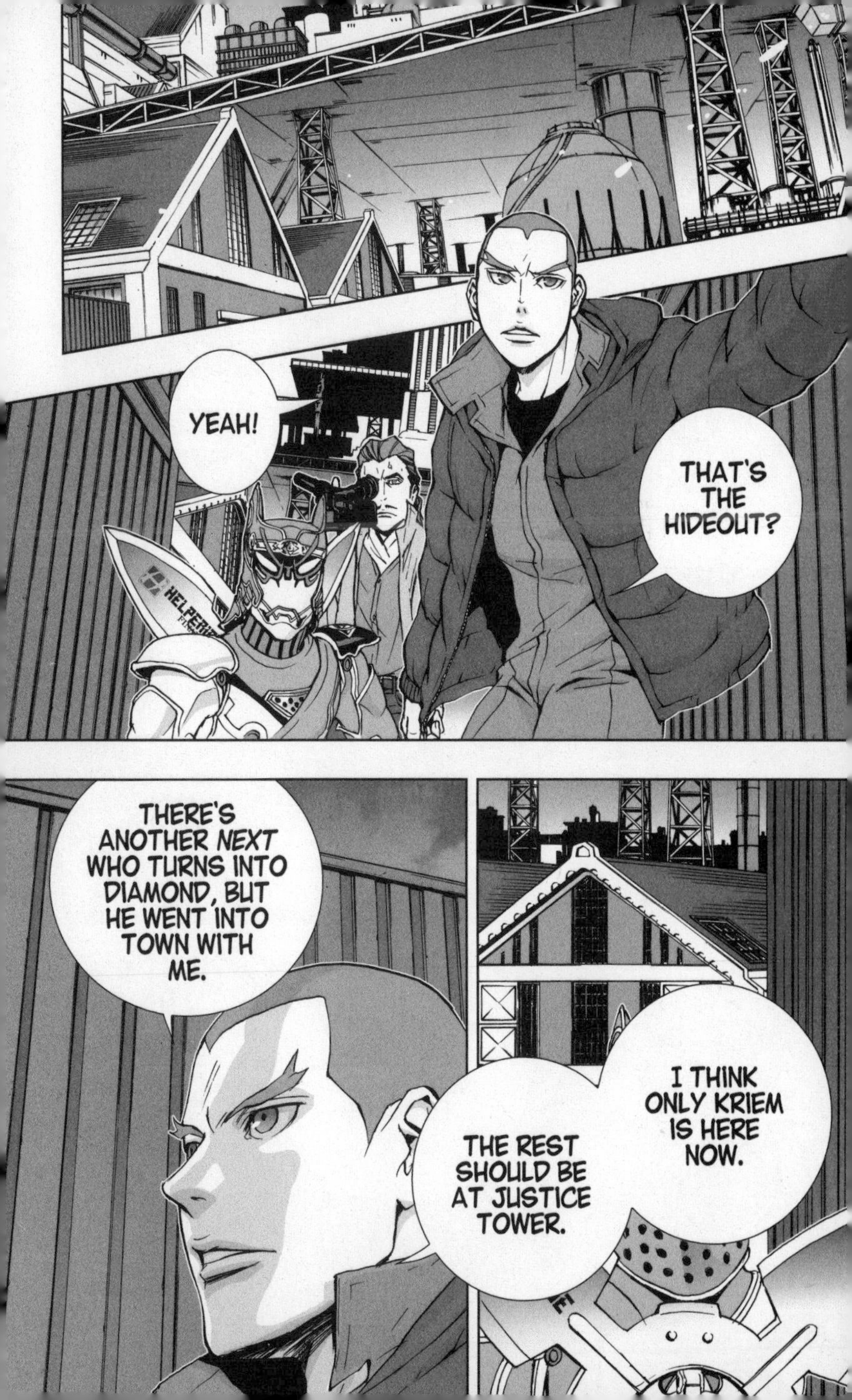
THAT'S THE HIDEOUT?
YEAH!
I THINK ONLY KRIEM IS HERE NOW.
THE REST SHOULD BE AT JUSTICE TOWER.
THERE'S ANOTHER NEXT WHO TURNS INTO DIAMOND, BUT HE WENT INTO TOWN WITH ME.

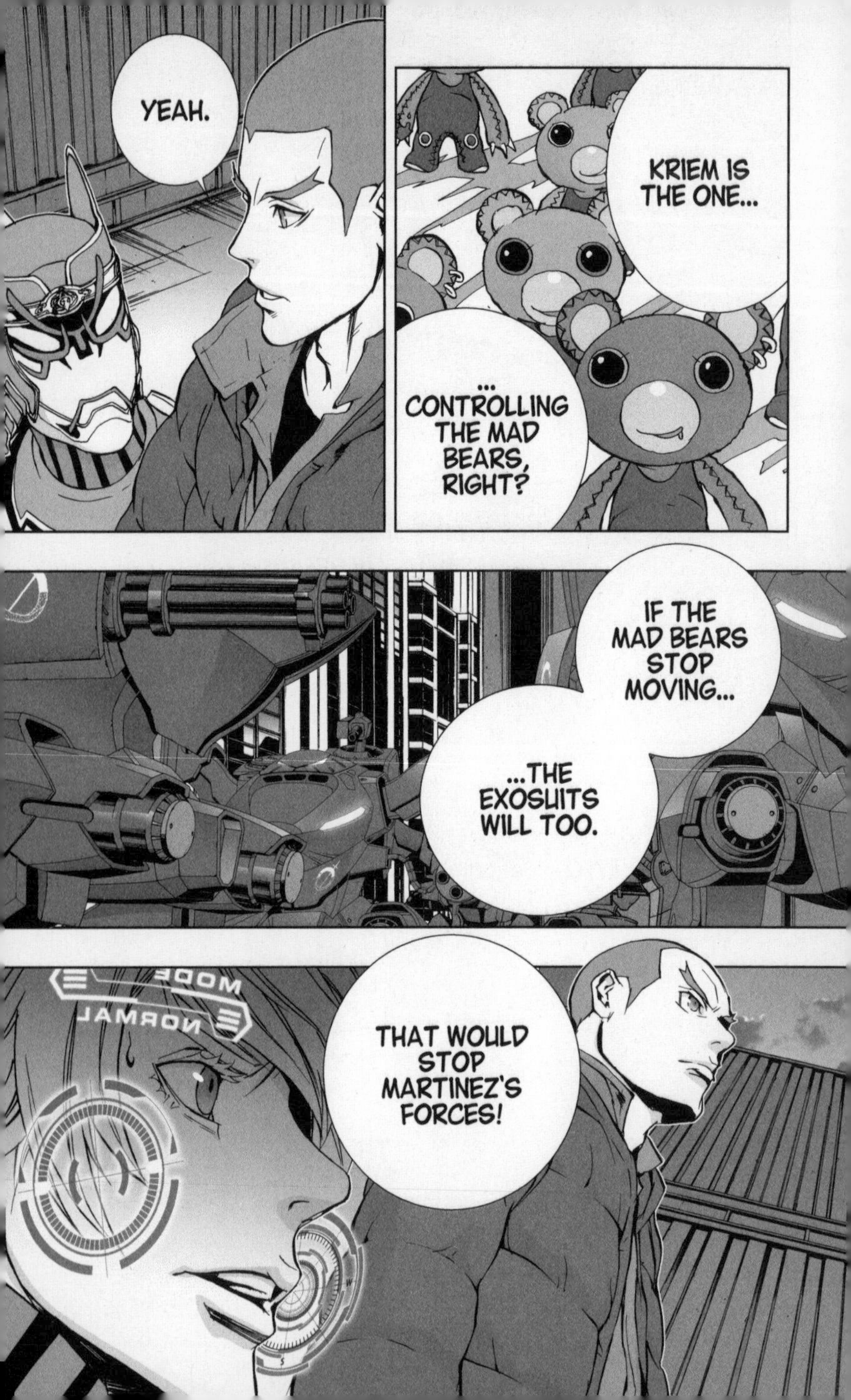
KRIEM IS THE ONE...
...CONTROLLING THE MAD BEARS, RIGHT?
YEAH.
IF THE MAD BEARS STOP MOVING...
...THE EXOSUITS WILL TOO.
THAT WOULD STOP MARTINEZ'S FORCES!

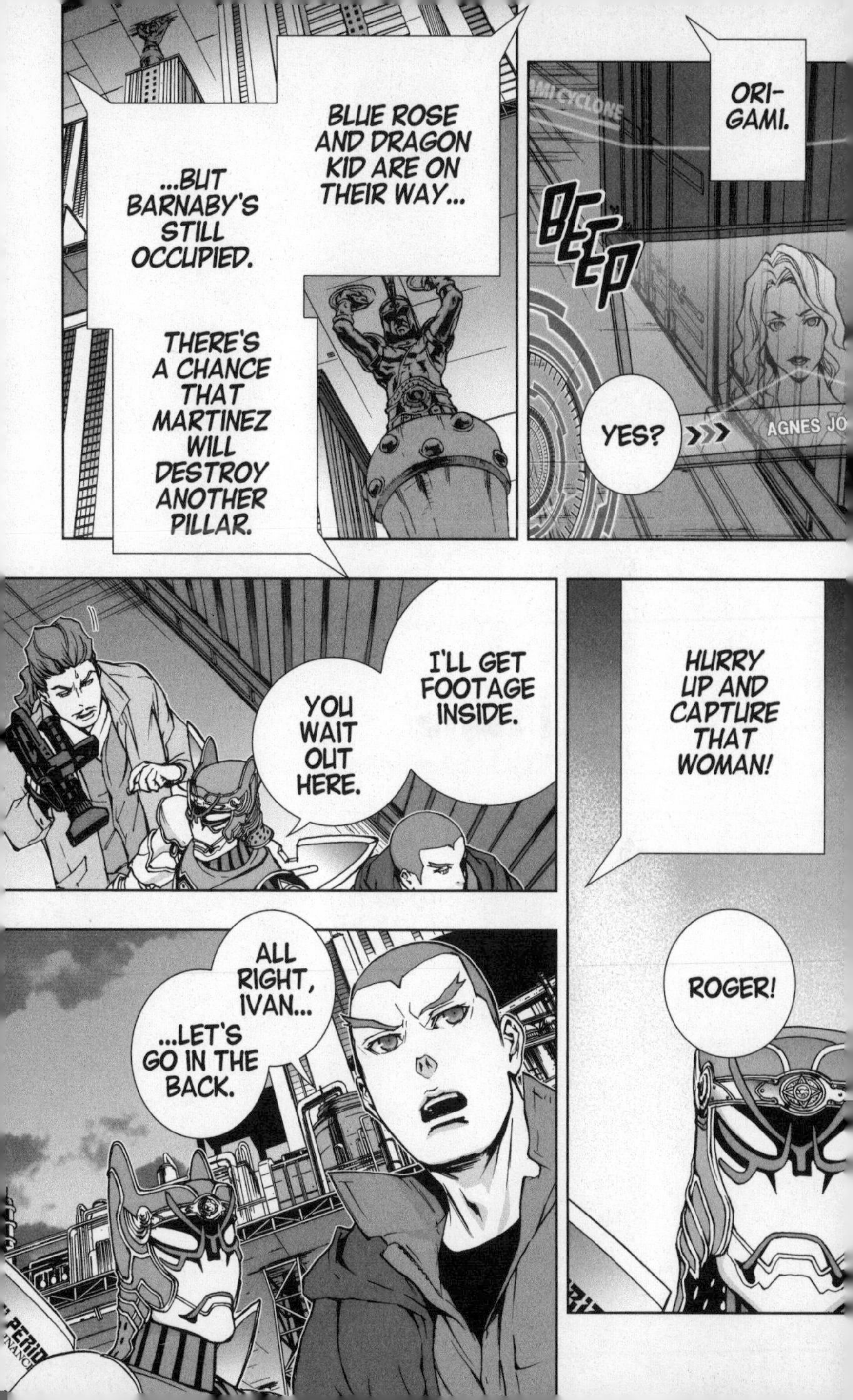
BEEP
ORI-GAMI.
YES?
BLUE ROSE AND DRAGON KID ARE ON THEIR WAY...
...BUT BARNABY'S STILL OCCUPIED.
THERE'S A CHANCE THAT MARTINEZ WILL DESTROY ANOTHER PILLAR.
HURRY UP AND CAPTURE THAT WOMAN!
ROGER!
I'LL GET FOOTAGE INSIDE.
YOU WAIT OUT HERE.
ALL RIGHT, IVAN...
...LET'S GO IN THE BACK.

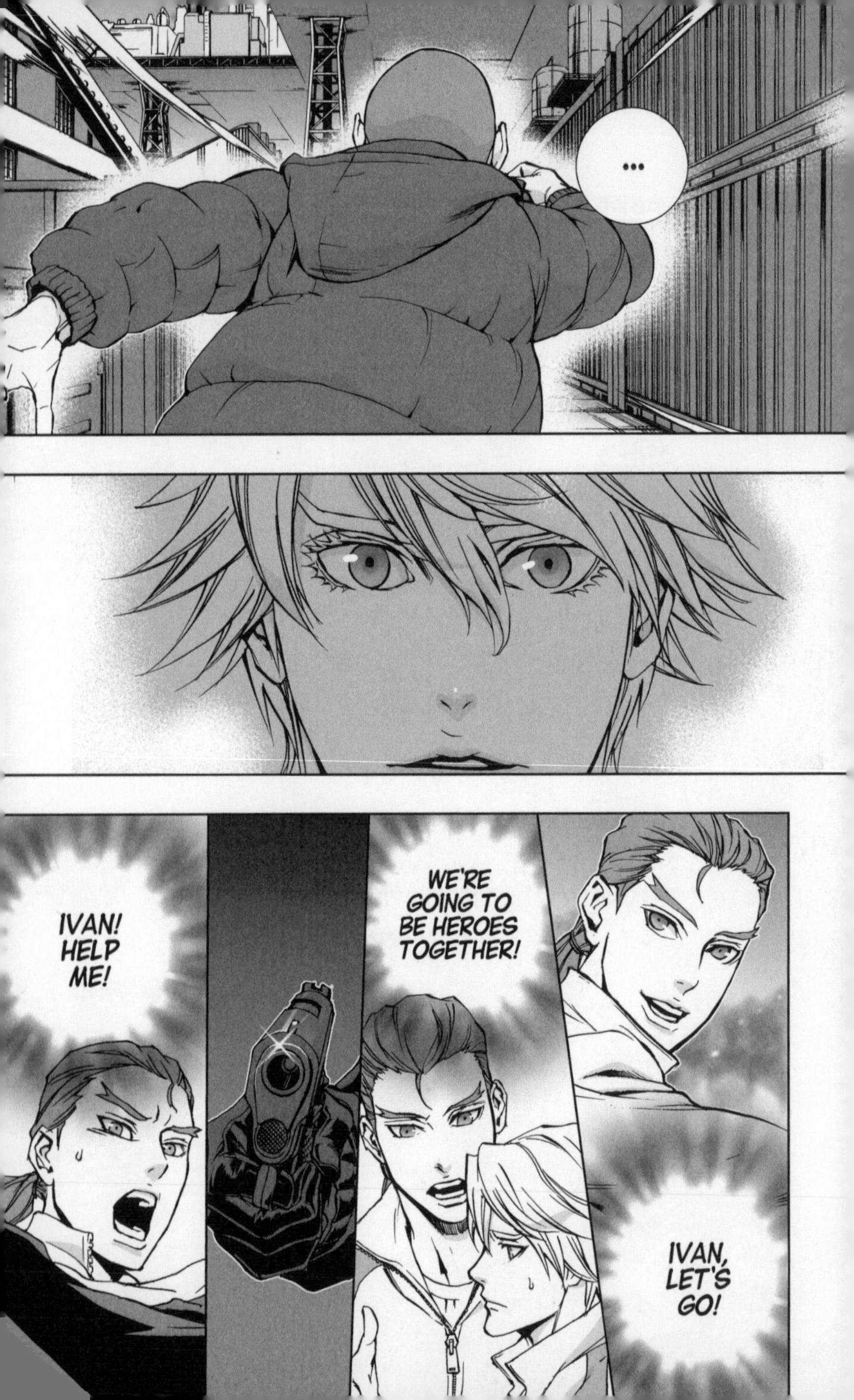
...
IVAN, LET'S GO!
WE'RE GOING TO BE HEROES TOGETHER!
IVAN! HELP ME!

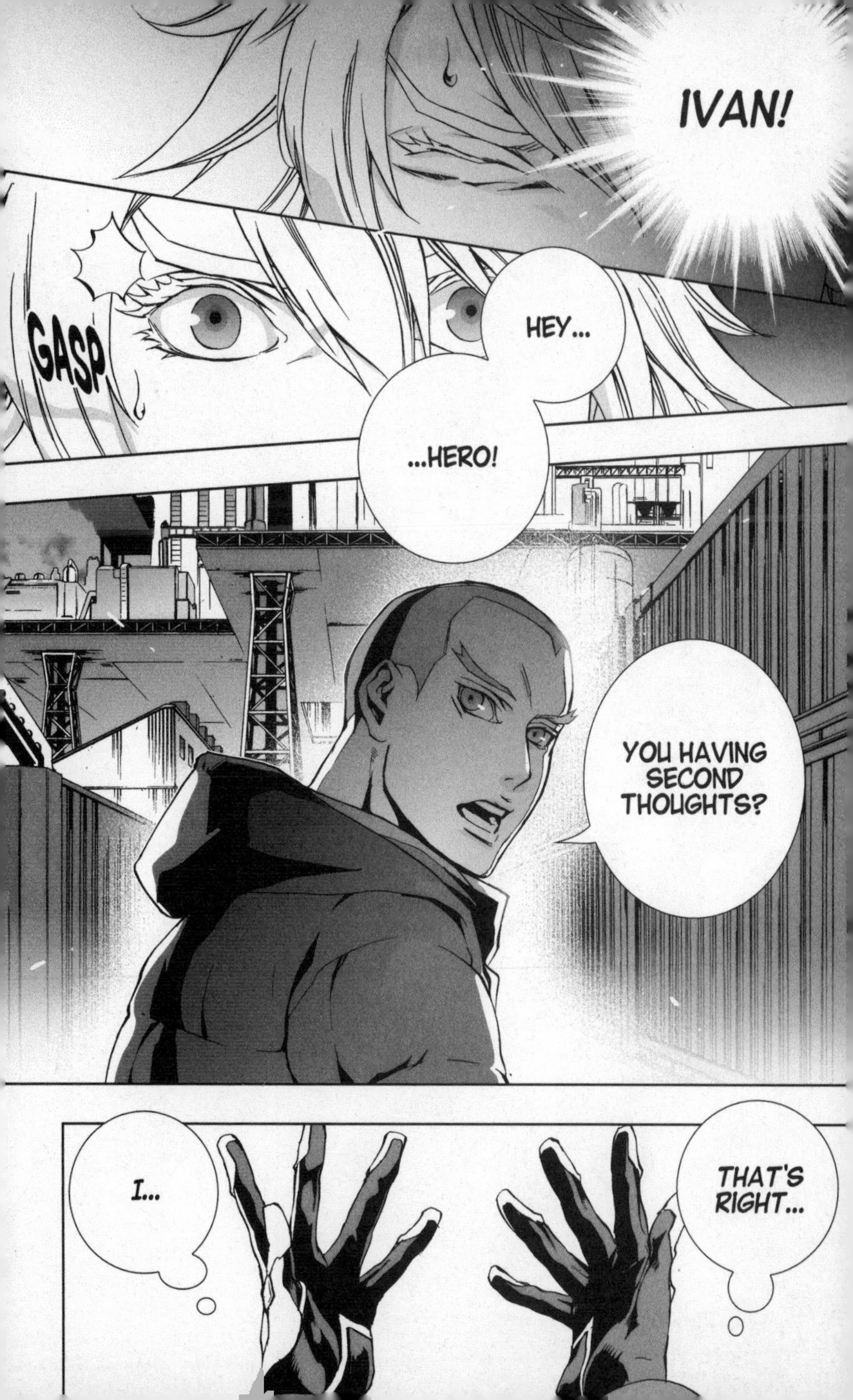
IVAN!
GASP
HEY...
...HERO!
YOU HAVING SECOND THOUGHTS?
THAT'S RIGHT...
I...

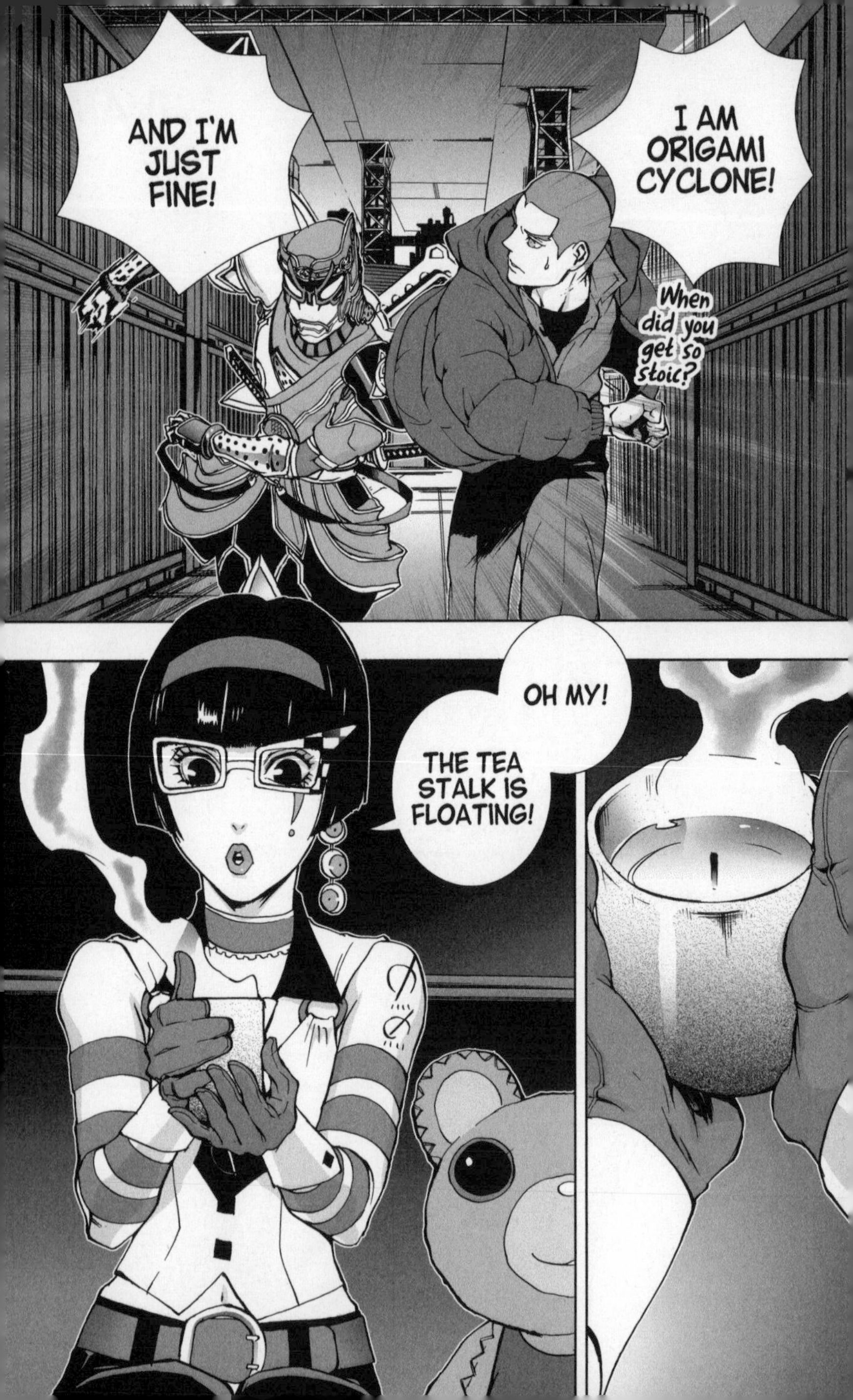
I AM ORIGAMI CYCLONE!
When did you get so stoic?
AND I'M JUST FINE!
OH MY!
THE TEA STALK IS FLOATING!

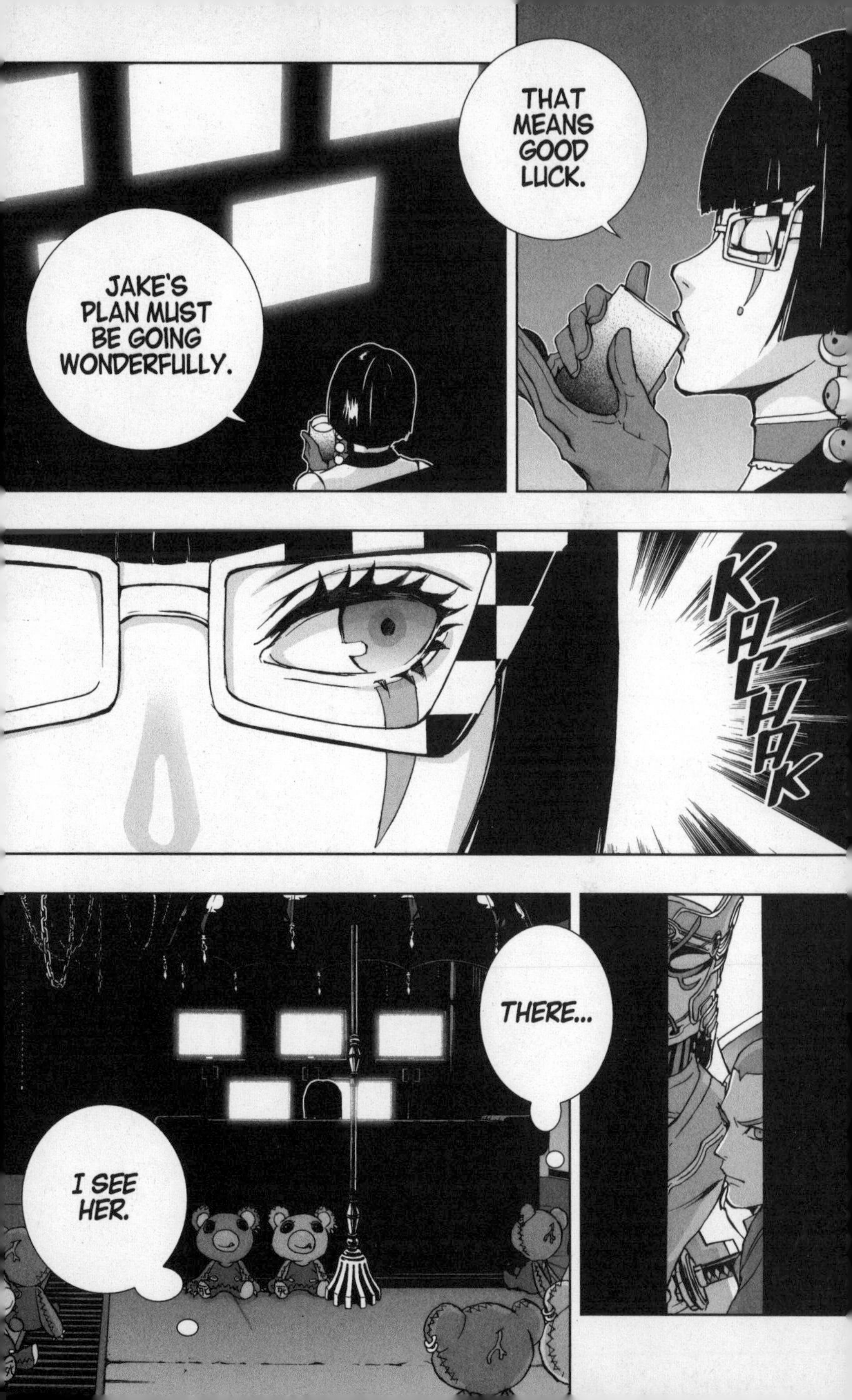
THAT MEANS GOOD LUCK.
JAKE'S PLAN MUST BE GOING WONDERFULLY.
KACHAK
THERE...
I SEE HER.

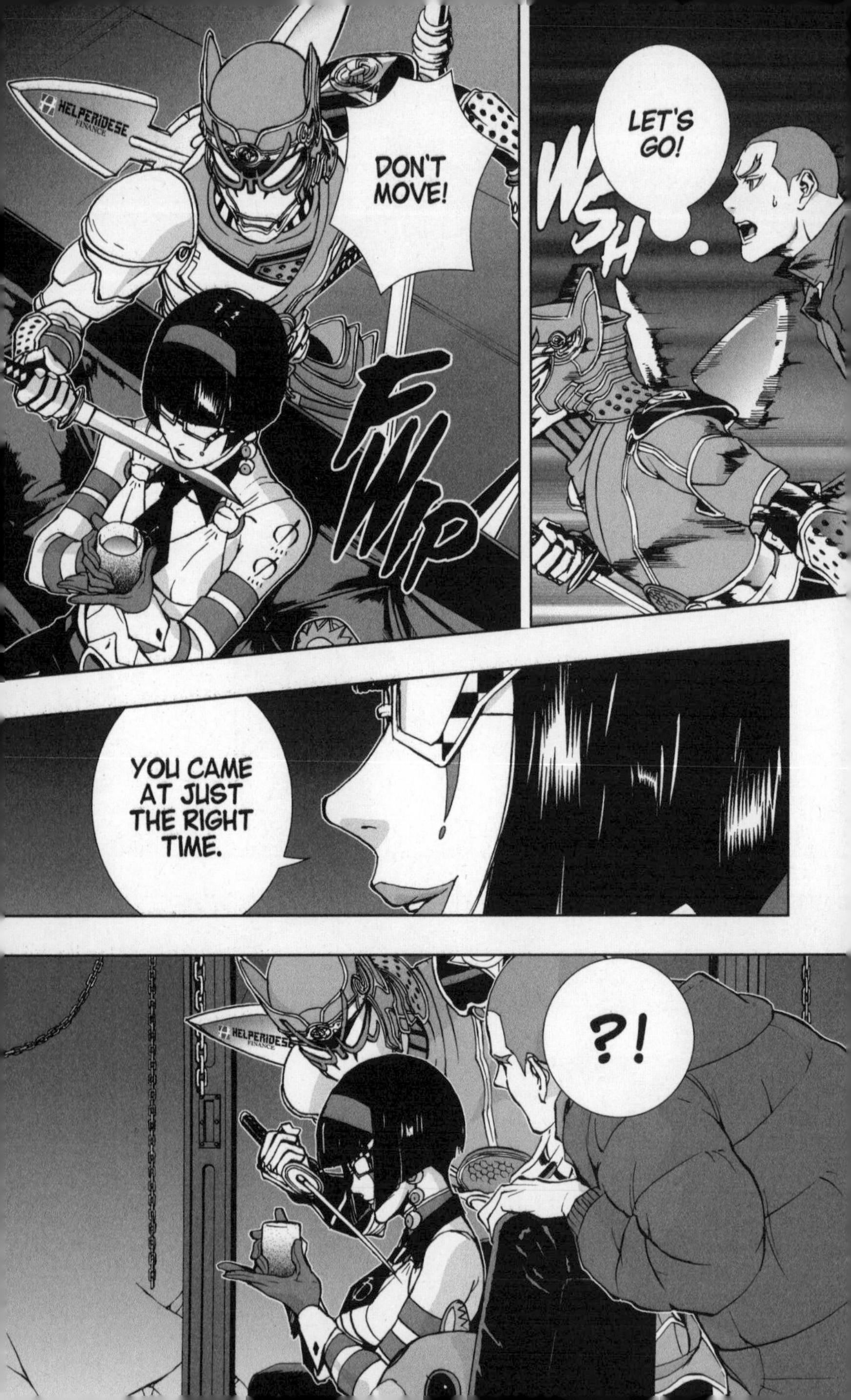
LET'S GO!
WSH
DON'T MOVE!
HELPERIDESE FINANCE
FWIP
YOU CAME AT JUST THE RIGHT TIME.
?!
HELPERIDESE FINANCE

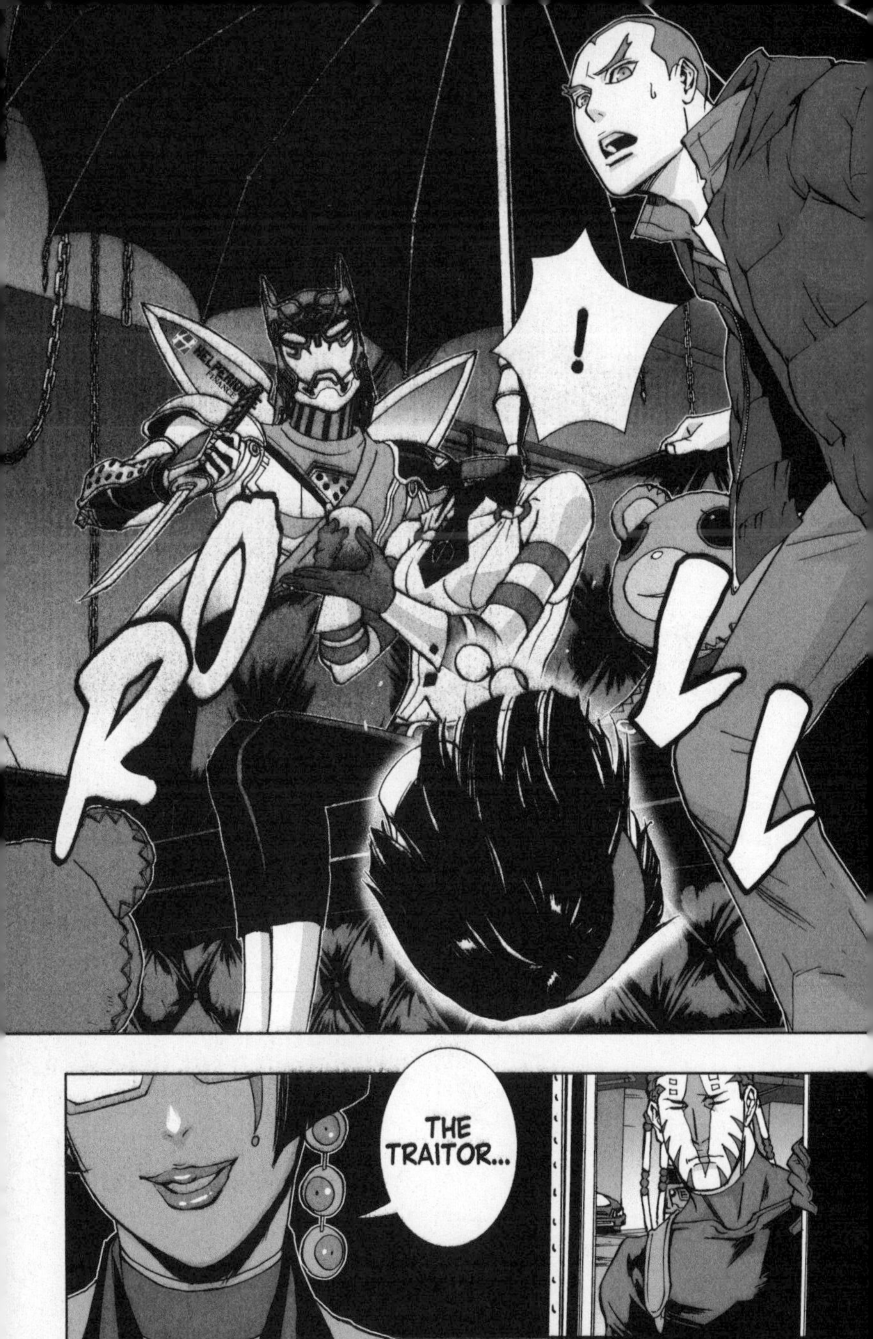
!
ROLL
THE TRAITOR...

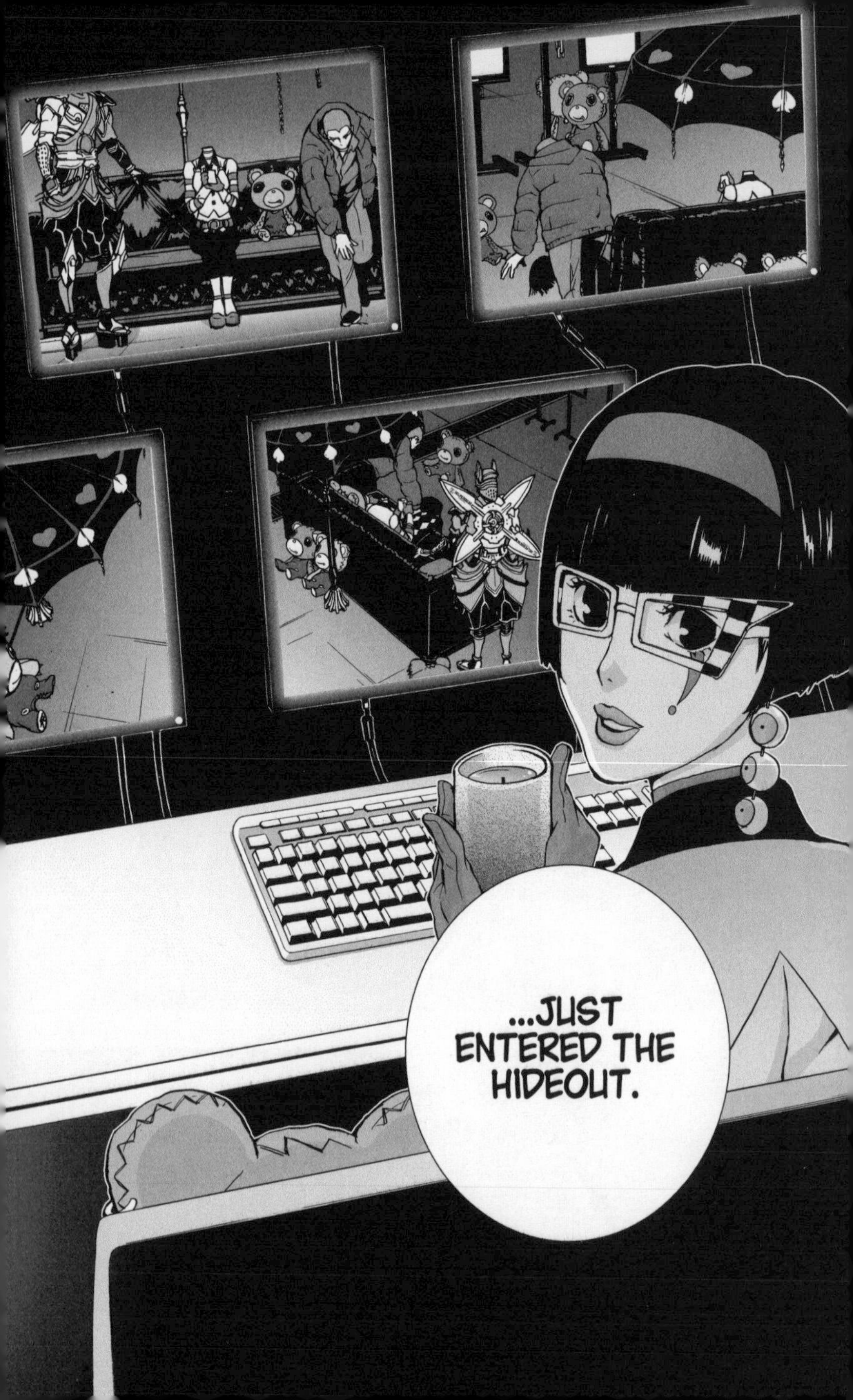
...JUST ENTERED THE HIDEOUT.

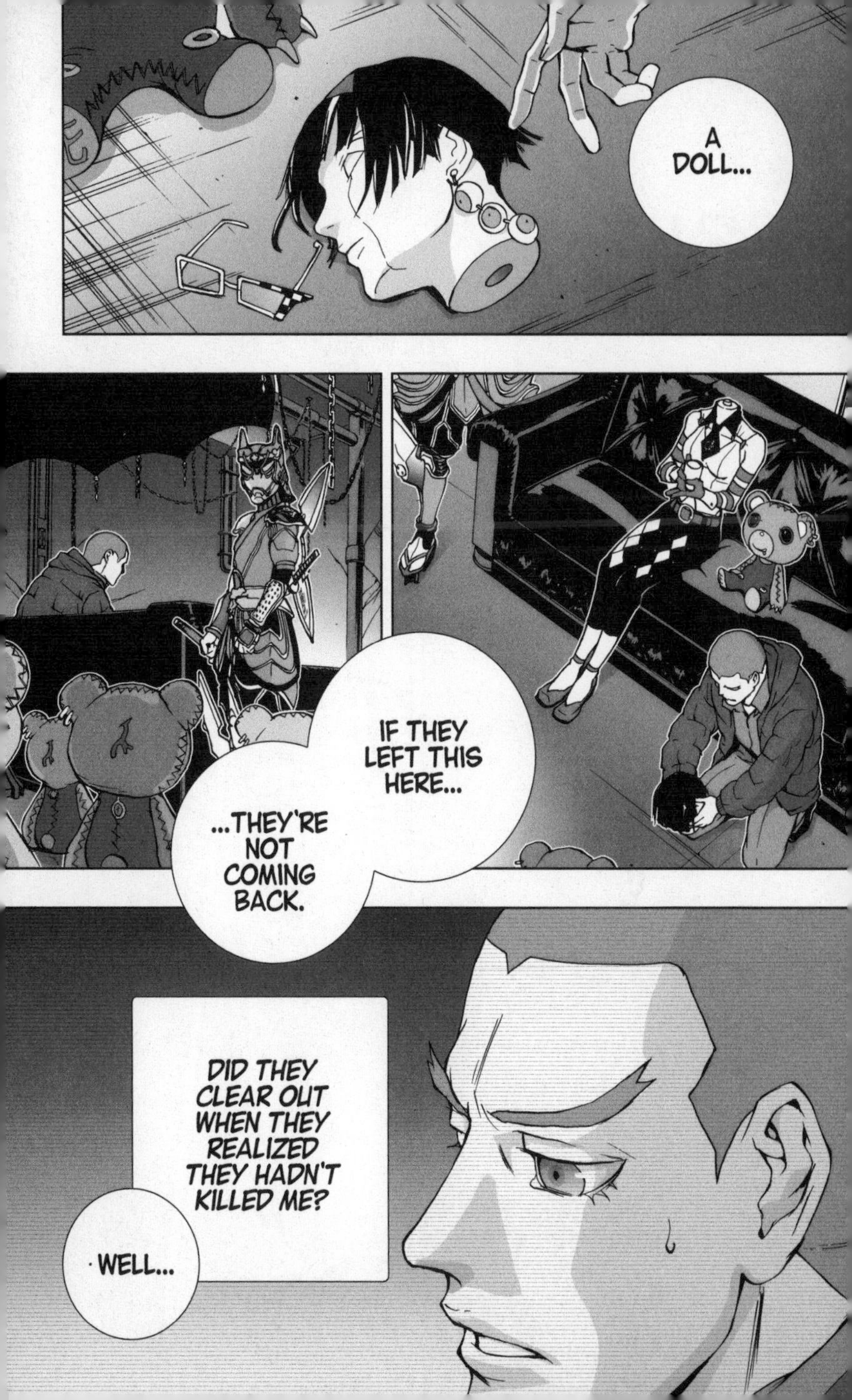
A DOLL...
IF THEY LEFT THIS HERE...
...THEY'RE NOT COMING BACK.
DID THEY CLEAR OUT WHEN THEY REALIZED THEY HADN'T KILLED ME?
WELL...

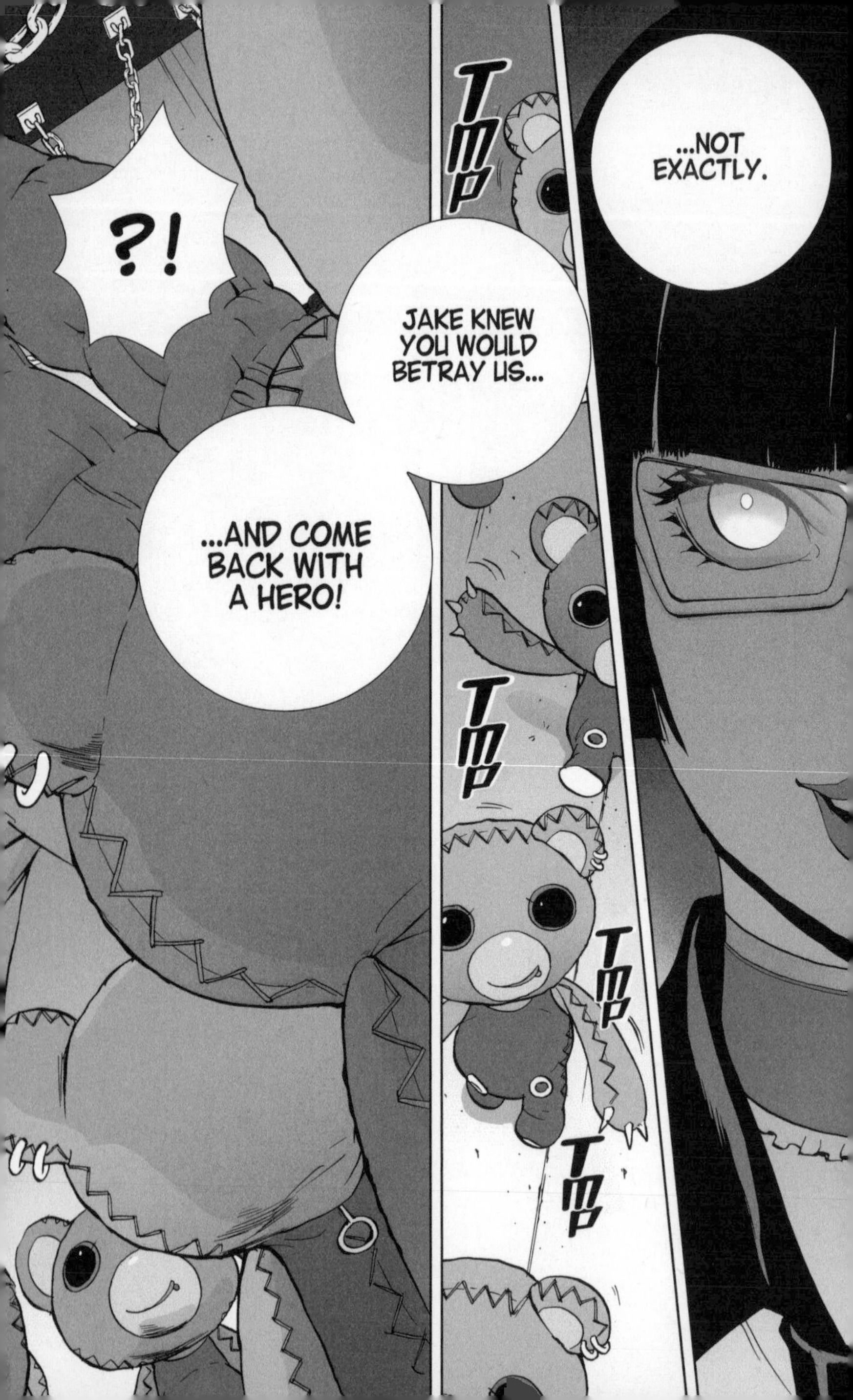
...NOT EXACTLY.
TMP
TMP
JAKE KNEW YOU WOULD BETRAY US...
...AND COME BACK WITH A HERO!
TMP
TMP
?!

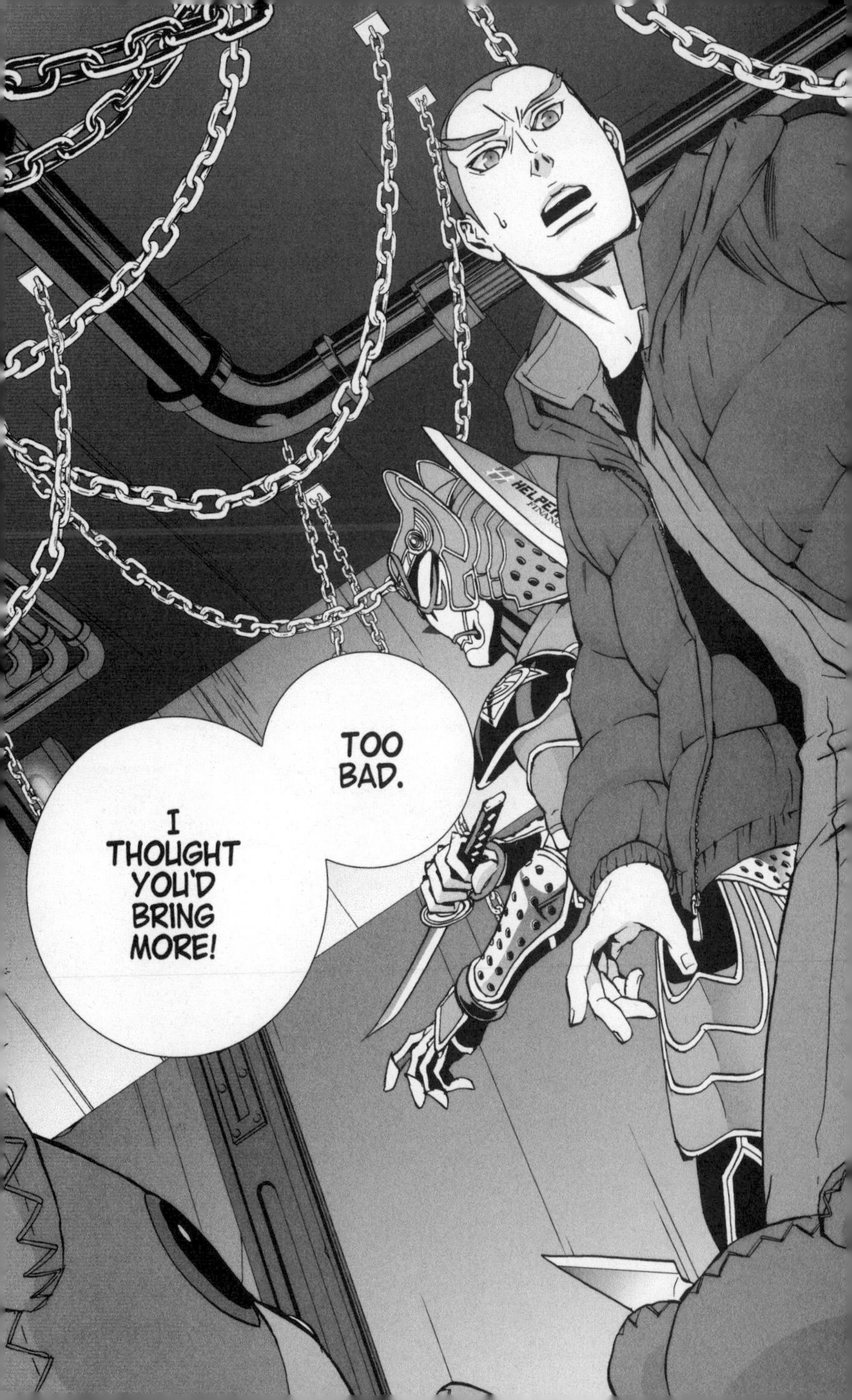
TOO BAD.
I THOUGHT YOU'D BRING MORE!

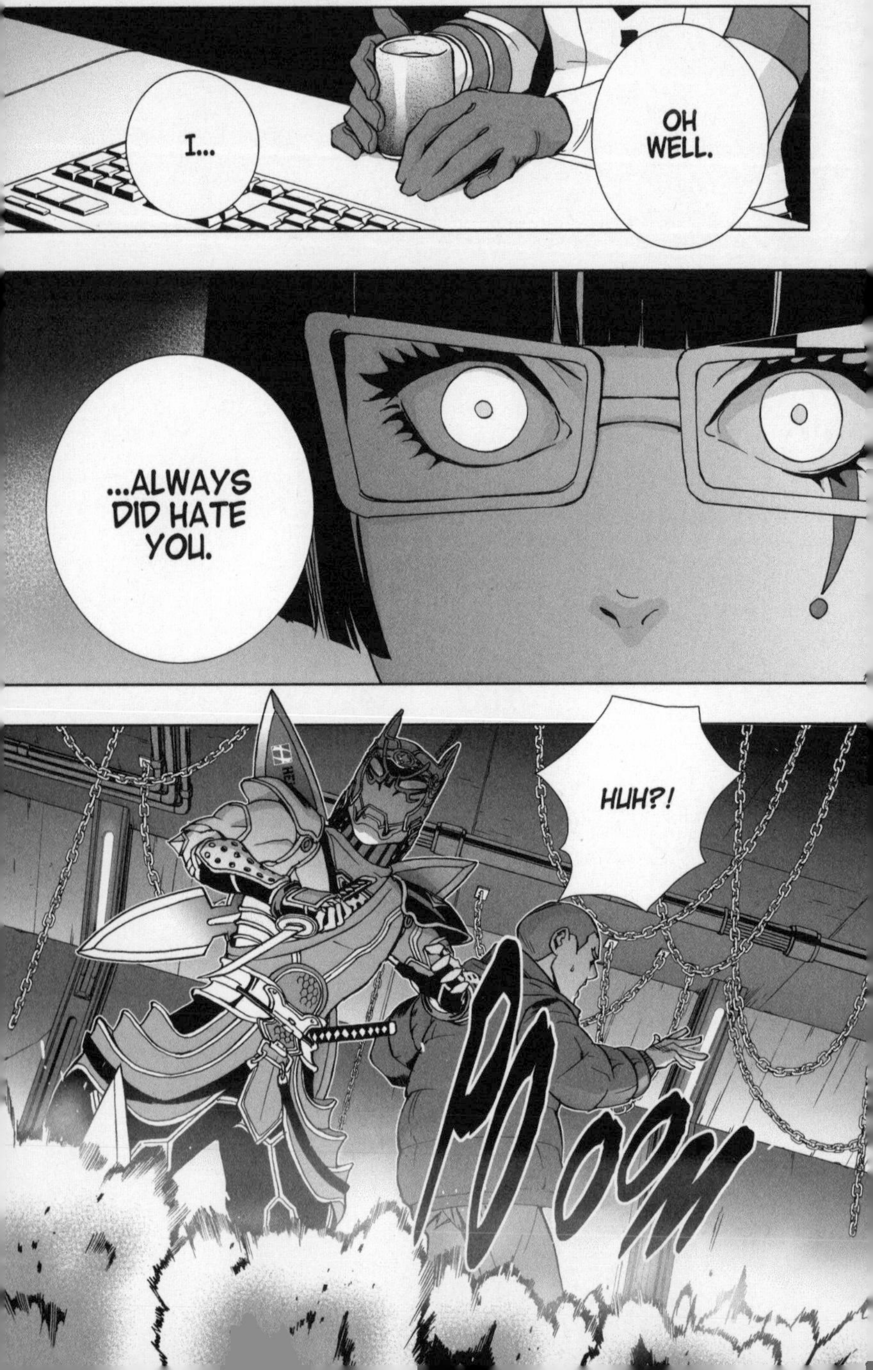
OH WELL.
I...
...ALWAYS DID HATE YOU.
HUH?!

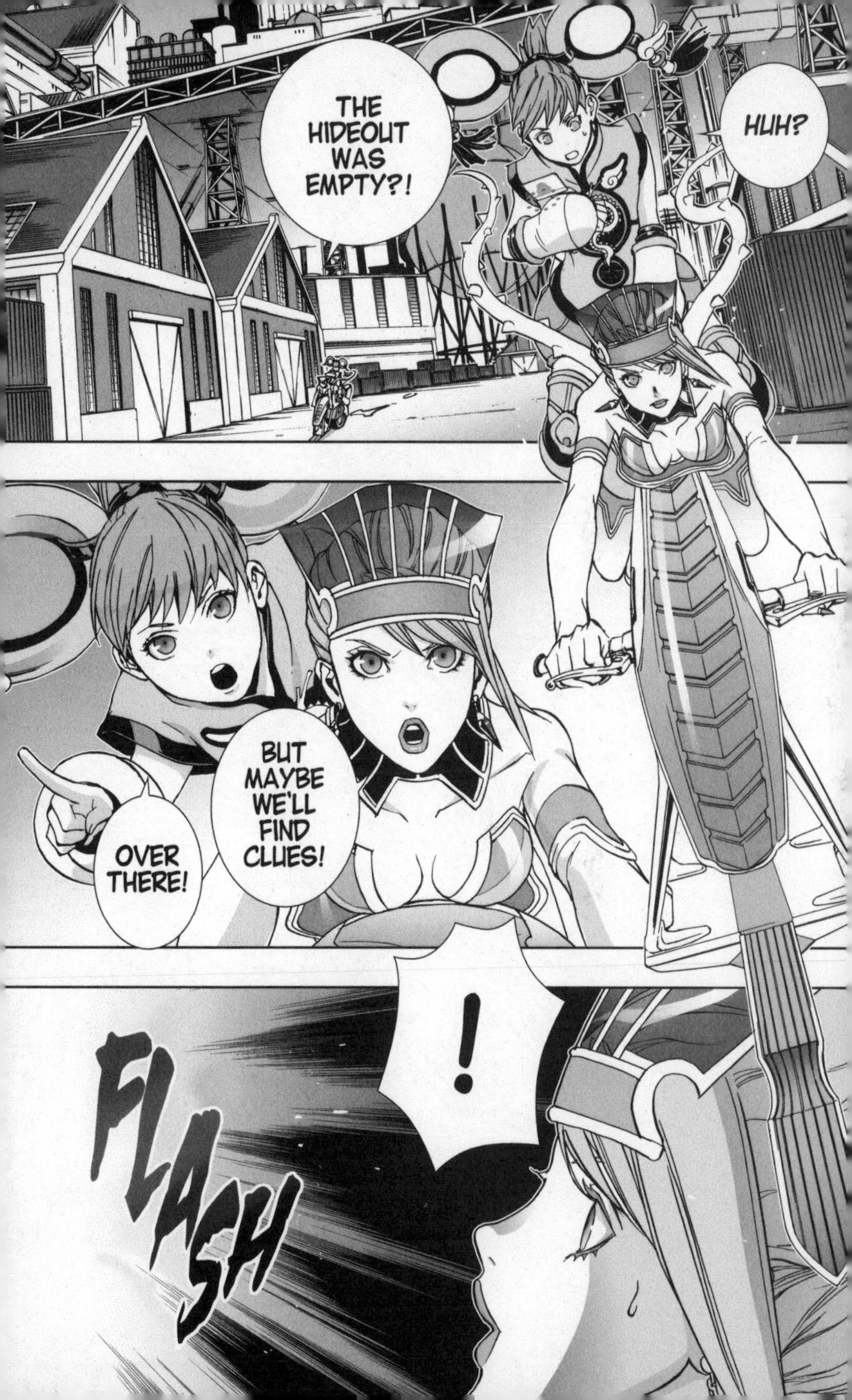
HUH?
THE HIDEOUT WAS EMPTY?!
BUT MAYBE WE'LL FIND CLUES!
OVER THERE!
!
FLASH

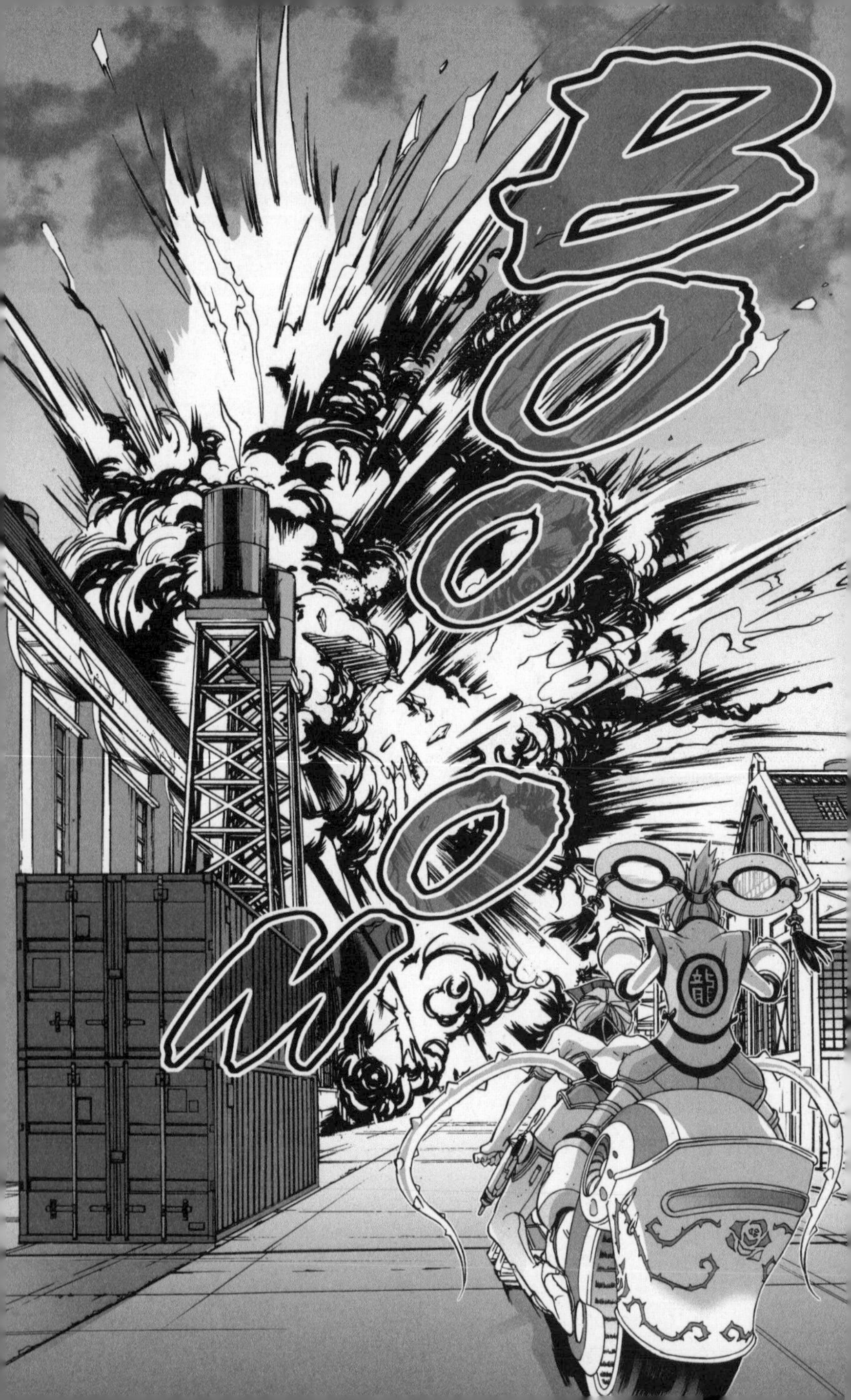
BOOOM

TIGER & BUNNY

TIGER&BUNNY

#29 Confidence Is a Plant of Slow Growth, Part 6

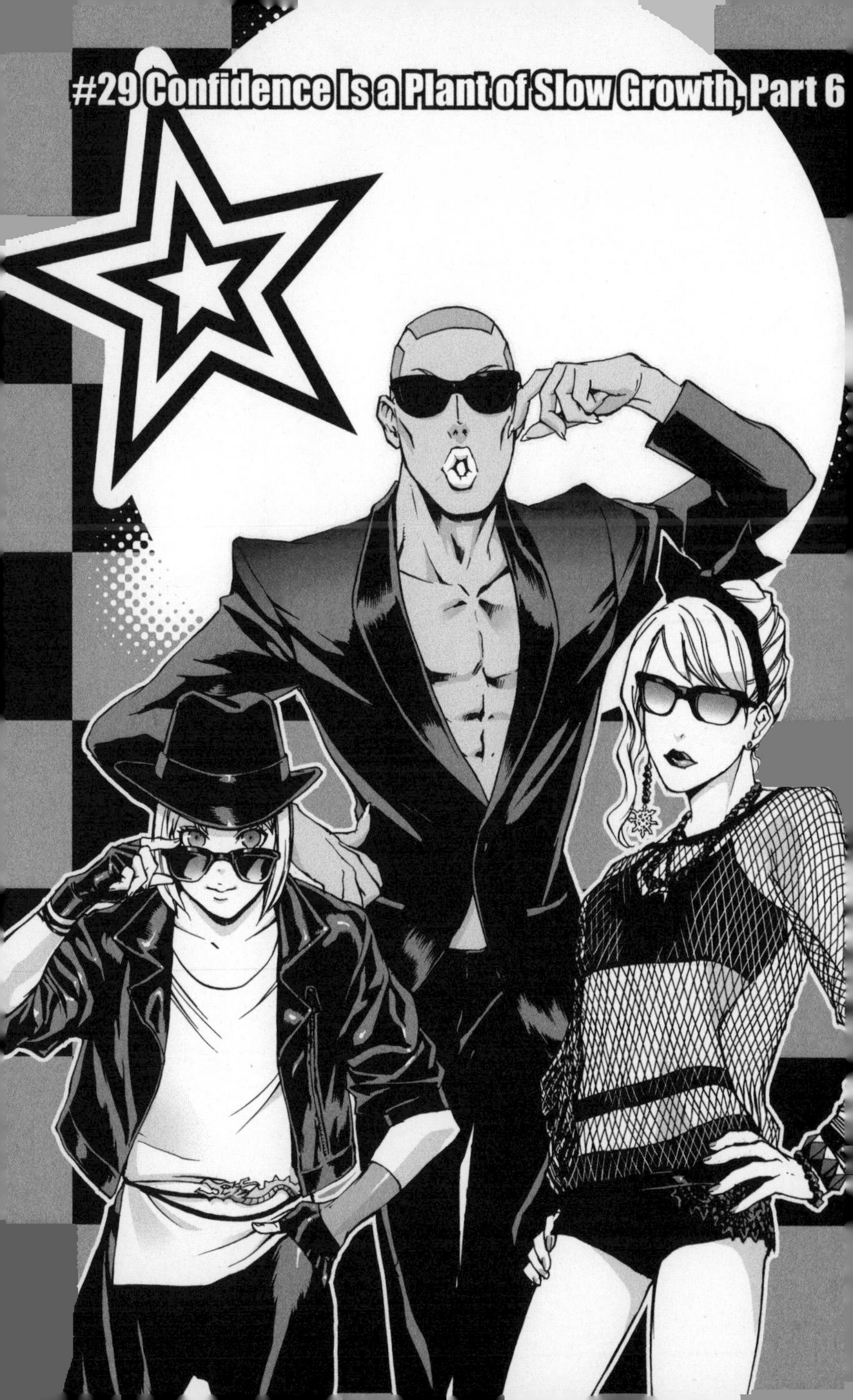

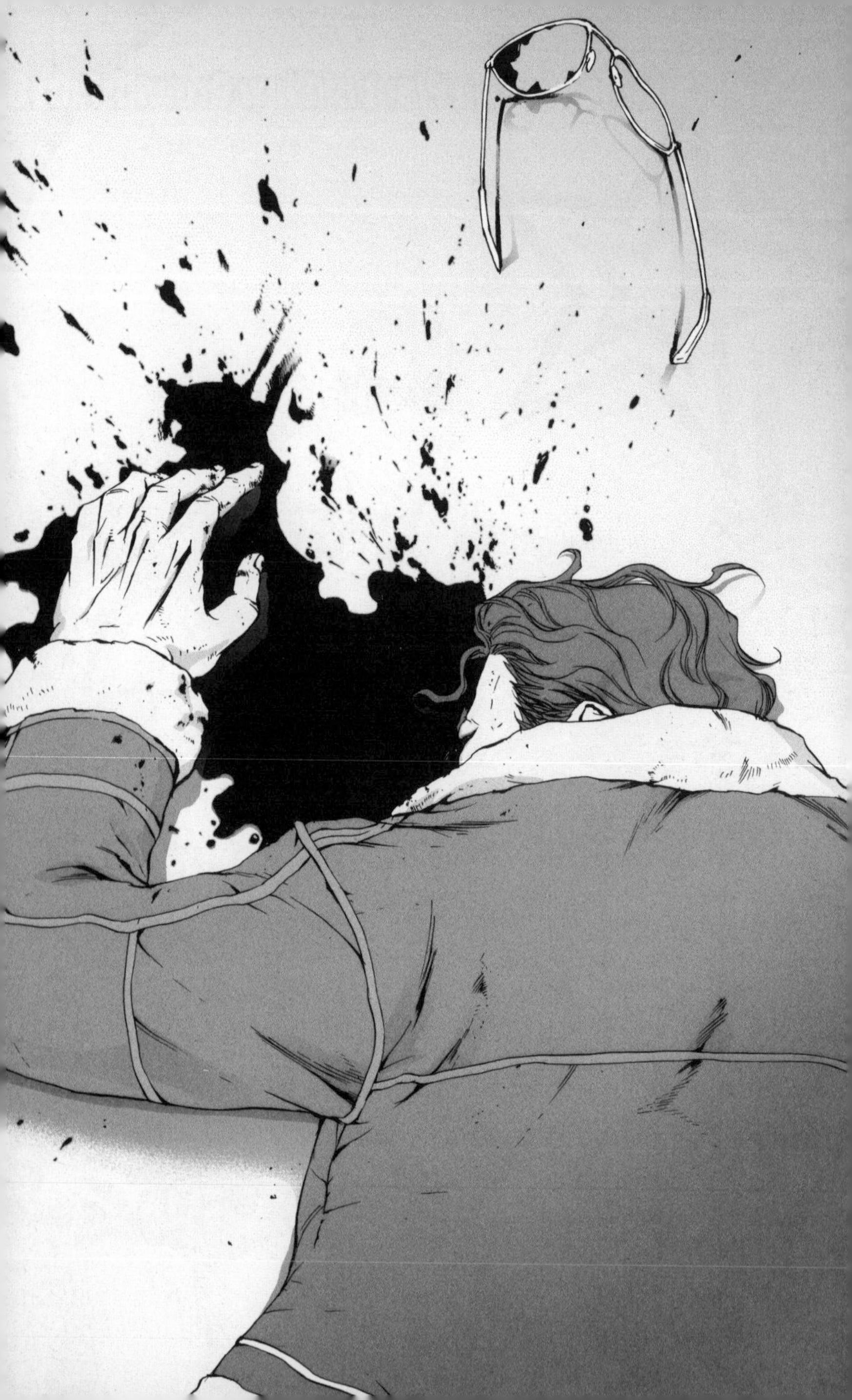

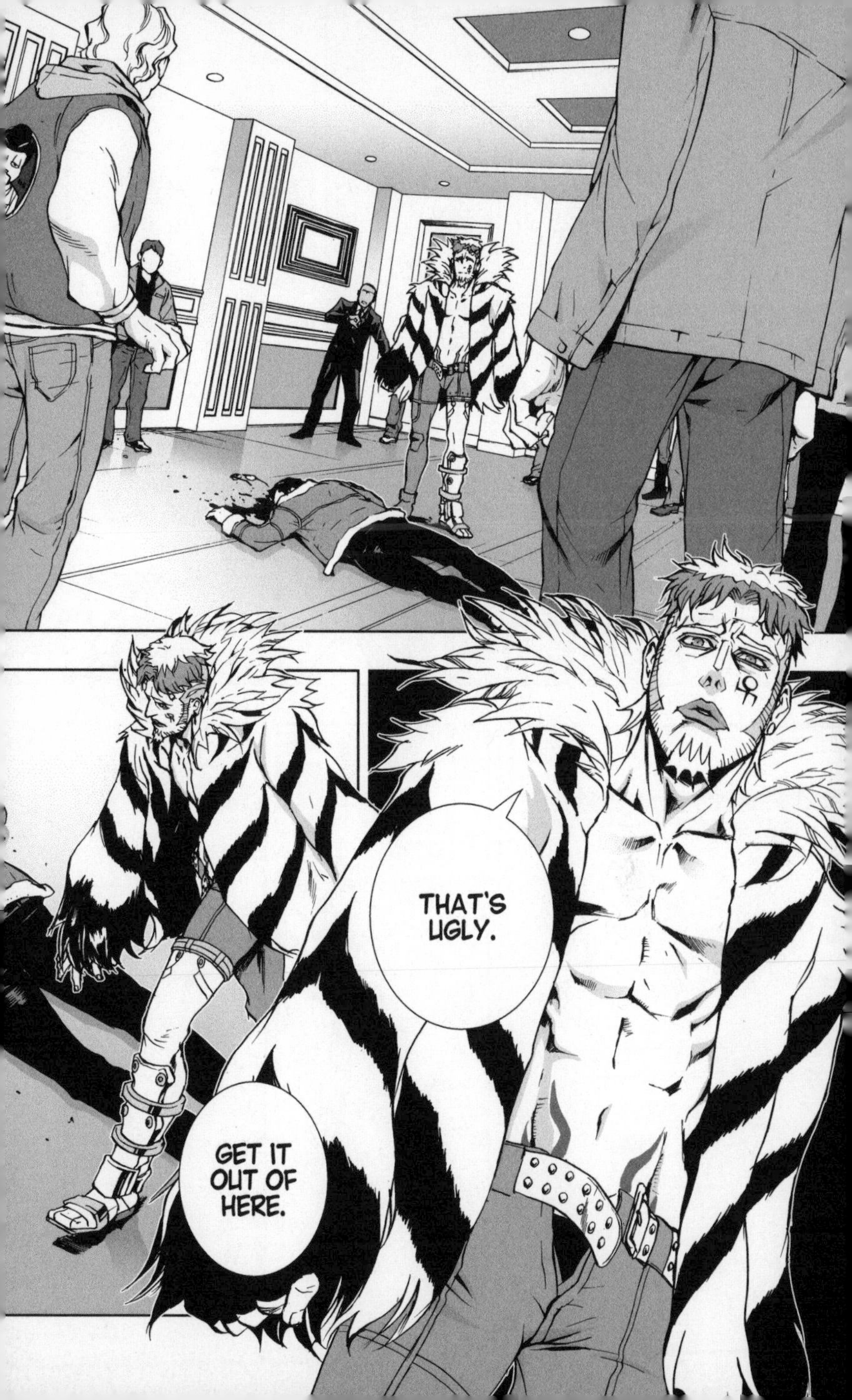
THAT'S UGLY.
GET IT OUT OF HERE.

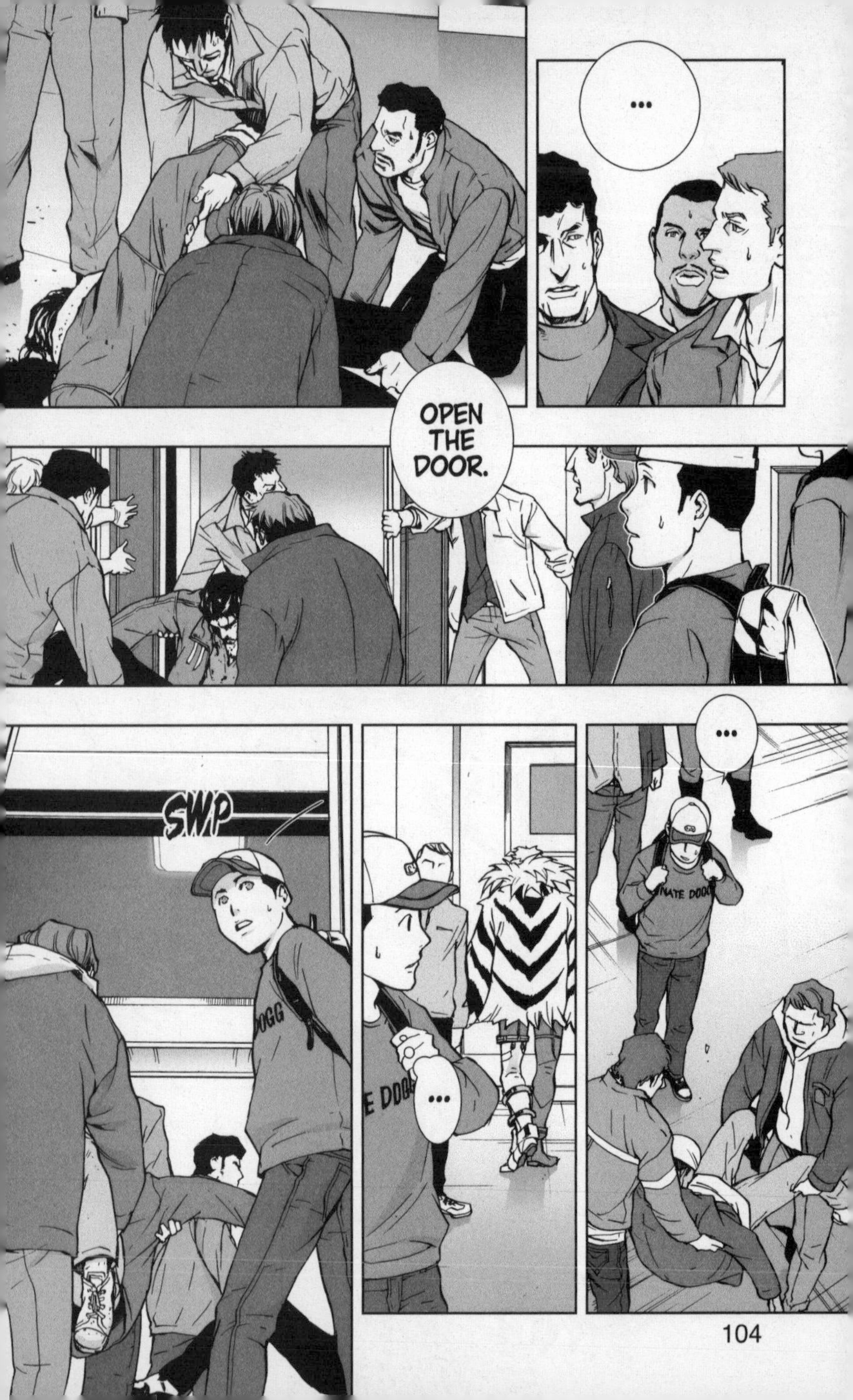
...
OPEN THE DOOR.
...
...
SWP

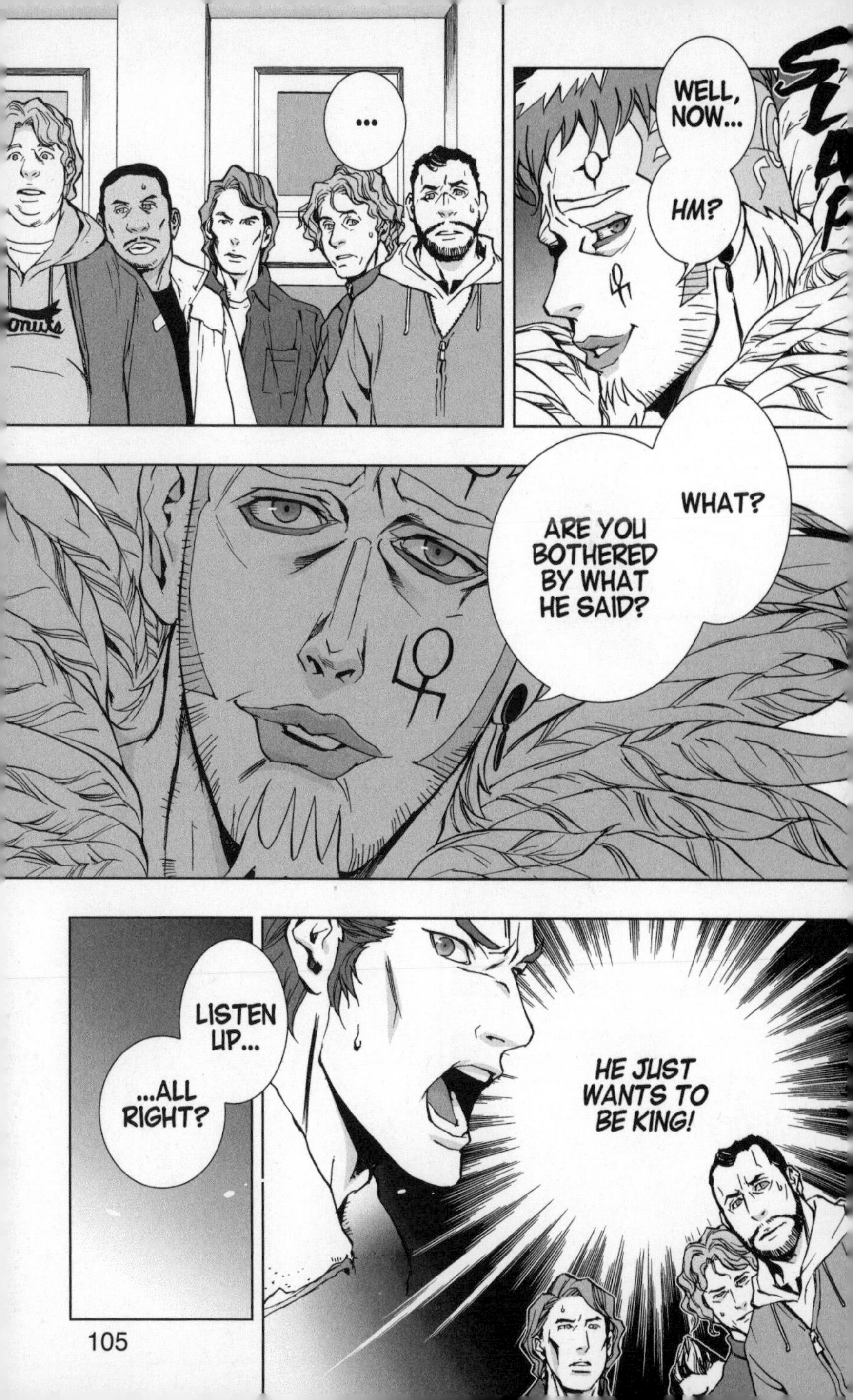
SLAP
WELL, NOW...
HM?
...
WHAT?
ARE YOU BOTHERED BY WHAT HE SAID?
LISTEN UP...
...ALL RIGHT?
HE JUST WANTS TO BE KING!

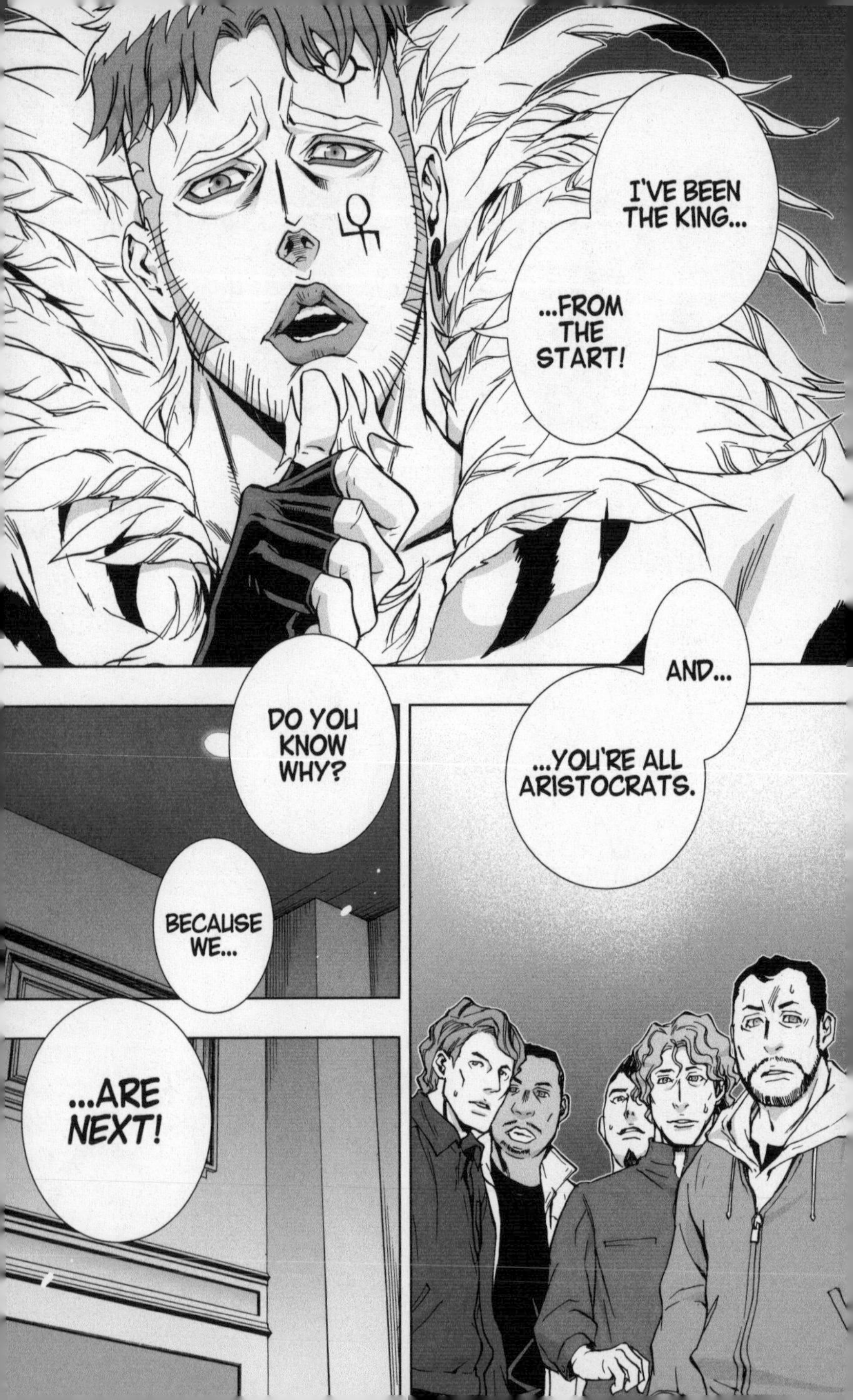
I'VE BEEN THE KING...
...FROM THE START!
AND...
...YOU'RE ALL ARISTOCRATS.
DO YOU KNOW WHY?
BECAUSE WE...
...ARE NEXT!

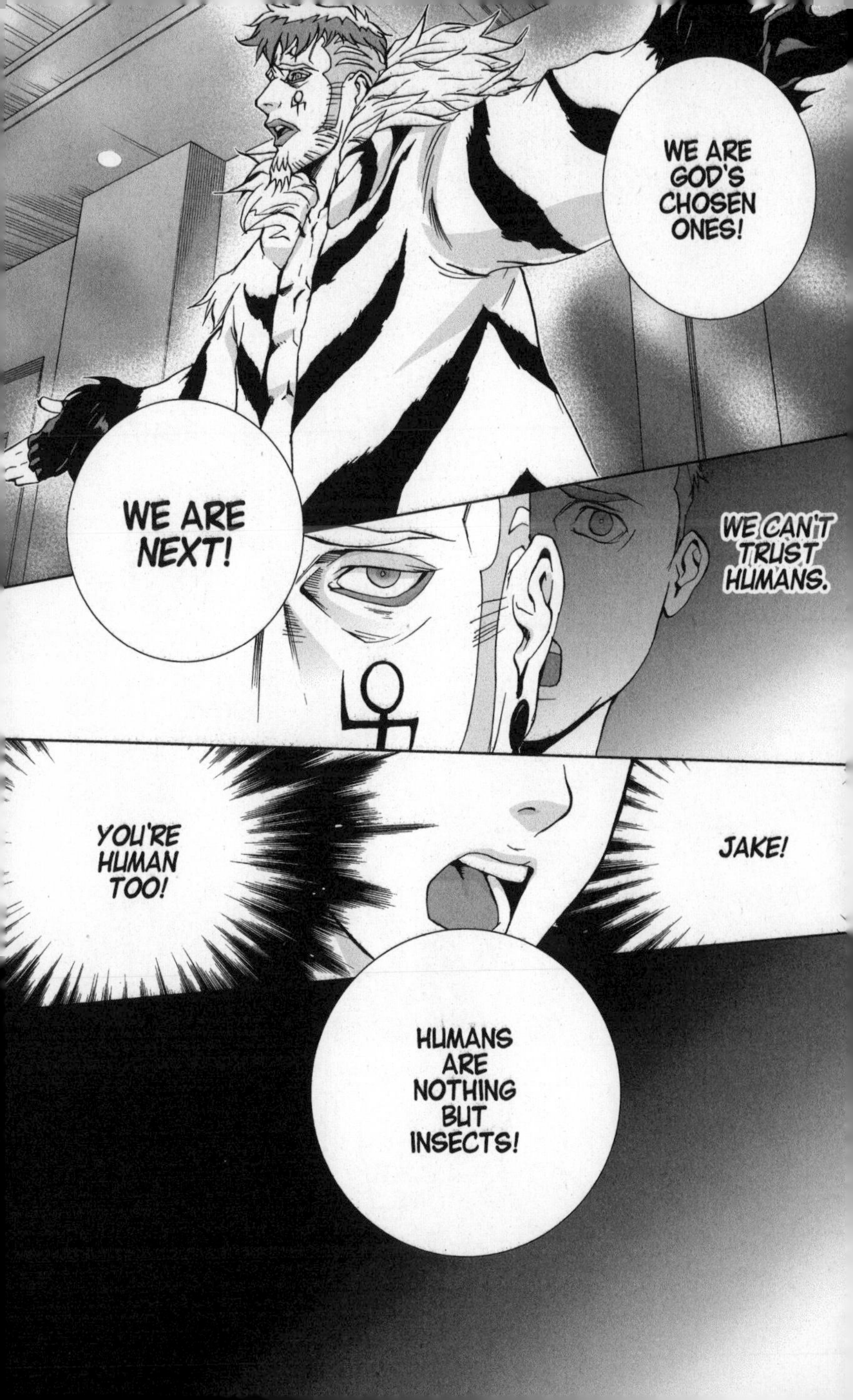
WE ARE GOD'S CHOSEN ONES!
WE ARE NEXT!
WE CAN'T TRUST HUMANS.
JAKE!
YOU'RE HUMAN TOO!
HUMANS ARE NOTHING BUT INSECTS!

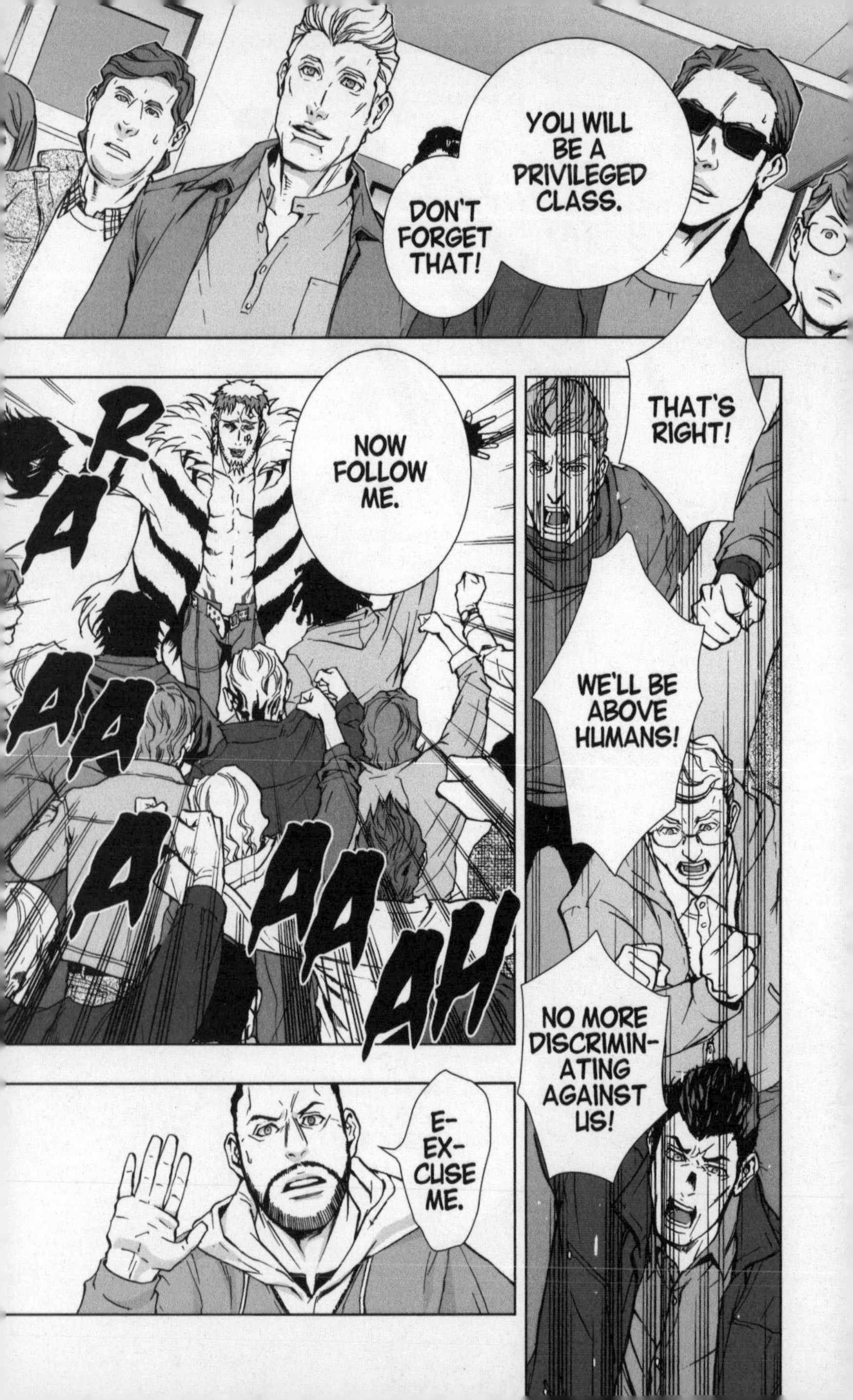
YOU WILL BE A PRIVILEGED CLASS.
DON'T FORGET THAT!
THAT'S RIGHT!
WE'LL BE ABOVE HUMANS!
NO MORE DISCRIMIN-ATING AGAINST US!
NOW FOLLOW ME.
RAAAAAAAH
E- EX-CUSE ME.

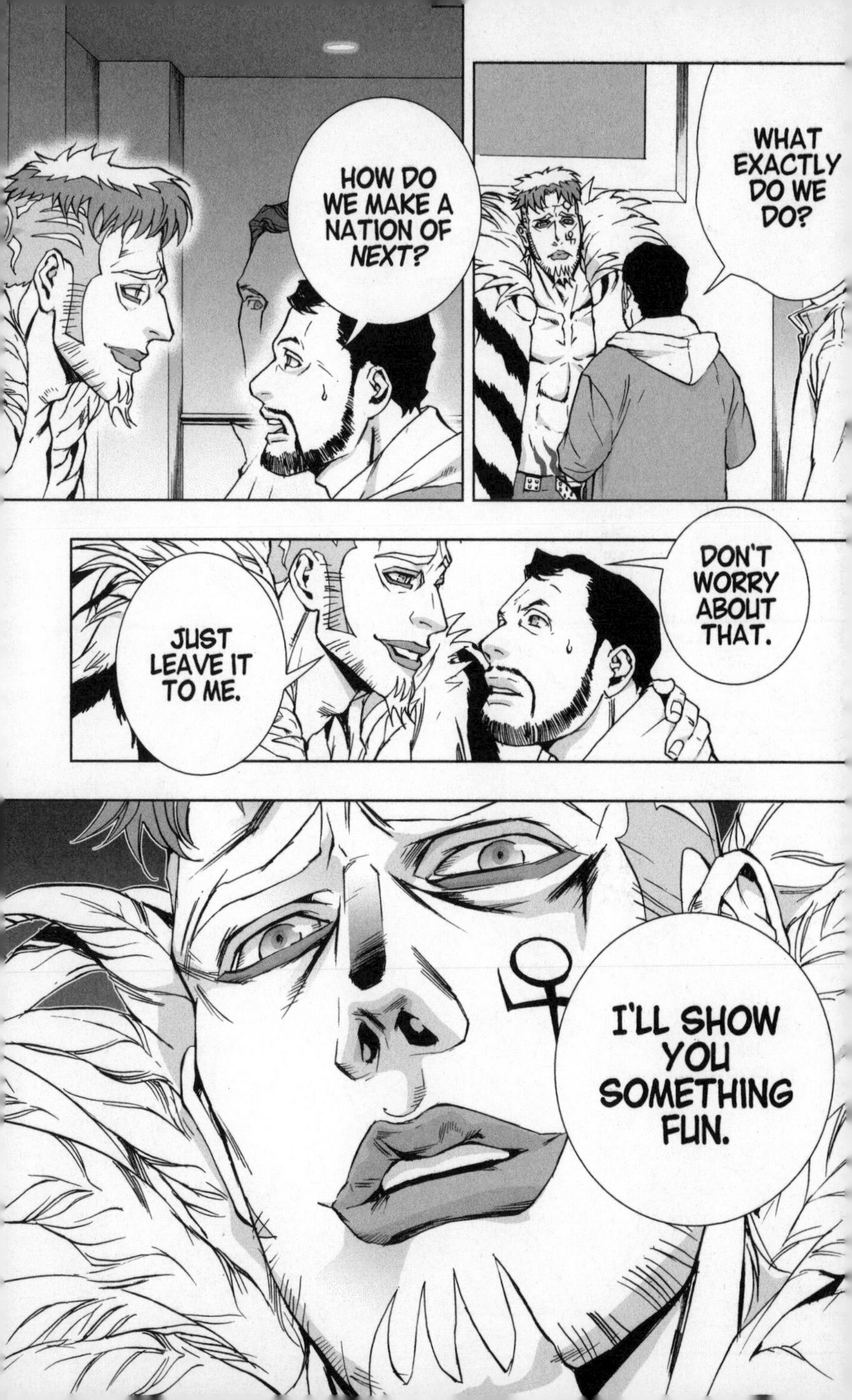
WHAT EXACTLY DO WE DO?
HOW DO WE MAKE A NATION OF NEXT?
DON'T WORRY ABOUT THAT.
JUST LEAVE IT TO ME.
I'LL SHOW YOU SOMETHING FUN.

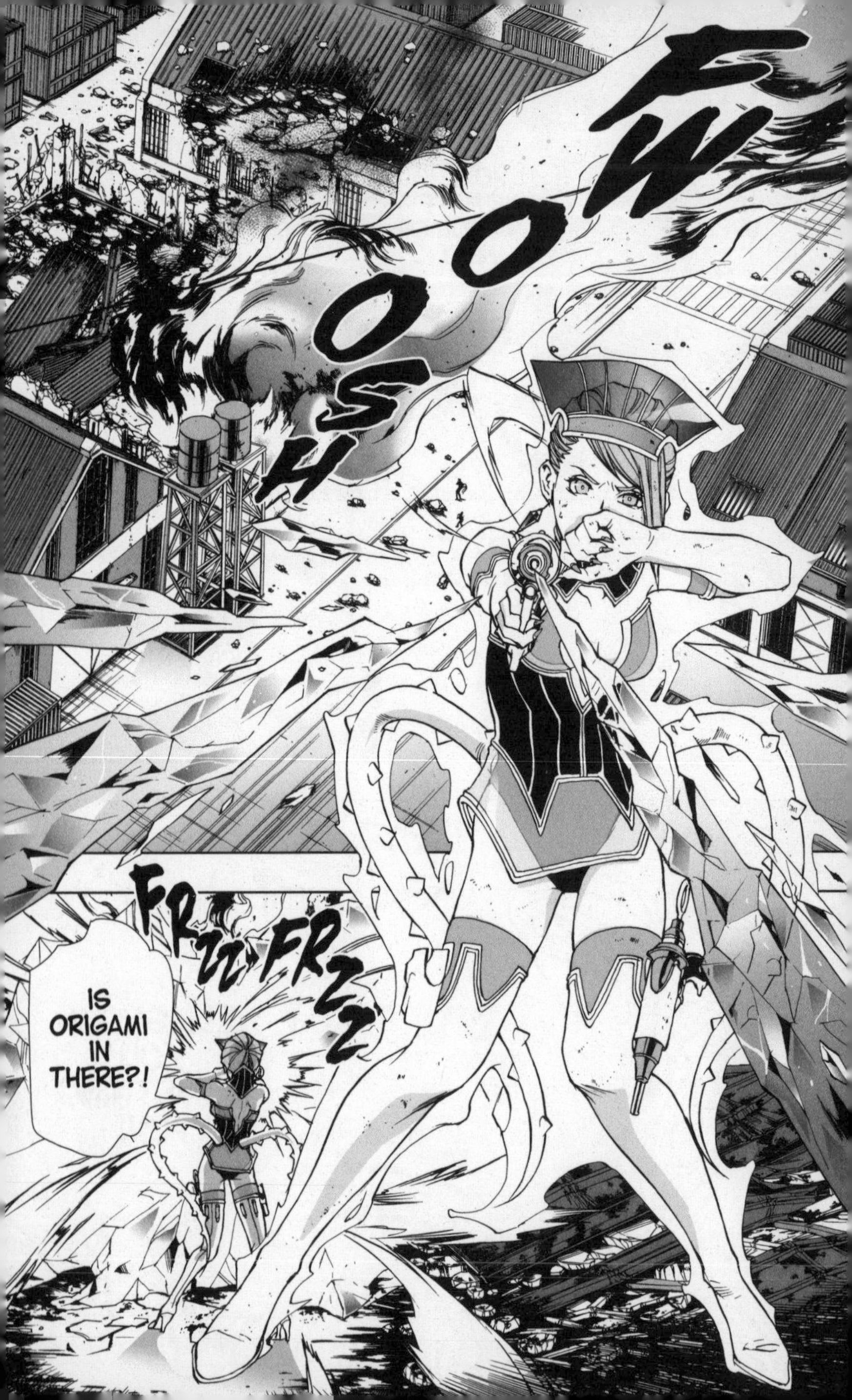
FWOOSH
FRZZ FRZZ
IS ORIGAMI IN THERE?!

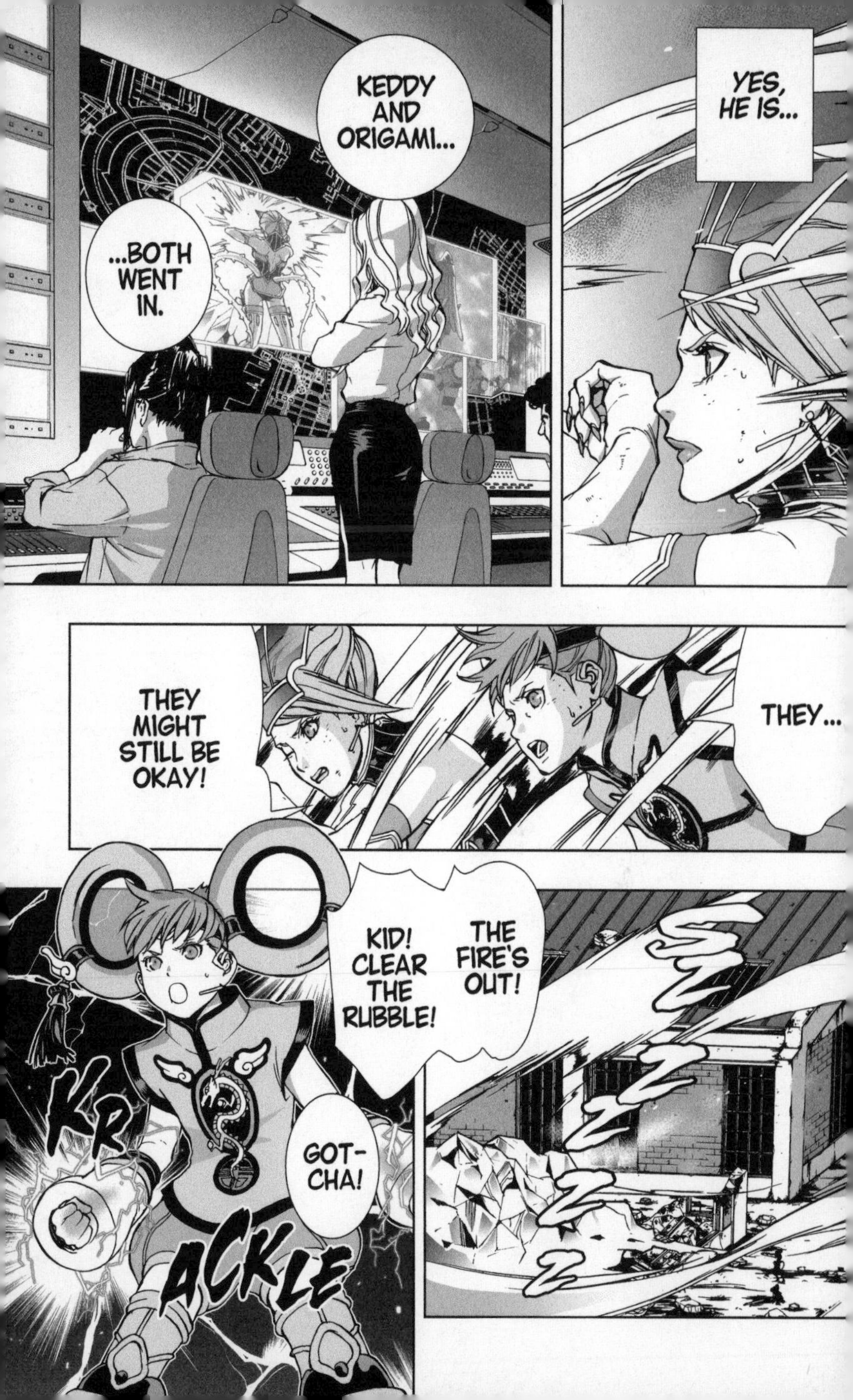
YES, HE IS...
KEDDY AND ORIGAMI...
...BOTH WENT IN.
THEY...
THEY MIGHT STILL BE OKAY!
THE FIRE'S OUT!
KID! CLEAR THE RUBBLE!
GOT-CHA!
KRACKLE

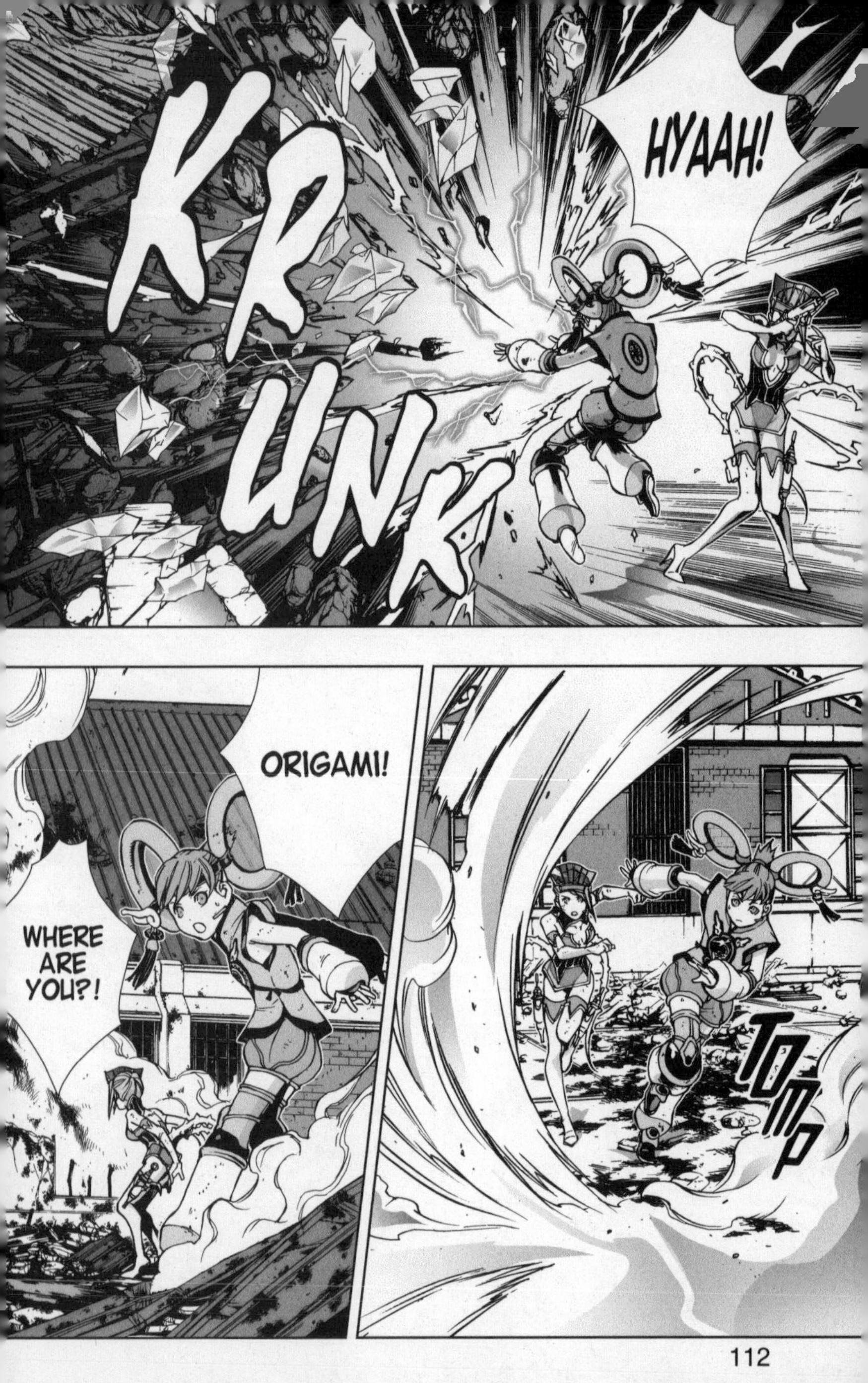
HYAAH!
KRUNK
TOMP
ORIGAMI!
WHERE ARE YOU?!

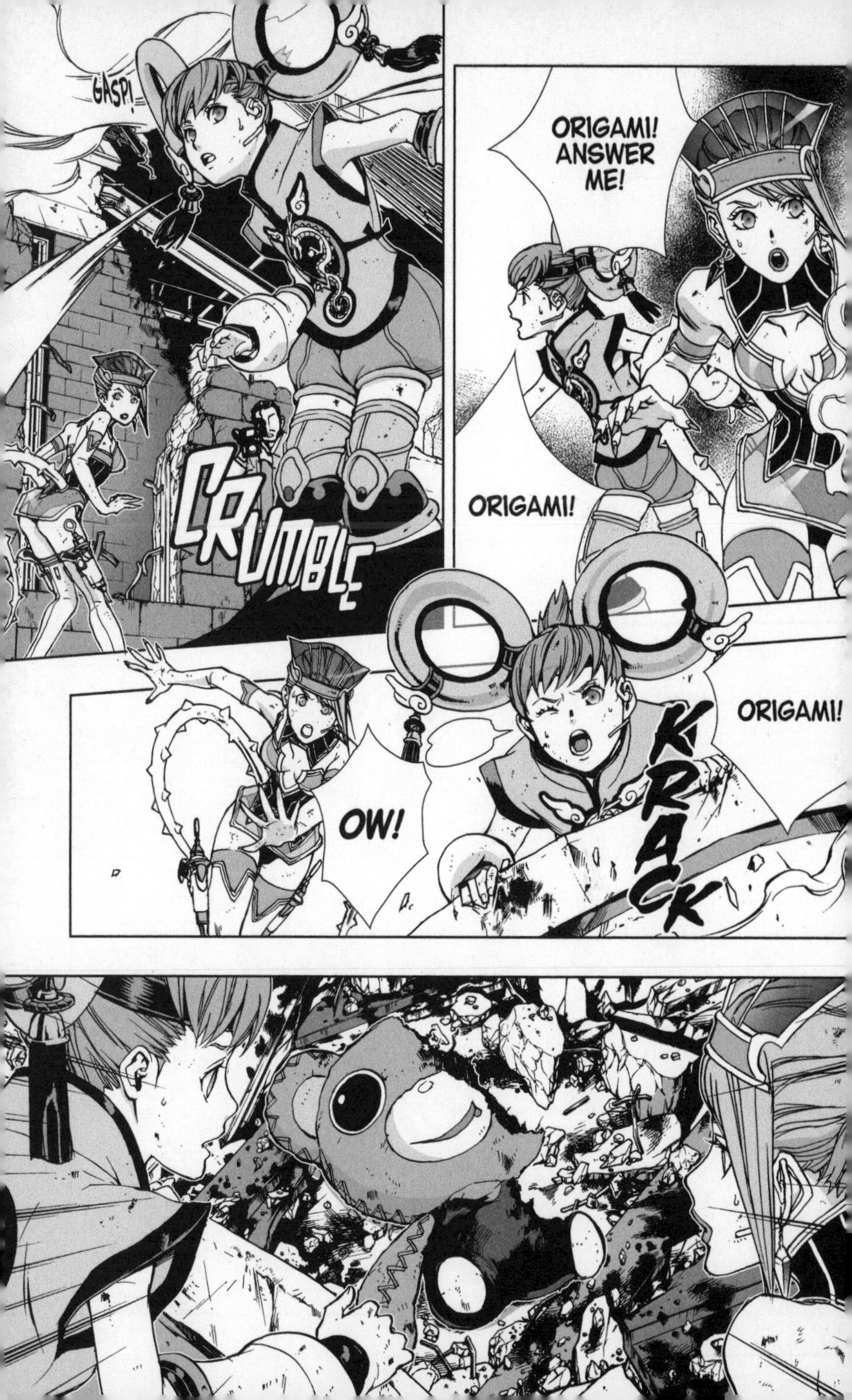
ORIGAMI! ANSWER ME!
ORIGAMI!
GASP!
CRUMBLE
ORIGAMI!
KRACK
OW!

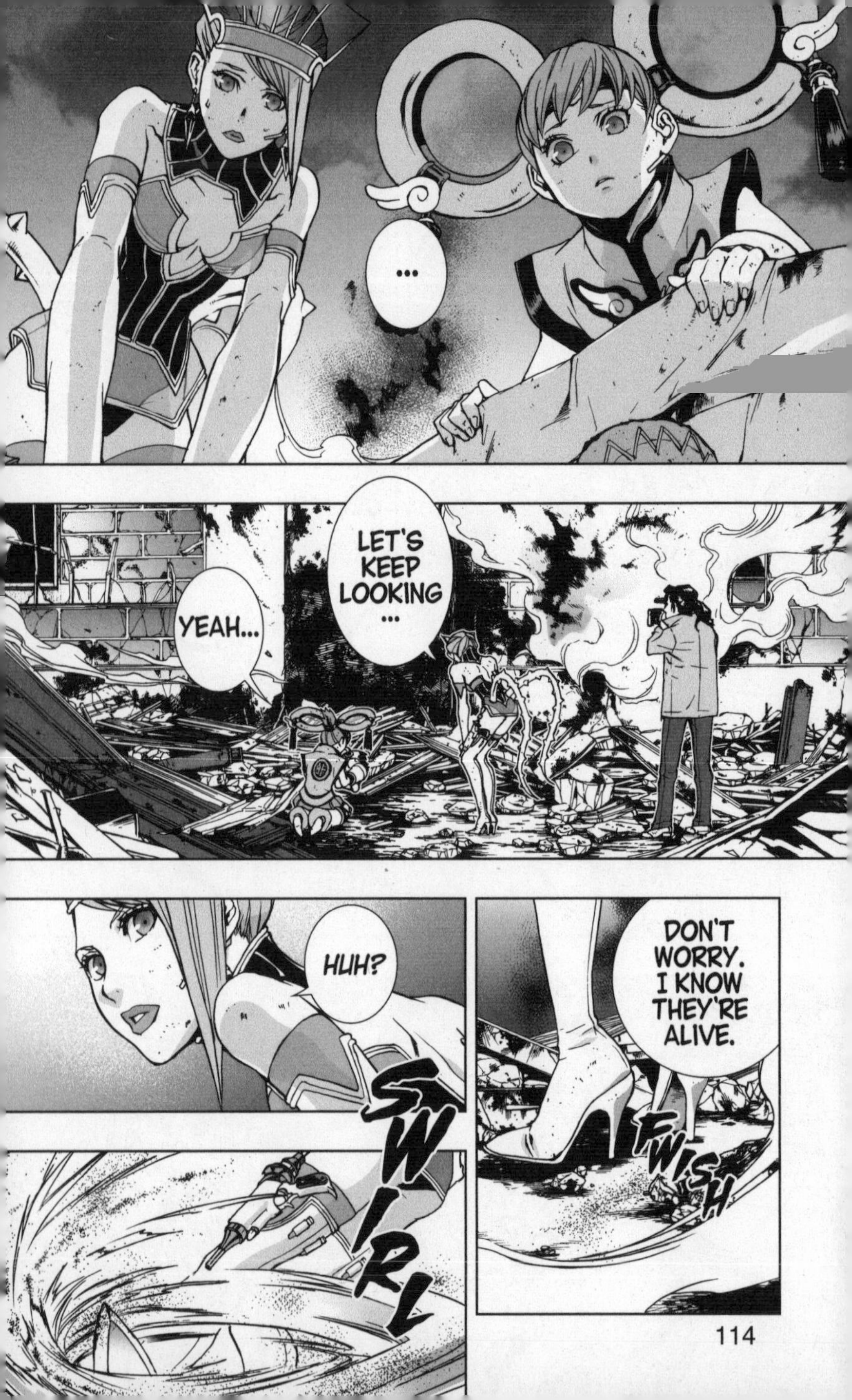
...
LET'S KEEP LOOKING ...
YEAH...
DON'T WORRY. I KNOW THEY'RE ALIVE.
FWISH
HUH?
SWIRL

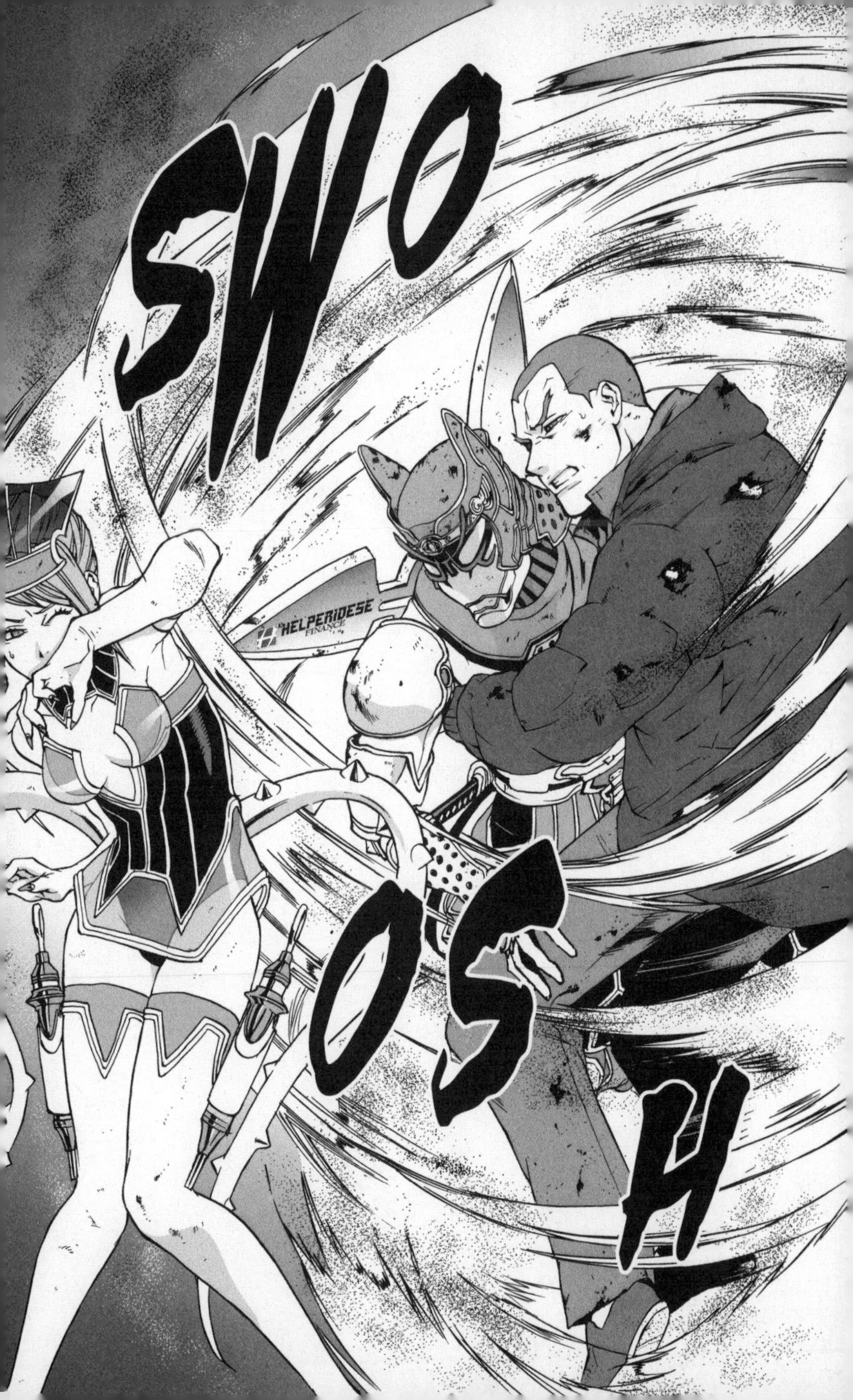
SWOOSH
HELPERIDESE FINANCE

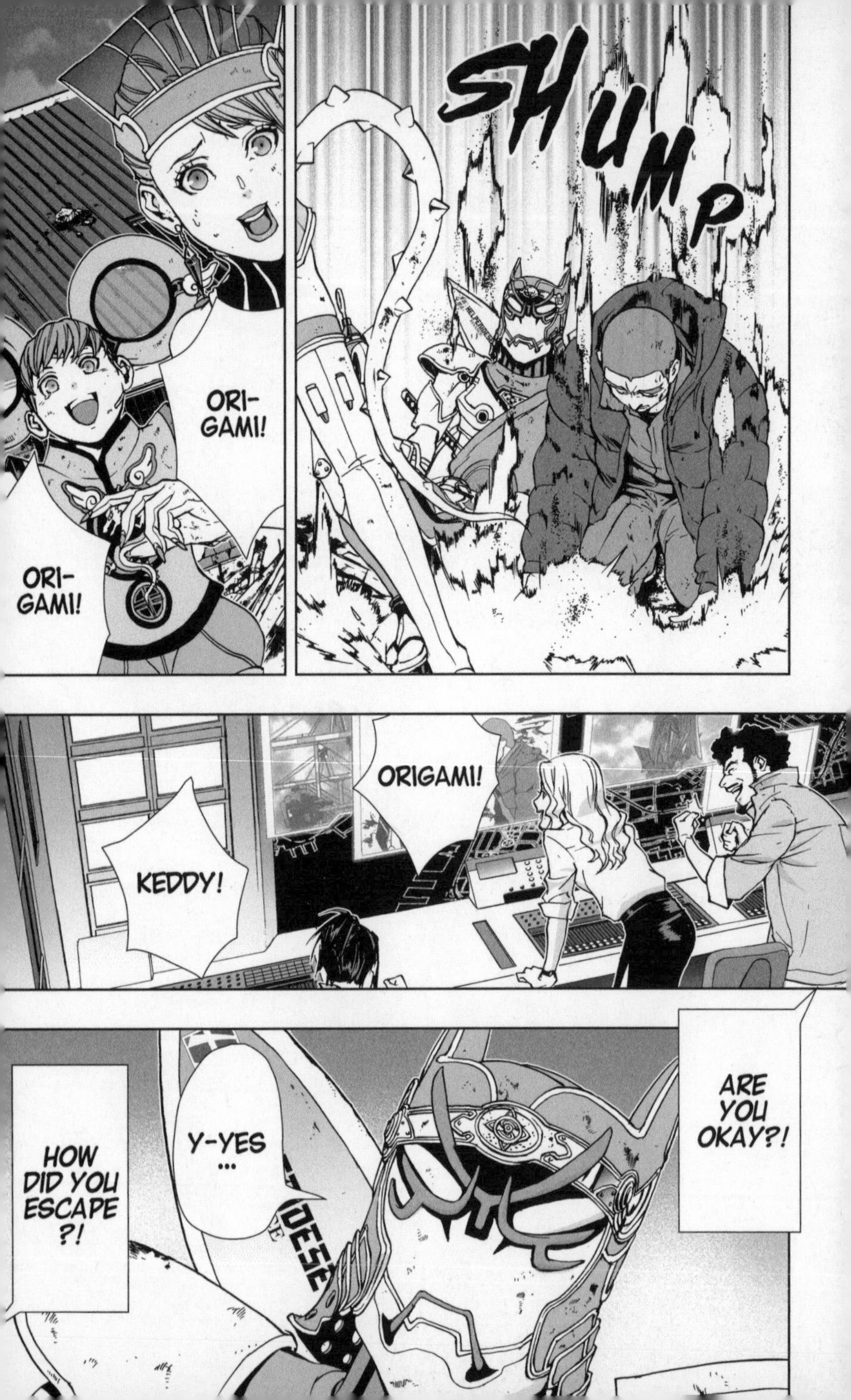
SHUMP
ORI-GAMI!
ORI-GAMI!
ORIGAMI!
KEDDY!
ARE YOU OKAY?!
Y-YES ...
HOW DID YOU ESCAPE ?!

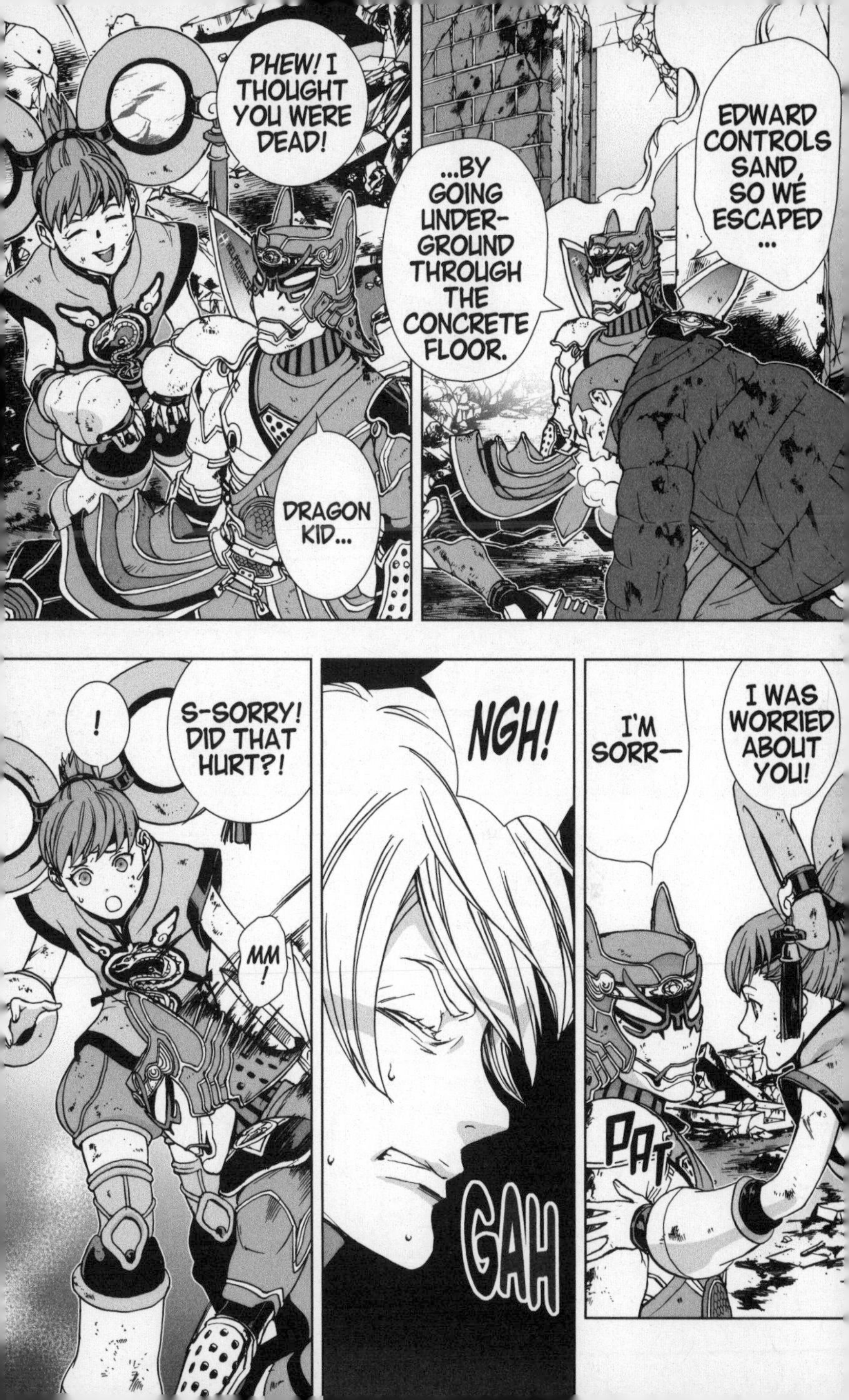
EDWARD CONTROLS SAND, SO WE ESCAPED...
...BY GOING UNDER-GROUND THROUGH THE CONCRETE FLOOR.
PHEW! I THOUGHT YOU WERE DEAD!
DRAGON KID...
I WAS WORRIED ABOUT YOU!
PAT
I'M SORR—
NGH!
GAH
!
S-SORRY! DID THAT HURT?!
MM!

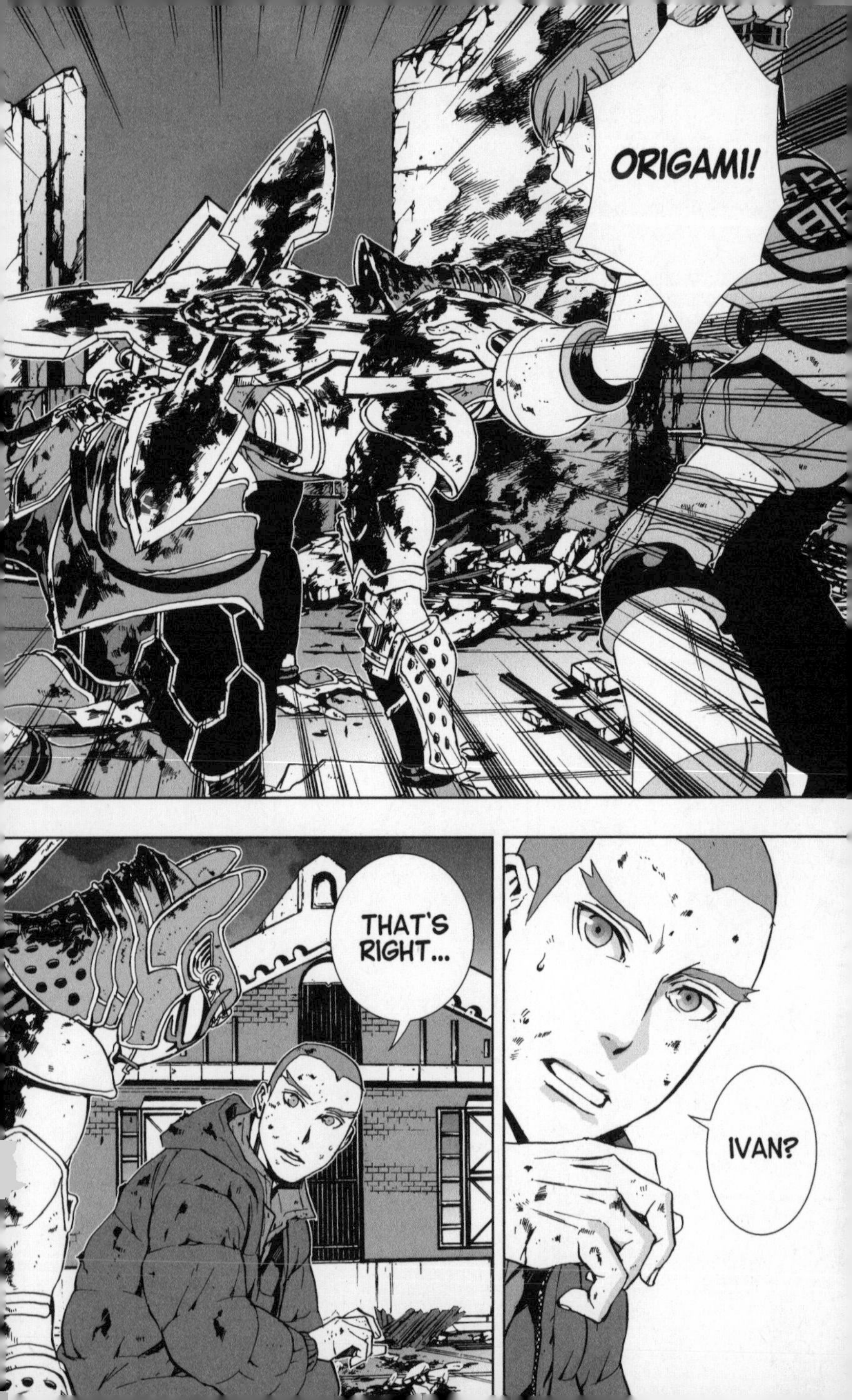
ORIGAMI!
IVAN?
THAT'S RIGHT...

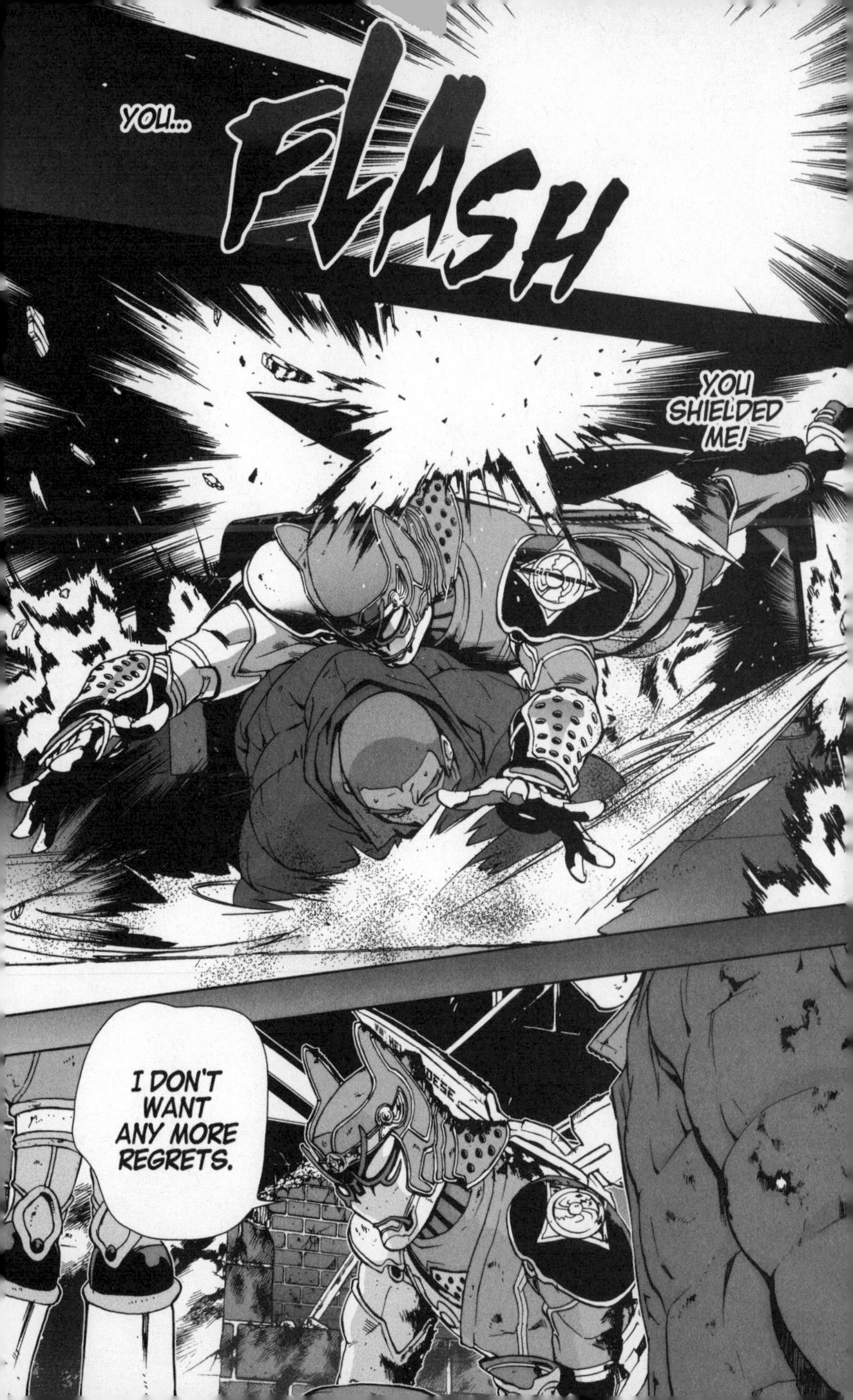
FLASH
YOU...
YOU SHIELDED ME!
I DON'T WANT ANY MORE REGRETS.

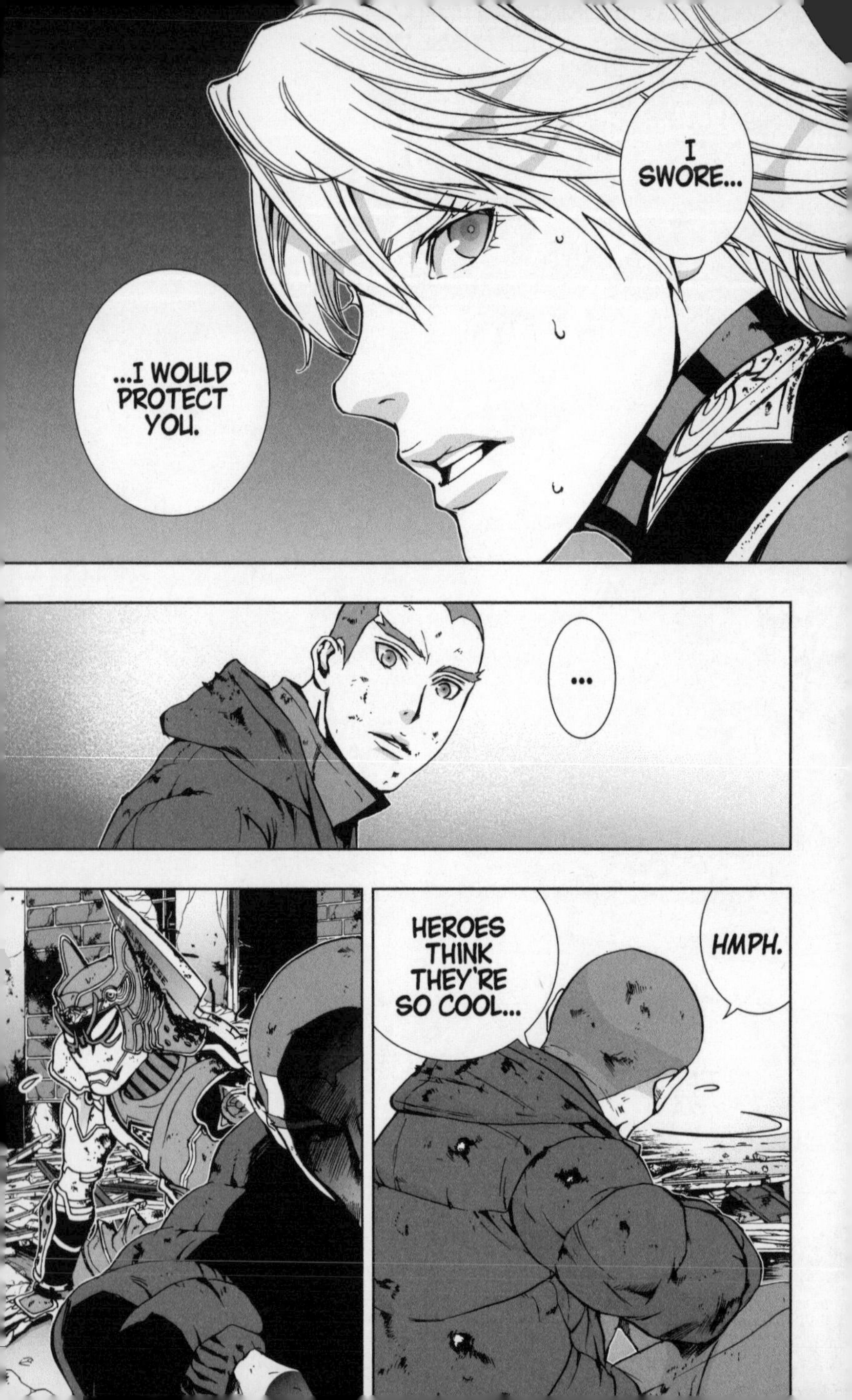
I SWORE...
...I WOULD PROTECT YOU.
...
HMPH.
HEROES THINK THEY'RE SO COOL...

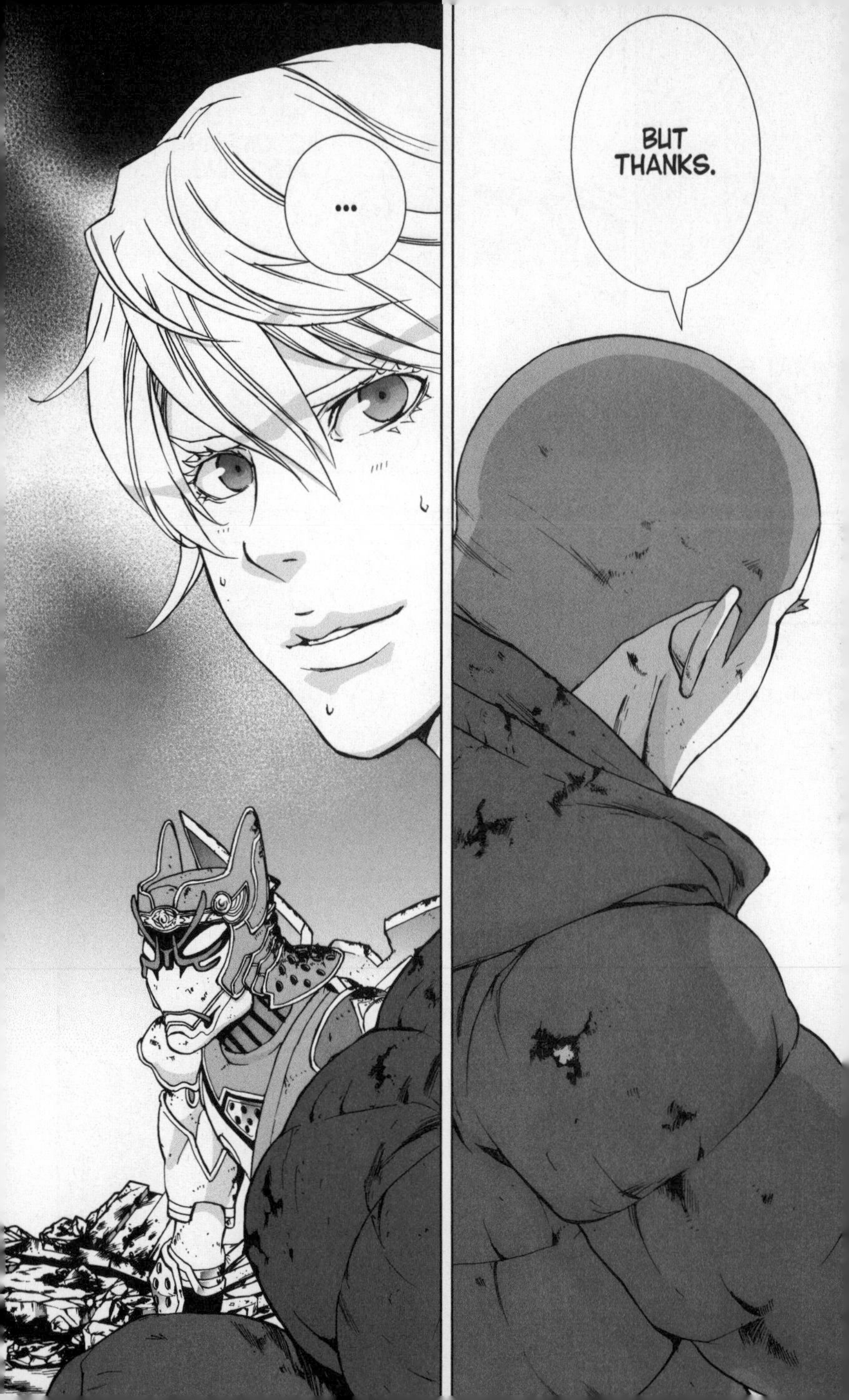
BUT THANKS.
...

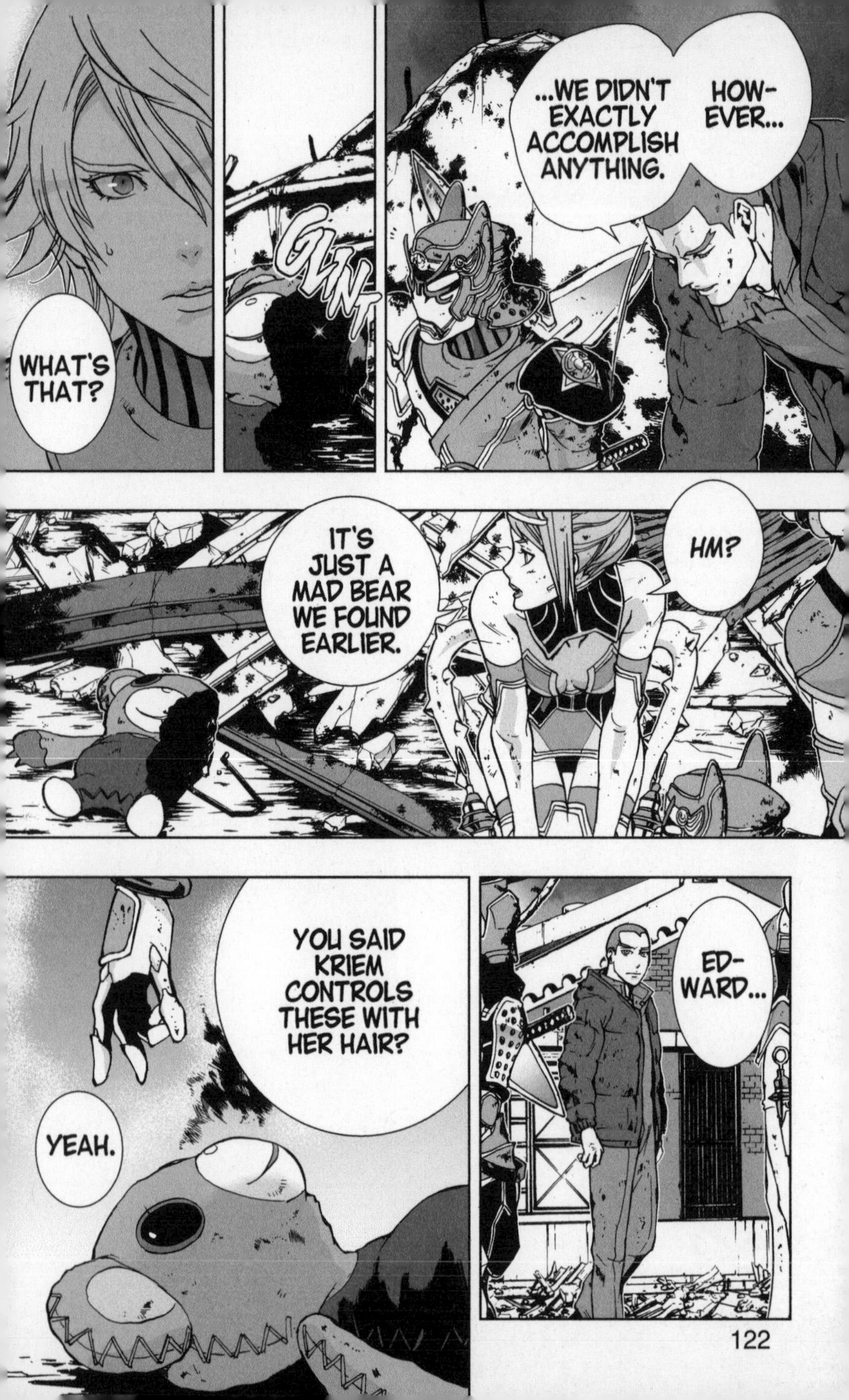
HOW-EVER...
...WE DIDN'T EXACTLY ACCOMPLISH ANYTHING.
GUNT
WHAT'S THAT?
HM?
IT'S JUST A MAD BEAR WE FOUND EARLIER.
ED-WARD...
YOU SAID KRIEM CONTROLS THESE WITH HER HAIR?
YEAH.

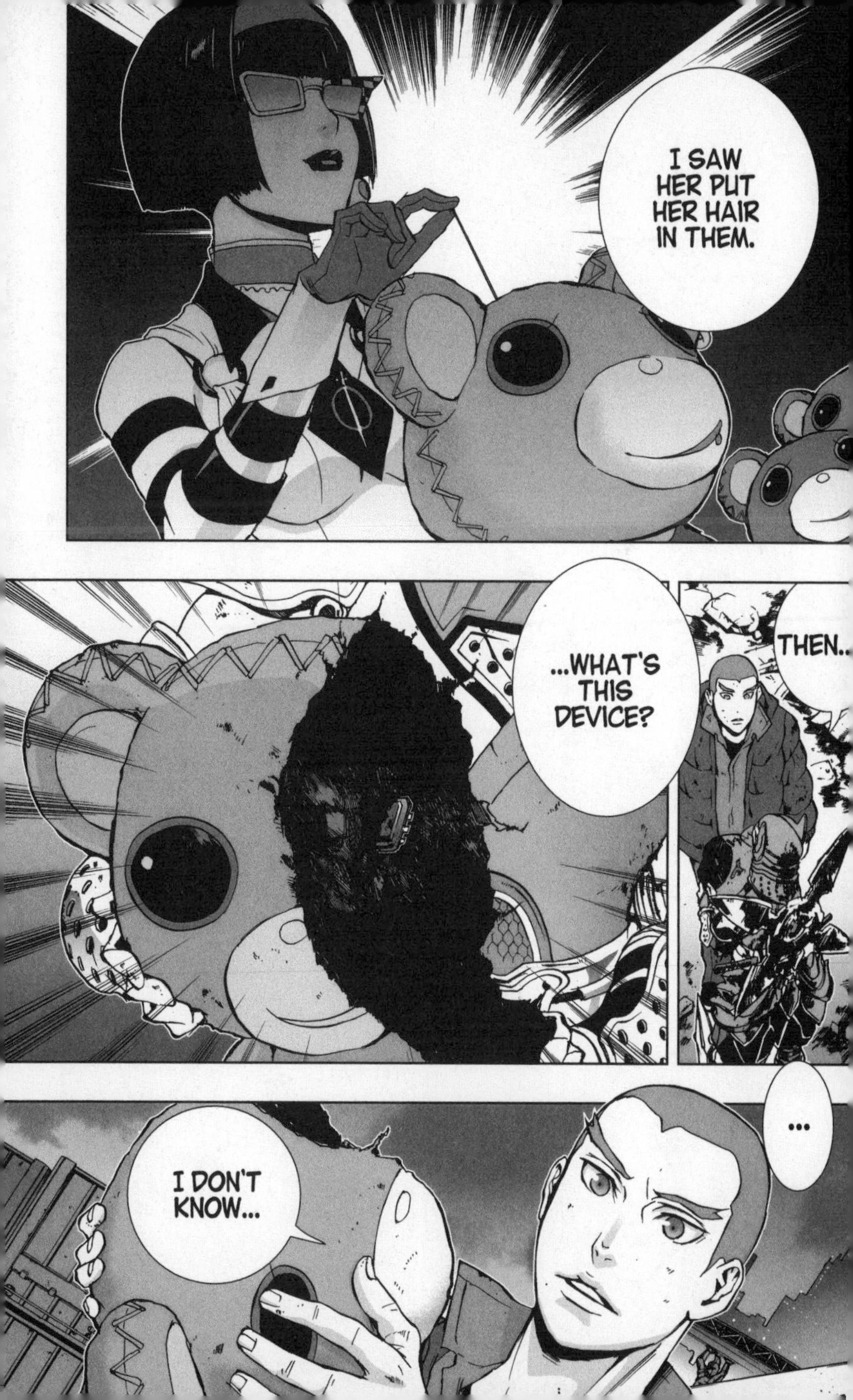
I SAW HER PUT HER HAIR IN THEM.
THEN...
...WHAT'S THIS DEVICE?
...
I DON'T KNOW...

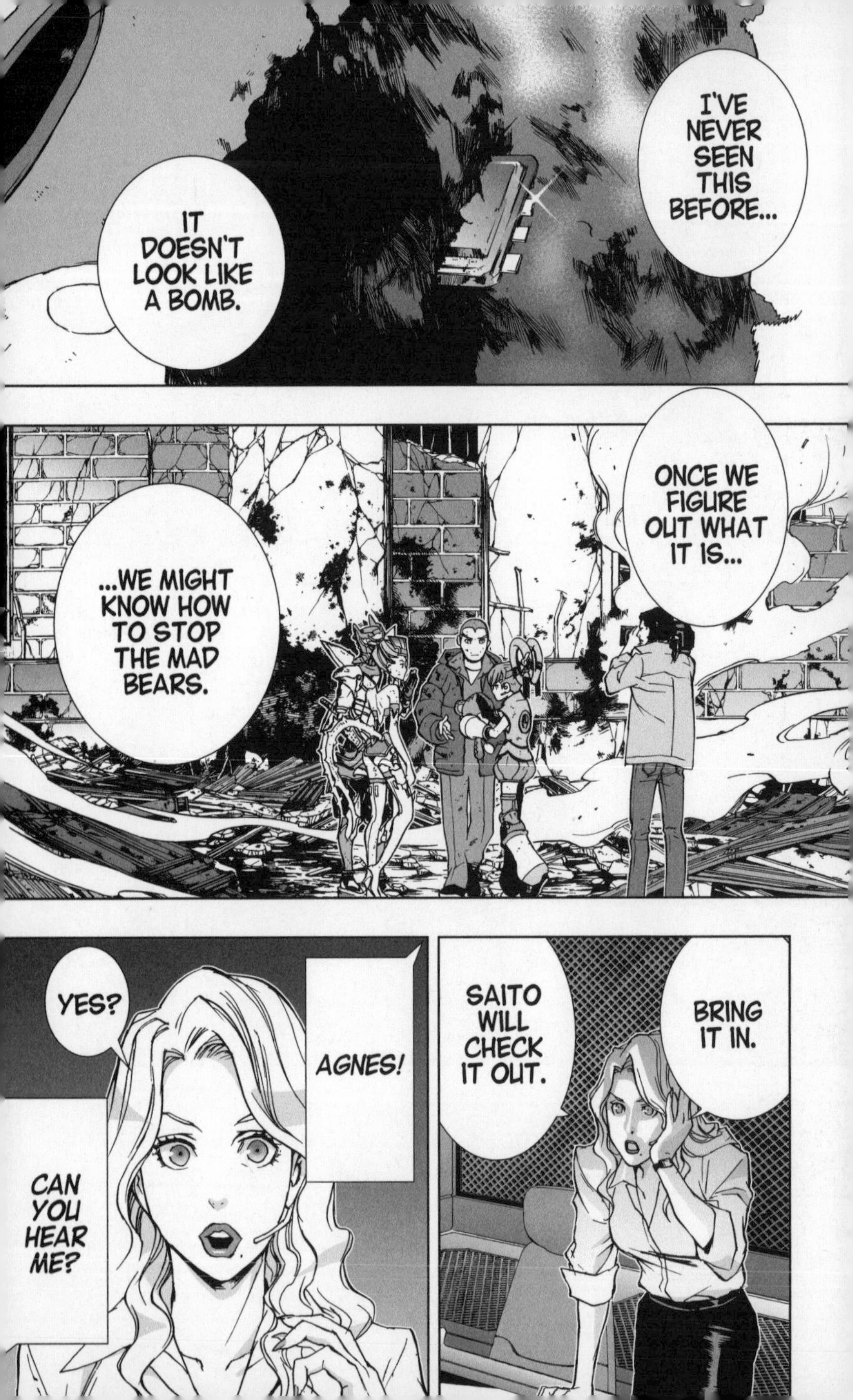
I'VE NEVER SEEN THIS BEFORE...
IT DOESN'T LOOK LIKE A BOMB.
ONCE WE FIGURE OUT WHAT IT IS...
...WE MIGHT KNOW HOW TO STOP THE MAD BEARS.
BRING IT IN.
SAITO WILL CHECK IT OUT.
AGNES!
CAN YOU HEAR ME?
YES?

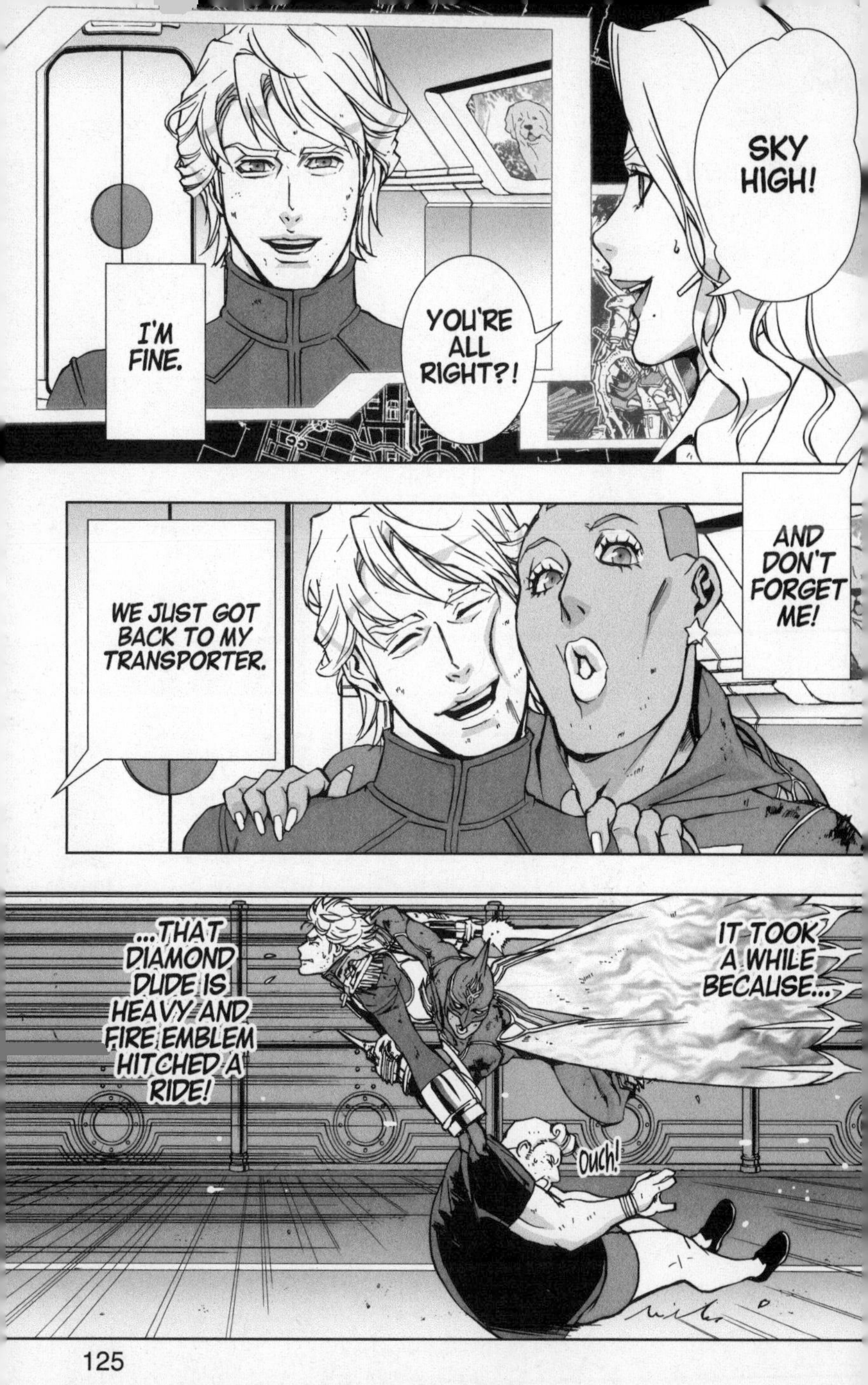
SKY HIGH!
YOU'RE ALL RIGHT?!
I'M FINE.
AND DON'T FORGET ME!
WE JUST GOT BACK TO MY TRANSPORTER.
IT TOOK A WHILE BECAUSE...
...THAT DIAMOND DUDE IS HEAVY AND FIRE EMBLEM HITCHED A RIDE!
OUCH!

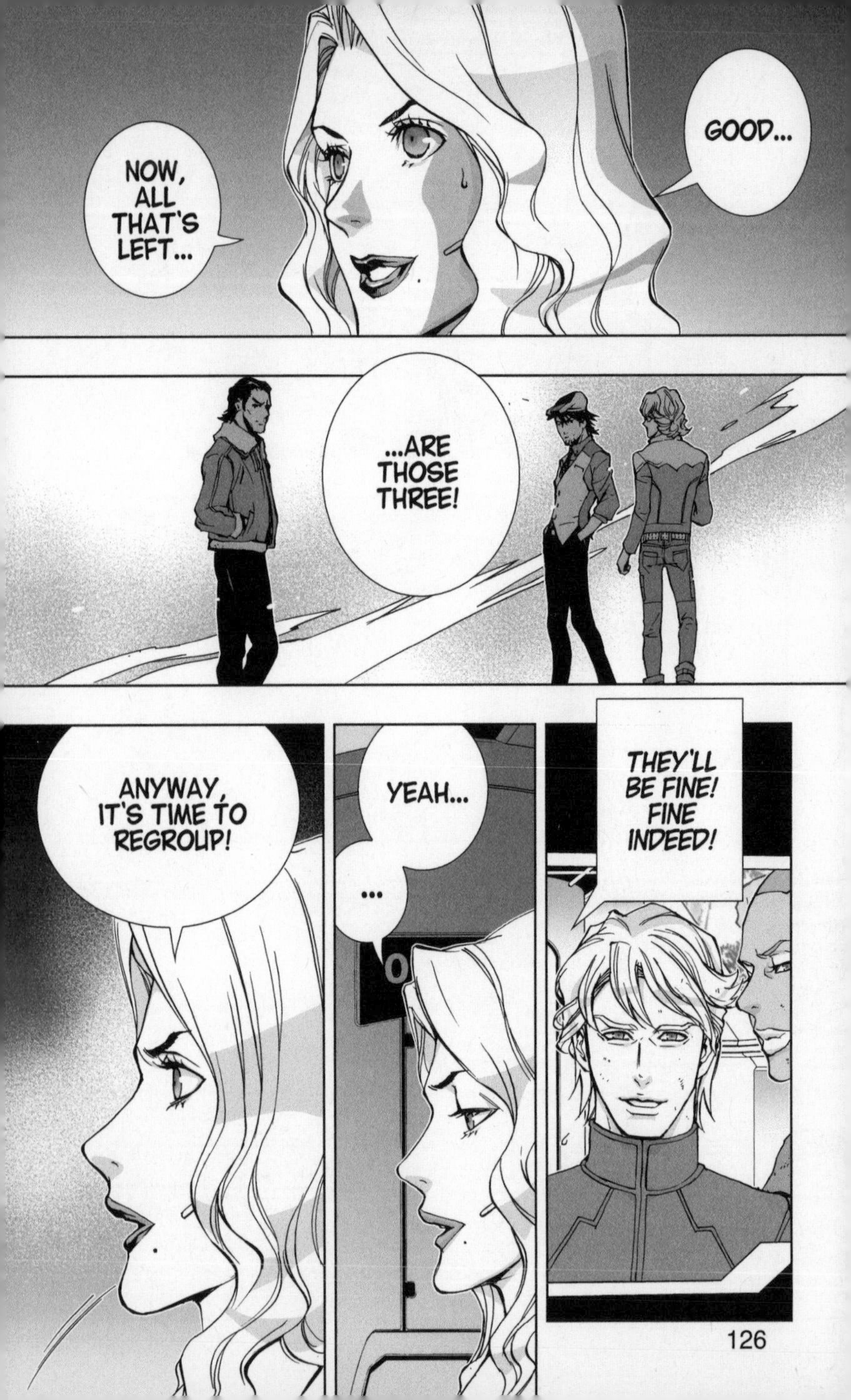
GOOD...
NOW, ALL THAT'S LEFT...
...ARE THOSE THREE!
THEY'LL BE FINE! FINE INDEED!
YEAH...
...
ANYWAY, IT'S TIME TO REGROUP!

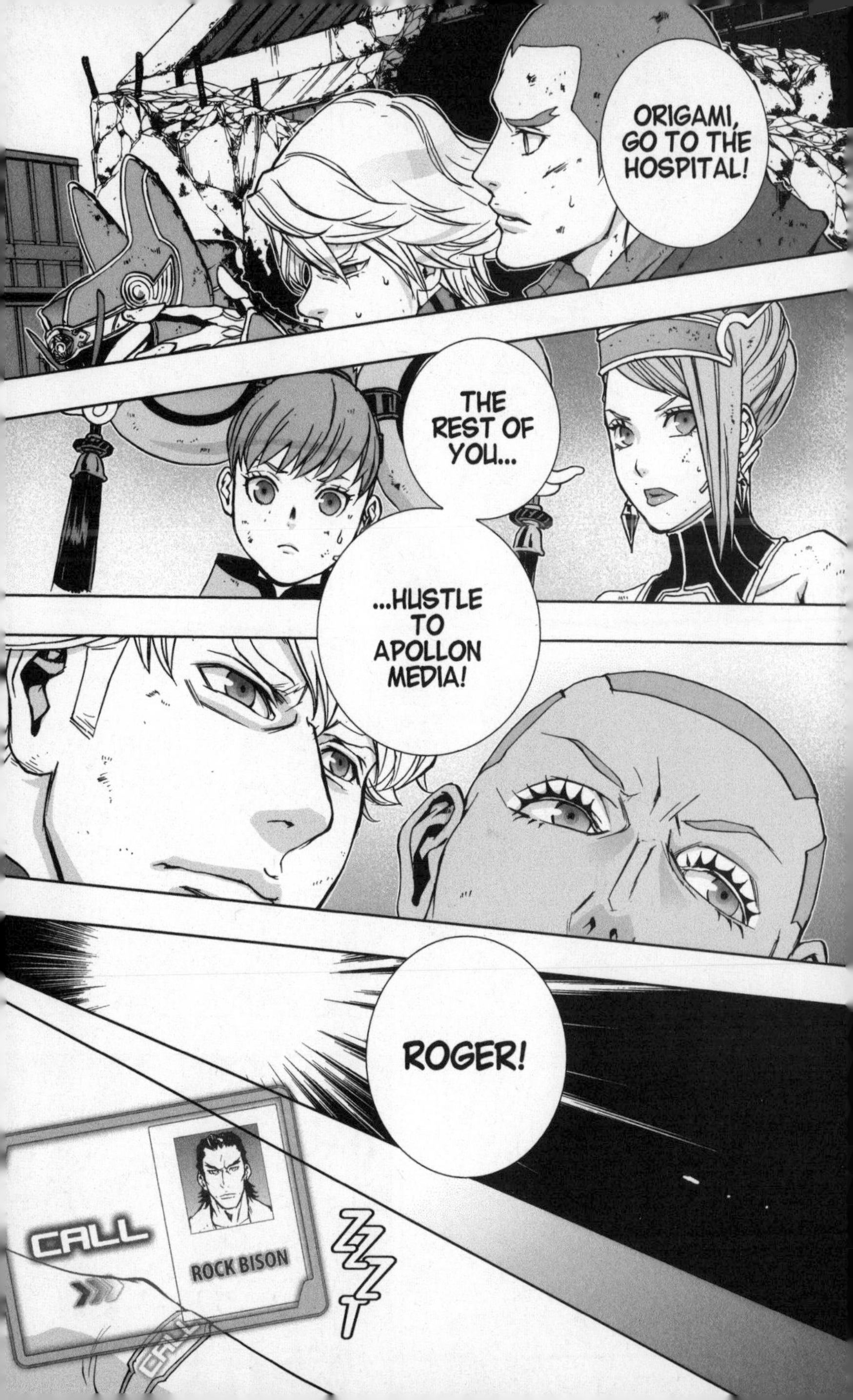
ORIGAMI, GO TO THE HOSPITAL!
THE REST OF YOU...
...HUSTLE TO APOLLON MEDIA!
ROGER!
CALL
ROCK BISON
ZZZT

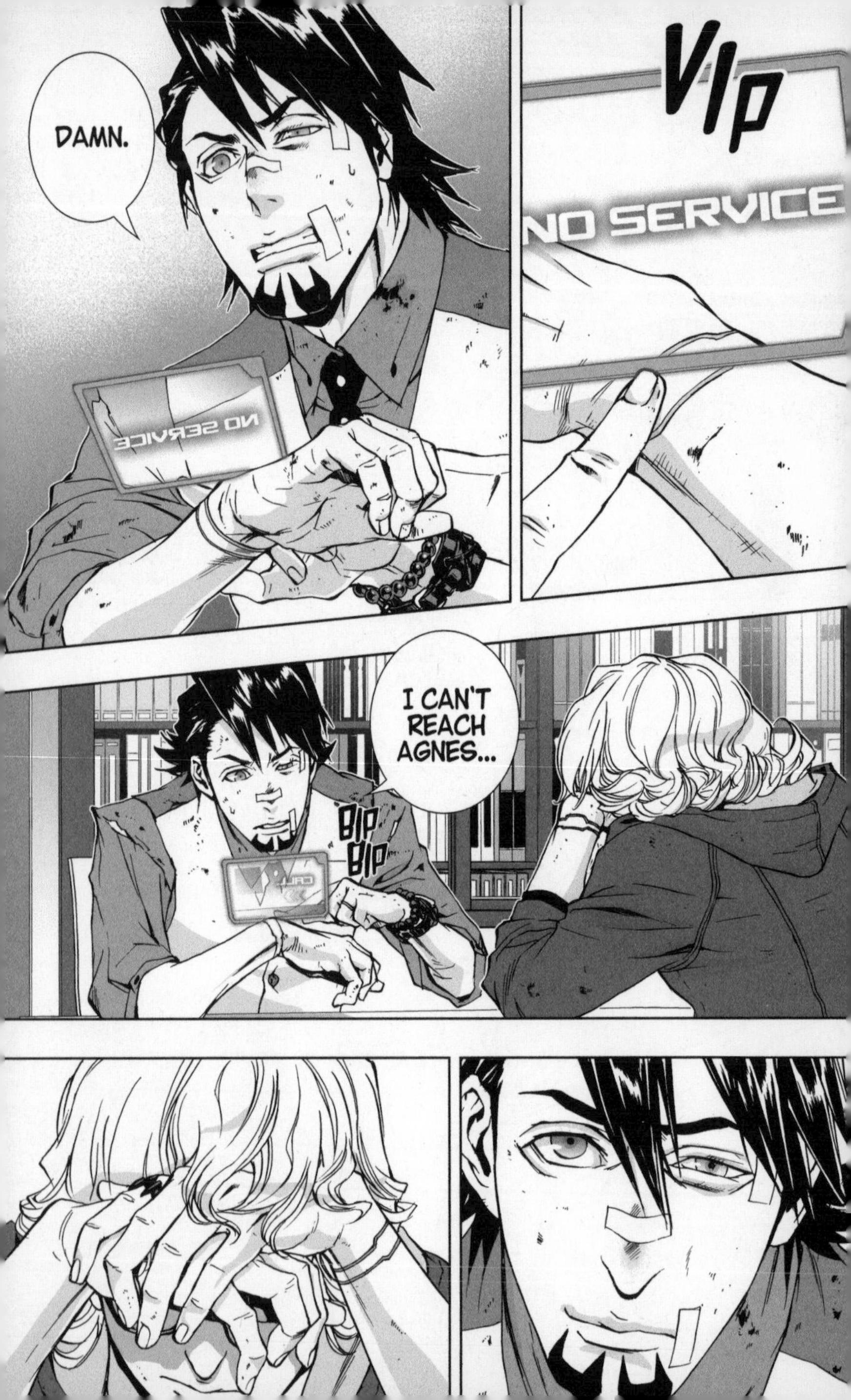
VIP
NO SERVICE
DAMN.
I CAN'T REACH AGNES...
BIP BIP

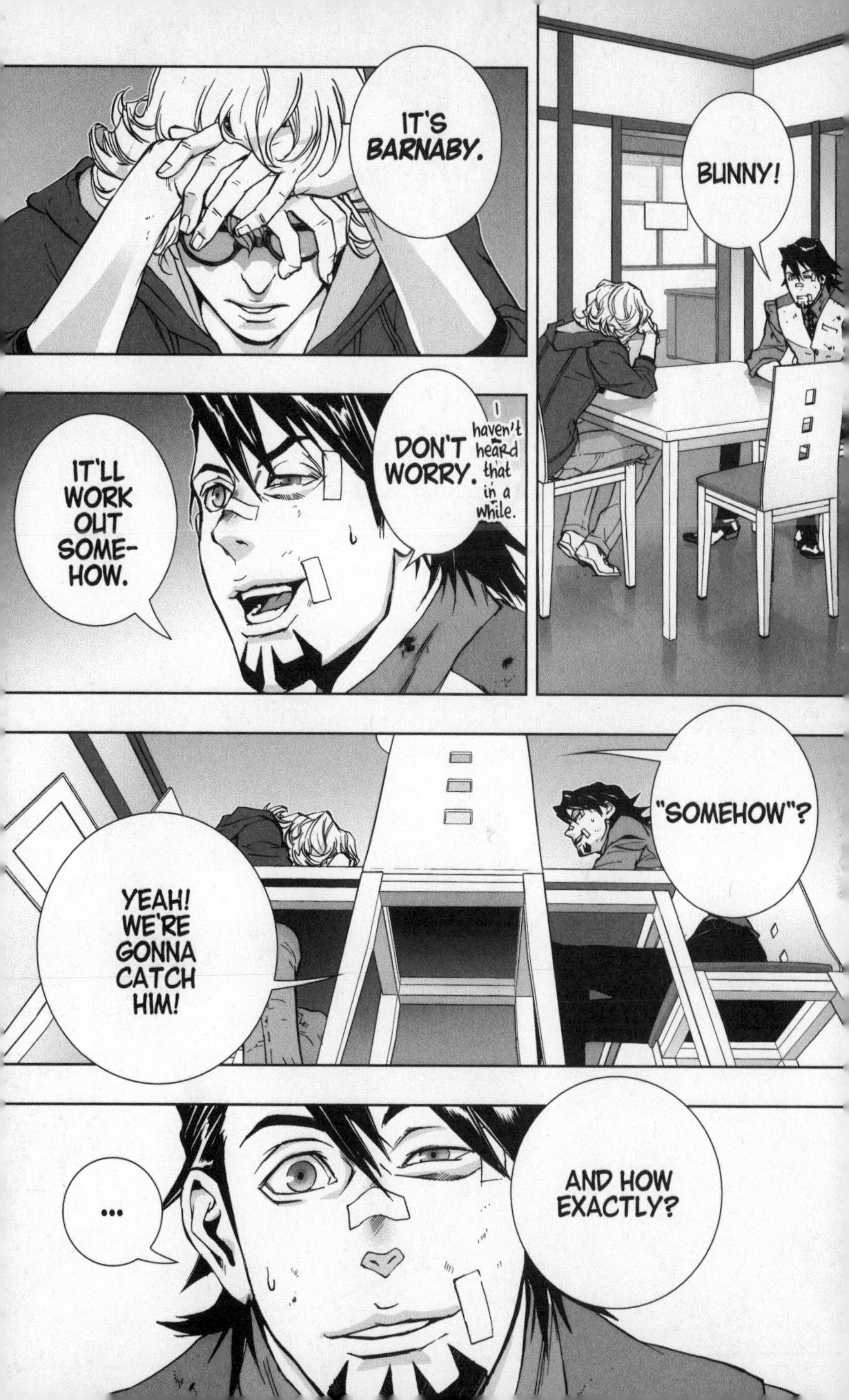
BUNNY!
IT'S BARNABY.
DON'T WORRY.
I haven't heard that in a while.
IT'LL WORK OUT SOME-HOW.
"SOMEHOW"?
YEAH! WE'RE GONNA CATCH HIM!
AND HOW EXACTLY?
...

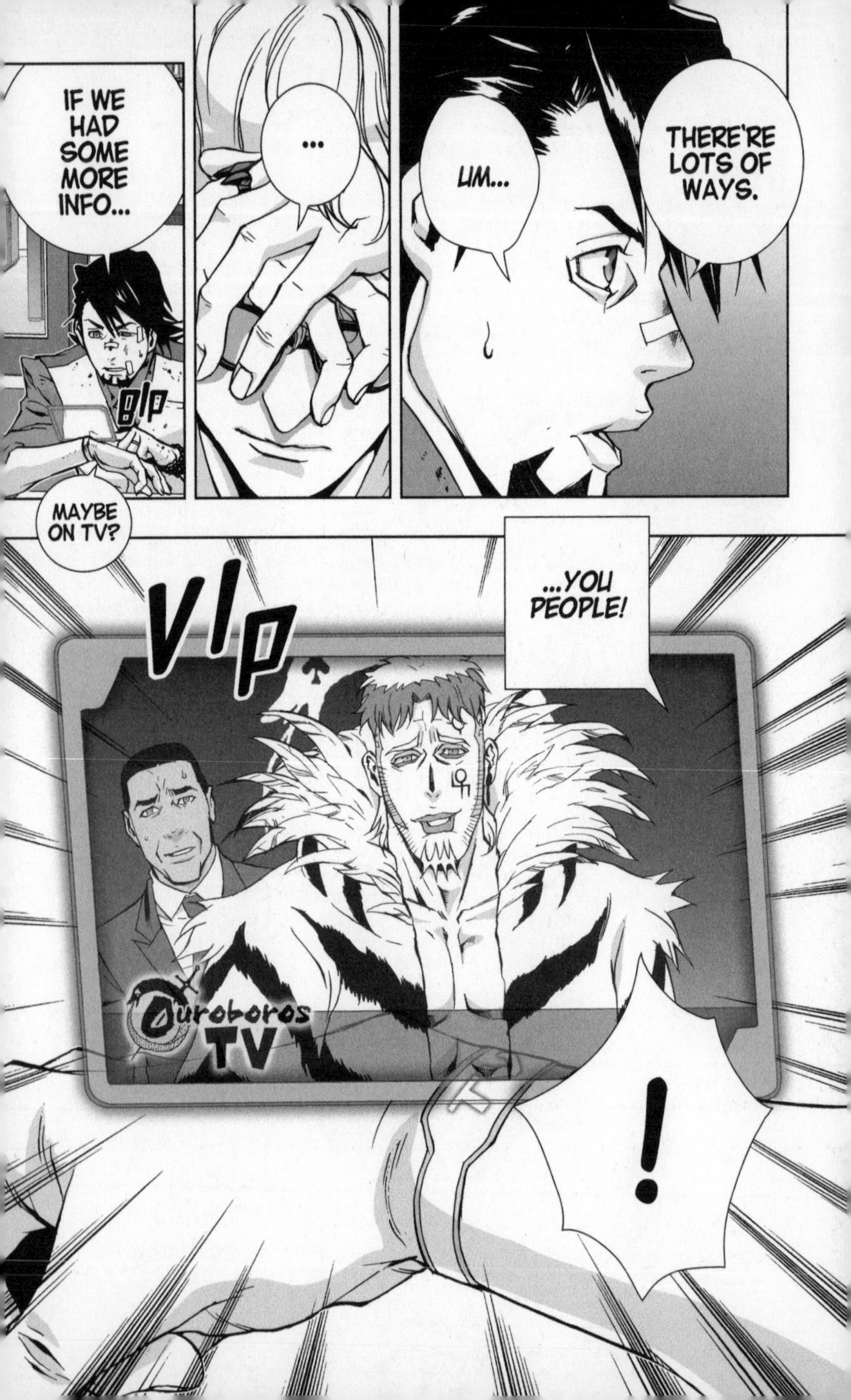
THERE'RE LOTS OF WAYS.
UM...
...
IF WE HAD SOME MORE INFO...
BIP
MAYBE ON TV?
...YOU PEOPLE!
VIP
Ouroboros TV
!

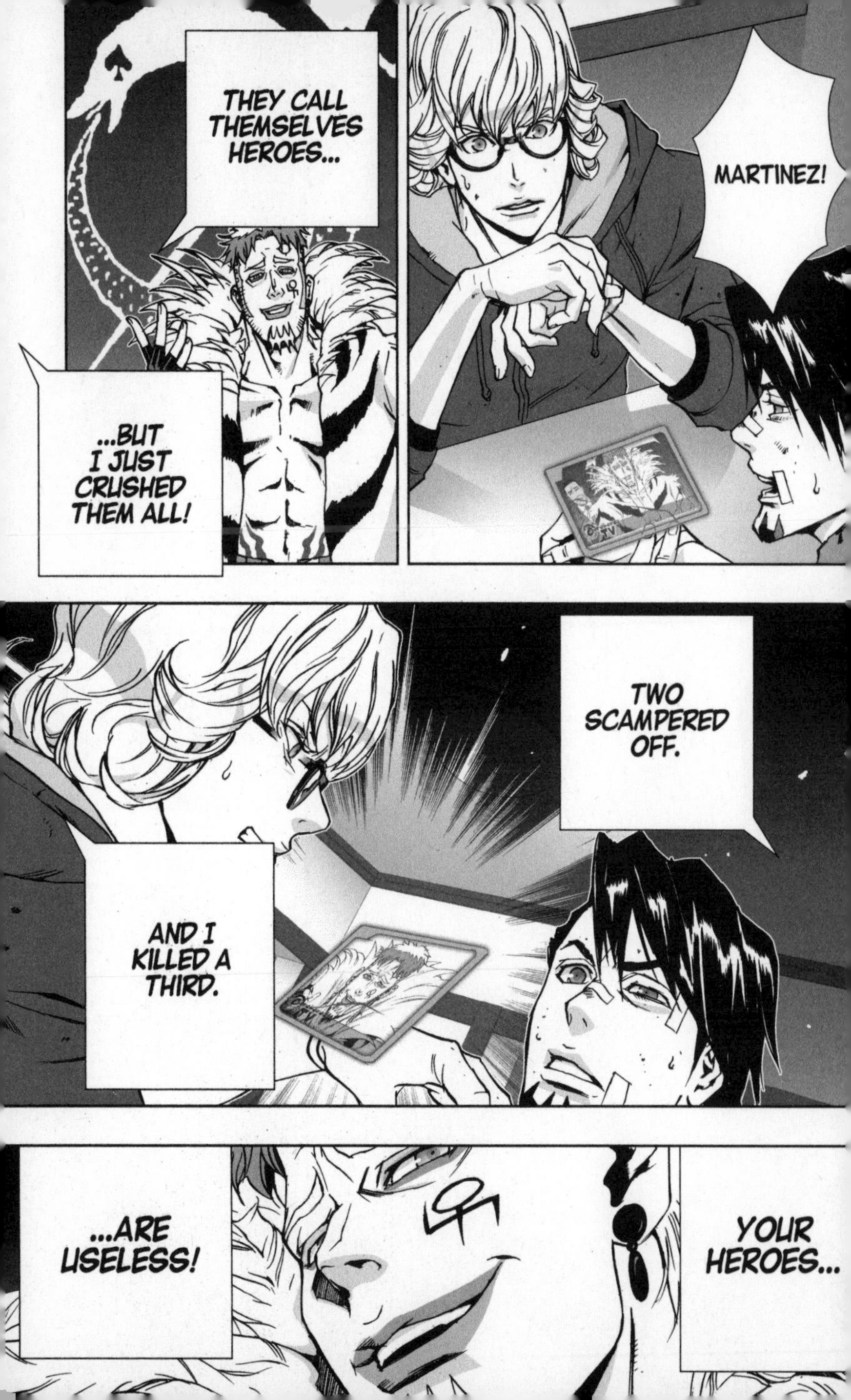
MARTINEZ!
THEY CALL THEMSELVES HEROES...
...BUT I JUST CRUSHED THEM ALL!
TWO SCAMPERED OFF.
AND I KILLED A THIRD.
YOUR HEROES...
...ARE USELESS!

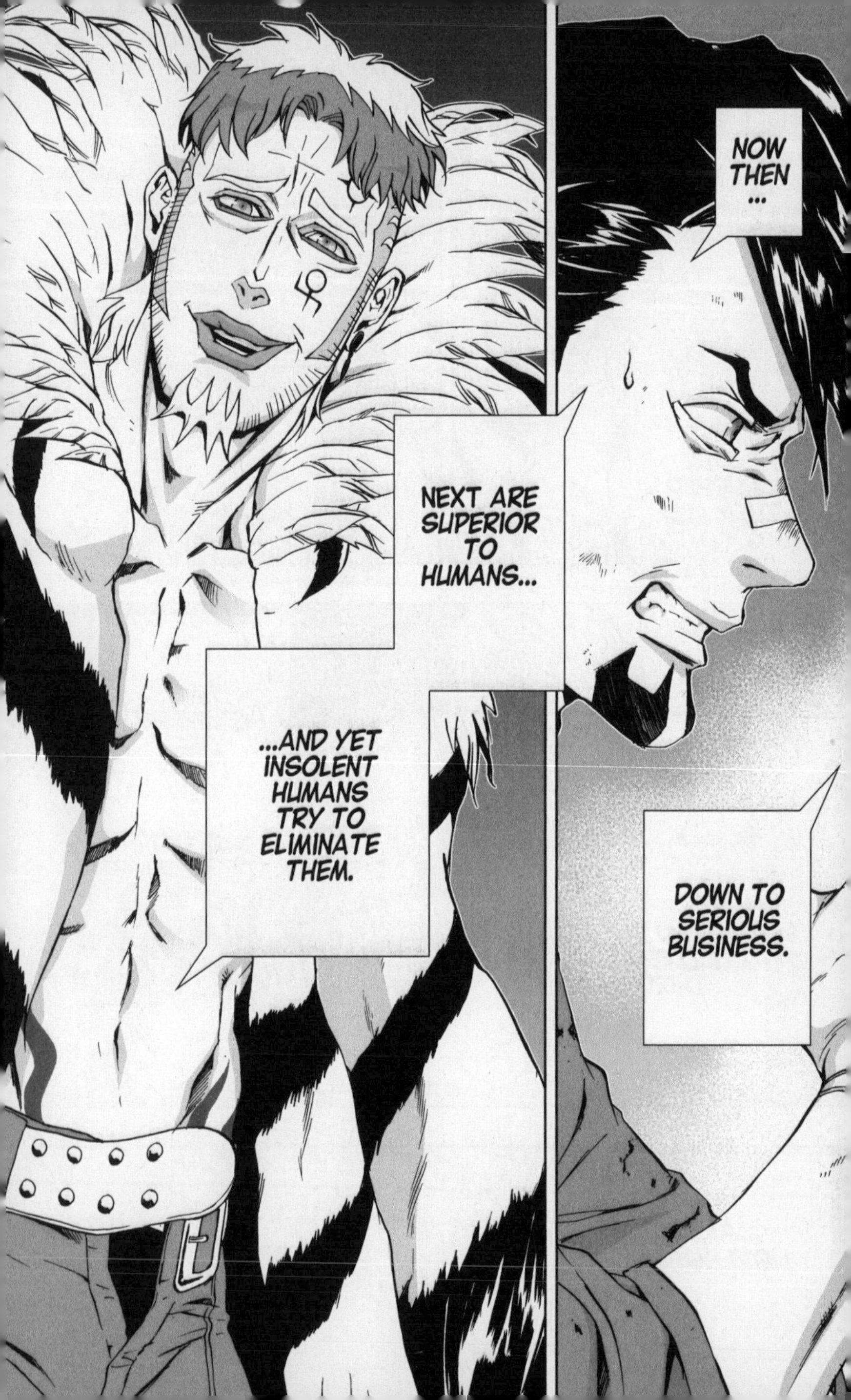
NOW THEN...
DOWN TO SERIOUS BUSINESS.
NEXT ARE SUPERIOR TO HUMANS...
...AND YET INSOLENT HUMANS TRY TO ELIMINATE THEM.

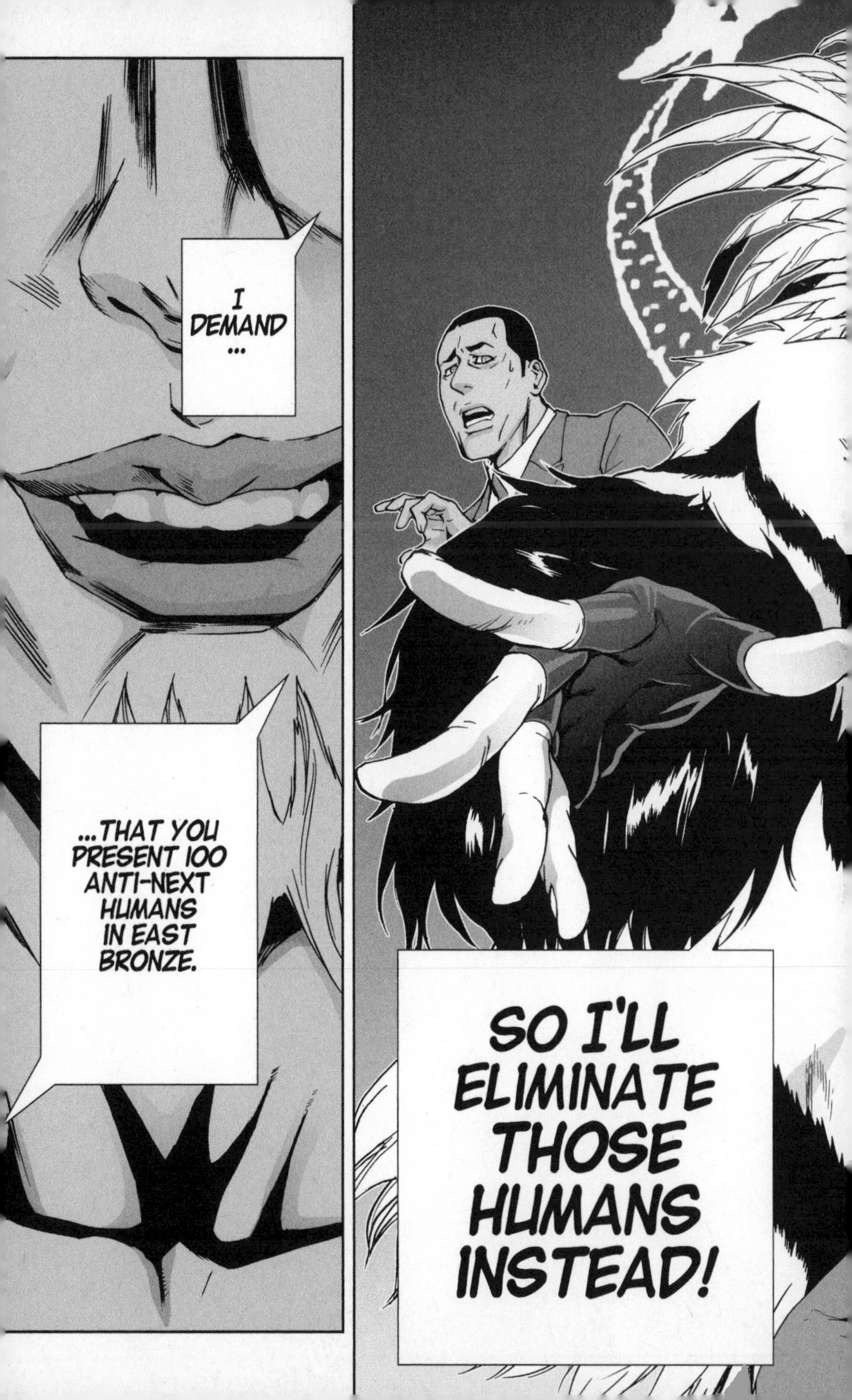
SO I'LL ELIMINATE THOSE HUMANS INSTEAD!
I DEMAND...
...THAT YOU PRESENT 100 ANTI-NEXT HUMANS IN EAST BRONZE.

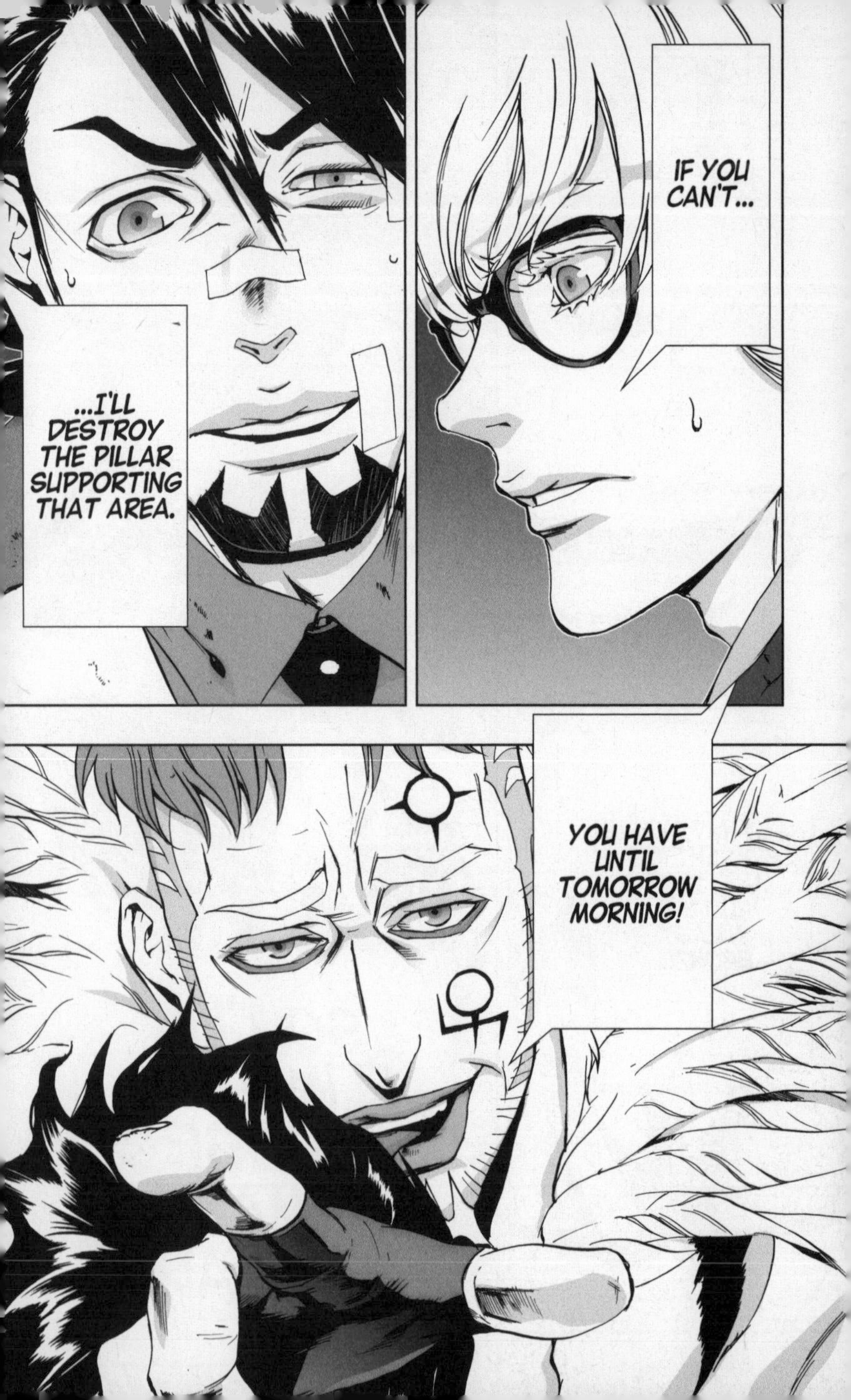
IF YOU CAN'T...
...I'LL DESTROY THE PILLAR SUPPORTING THAT AREA.
YOU HAVE UNTIL TOMORROW MORNING!

#30 Confidence Is a Plant of Slow Growth, Part 7

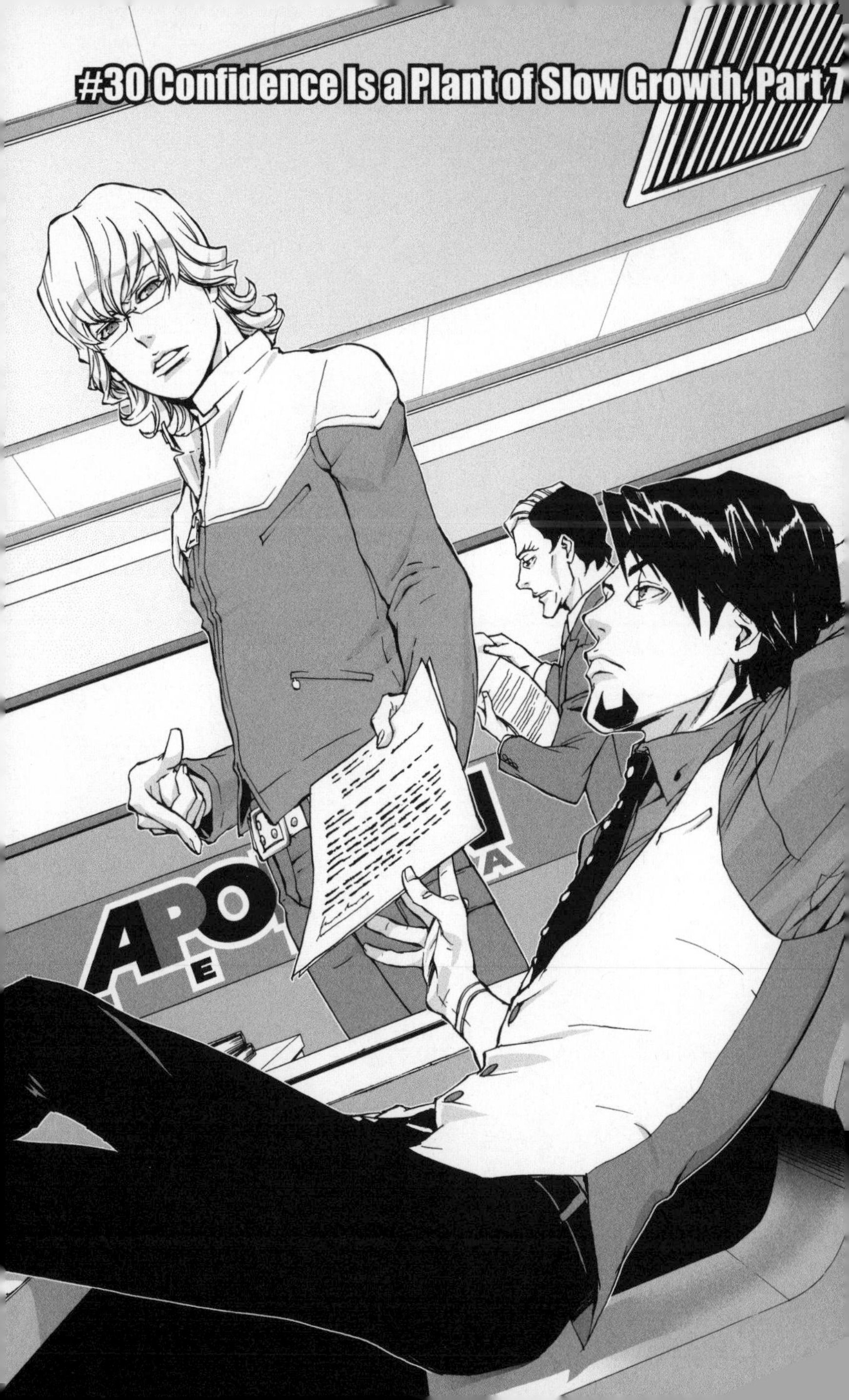

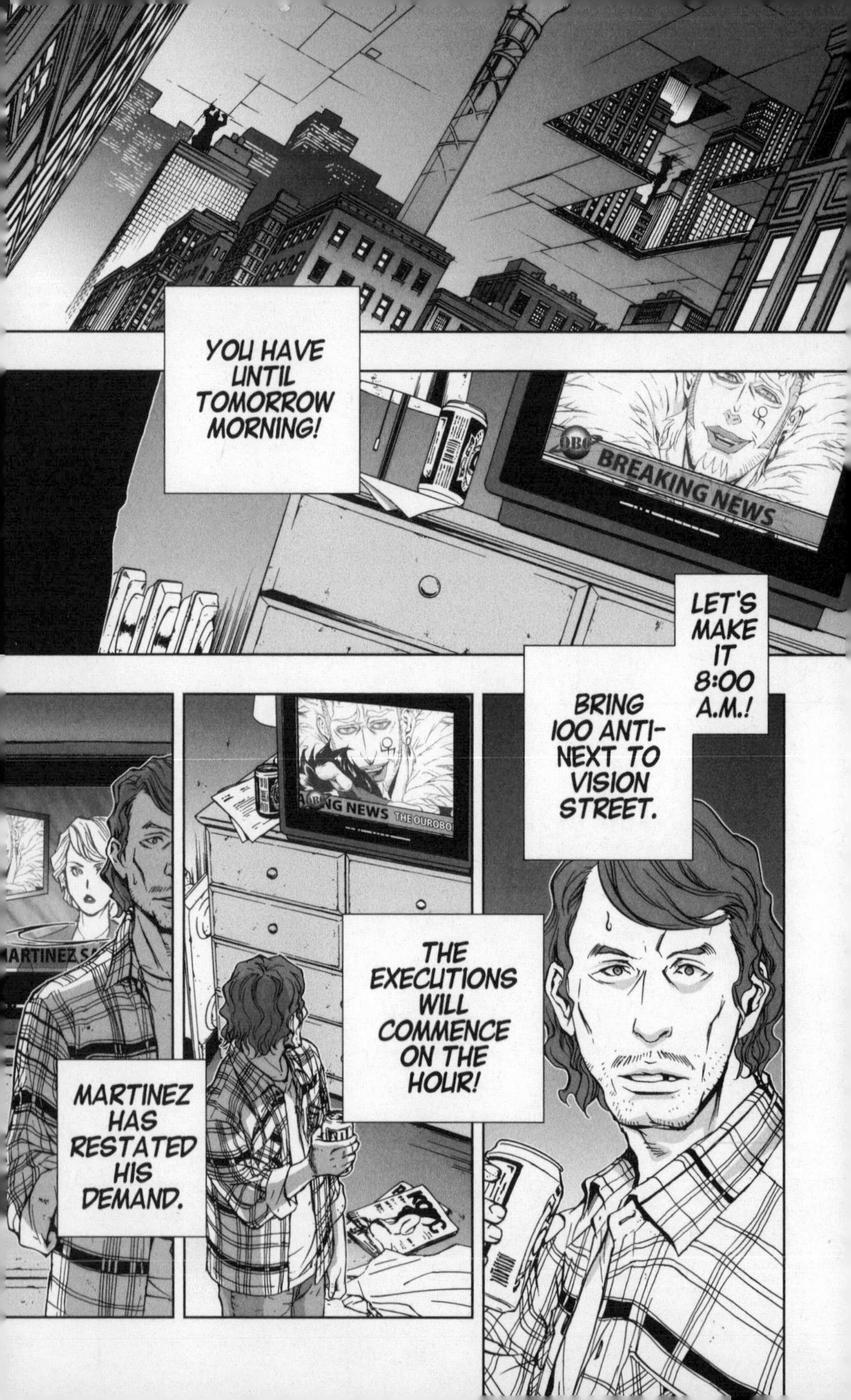
YOU HAVE UNTIL TOMORROW MORNING!
BREAKING NEWS
LET'S MAKE IT 8:00 A.M.!
BRING 100 ANTI-NEXT TO VISION STREET.
THE EXECUTIONS WILL COMMENCE ON THE HOUR!
MARTINEZ HAS RESTATED HIS DEMAND.

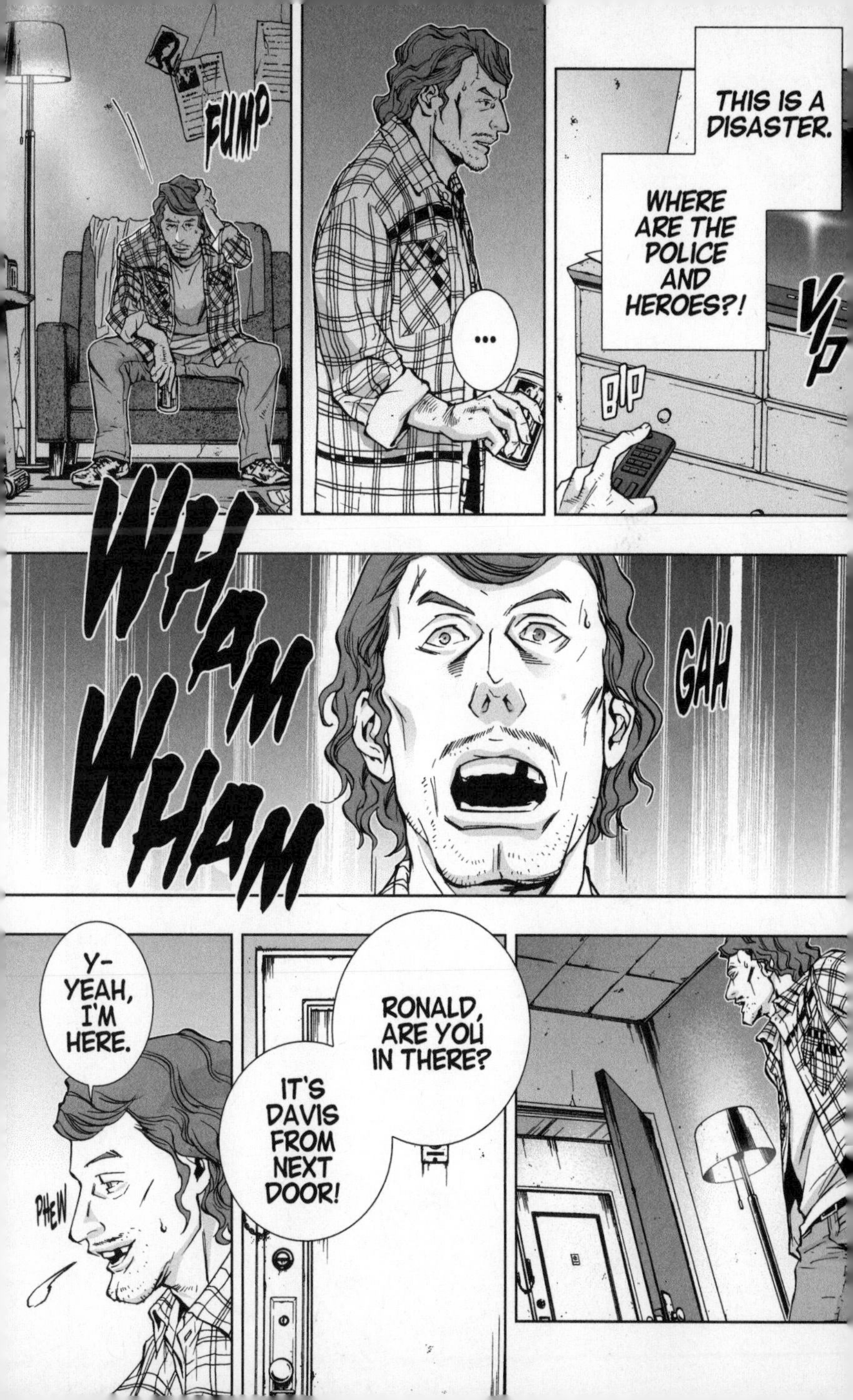
THIS IS A DISASTER.
WHERE ARE THE POLICE AND HEROES?!
VIP
BLIP
...
FUMP
WHAM WHAM WHAM
GAH
RONALD, ARE YOU IN THERE?
IT'S DAVIS FROM NEXT DOOR!
Y-YEAH, I'M HERE.
PHEW

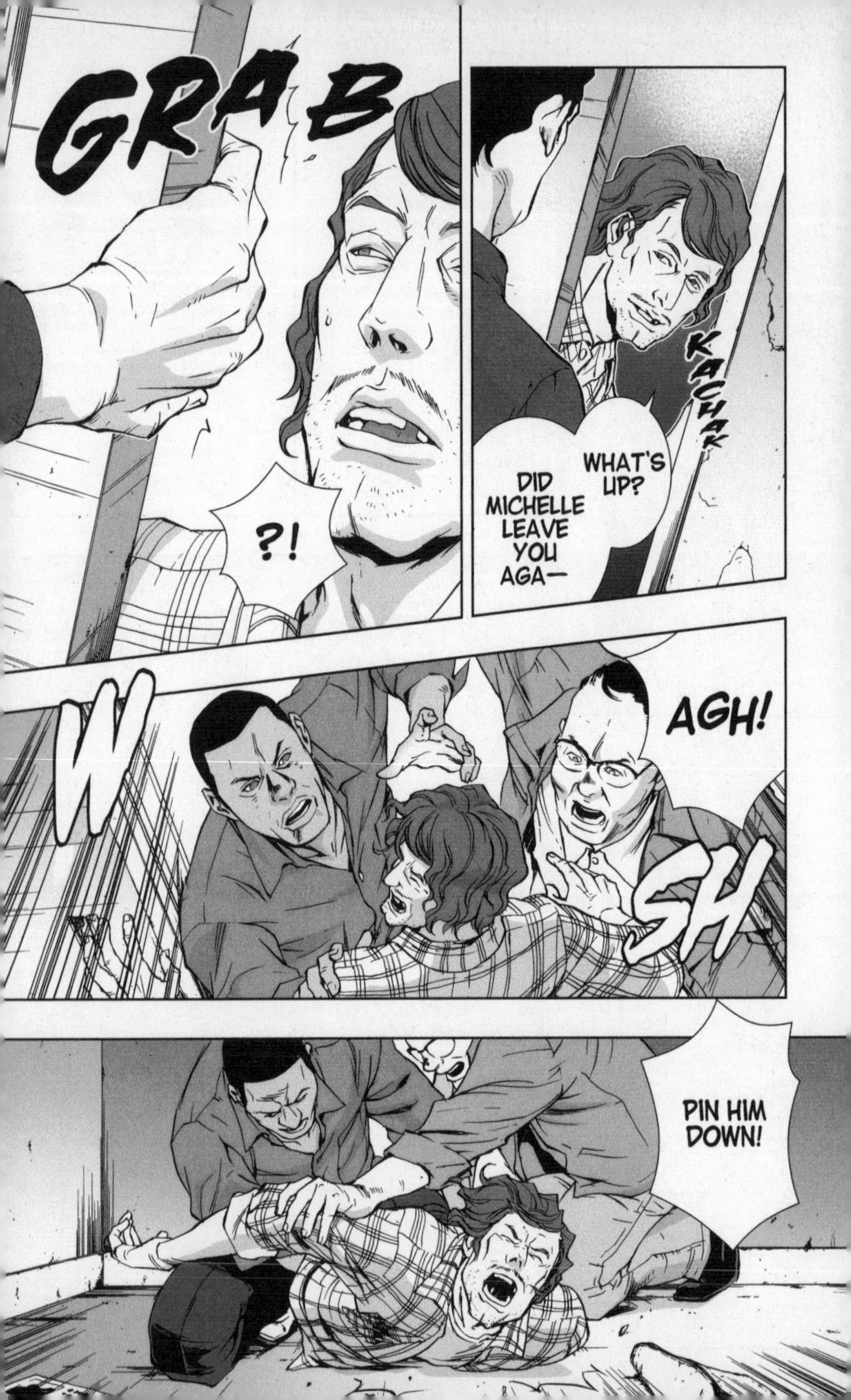
KACHAK
WHAT'S UP?
DID MICHELLE LEAVE YOU AGA—
GRAB
?!
AGH!
WSH
PIN HIM DOWN!

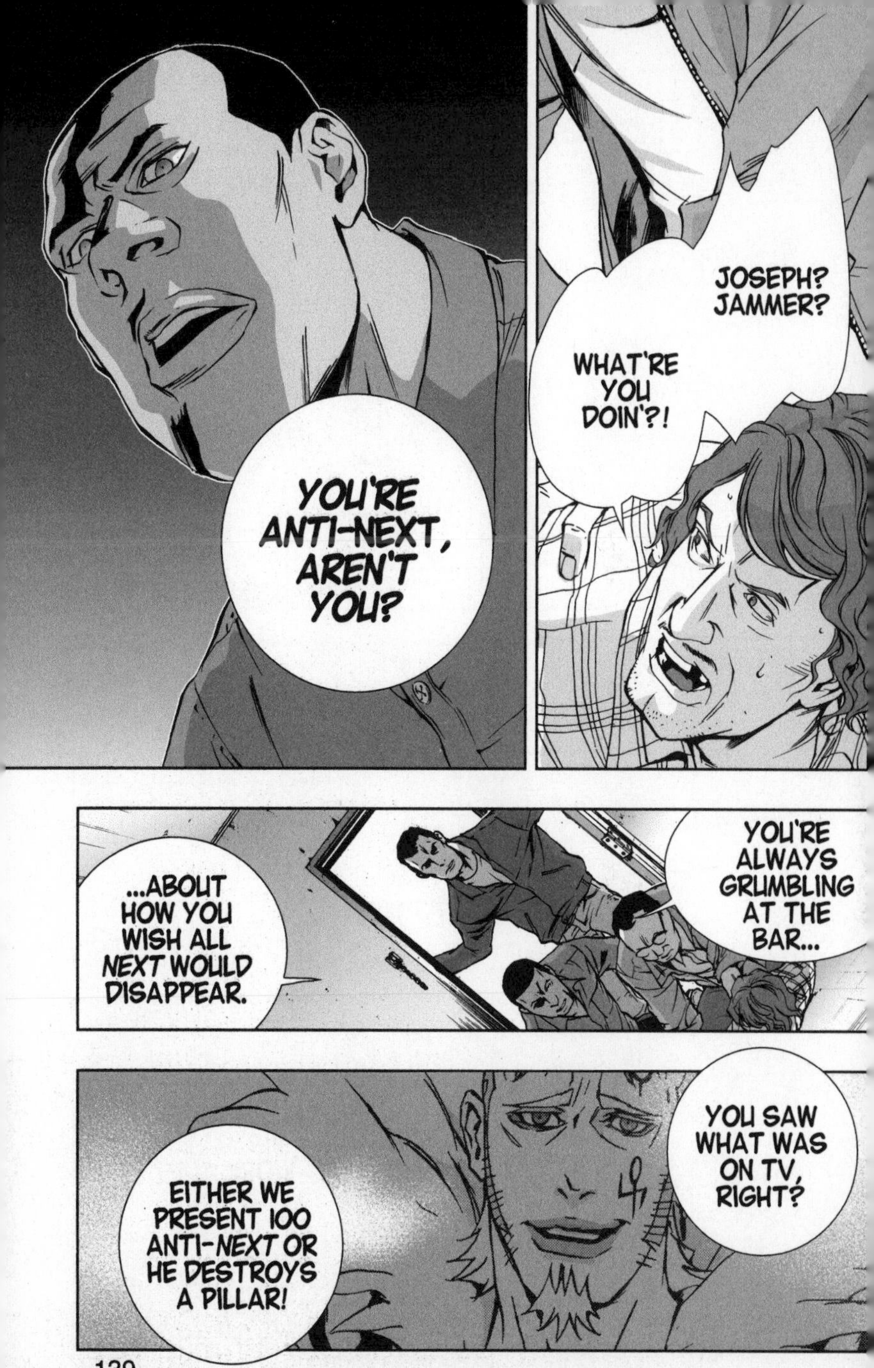
JOSEPH? JAMMER?
WHAT'RE YOU DOIN'?!
YOU'RE ANTI-NEXT, AREN'T YOU?
YOU'RE ALWAYS GRUMBLING AT THE BAR...
...ABOUT HOW YOU WISH ALL NEXT WOULD DISAPPEAR.
YOU SAW WHAT WAS ON TV, RIGHT?
EITHER WE PRESENT 100 ANTI-NEXT OR HE DESTROYS A PILLAR!

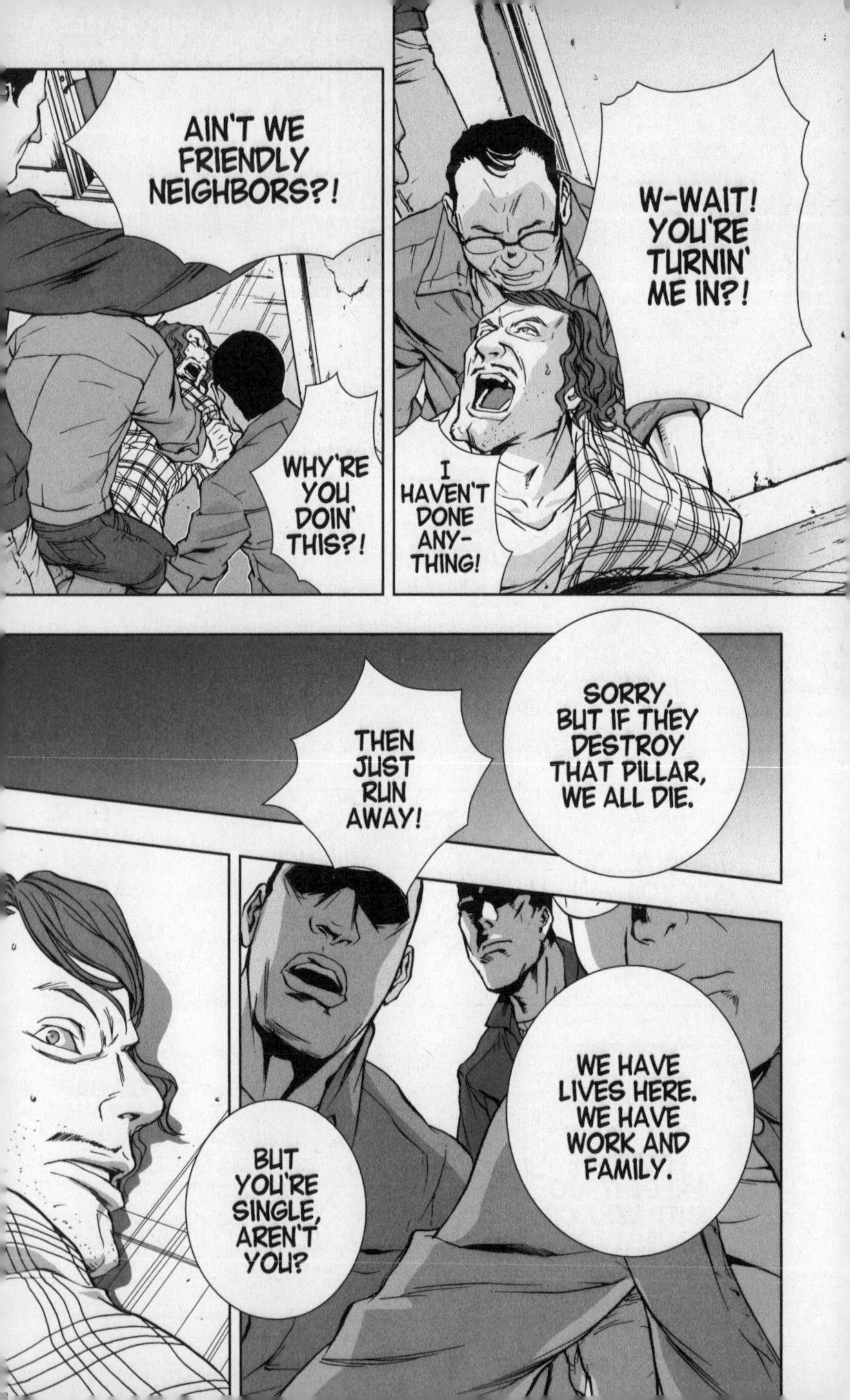
W-WAIT! YOU'RE TURNIN' ME IN?!
I HAVEN'T DONE ANY-THING!
AIN'T WE FRIENDLY NEIGHBORS?!
WHY'RE YOU DOIN' THIS?!
SORRY, BUT IF THEY DESTROY THAT PILLAR, WE ALL DIE.
THEN JUST RUN AWAY!
WE HAVE LIVES HERE. WE HAVE WORK AND FAMILY.
BUT YOU'RE SINGLE, AREN'T YOU?

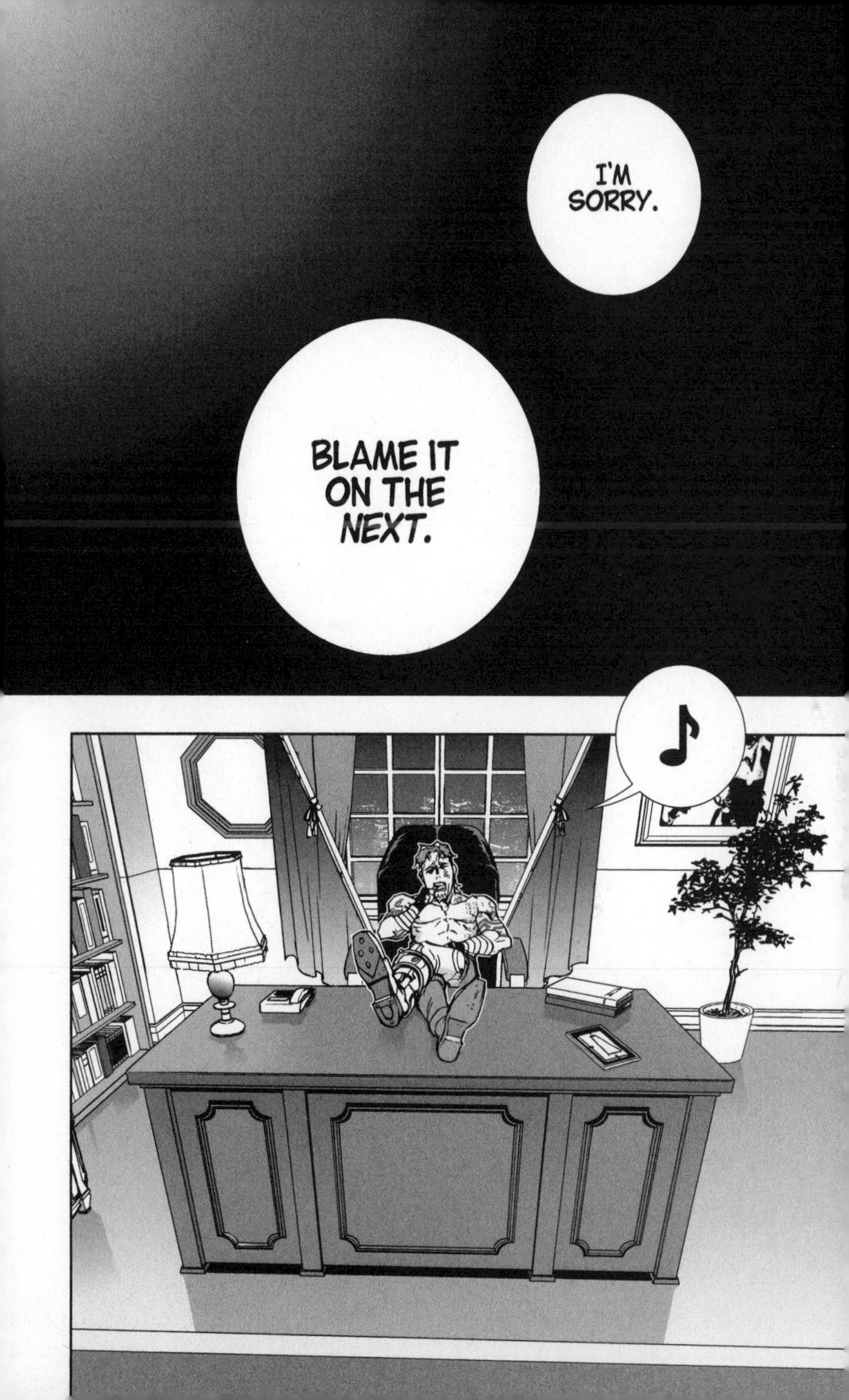
I'M SORRY.
BLAME IT ON THE NEXT.
♪

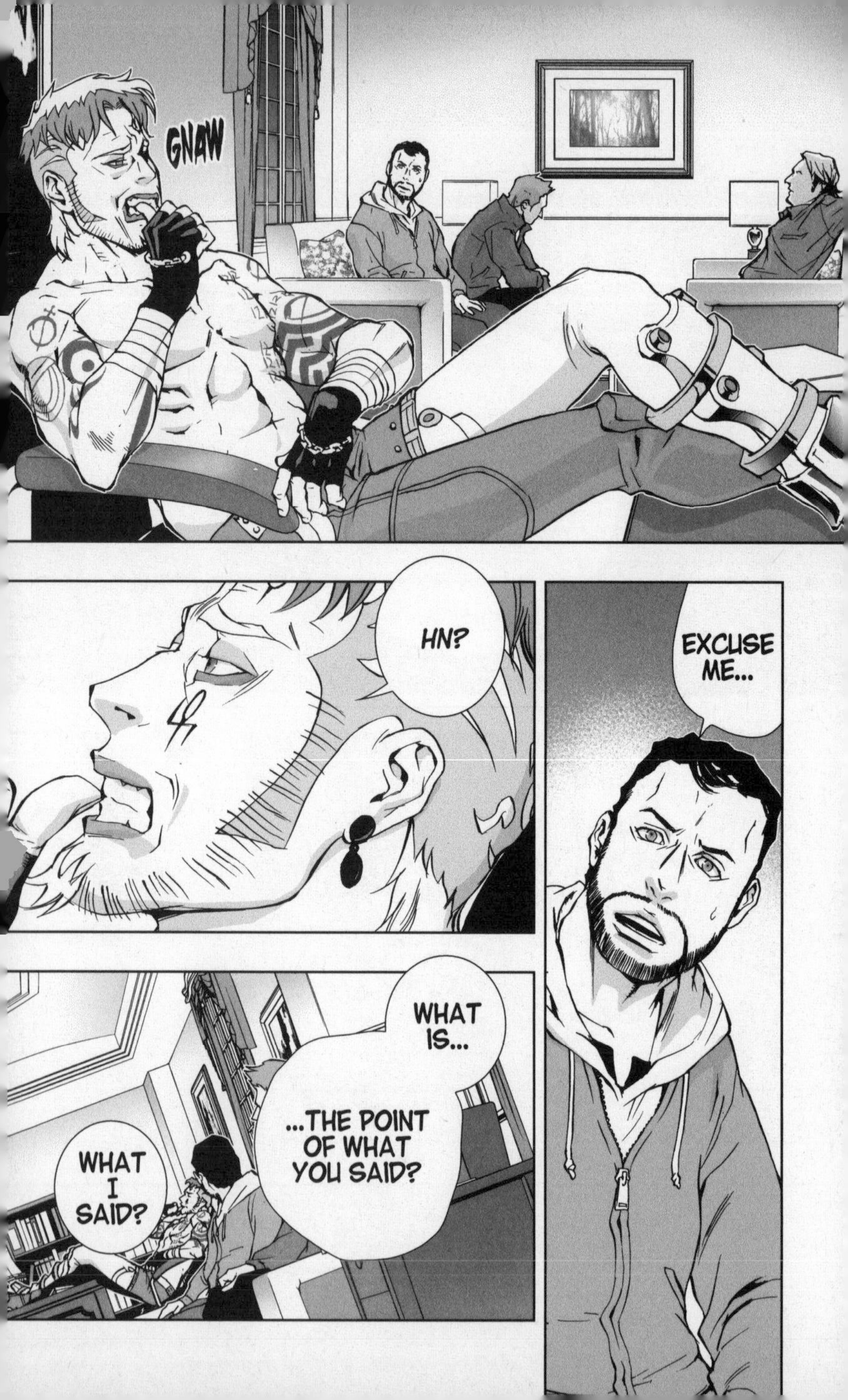
GNAW
EXCUSE ME...
HN?
WHAT IS...
...THE POINT OF WHAT YOU SAID?
WHAT I SAID?

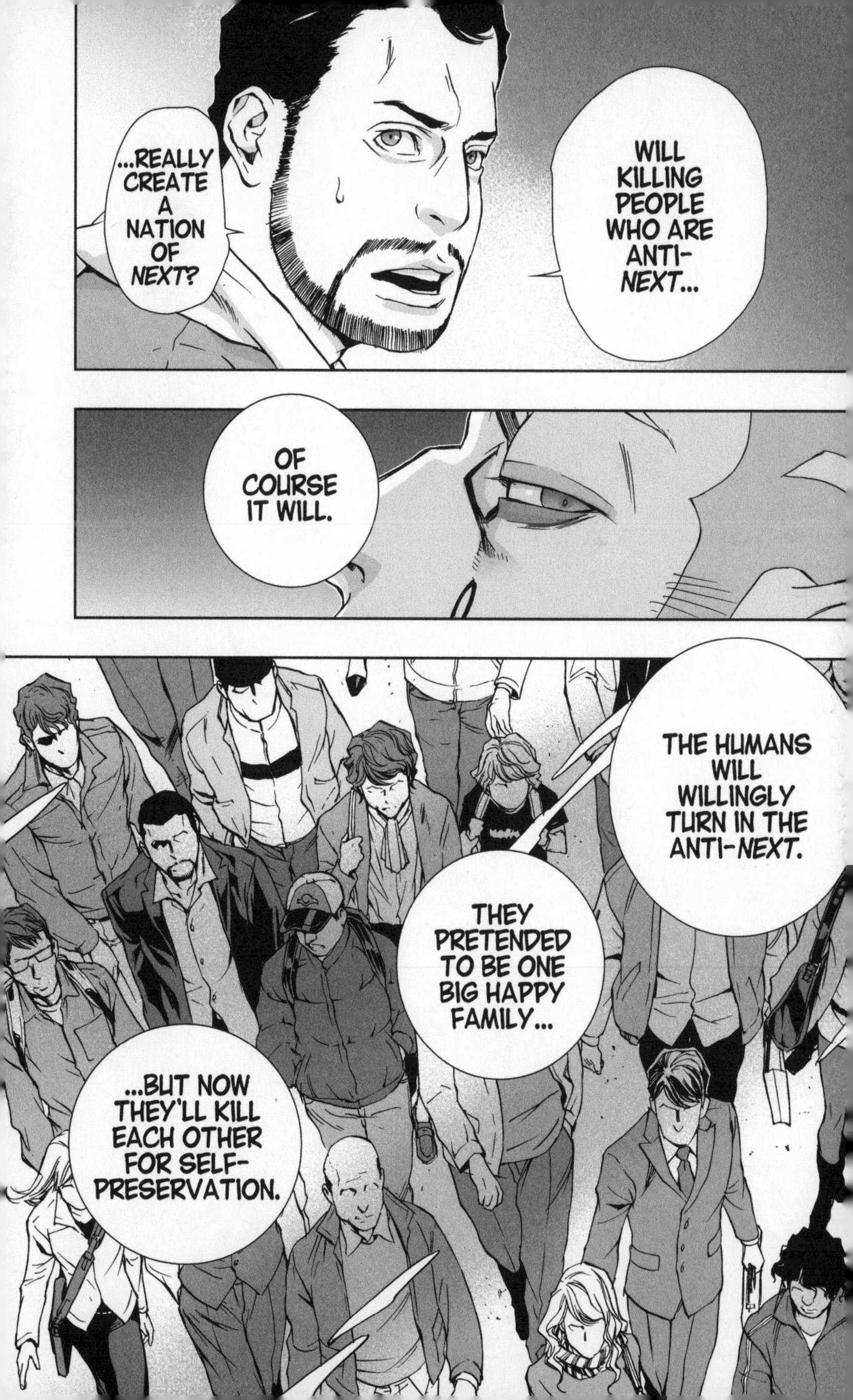
WILL KILLING PEOPLE WHO ARE ANTI-NEXT...
...REALLY CREATE A NATION OF NEXT?
OF COURSE IT WILL.
THE HUMANS WILL WILLINGLY TURN IN THE ANTI-NEXT.
THEY PRETENDED TO BE ONE BIG HAPPY FAMILY...
...BUT NOW THEY'LL KILL EACH OTHER FOR SELF-PRESERVATION.

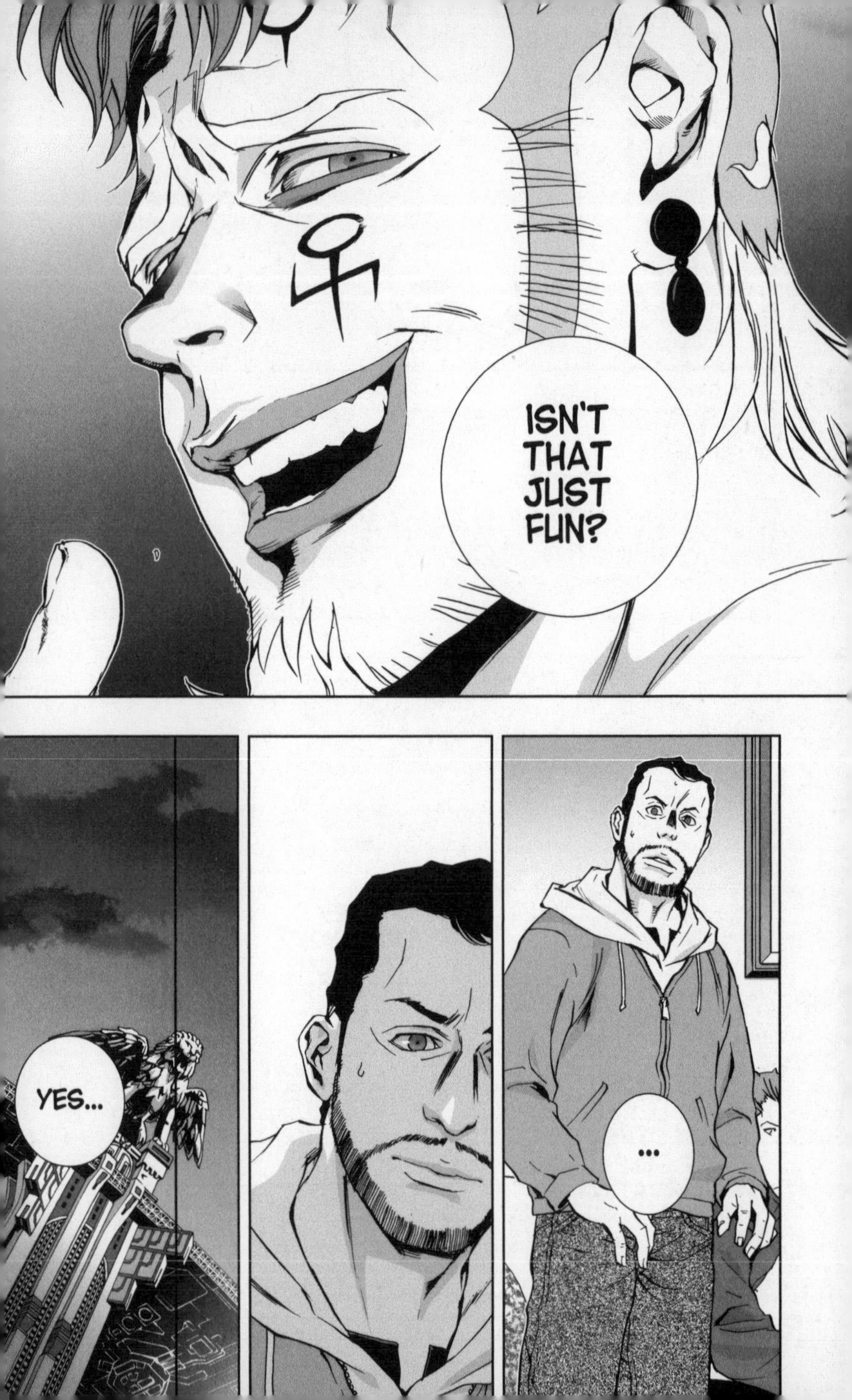
ISN'T THAT JUST FUN?
...
YES...

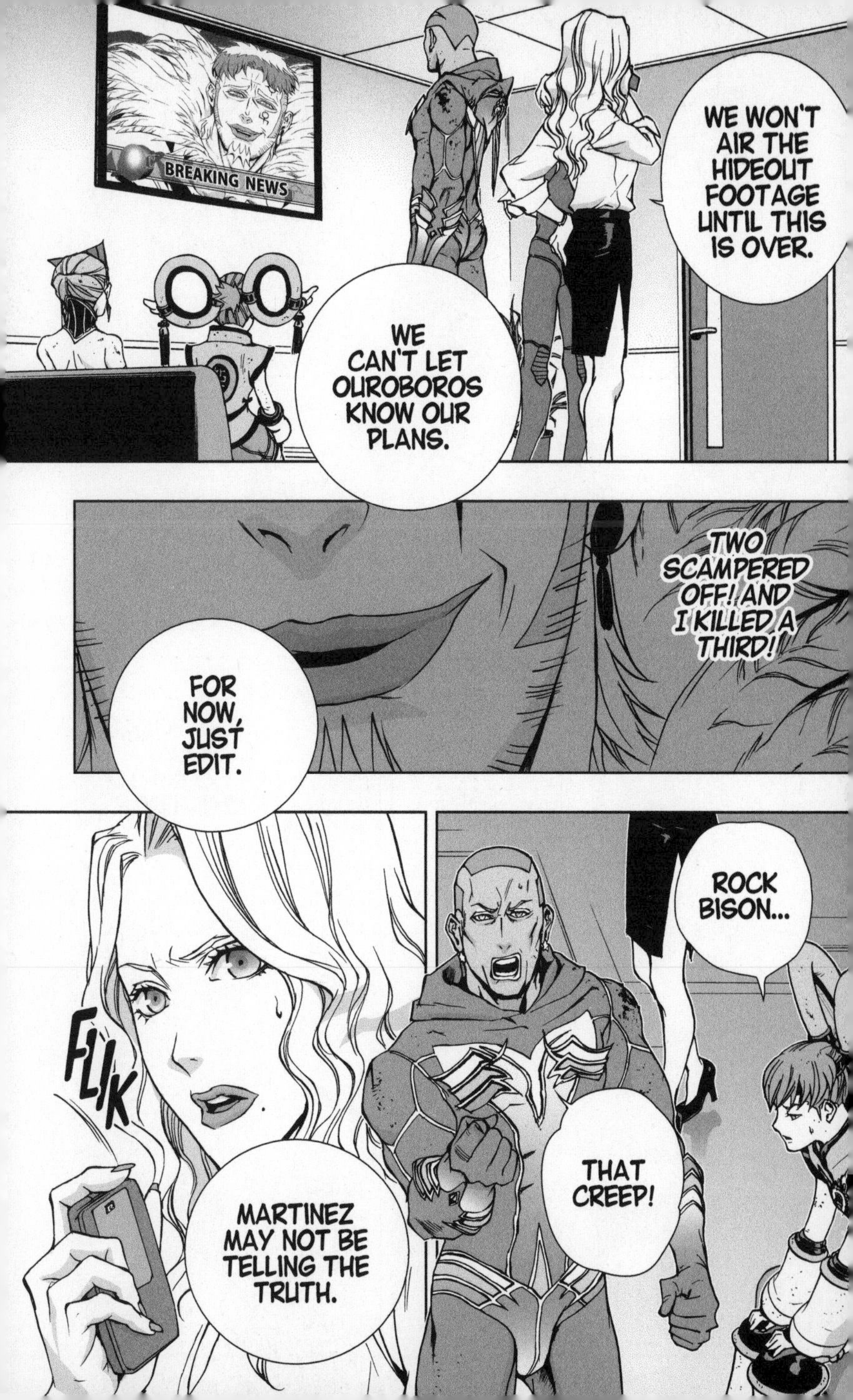
WE WON'T AIR THE HIDEOUT FOOTAGE UNTIL THIS IS OVER.
BREAKING NEWS
WE CAN'T LET OUROBOROS KNOW OUR PLANS.
TWO SCAMPERED OFF! AND I KILLED A THIRD!
FOR NOW, JUST EDIT.
ROCK BISON...
THAT CREEP!
FLIK
MARTINEZ MAY NOT BE TELLING THE TRUTH.

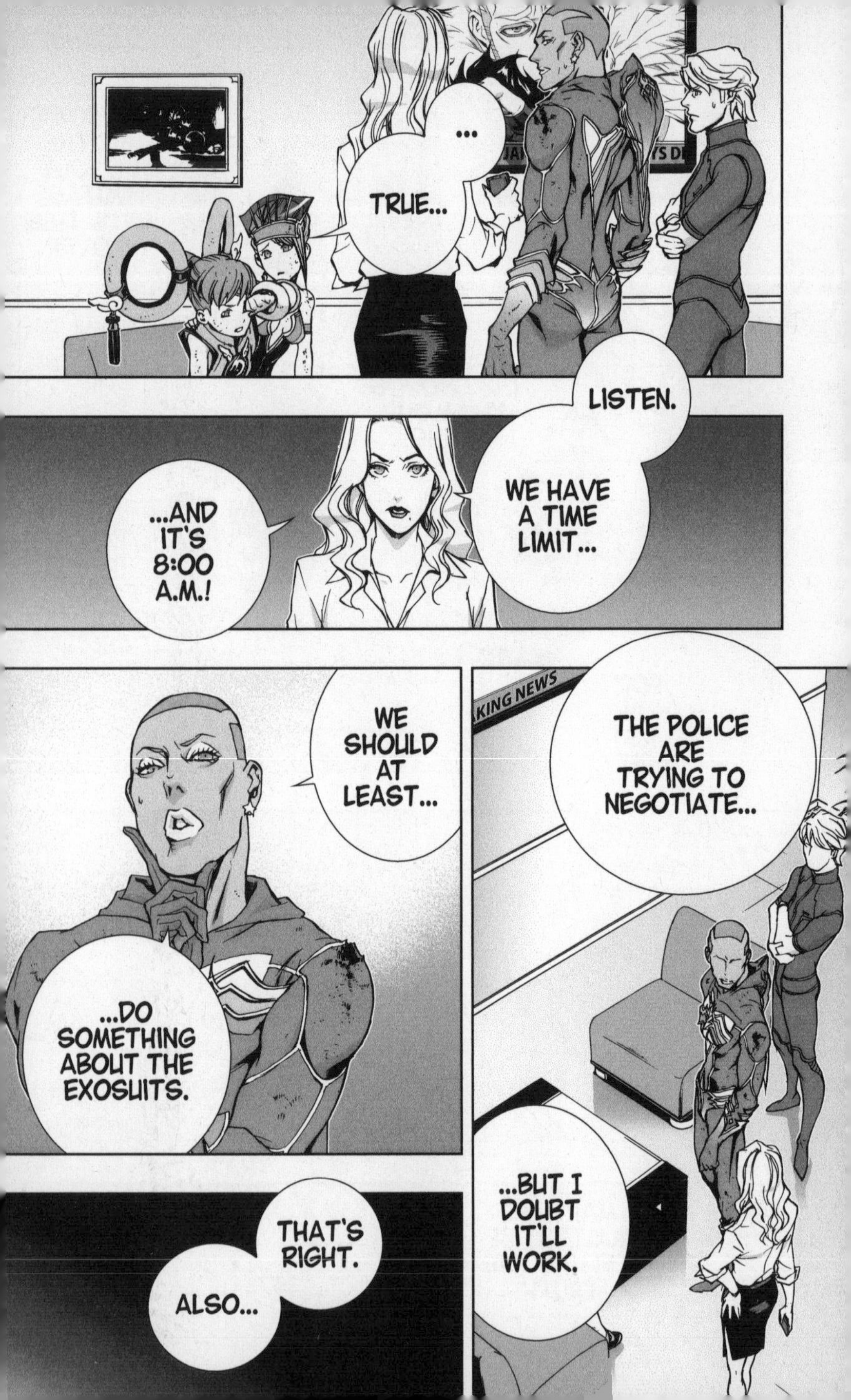
...
TRUE...
LISTEN.
WE HAVE A TIME LIMIT...
...AND IT'S 8:00 A.M.!
THE POLICE ARE TRYING TO NEGOTIATE...
...BUT I DOUBT IT'LL WORK.
WE SHOULD AT LEAST...
...DO SOMETHING ABOUT THE EXOSUITS.
THAT'S RIGHT.
ALSO...

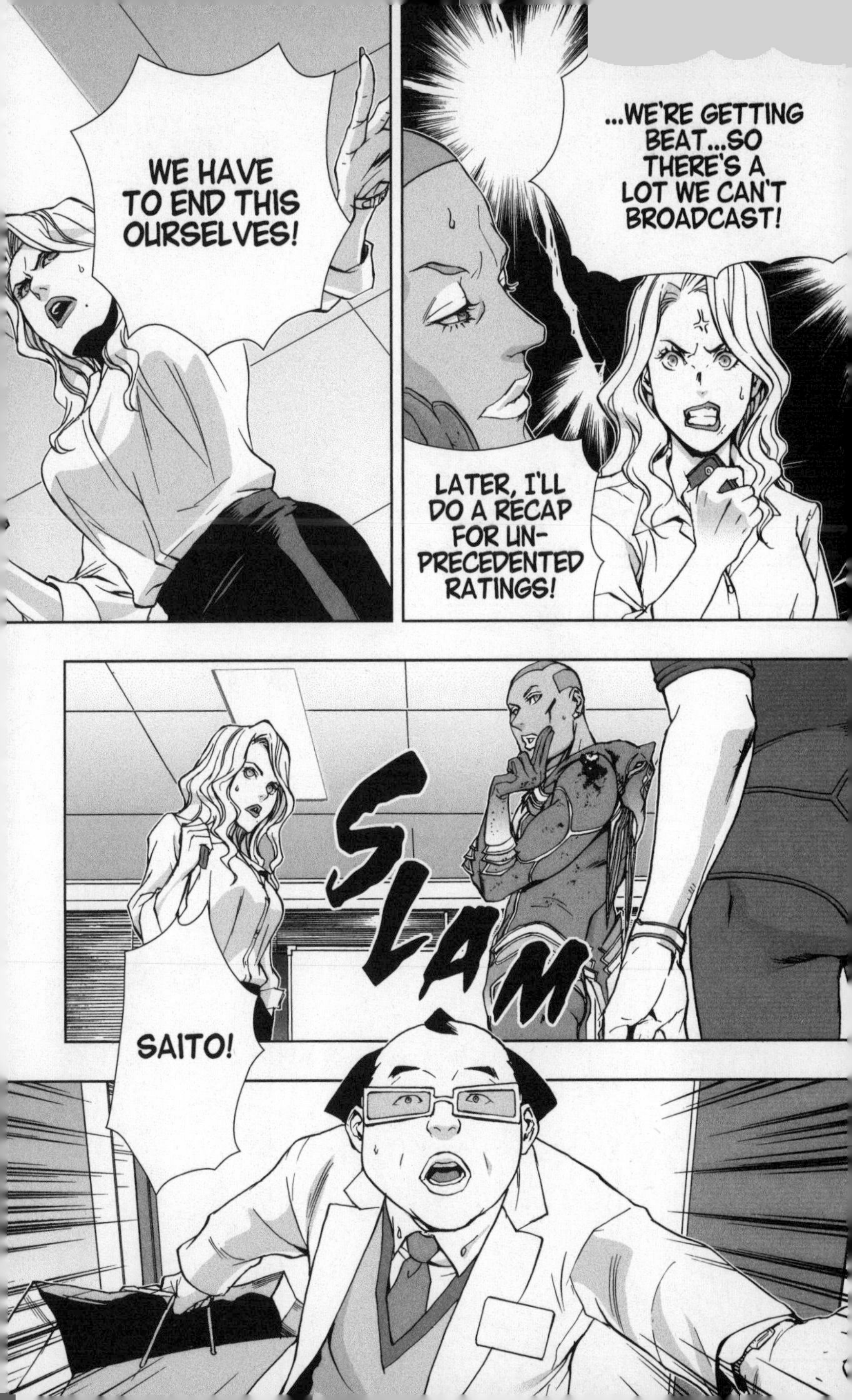
...WE'RE GETTING BEAT...SO THERE'S A LOT WE CAN'T BROADCAST!
LATER, I'LL DO A RECAP FOR UN-PRECEDENTED RATINGS!
WE HAVE TO END THIS OURSELVES!
SLAM
SAITO!

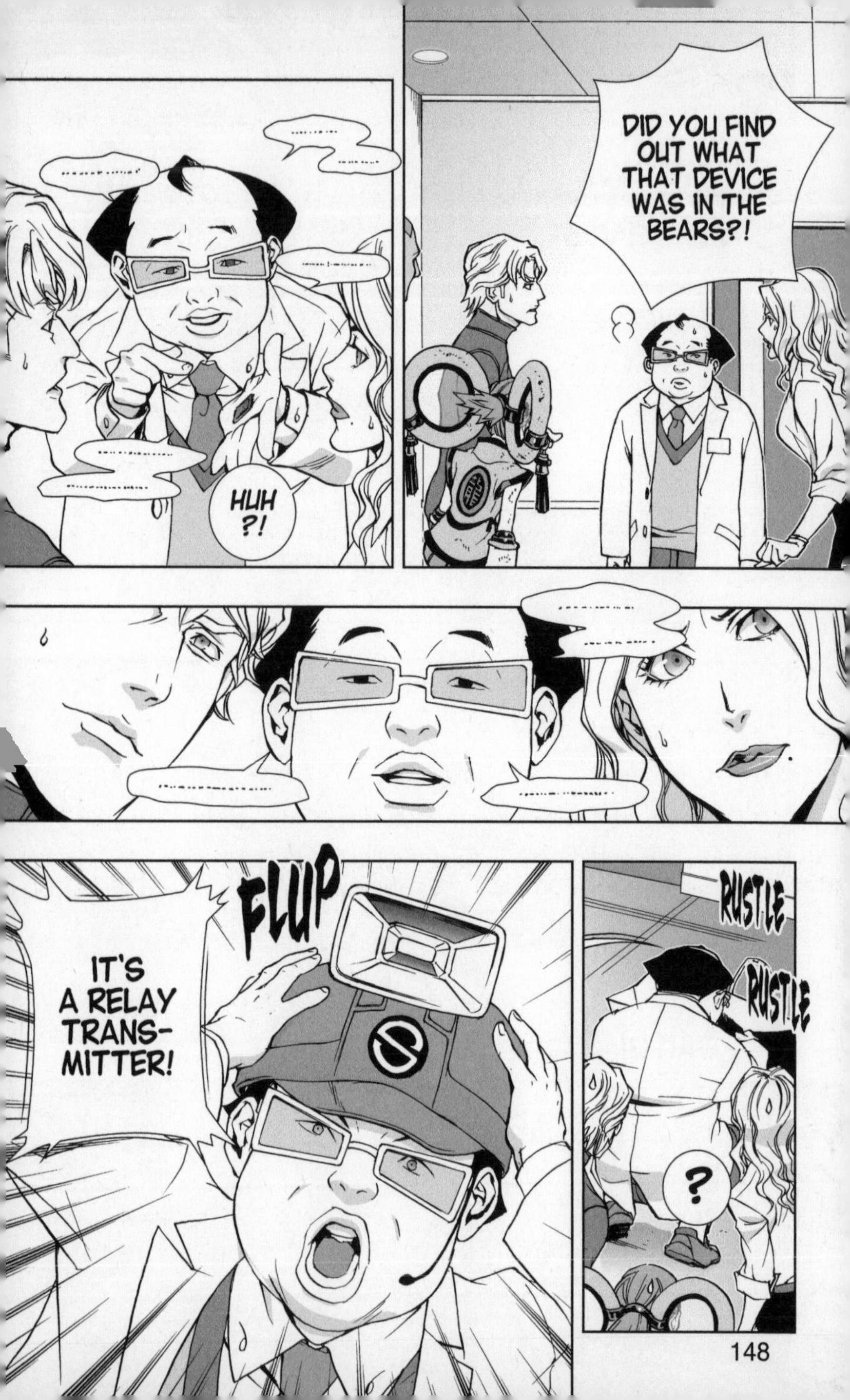
DID YOU FIND OUT WHAT THAT DEVICE WAS IN THE BEARS?!
HUH ?!
RUSTLE
RUSTLE
?
FLUP
IT'S A RELAY TRANS-MITTER!

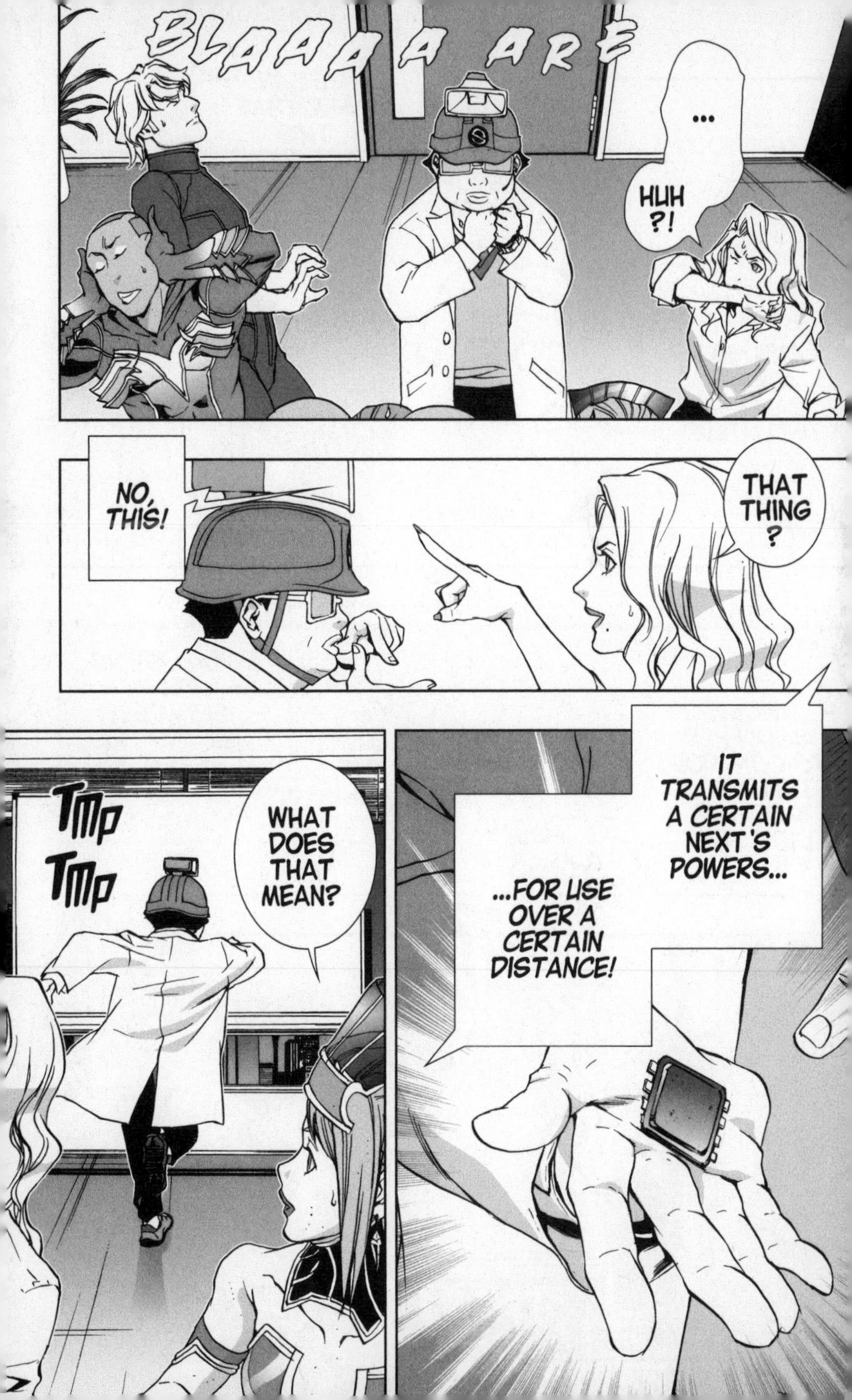
...
HUH ?!
BLAAAA ARE
THAT THING ?
NO, THIS!
IT TRANSMITS A CERTAIN NEXT'S POWERS...
...FOR USE OVER A CERTAIN DISTANCE!
WHAT DOES THAT MEAN?
TMP TMP

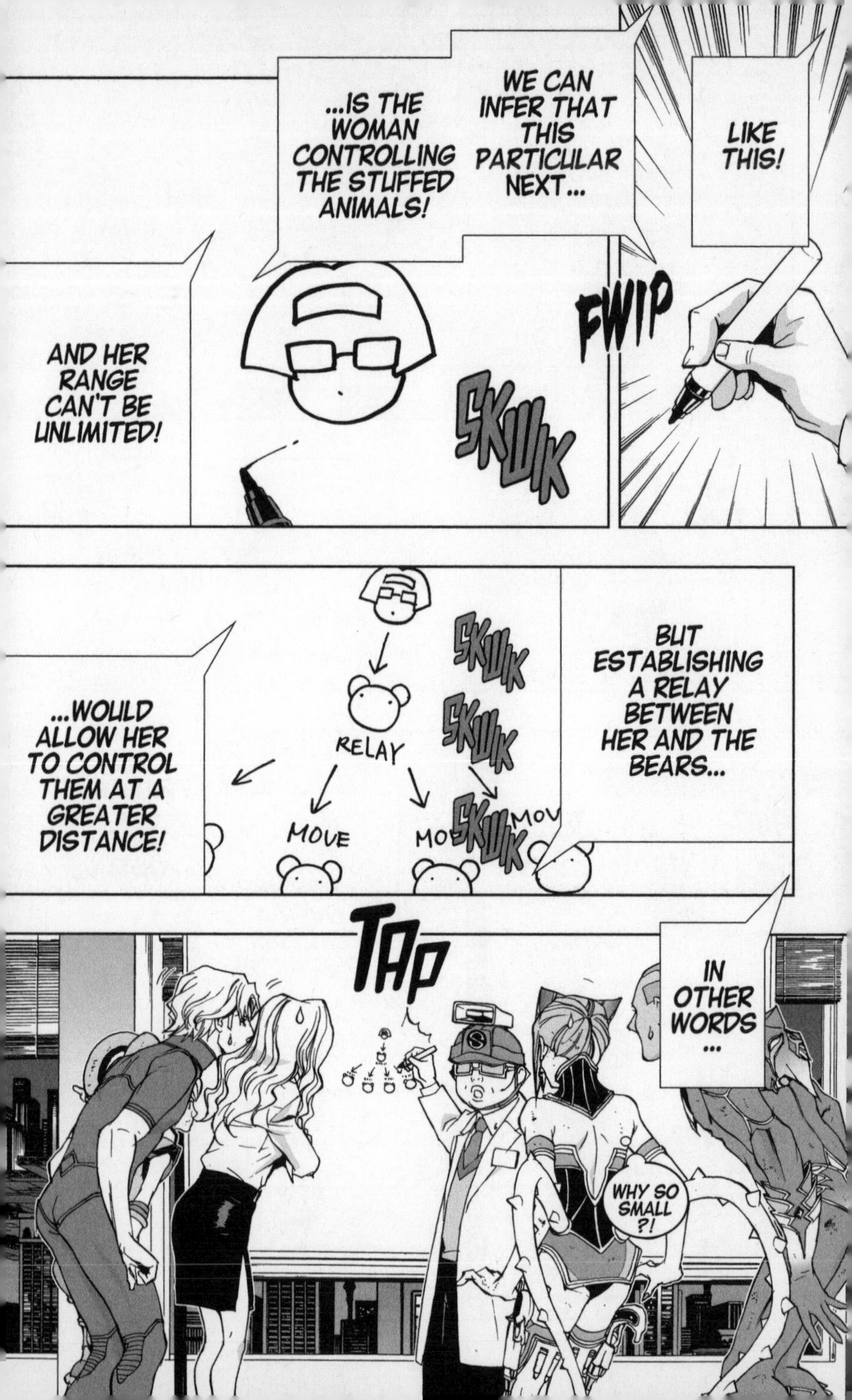
LIKE THIS!
FWIP
WE CAN INFER THAT THIS PARTICULAR NEXT...
...IS THE WOMAN CONTROLLING THE STUFFED ANIMALS!
SKWIK
AND HER RANGE CAN'T BE UNLIMITED!
BUT ESTABLISHING A RELAY BETWEEN HER AND THE BEARS...
SKWIK
SKWIK
SKWIK
RELAY
MOVE
MOVE
...WOULD ALLOW HER TO CONTROL THEM AT A GREATER DISTANCE!
IN OTHER WORDS...
TAP
WHY SO SMALL?!

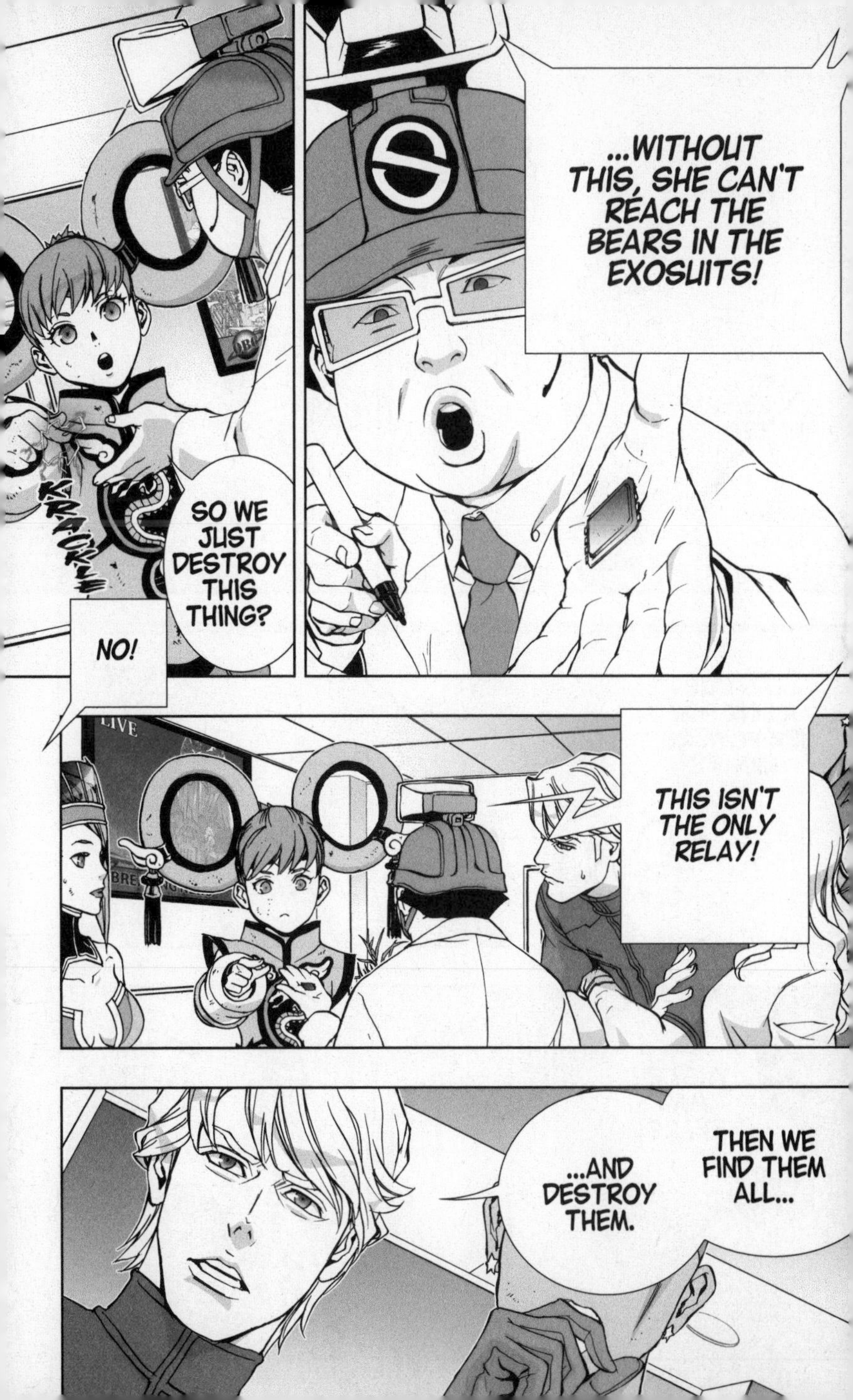
...WITHOUT THIS, SHE CAN'T REACH THE BEARS IN THE EXOSUITS!
SO WE JUST DESTROY THIS THING?
KRACKLE
NO!
THIS ISN'T THE ONLY RELAY!
THEN WE FIND THEM ALL...
...AND DESTROY THEM.

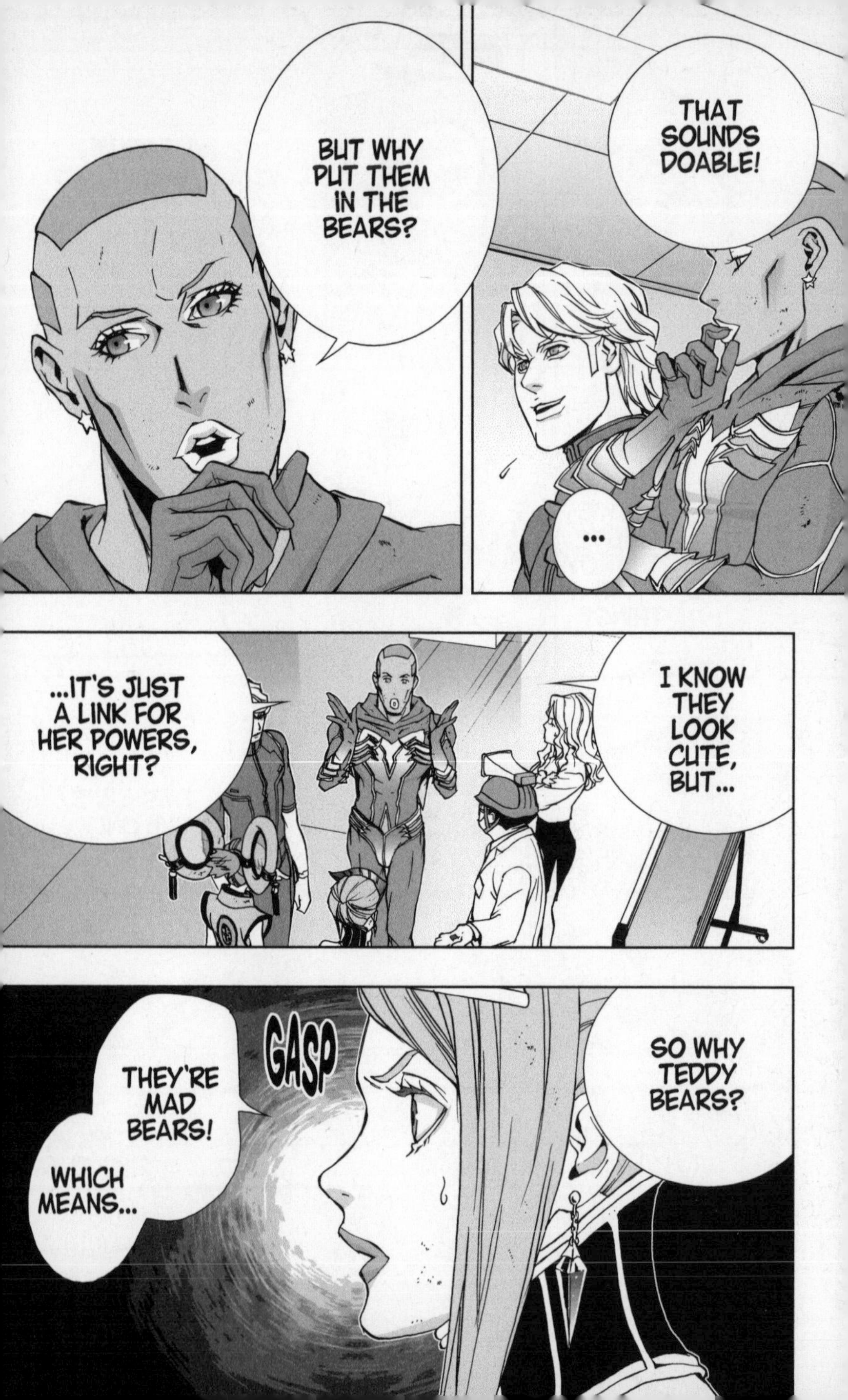
THAT SOUNDS DOABLE!
...
BUT WHY PUT THEM IN THE BEARS?
I KNOW THEY LOOK CUTE, BUT...
...IT'S JUST A LINK FOR HER POWERS, RIGHT?
SO WHY TEDDY BEARS?
GASP
THEY'RE MAD BEARS!
WHICH MEANS...

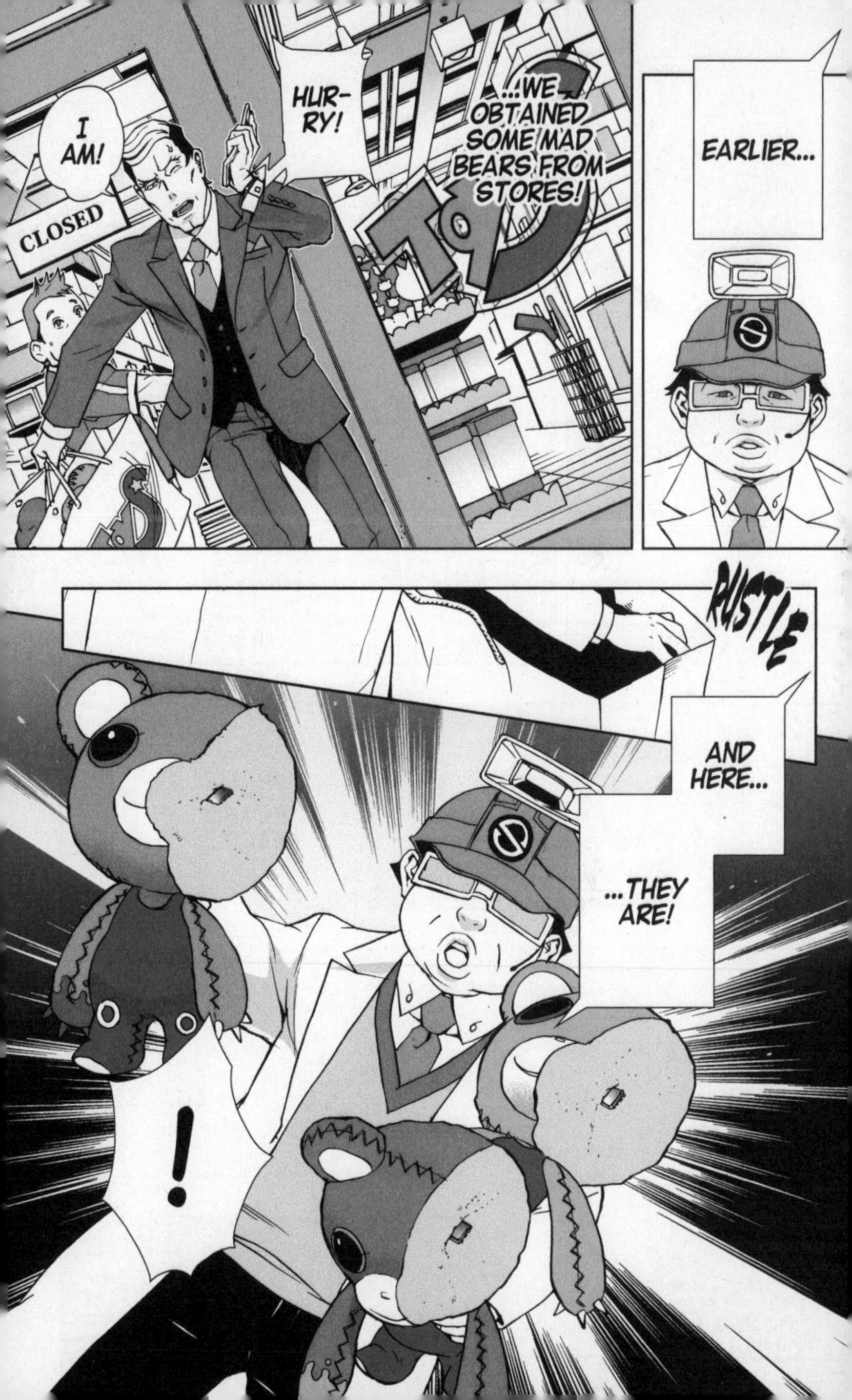
EARLIER...
...WE OBTAINED SOME MAD BEARS FROM STORES!
HUR-RY!
I AM!
CLOSED
RUSTLE
AND HERE...
...THEY ARE!
!

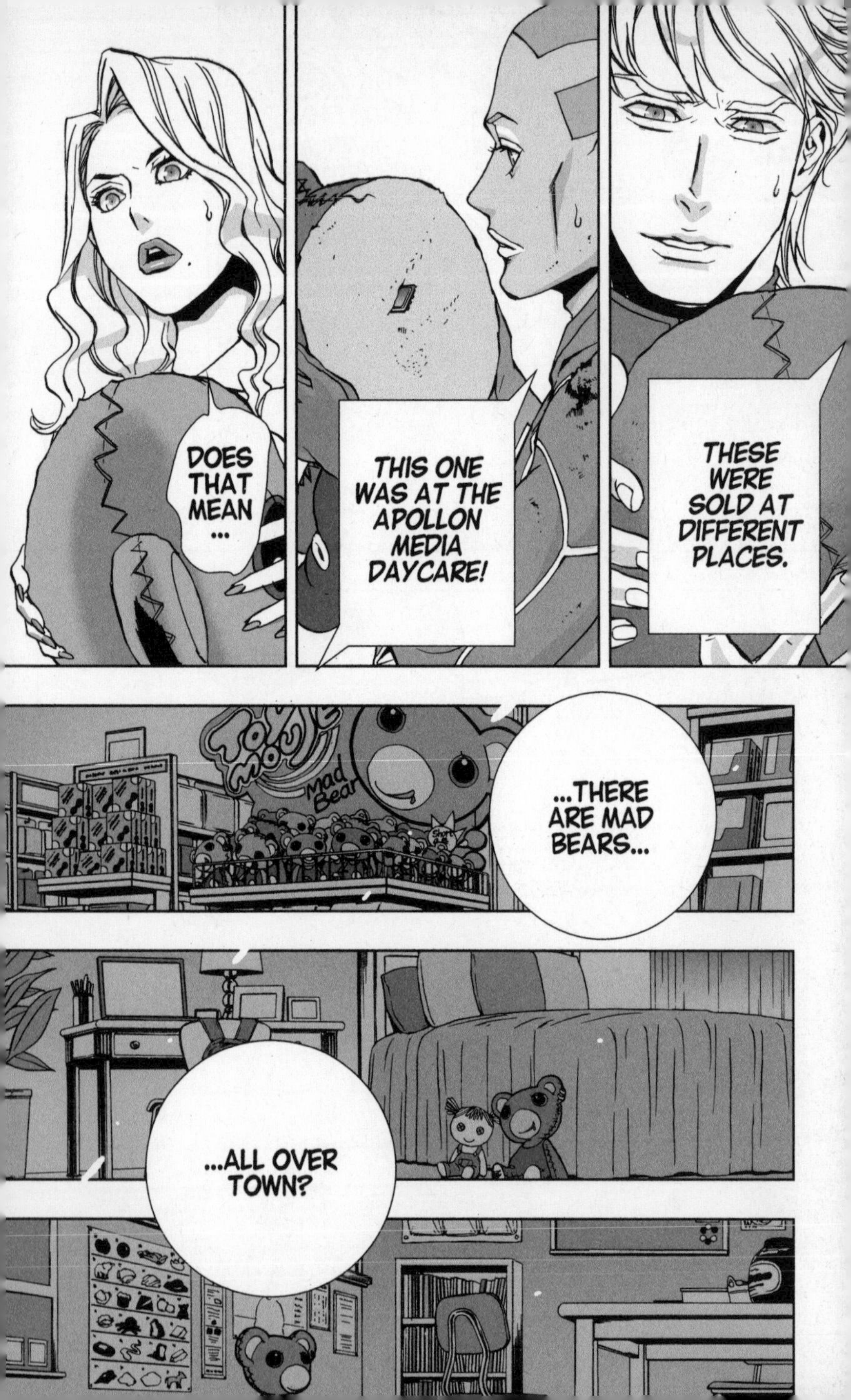
THESE WERE SOLD AT DIFFERENT PLACES.
THIS ONE WAS AT THE APOLLON MEDIA DAYCARE!
DOES THAT MEAN ...
Mad Bear
...THERE ARE MAD BEARS...
...ALL OVER TOWN?

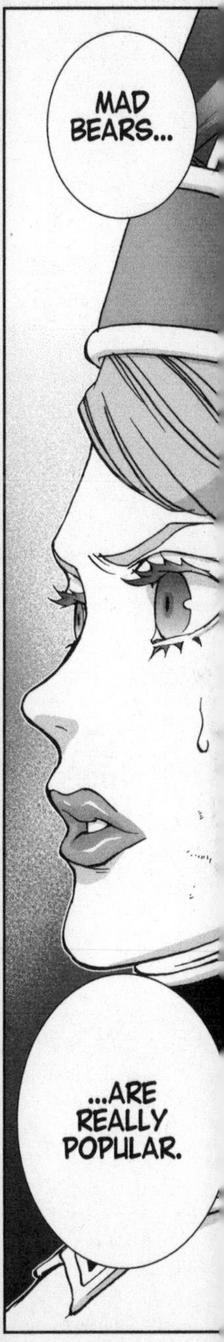
MAD BEARS...
...ARE REALLY POPULAR.
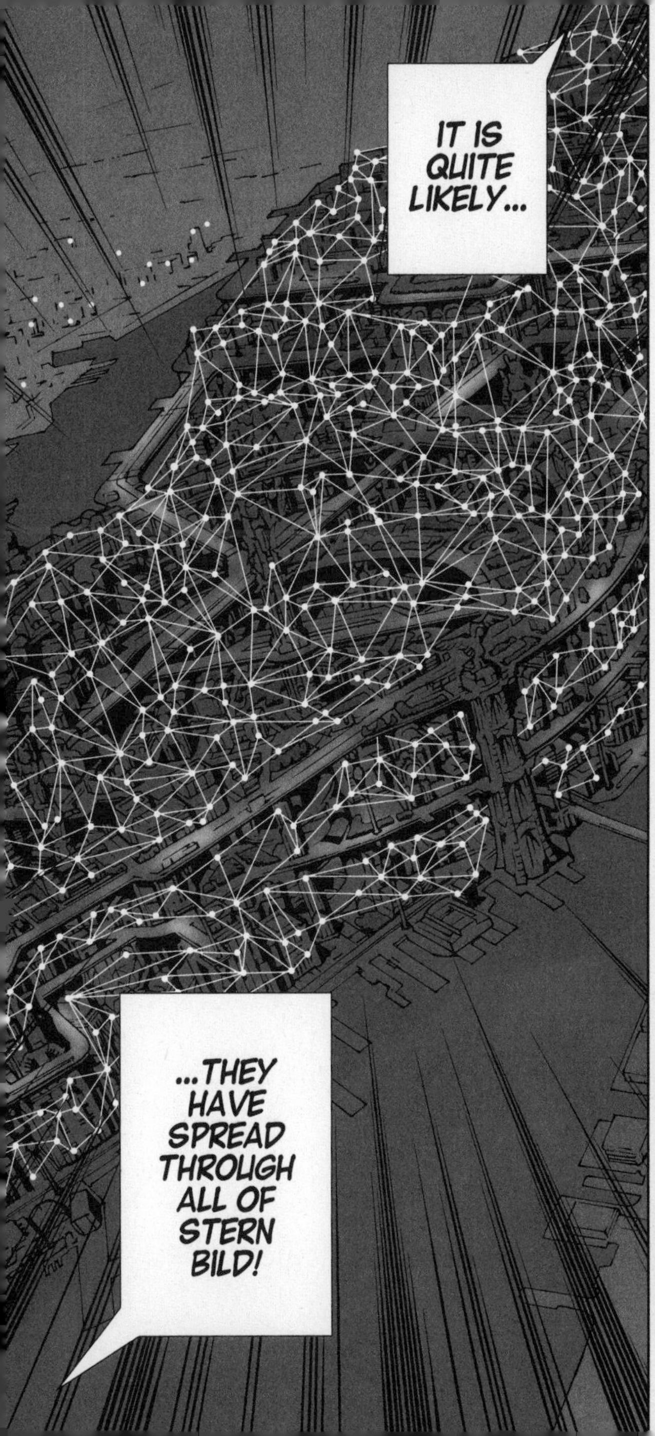
IT IS QUITE LIKELY...
...THEY HAVE SPREAD THROUGH ALL OF STERN BILD!

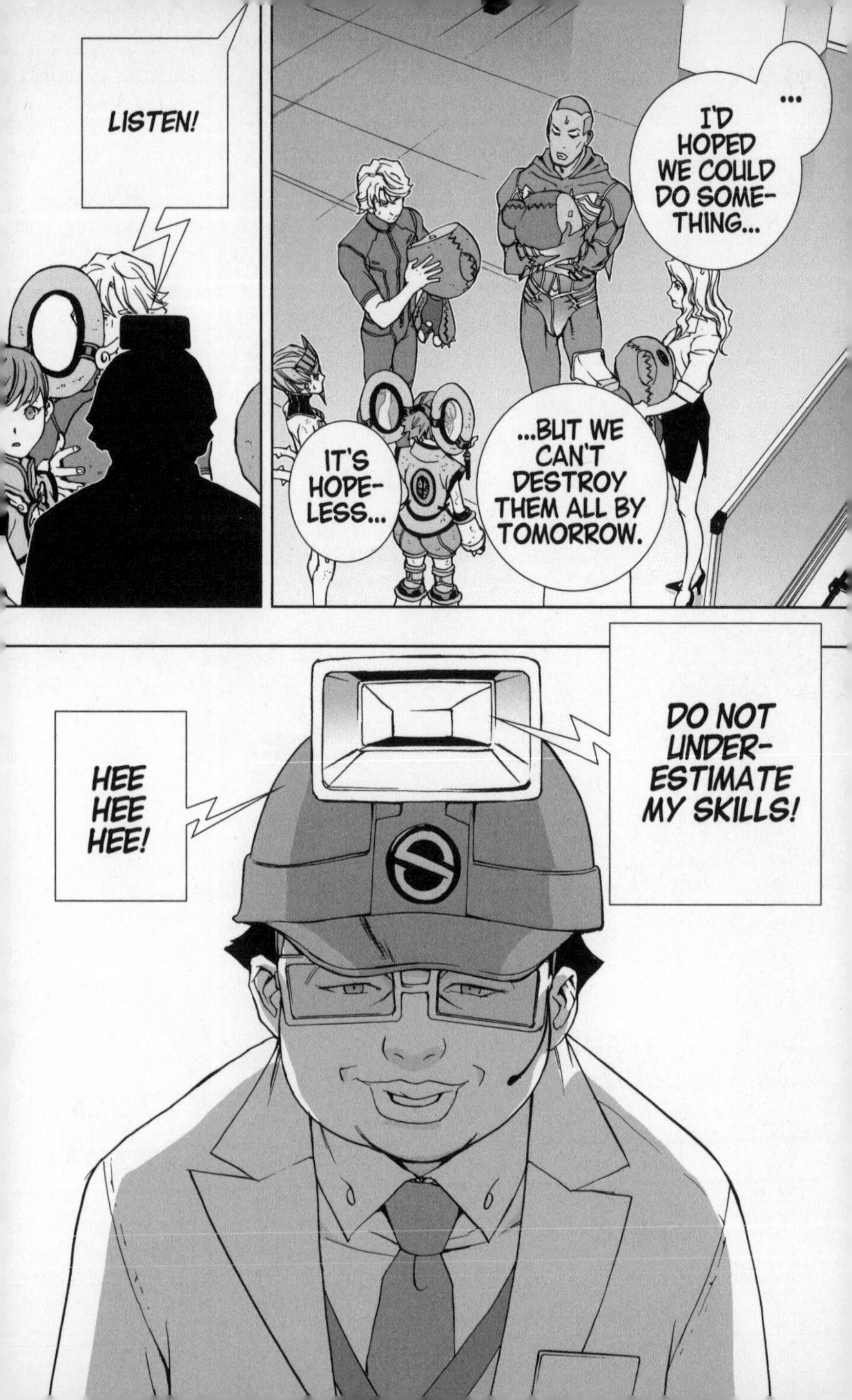
...
I'D HOPED WE COULD DO SOME-THING...
...BUT WE CAN'T DESTROY THEM ALL BY TOMORROW.
IT'S HOPE-LESS...
LISTEN!
DO NOT UNDER-ESTIMATE MY SKILLS!
HEE HEE HEE!

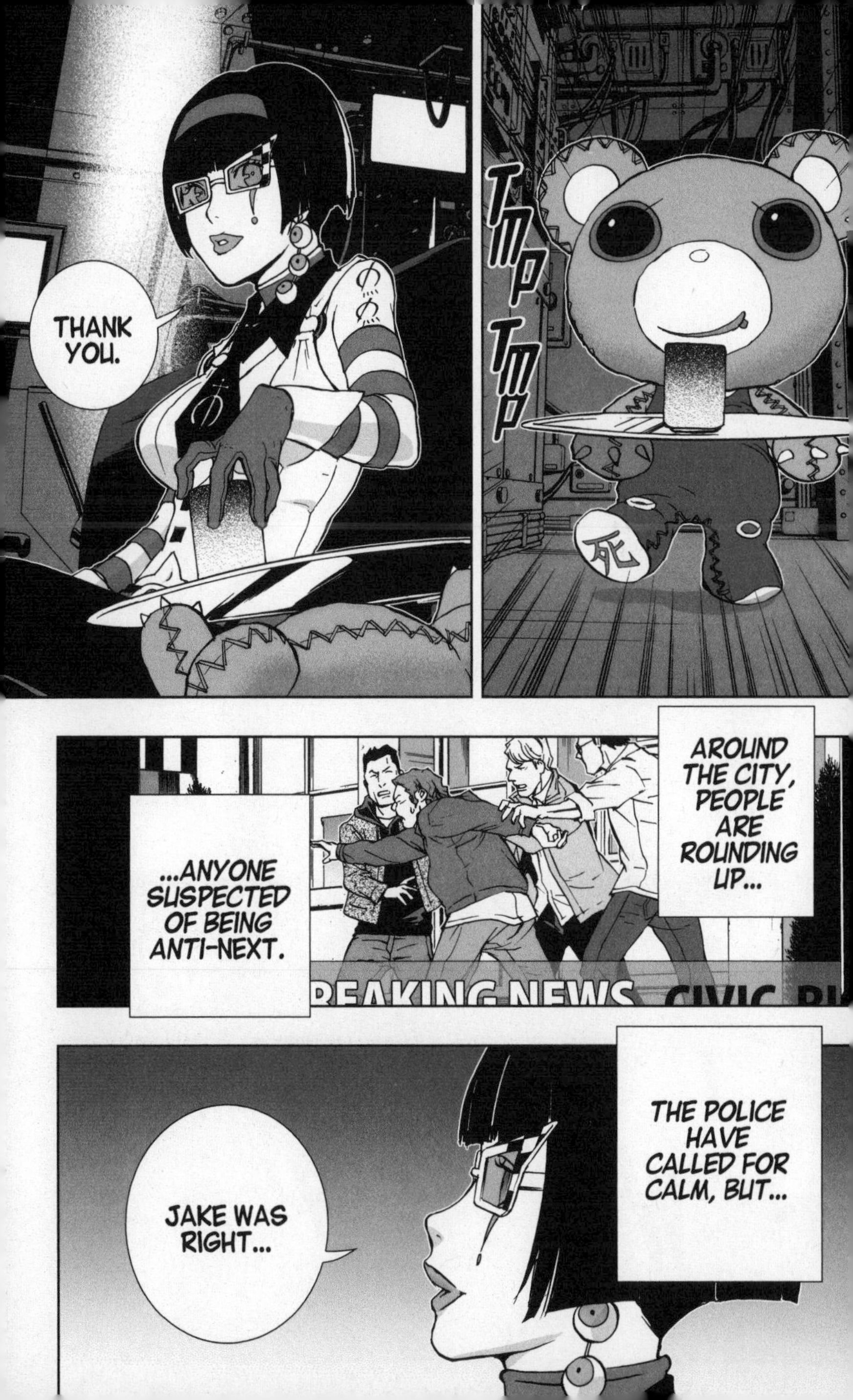
TMP TMP
THANK YOU.
AROUND THE CITY, PEOPLE ARE ROUNDING UP...
...ANYONE SUSPECTED OF BEING ANTI-NEXT.
THE POLICE HAVE CALLED FOR CALM, BUT...
JAKE WAS RIGHT...

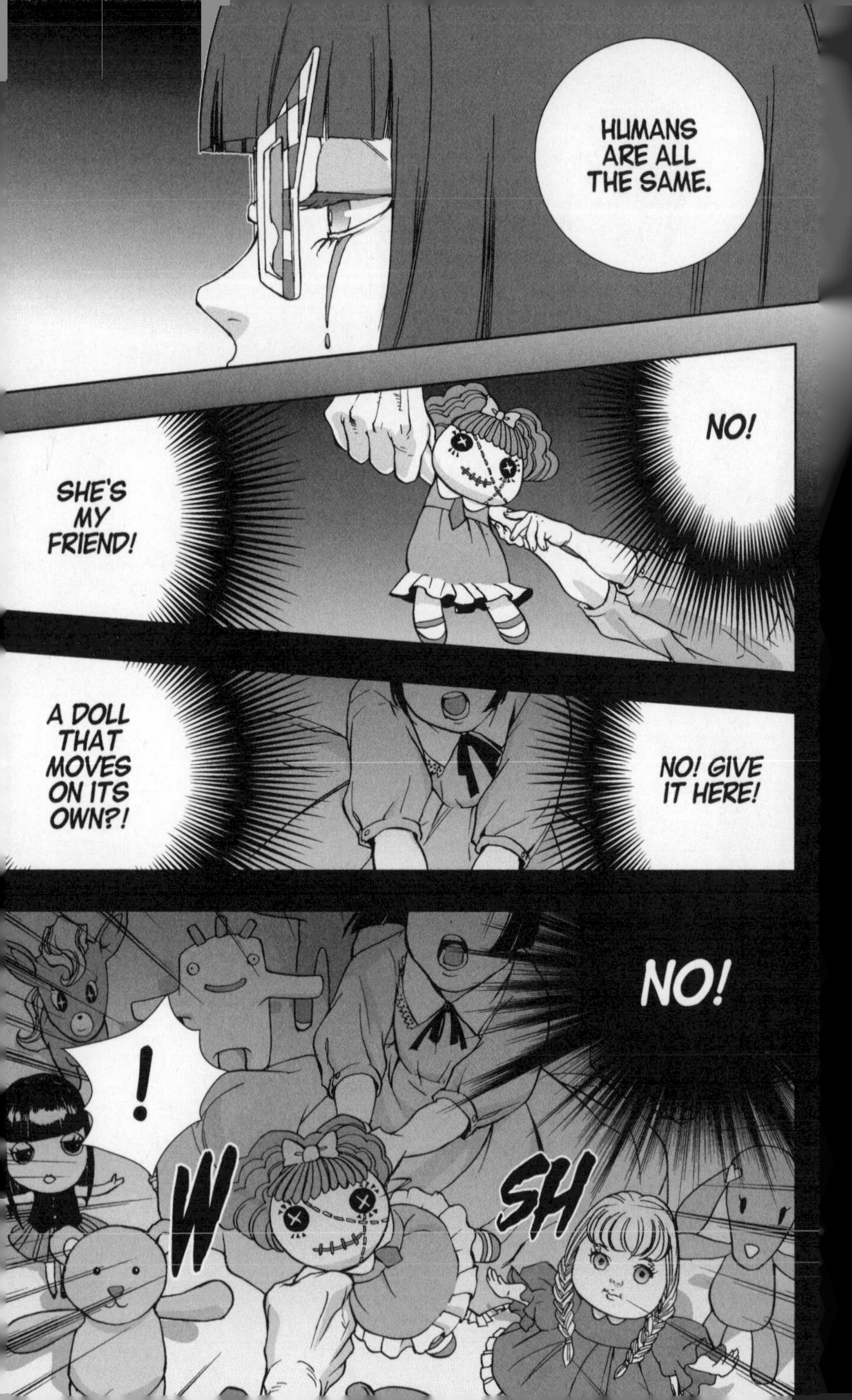
HUMANS ARE ALL THE SAME.
NO!
SHE'S MY FRIEND!
NO! GIVE IT HERE!
A DOLL THAT MOVES ON ITS OWN?!
NO!
!
W SH

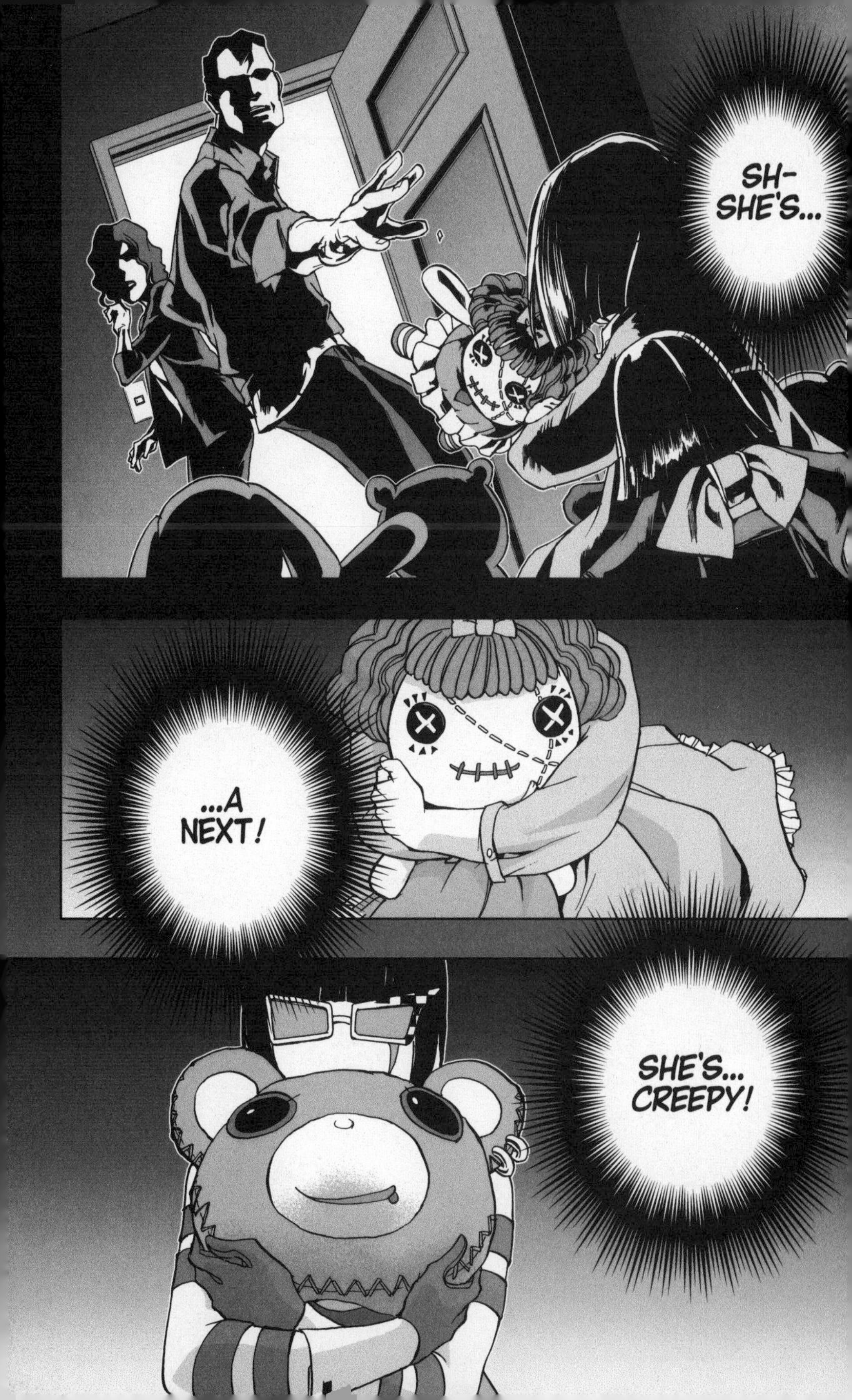
SH-
SHE'S...
...A NEXT!
SHE'S... CREEPY!

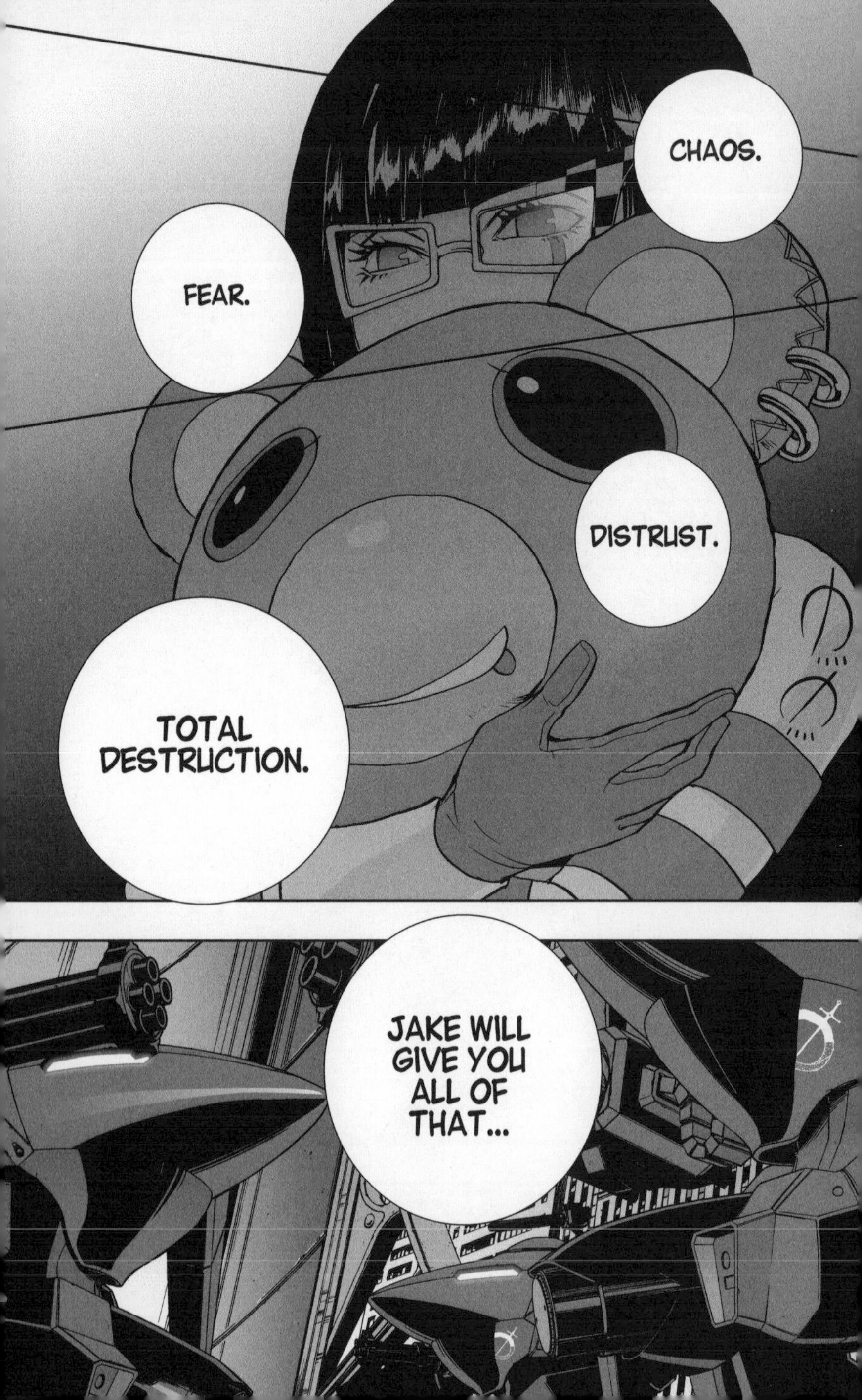
CHAOS.
FEAR.
DISTRUST.
TOTAL DESTRUCTION.
JAKE WILL GIVE YOU ALL OF THAT...

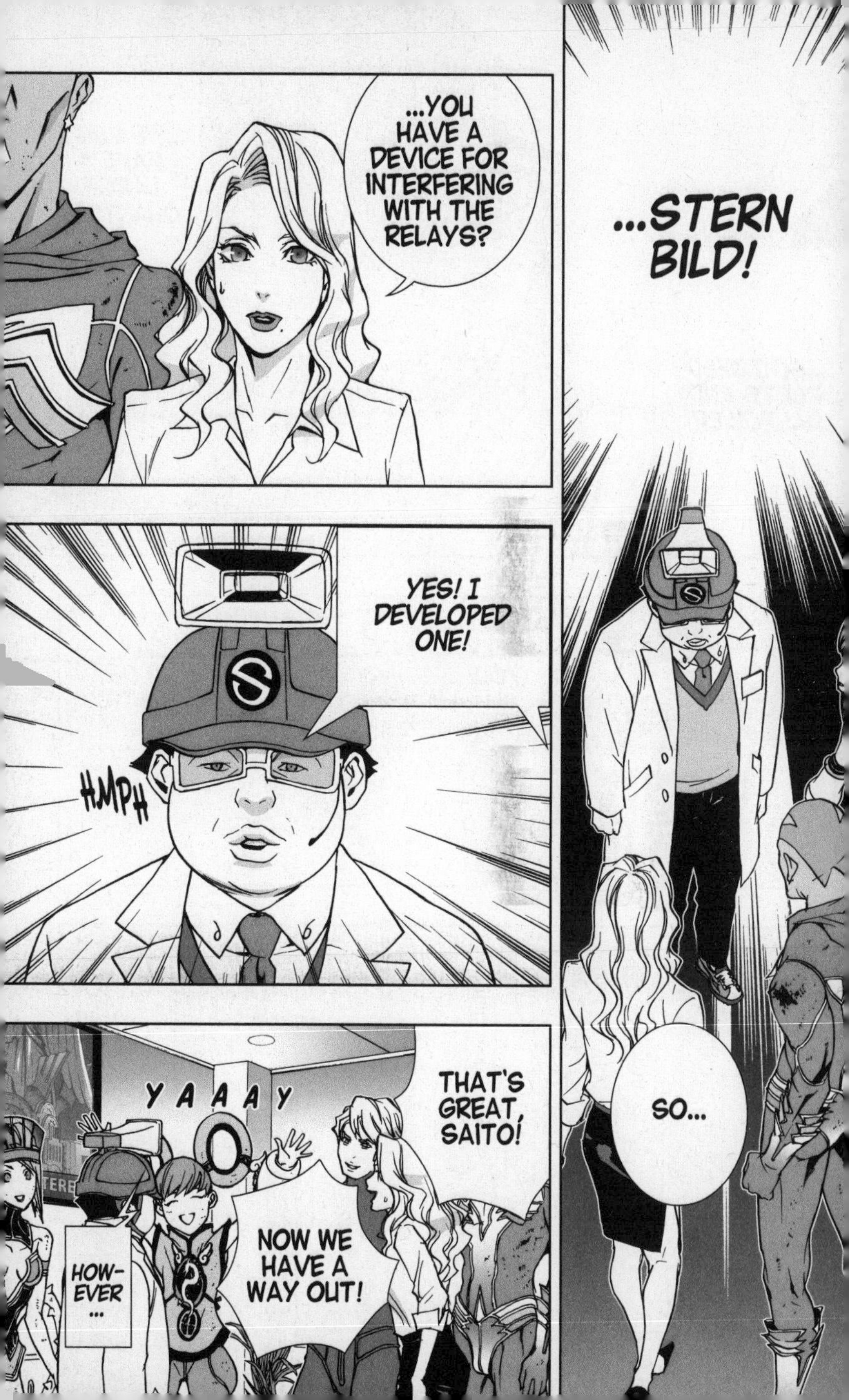
...STERN BILD!
SO...
...YOU HAVE A DEVICE FOR INTERFERING WITH THE RELAYS?
YES! I DEVELOPED ONE!
HMPH
THAT'S GREAT, SAITO!
YAAAY
NOW WE HAVE A WAY OUT!
HOW-EVER...

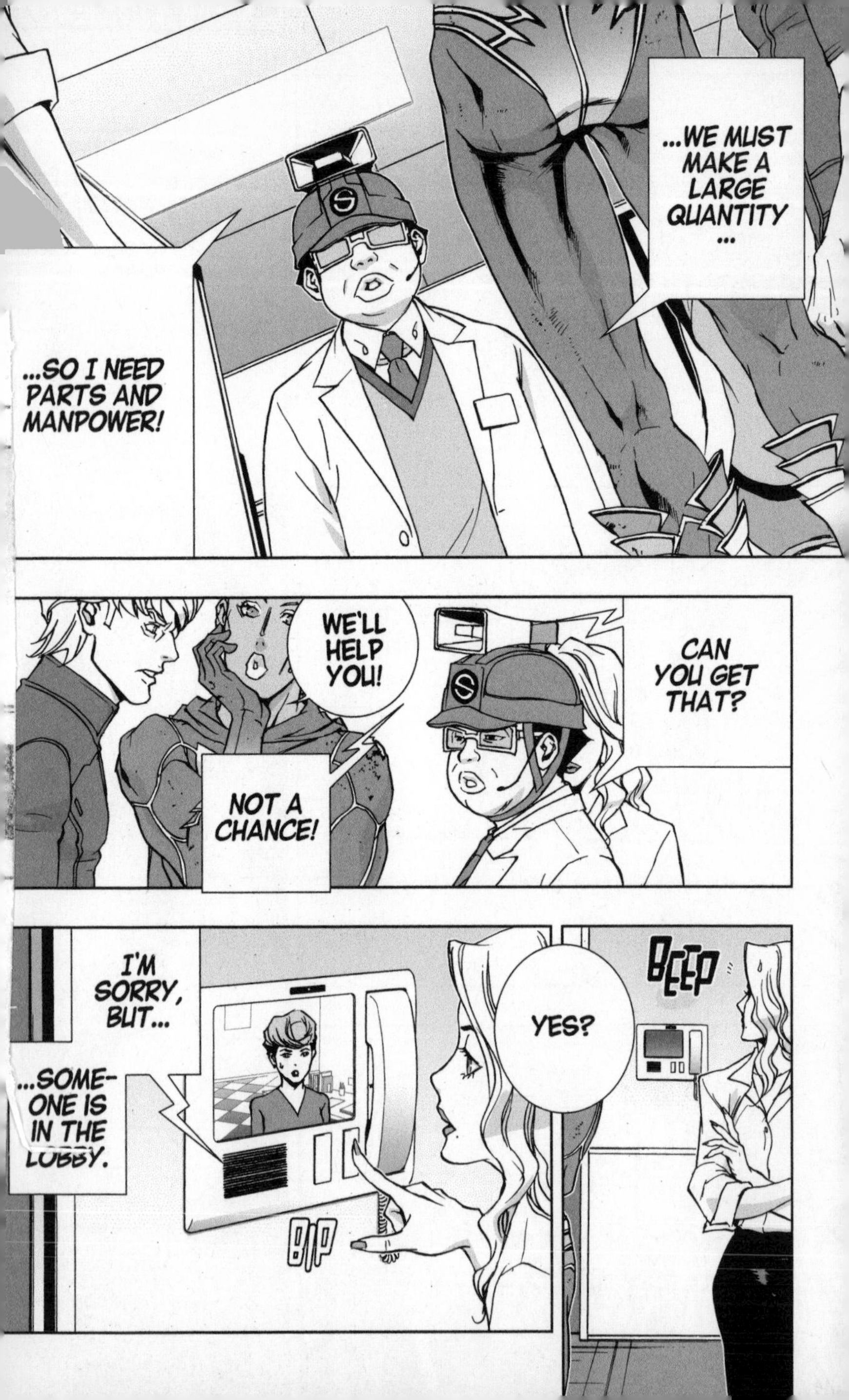
...WE MUST MAKE A LARGE QUANTITY...
...SO I NEED PARTS AND MANPOWER!
CAN YOU GET THAT?
WE'LL HELP YOU!
NOT A CHANCE!
BEEP
YES?
BIP
I'M SORRY, BUT...
...SOME-ONE IS IN THE LOBBY.

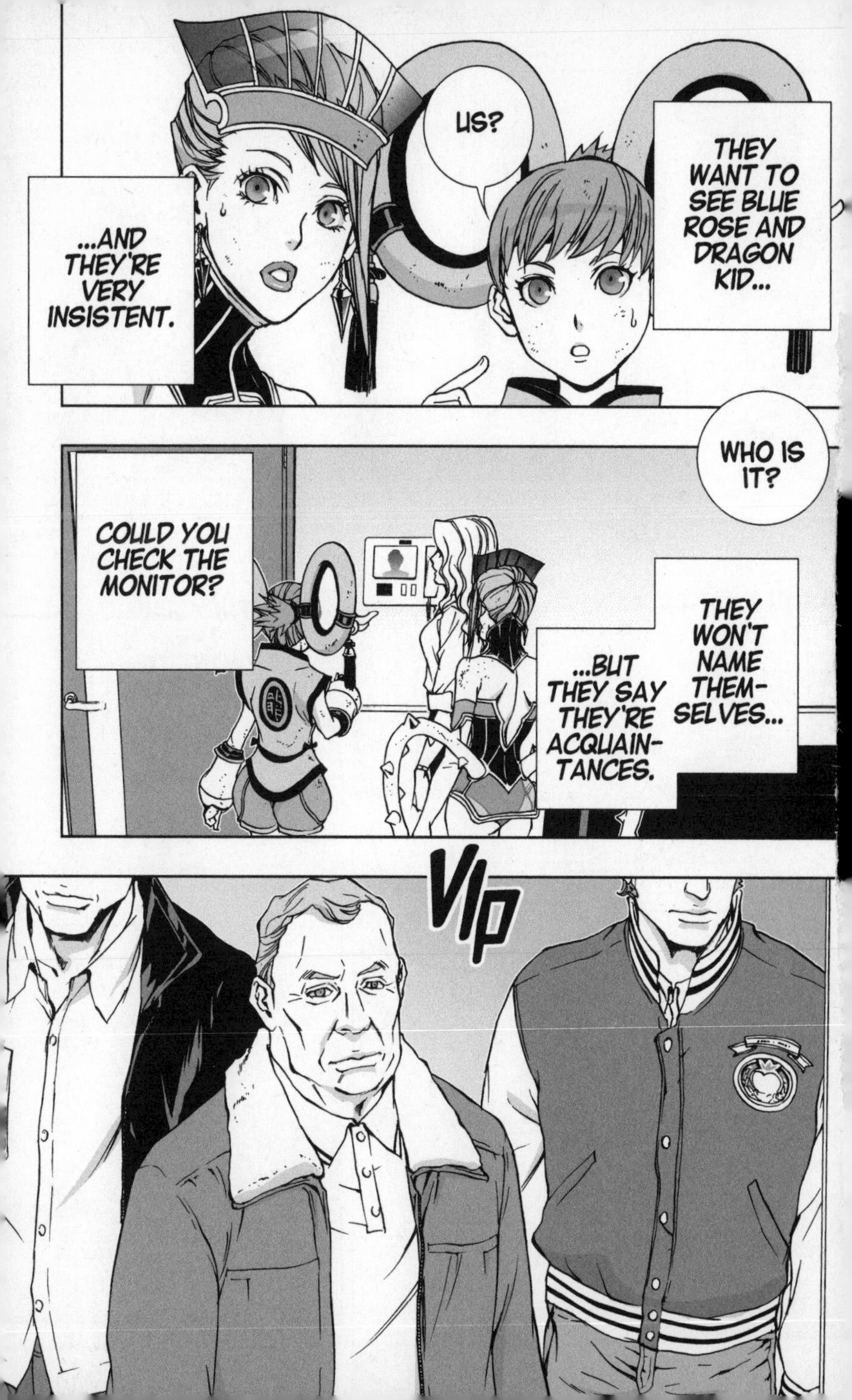
THEY WANT TO SEE BLUE ROSE AND DRAGON KID...
US?
...AND THEY'RE VERY INSISTENT.
WHO IS IT?
THEY WON'T NAME THEM-SELVES...
...BUT THEY SAY THEY'RE ACQUAIN-TANCES.
COULD YOU CHECK THE MONITOR?
VIP

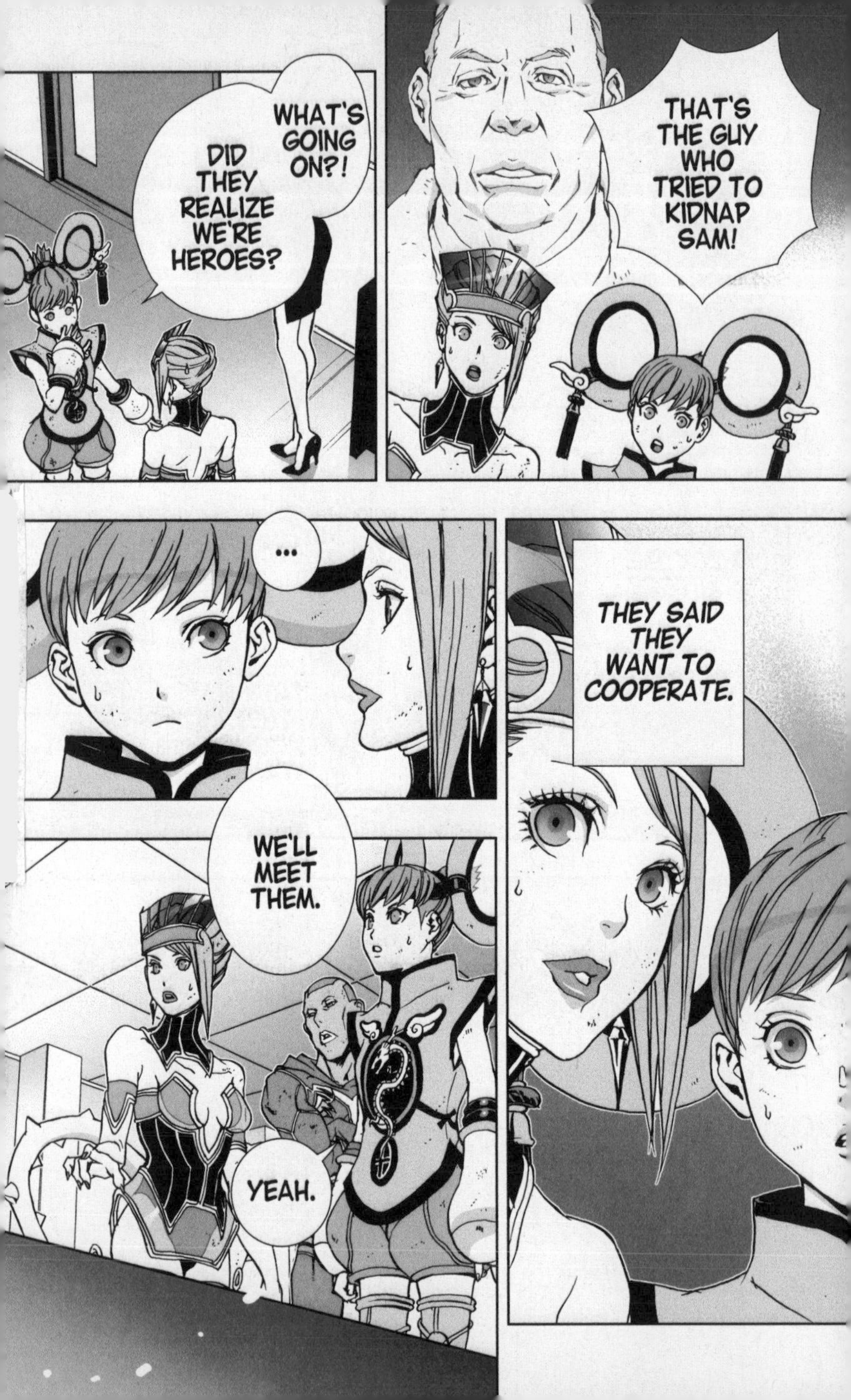
THAT'S THE GUY WHO TRIED TO KIDNAP SAM!
WHAT'S GOING ON?!
DID THEY REALIZE WE'RE HEROES?
THEY SAID THEY WANT TO COOPERATE.
...
WE'LL MEET THEM.
YEAH.

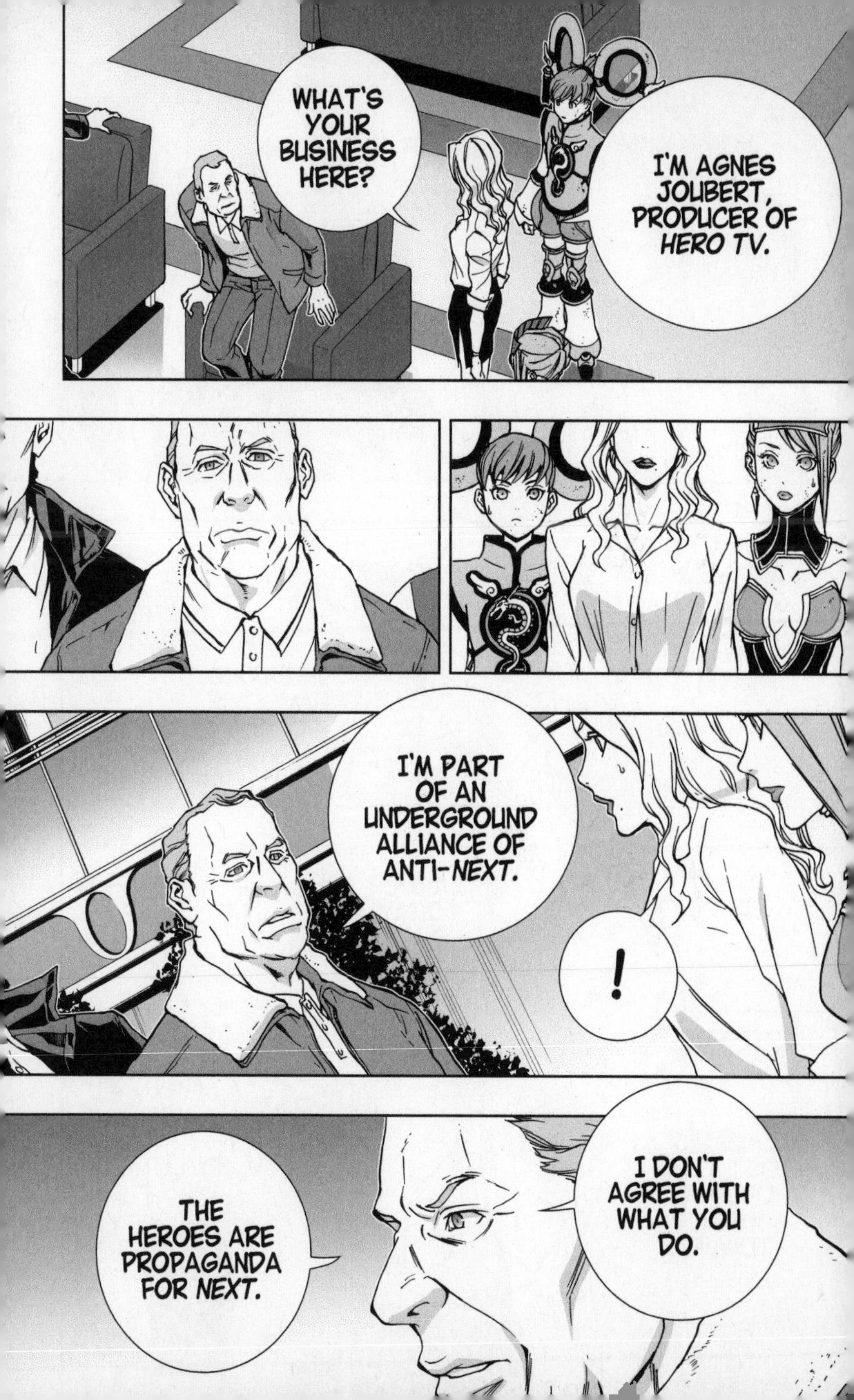
WHAT'S YOUR BUSINESS HERE?
I'M AGNES JOUBERT, PRODUCER OF HERO TV.
I'M PART OF AN UNDERGROUND ALLIANCE OF ANTI-NEXT.
!
I DON'T AGREE WITH WHAT YOU DO.
THE HEROES ARE PROPAGANDA FOR NEXT.

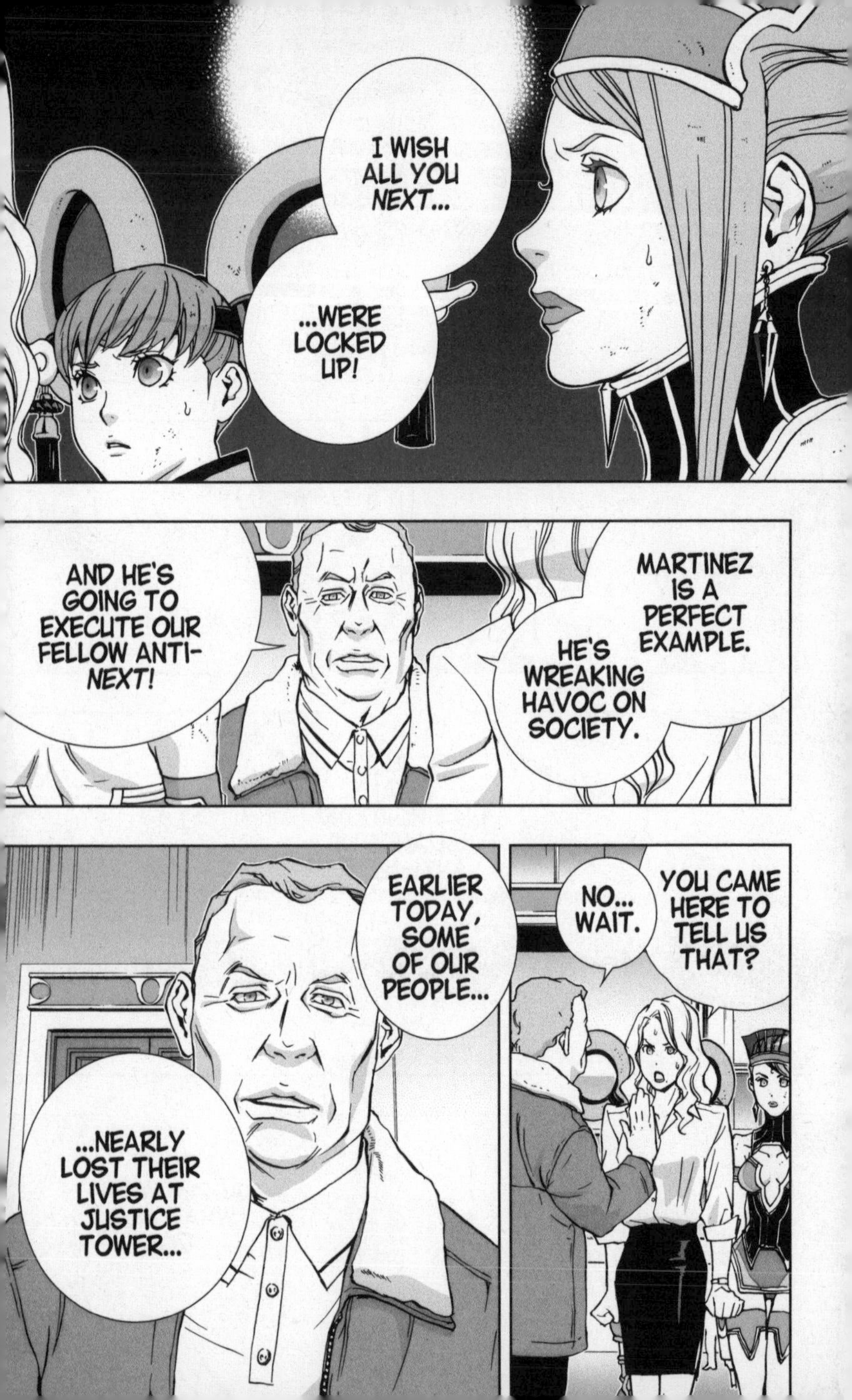
I WISH ALL YOU NEXT...
...WERE LOCKED UP!
MARTINEZ IS A PERFECT EXAMPLE.
HE'S WREAKING HAVOC ON SOCIETY.
AND HE'S GOING TO EXECUTE OUR FELLOW ANTI-NEXT!
YOU CAME HERE TO TELL US THAT?
NO... WAIT.
EARLIER TODAY, SOME OF OUR PEOPLE...
...NEARLY LOST THEIR LIVES AT JUSTICE TOWER...

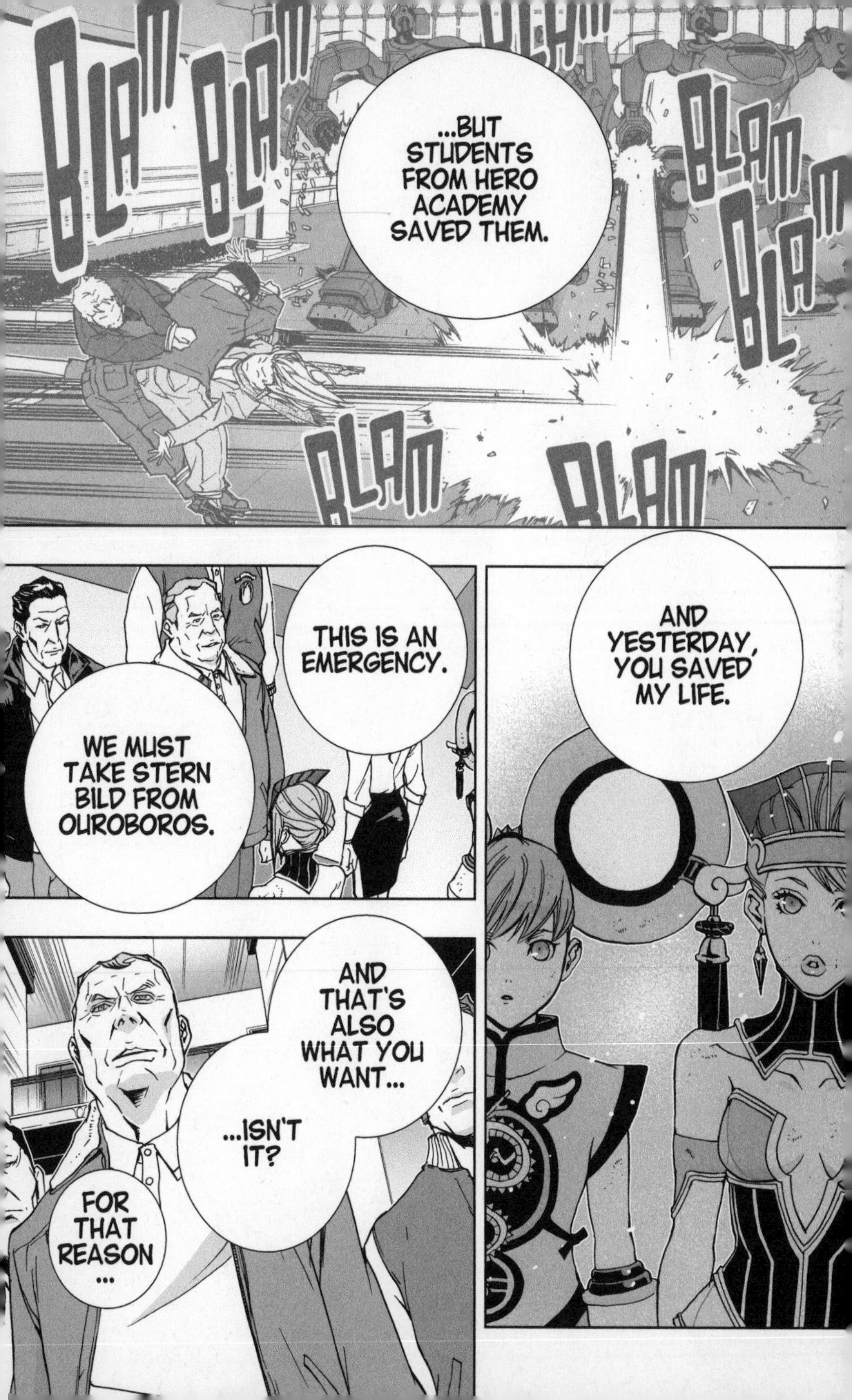
BLAM
BLAM
...BUT STUDENTS FROM HERO ACADEMY SAVED THEM.
BLAM
BLAM
BLAM
BLAM
AND YESTERDAY, YOU SAVED MY LIFE.
THIS IS AN EMERGENCY.
WE MUST TAKE STERN BILD FROM OUROBOROS.
AND THAT'S ALSO WHAT YOU WANT...
...ISN'T IT?
FOR THAT REASON ...

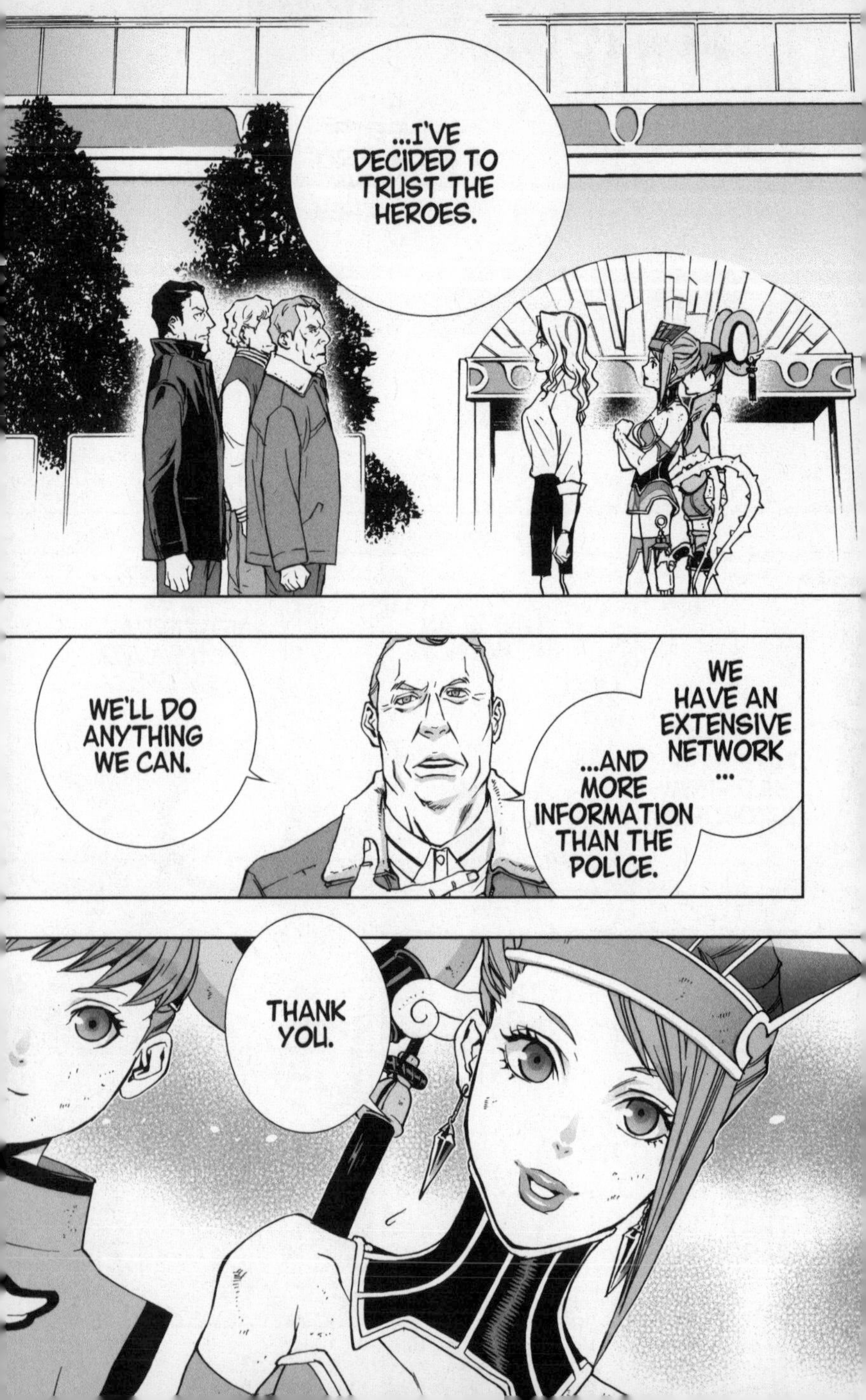
...I'VE DECIDED TO TRUST THE HEROES.
WE HAVE AN EXTENSIVE NETWORK ...
...AND MORE INFORMATION THAN THE POLICE.
WE'LL DO ANYTHING WE CAN.
THANK YOU.

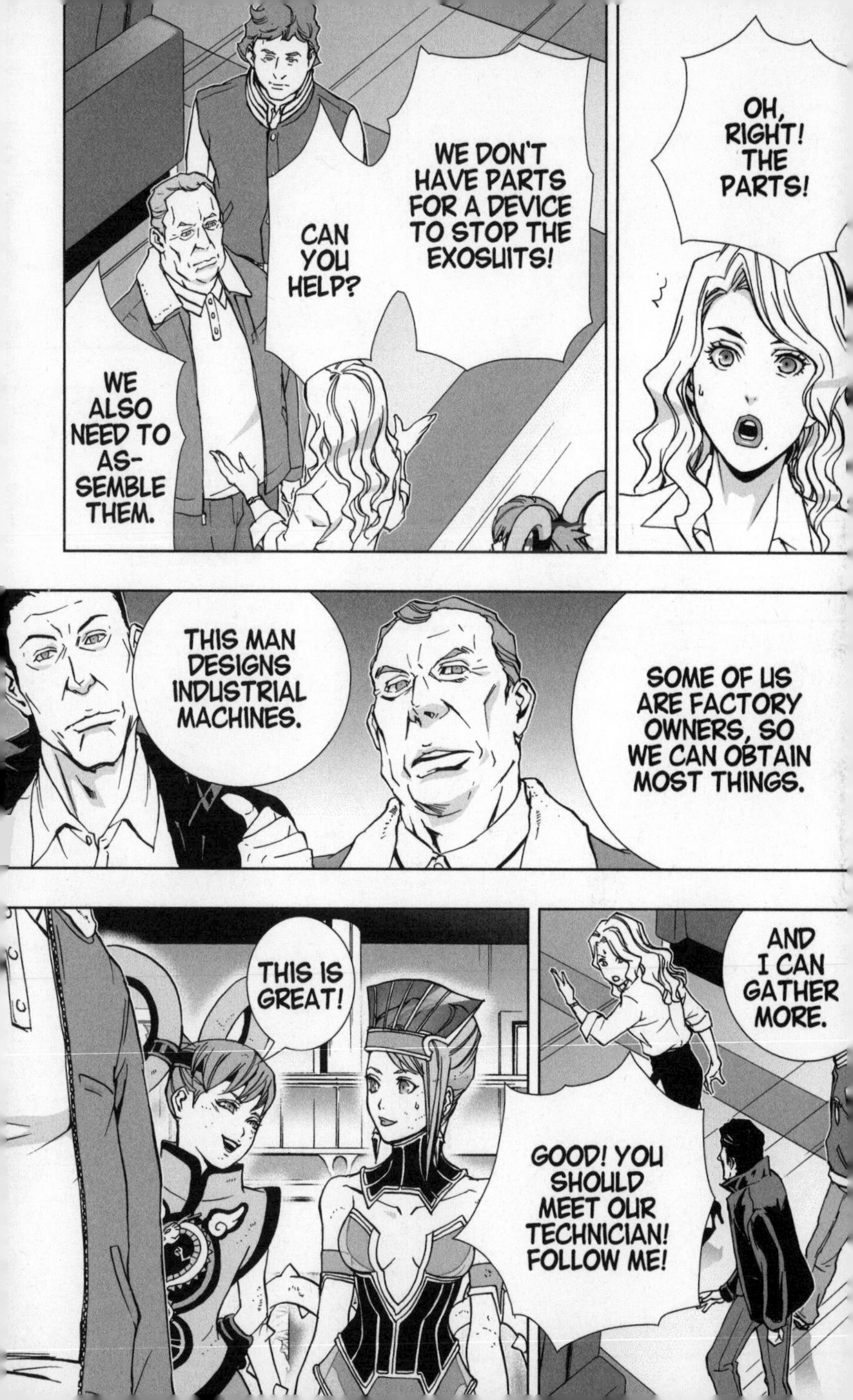
OH, RIGHT! THE PARTS!
WE DON'T HAVE PARTS FOR A DEVICE TO STOP THE EXOSUITS!
CAN YOU HELP?
WE ALSO NEED TO AS-SEMBLE THEM.
SOME OF US ARE FACTORY OWNERS, SO WE CAN OBTAIN MOST THINGS.
THIS MAN DESIGNS INDUSTRIAL MACHINES.
AND I CAN GATHER MORE.
THIS IS GREAT!
GOOD! YOU SHOULD MEET OUR TECHNICIAN! FOLLOW ME!

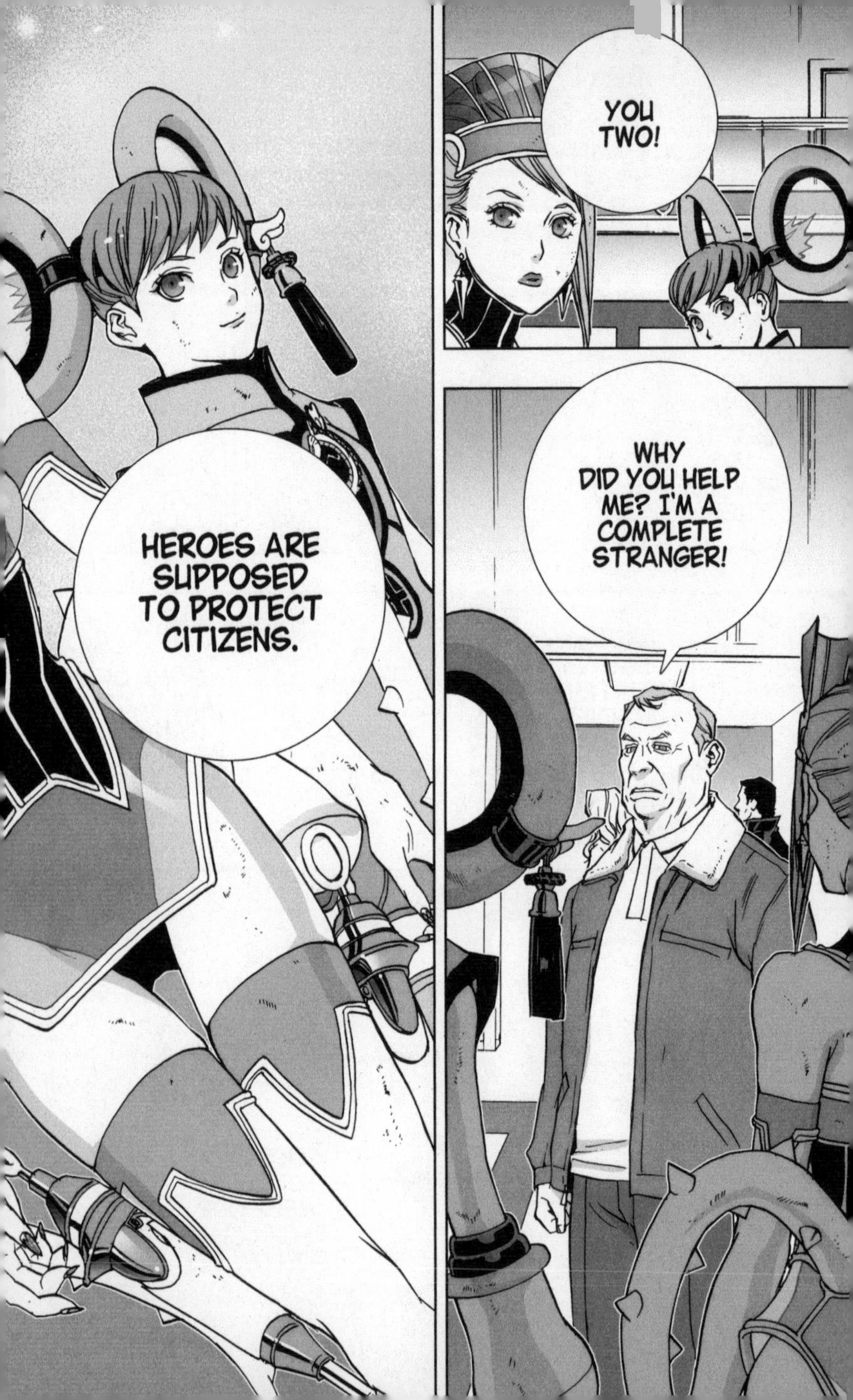
YOU TWO!
WHY DID YOU HELP ME? I'M A COMPLETE STRANGER!
HEROES ARE SUPPOSED TO PROTECT CITIZENS.

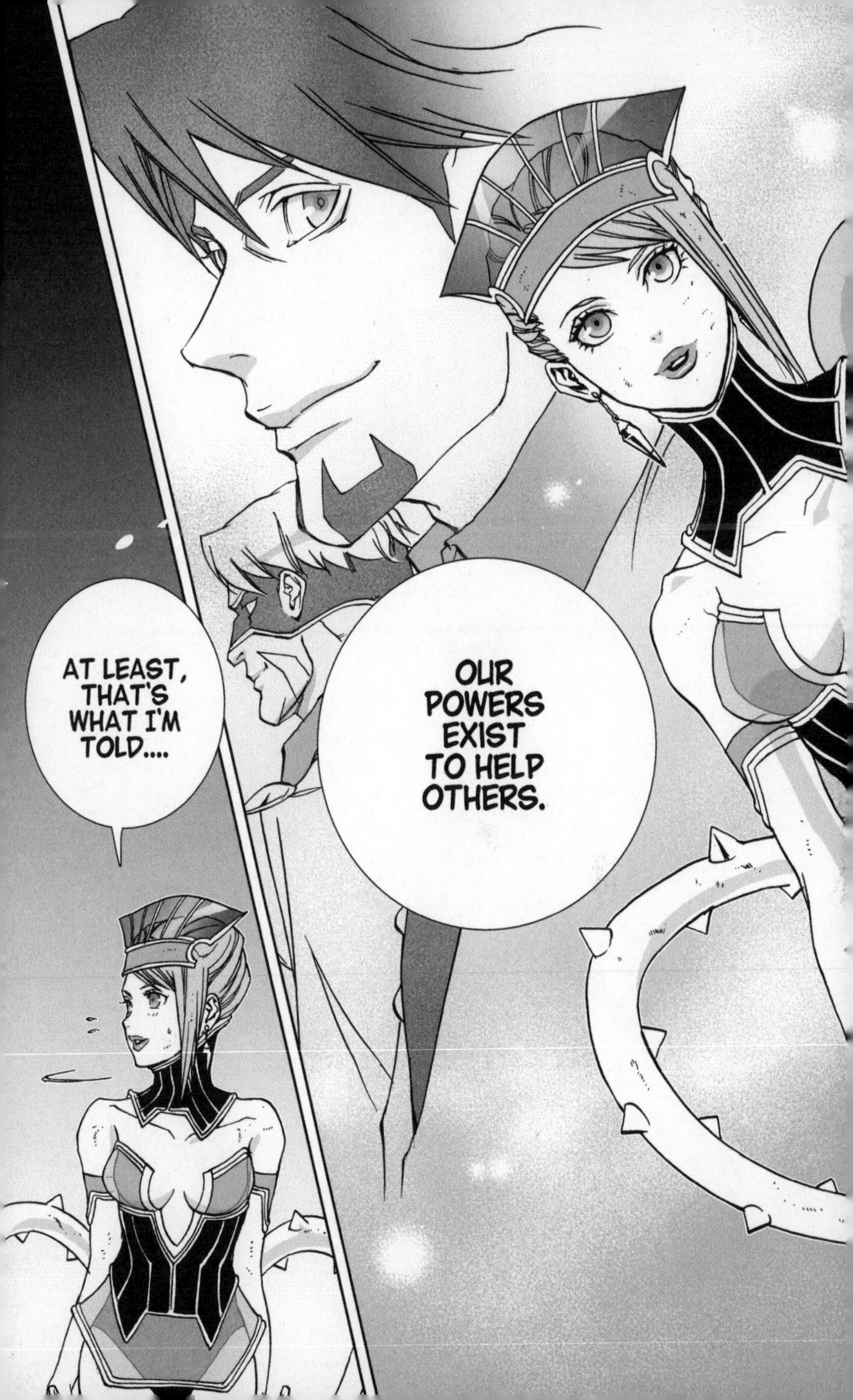
OUR POWERS EXIST TO HELP OTHERS.
AT LEAST, THAT'S WHAT I'M TOLD....

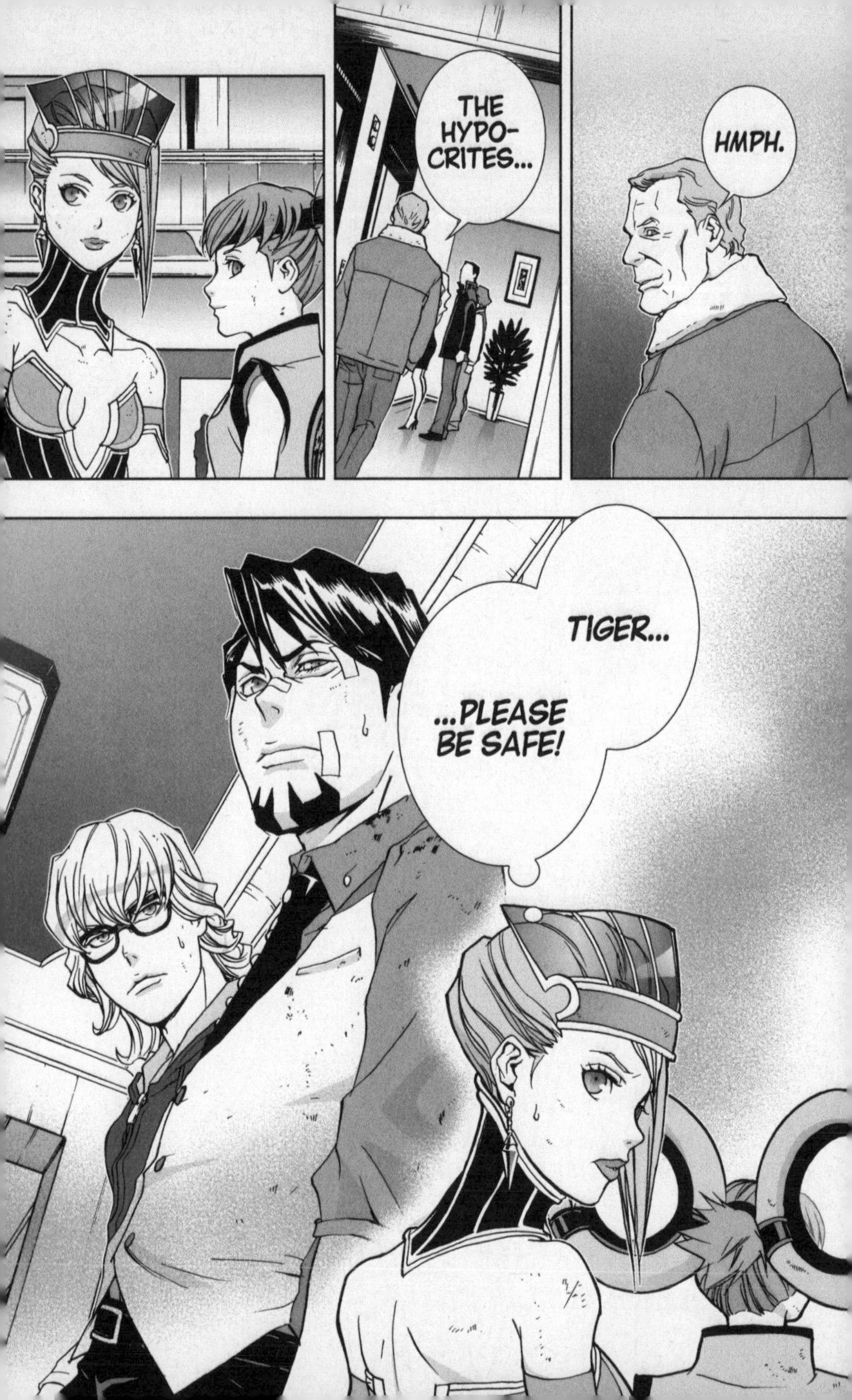
HMPH.
THE HYPOCRITES...
TIGER...
...PLEASE BE SAFE!

TIGER&BUNNY
To Be Continued

Mizuki Sakakibara

Assistants
Ayako Mayuzumi
Beth
Eri Saito
Sachiko Ito
Fuku

MIZUKI SAKAKIBARA

Mizuki Sakakibara's American comics debut was Marvel's *Exile* in 2002. Currently, *TIGER & BUNNY* is serialized in *Newtype Ace* magazine by Kadokawa Shoten.

MASAFUMI NISHIDA

Story director. *TIGER & BUNNY* was his first work as a TV animation scriptwriter. He is well known for the movie *Gachi☆Boy* and the Japanese TV dramas *Maoh*, *Kaibutsu-kun*, and *Youkai Ningen Bem*.

MASAKAZU KATSURA

Original character designer. Masakazu Katsura is well known for the manga series *WING MAN*, *Denei Shojo* (*Video Girl Ai*), *I"s*, and *ZETMAN*. Katsura's works have been translated into several languages, including Chinese and French, as well as English.

TIGER&BUNNY 7

VIZ Media Edition

Art **MIZUKI SAKAKIBARA**
Planning / Original Story **SUNRISE**
Original Script **MASAFUMI NISHIDA**
Original Character and Hero Design **MASAKAZU KATSURA**

TIGER & BUNNY Volume 7
© Mizuki SAKAKIBARA 2014
© SUNRISE/T&B PARTNERS, MBS
Edited by KADOKAWA SHOTEN
First published in Japan in 2014 by KADOKAWA CORPORATION, Tokyo.
English translation rights arranged with KADOKAWA CORPORATION, Tokyo.

Translation & English Adaptation **LABAAMEN & JOHN WERRY, HC LANGUAGE SOLUTIONS**
Touch-up Art & Lettering **STEPHEN DUTRO**
Design **FAWN LAU**
Editor **JENNIFER LEBLANC**

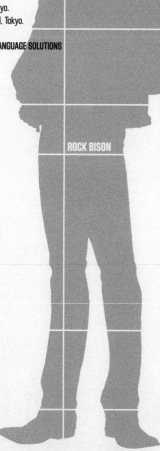

ROCK BISON

Printed in the U.S.A.

Published by VIZ Media, LLC
P.O. Box 77010
San Francisco, CA 94107

10 9 8 7 6 5 4 3 2 1
First printing, July 2015

YOU'RE READING THE
WRONG WAY!

Tiger & Bunny reads from right to left, starting in the upper-right corner. Japanese is read from right to left, meaning that action, sound effects, and word-balloon order are completely reversed from English order.

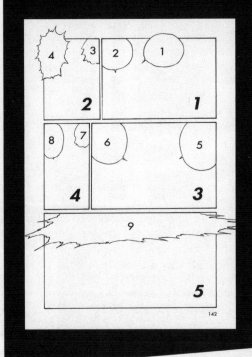